1992 CARS

Contents

Introduction

1992 Cars covers more than 175 passenger cars, passenger vans, and sport-utility vehicles, listing the major changes for each model, a summary of key features, and specifications for all available body styles, engines, and transmissions.

We have combined similar models, such as the Mercury Grand Marquis and Ford Crown Victoria, into one report so that we can cover more vehicles in the same amount of space. The Crown Victoria and Grand Marquis are built from the same design, use the same engine and transmission, and have similar styling. Their main differences are in interior trim, optional equipment, and prices, so we've provided separate price lists for both brands. We have not combined all similar vehicles, but in our reports we mention other models that are built from the same design. This should help you make a shopping list of cars that fit your needs and meet your budget.

Information in the specifications charts is provided by the manufacturers, except for the fuel economy estimates, which are furnished by the federal Environmental Protection Agency.

KEY TO SPECIFICATIONS

Notchback = coupe or sedan with a separate trunk. **Hatchback** = coupe or sedan with a rear liftgate. **Wheelbase** = distance between the front and rear wheels. **Curb weight** = weight of base models, not including optional equipment. **Engines: ohv** = overhead valve; **ohc** = overhead cam; **dohc** = double overhead cam; **I** = inline cylinders; **V** = cylinders in V configuration; **flat** = horizontally opposed cylinders; **bbl.** = barrel (carburetor); **TBI** = throttle-body (single-point) fuel injection; **PFI** = port (multi-point) fuel injection; **rpm** = revolutions per minute; **OD** = overdrive transmission; **S** = standard; **O** = optional; **NA** = not available.

How Cars Are Rated

The Ratings Chart at the end of this book includes numerical ratings in 16 categories for each car line. In cases where a certain model, body style, engine, or other feature affected the ratings, that is noted in the chart. The ratings apply only to the specific model that was tested by the editors. For example, the ratings for the Toyota Camry XLE apply only to those with the optional V-6 engine and anti-lock brakes (ABS). A Camry with the standard 4-cylinder engine may not score as highly in acceleration, and one without ABS may not score as highly in braking.

While the total points awarded to each model or car line is an important indication of a vehicle's overall capabilities, the editors encourage readers to study the ratings in individual categories. Large cars tend to earn more points because they have spacious interiors, roomy trunks, and wide doorways that allow easy entry/exit. That gives them a built-in advantage over small cars in the rating scale. However, small cars typically earn higher marks for fuel economy, while sporty cars score well in steering/handling, and cars with ABS score higher in braking. The individual reader should determine which categories are the most important in making a buying decision.

Price Information

The latest available prices have been provided for all models and optional equipment offered by the manufacturers. In most cases, the editors were able to provide dealer invoice prices and our estimated low prices. In some cases, only suggested retail prices were available; with some models that hadn't yet gone on sale (such as the Oldsmobile Achieva), no prices were available. In all cases, the prices are subject to change by the manufacturers.

If the prices in this book don't match what you see in a dealer's showroom, or if a salesman claims our prices are incorrect, contact us and we'll do what we can to help you out (the address is listed below).

The dealer invoice prices are what the dealer pays the manufacturer for the car and factory- or port-installed options. The dealer's costs of preparing a car for delivery to the consumer are included in the invoice price of all domestic cars. On some imported vehicles, this cost may not be included in the dealer invoice. The destination charge is not included in either the suggested retail or dealer invoice prices, so it must be added to the total cost of the vehicle.

Invoice prices do not include any advertising fees charged to dealers. Most dealers try to pass advertising fees on to their customers. Since it's their cost of doing business—not yours—you should strongly argue against paying these fees. Shop at other dealers; they may not try to charge you for advertising.

The low prices listed in this book are estimates based on national market conditions for each model. Cars that are in high demand and short supply will likely sell at or near suggested retail price. Cars in low demand and high supply will be sold at much larger discounts, or closer to dealer invoice. Certain cars are in much higher demand in certain areas. For example, a 4-wheel-drive station wagon will be in great demand in the Denver area, while there may be little interest in this 4WD model in the Sun Belt. On the other hand, convertibles are always "in season" in Phoenix.

To determine local market conditions for the vehicles you're interested in, we encourage you to shop for the same car at three or more dealers. If all the dealers have only a few of a given model in stock and show little inclination to discount their prices, you're shopping in a seller's market, so you should expect to pay close to suggested retail. On the other hand, if all the dealers have lots of cars in stock and seem eager to bargain, then you are in the driver's seat on price.

With most cars these days, it is a buyer's market. Take advantage of this by letting the dealers know that you've been shopping elsewhere and that price will be an important factor in your decision.

However, before you buy any car, test drive it. Don't choose your next car on price alone. Buy the car that feels right for you when you're behind the wheel. Since you're going to be the one who has to live with this vehicle, make sure that it fits your needs. We strongly suggest you test drive the same vehicle you're planning to buy.

The editors invite your questions and comments. Address them to:

Consumer Guide®
7373 N. Cicero Ave.
Lincolnwood, IL 60646

Acura Integra

Acura Integra RS 3-door

Last redesigned for 1990, the subcompact front-drive Integra is treated to a mild facelift and a few more horsepower for 1992. Model offerings are unchanged: 3-door hatchback coupe and 4-door notchback in base RS, mid-level LS, and sporty GS trim. There's still no driver-side air bag. All Integras use a 1.8-liter twin-cam 4-cylinder engine rated at 140 horsepower, 10 more than last year. It is coupled to a standard 5-speed manual or optional 4-speed automatic transmission. Four-wheel disc brakes are standard, but GS models remain the only Integras with an anti-lock brake system; ABS is not available elsewhere even at extra cost. The 4-door Integra is about 3.5 inches longer than the coupe, making it a compact sedan. Integra's smooth 1.8-liter engine furnishes zesty acceleration with the 5-speed manual transmission, but is much less lively with automatic. Our test 5-speed hatchback ran to 60 mph in a brisk 9.0 seconds, a trip that took our automatic 4-door a leisurely 11.5 seconds. Fuel economy is good with either transmission, around 23-25 mpg around town and well into the 30s on the highway. The ride is fairly supple, and in turns, there's minimal body roll and good grip. The analog instruments are well marked and unobscured, the controls are simple and fall easily to hand. A low driving position emphasizes this car's sporty bent. The hatchback's rear seat is best left to kids and cargo, but the longer 4-door offers enough room for a pair of adults to fit comfortably. The Acura is built quite solidly, should be reliable, and is likely to enjoy good resale value.

Specifications

	3-door hatchback	4-door notchback
Wheelbase, in.	100.4	102.4
Overall length, in.	172.9	176.5
Overall width, in.	67.4	67.4
Overall height, in.	52.2	52.8
Curb weight, lbs.	2560	2606
Cargo vol., cu. ft.	16.2	11.2
Fuel capacity, gals.	13.2	13.2
Seating capacity	4	5
Front head room, in.	38.5	38.7
Front leg room, max., in.	41.8	41.6
Rear head room, in.	34.7	36.8
Rear leg room, min., in.	28.6	31.7

Powertrain layout: transverse front engine/front-wheel drive.

Engines

	dohc I-4
Size, liters/cu. in.	1.8/112
Fuel delivery	PFI
Horsepower @ rpm	140 @ 6300
Torque (lbs./ft.) @ rpm	126 @ 5000
Availability	S

EPA city/highway mpg

5-speed OD manual	NA
4-speed OD automatic	NA

Assembly point: Suzuka, Japan.

Prices

Acura Integra	Retail Price	Dealer Invoice	Low Price
RS 3-door hatchback, 5-speed	$12100	$10164	$11225
RS 3-door hatchback, automatic	12825	10773	11950
LS 3-door hatchback, 5-speed	13975	11739	13100
LS 3-door hatchback, automatic	14700	12348	13825
LS Special 3-door, 5-speed	14675	12327	13800

	Retail Price	Dealer Invoice	Low Price
GS 3-door hatchback, 5-speed	16105	13528	15230
GS 3-door hatchback, automatic	16830	14137	15955
GS 3-door, 5-speed, leather interior	16605	13948	15730
GS 3-door, automatic, leather interior . . .	17330	14557	16455
RS 4-door notchback, 5-speed	13025	10941	12025
RS 4-door notchback, automatic	13750	11550	12750
LS 4-door notchback, 5-speed	14725	12639	13725
LS 4-door notchback, automatic	15450	12978	14450
GS 4-door notchback, 5-speed	16645	13982	15645
GS 4-door notchback, automatic	17370	14591	16370
GS 4-door, 5-speed, leather interior	17145	14402	16145
GS 4-door, automatic, leather interior . . .	17870	15011	16870
Destination charge	325	325	325

Standard equipment:

RS: 1.8-liter DOHC 16-valve PFI 4-cylinder engine, 5-speed manual or 4-speed automatic transmission, 4-wheel disc brakes, power steering, motorized front shoulder belts, cloth reclining front bucket seats, split folding rear seat, tinted glass, remote fuel door and decklid/hatch releases, dual outside mirrors, fog lights, rear defogger, rear wiper/washer (hatchback), tachometer, coolant temperature gauge, tilt steering column, intermittent wipers, door pockets, cargo cover (hatchback), 195/60R14 85H tires. **LS** adds: power mirrors, power windows, power locks (4-door), power sunroof (hatchback), AM/FM cassette with power antenna, driver's-seat lumbar support adjustment, cruise control, map lights (hatchback). **LS Special** adds: color-keyed spolier and dual power mirrors, leather-wrapped steering wheel, alloy wheels. **GS** adds to LS: anti-lock brakes, map lights, adjustable side bolsters on driver's seat, power sunroof, alloy wheels.

OPTIONS are available as dealer-installed accessories.

Acura Legend

A passenger-side air bag is standard on an additional Legend model for 1992. Legend sedans come in base, L, and LS models. The coupe comes in L and LS guise. It's shorter than the 4-door by nearly three inches overall and by 2.4 inches in wheelbase. Appearance is unchanged for 1992, but L models of both body styles get the standard passenger air bag previously reserved for LS versions. All Legends retain a standard driver-side air bag and anti-lock

Prices are accurate at time of publication; subject to manufacturer's change.

Acura Legend LS Sedan

Specifications

	2-door notchback	4-door notchback
Wheelbase, in.	111.4	114.6
Overall length, in.	192.5	194.9
Overall width, in.	71.3	71.3
Overall height, in.	53.5	55.1
Curb weight, lbs.	3408	3455
Cargo vol., cu. ft.	14.1	14.8
Fuel capacity, gals.	18.0	18.0
Seating capacity	5	5
Front head room, in.	37.3	38.5
Front leg room, max., in.	42.9	42.7
Rear head room, in.	35.9	36.5
Rear leg room, min., in.	28.7	33.5

Powertrain layout: longitudinal front engine/front-wheel drive.

Engines

	ohc V-6
Size, liters/cu. in.	3.2/196
Fuel delivery	PFI
Horsepower @ rpm	200 @ 5500
Torque (lbs./ft.) @ rpm	210 @ 4500
Availability	S

EPA city/highway mpg

5-speed OD manual	18/26
4-speed OD automatic	19/24

Assembly point: Sayama, Japan.

brakes. Power for all models comes from a 200-horsepower 3.2-liter 24-valve V-6 mated to a 5-speed manual or 4-speed automatic transmission. In all-out acceleration, the Acura holds its own against the costlier V-8 Lexus LS 400 and Infiniti Q45. Our automatic-transmission Legend sedan ran 0-60 mph in just 7.6 seconds—fractionally faster than its competitors. Where the Legend's powertrain doesn't quite match up is in overall smoothness. There's ample power for passing, but the automatic's gear changes border on harsh going from first to second and downshifting in the 40-60-mph range. Come time to stop, the standard ABS feels strong and secure. Fast turns bring on some body lean, but grip, balance, and control are laudable. The taut ride is never harsh, but falls short of the suppleness over bumps displayed by brands such as BMW or Mercedes-Benz. Instruments and controls are the usual Honda combination of logical placement and feather-touch feel. Some taller testers complained that the adjustable driver's seat cushion doesn't lower enough to give adequate head room, and others said the steering wheel, which telescopes but doesn't tilt, crowds the thighs.

Prices

Acura Legend	Retail Price	Dealer Invoice	Low Price
L 2-door coupe, 5-speed	$30900	$25338	—
L 2-door coupe, automatic	31700	25994	—
L 2-door w/leather trim, 5-speed	32400	26568	—
L 2-door w/leather trim, automatic	33200	27224	—
LS 2-door coupe, 5-speed	35500	29110	—
LS 2-door coupe, automatic	36300	29766	—
4-door notchback, 5-speed	27250	22345	—
4-door notchback, automatic	28050	23001	—
L 4-door notchback, 5-speed	29250	23985	—
L 4-door notchback, automatic	30050	24641	—
L 4-door w/leather trim, 5-speed	30750	25215	—
L 4-door w/leather trim, automatic	31550	25871	—
LS 4-door notchback, 5-speed	34050	27921	—
LS 4-door notchback, automatic	34850	28577	—
Destination charge	325	325	325

Low price not available at time of publication.

Prices are accurate at time of publication; subject to manufacturer's change.

Standard equipment:

3.2-liter SOHC 24-valve PFI V-6, 5-speed manual or 4-speed automatic transmission, anti-lock 4-wheel disc brakes, power steering, driver-side air bag, air conditioning, fabric reclining front bucket seats, driver-seat lumbar support and power height adjustments, power windows and locks, cruise control, telescopic steering column, tinted glass, power mirrors, AM/FM cassette with power diversity antenna, security system, intermittent wipers, bodyside moldings, rear defogger, remote fuel door and decklid releases, lighted visor mirrors, front door pockets, center console with armrest and covered storage, folding rear armrest, digital clock, 205/60R15 90V tires on alloy wheels. **L** adds: power sunroof, power driver's seat, upgraded audio system with EQ and steering-wheel-mounted auxiliary controls, heated mirrors, cellular phone pre-wire, map lights. **LS** adds: passenger airbag, leather trim, automatic climate control, heated front seats, Acura/Bose audio system, illuminated entry, walnut interior trim, power passenger seat.

OPTIONS are available as dealer-installed accessories.

Acura NSX

Acura NSX

Launched with fanfare in the summer of 1990, Acura's mid-engine coupe commanded prices way above sticker during 1991. NSX is predictably unchanged for 1992, but prices may well be raised above the suggested $62,000 with 5-speed manual transmission, $66,000 with 4-speed automatic, both new highs for a Japanese model. A maximum of 3000 units per year are destined for U.S. sale, and only

5000 will be available worldwide. NSX remains a no-options high-performance sports car powered by a twin-cam 3.0-liter V-6 mounted sideways behind a 2-seat cockpit. Horsepower is 270 with manual, 252 with automatic. The body, engine, and the fully independent suspension are made of weight-saving aluminum. Standard features include 4-wheel anti-lock disc brakes, driver-side air bag, traction control, leather upholstery, Acura/Bose audio system, automatic climate control, and power seats, windows and door locks. Power steering, electrically driven, is exclusive to the automatic model. While exotic cars are supposed to be hard to live with, Honda breaks the rules with the

Specifications

	2-door notchback
Wheelbase, in.	99.6
Overall length, in.	173.4
Overall width, in.	71.3
Overall height, in.	46.1
Curb weight, lbs.	3010
Cargo vol., cu. ft.	5.0
Fuel capacity, gals.	18.5
Seating capacity	2
Front head room, in.	36.3
Front leg room, max., in.	44.3
Rear head room, in.	—
Rear leg room, min., in.	—

Powertrain layout: transverse mid engine/rear-wheel drive.

Engines

	dohc V-6
Size, liters/cu. in.	3.0/182
Fuel delivery	PFI
Horsepower @ rpm	270 @ 7100[1]
Torque (lbs./ft.) @ rpm	210 @ 5300
Availability	S

EPA city/highway mpg

5-speed OD manual	19/24
4-speed OD automatic	18/24

1. 252 @ 6600 with automatic.

Assembly point: Tochigi, Japan.

Prices are accurate at time of publication; subject to manufacturer's change.

NSX. Getting in and out is fairly easy, there's adequate room inside, the cockpit is comfortable and well laid out, and visibility is good enough to take the drama out of rush-hour lane changes. The engine runs Honda-smooth, and with the slick, short-throw 5-speed, Acura claims a 0-60 mph time of 5.6 seconds and a top speed of 168. The well-behaved automatic is only slightly less rewarding. Traction control is a boon in the wet; a dash button can turn it off. Precise steering, glue-like grip, taut suspension, and anchor-like brakes make for extraordinary reflexes and control. You feel most every bump and tar strip and the tires roar over most surfaces, but the ride and sound levels are compliant enough to qualify this as an everyday sports car.

Prices

	Retail Price	Dealer Invoice	Low Price
Acura NSX			
2-door notchback, 5-speed	$62000	$50840	—
2-door notchback, automatic	66000	54120	—
Destination charge	600	600	600

Low price not available at time of publication.

Standard equipment:

3.0-liter DOHC 24-valve PFI V-6, 5-speed manual or 4-speed automatic transmission, anti-lock 4-wheel disc brakes, power steering (with automatic), traction control, driver-side air bag, automatic climate control, leather power seats, power windows and locks, cruise control, power mirrors, Acura/Bose AM/FM cassette with diversity antenna system, power antenna, center console, tachometer, coolant temperature and oil pressure gauges, voltmeter, trip odometer, tilt/telescopic steering column, intermittent wipers, rear defogger, remote fuel door and decklid releases, digital clock, 205/50ZR15 front and 225/50ZR16 rear tires on forged alloy wheels.

Acura Vigor

Announced last spring as a 1992 model, Vigor fills the size/price gap between Acura's entry-level Integra and luxury Legend. It's a front-drive 4-door derived from the Honda Accord sedan, but sports frameless door glass *a la* Integra and a wheelbase stretched 2.7 inches from Accord's, to 110.4.

Acura Vigor GS

The last helps accommodate a 176-horsepower 2.5-liter 20-valve inline 5-cylinder engine mounted longitudinally. A 5-speed manual transmission is standard, a 4-speed automatic is optional. Vigor comes in LS and upgraded GS guise. Standard equipment on both includes 4-wheel anti-lock disc brakes, driver-side air bag, automatic climate control, a theft-deterrent system, cruise control, and power windows/mirrors/door locks. Acceleration is strong enough to put the car solidly in the sport-sedan category. The willing 5-cylinder has adequate power at low engine speeds and comes alive over 3000 rpm or so, pushing you back in your seat as it runs all the way to the 6800-rpm redline. Its voice is raspy, however, and some testers brand it somewhat rough-running. Vigor requires premium fuel and we averaged 21.5 mpg in mixed city and highway driving. A satisfyingly flat ride is the rule, and though Vigor's firm suspension can feel choppy over poor pavement, it's not bone-jarring. The driver sits low before a concise array of analog gauges and logically arranged, smooth-working controls. Room in front is good, but the rear seat has a serious shortage of leg room. Most comparable sedans in the mid-$20,000 class have V-6 engines that feel more refined. Still, if a large rear seat isn't a must, you may find a lot to like here.

Specifications

	4-door notchback
Wheelbase, in.	110.4
Overall length, in.	190.4
Overall width, in.	70.1
Overall height, in.	53.9
Curb weight, lbs.	3150
Cargo vol., cu. ft.	14.2
Fuel capacity, gals.	17.2
Seating capacity	5
Front head room, in.	38.8
Front leg room, max., in.	43.7
Rear head room, in.	36.2
Rear leg room, min., in.	30.3

Powertrain layout: longitudinal front engine/front-wheel drive.

Engines

	ohc I-5
Size, liters/cu. in.	2.5/152
Fuel delivery	PFI
Horsepower @ rpm	176 @ 6300
Torque (lbs./ft.) @ rpm	170 @ 3900
Availability	S

EPA city/highway mpg

5-speed OD manual	20/26
4-speed OD automatic	20/25

Assembly point: Saitama, Japan.

Prices

Acura Vigor	Retail Price	Dealer Invoice	Low Price
LS 4-door notchback, 5-speed	$23265	$19310	—
LS 4-door notchback, automatic	24015	19932	—
GS 4-door notchback, 5-speed	25250	20958	—
GS 4-door notchback, automatic	26000	21580	—

Low price not available at time of publication.

Standard equipment:

LS: 2.5-liter PFI 5-cylinder engine, 5-speed manual or 4-speed automatic transmission, anti-lock 4-wheel disc brakes, power steering, driver's side airbag, air conditioning, tinted glass, power windows, door locks and mirrors, cruise control, theft-deterrent system, illuminated entry system, tachometer, digital clock, cloth upholstery, tilt steering wheel, rear window defogger, 8-speaker AM/FM cassette, power antenna, alloy wheels, 205/60HR15 all-season tires. **GS** adds: leather upholstery, power monroof, digital signal processor.

OPTIONS are available as dealer-installed accessories.

Audi 80 and 100

Audi 100 S

For 1992, Audi carries the 80-series over with few changes, and drops the 90 series in preparation for a new 90 model scheduled for introduction in the spring of 1992. Meanwhile, the front-drive Audi 100 premium sedan receives a redesigned body and a V-6 engine to replace the inline-5 used previously. The entry-level 80, which will be discontinued when the new 90 debuts, gains anti-lock brakes as standard equipment, and a power sunroof to replace a manual version on the option list. The redesigned 100 is virtually identical in size to the previous model, and Audi is taking aim at the Acura Legend with three front-drive

Prices are accurate at time of publication; subject to manufacturer's change.

versions: 100, 100 S, and 100 CS. All come with a driver-side air bag and 4-wheel anti-lock disc brakes. They also carry the same powertrain: a 2.8-liter V-6 rated at 172 horsepower, and 5-speed manual or 4-speed automatic transmission. All-wheel-drive Quattro versions (including a wagon) are scheduled for introduction in March, and will be offered with automatic transmission for the first time. A new S4 model based on the 100 Quattro will also debut in March, equipped with 5-speed only and carrying a turbocharged 5-cylinder engine with 227 horsepower. The 100's new 2.8-

Specifications

	80 4-door notchback	100 4-door notchback
Wheelbase, in.	100.2	105.8
Overall length, in.	176.3	192.6
Overall width, in.	66.7	70.0
Overall height, in.	54.8	56.3
Curb weight, lbs.	2906	3385
Cargo vol., cu. ft.	10.2	16.4
Fuel capacity, gals.	15.9	21.1
Seating capacity	5	5
Front head room, in.	37.8	38.4
Front leg room, max., in.	42.2	42.2
Rear head room, in.	37.2	37.6
Rear leg room, min., in.	32.2	34.8

Powertrain layout: longitudinal front engine/front-wheel drive or permanent 4WD.

Engines

	dohc I-5	ohc V-6
Size, liters/cu. in.	2.3/141	2.8/169
Fuel delivery	PFI	PFI
Horsepower @ rpm	130 @ 5500	172 @ 5500
Torque (lbs./ft.) @ rpm	140 @ 4500	184 @ 3000
Availability	S[1]	S[2]

EPA city/highway mpg

5-speed OD manual	20/26	19/26
4-speed OD automatic	18/25	17/25

1. 80.   2. 100.

Assembly point: Neckarsulm, Germany.

liter V-6, while smaller than most engines in this class, delivers adequate acceleration. The 5-speed manual transmission is very smooth and precise, but the automatic is less appealing; it's often caught in too high a gear, and shift action is a bit harsh. Handling and roadholding rank at or near the top of this class, but the price is paid with a ride that seems to transmit every little bump through to the passenger compartment. Interior appointments are first rate, and rear passengers are given plenty of room.

Prices

Audi 80	Retail Price	Dealer Invoice	Low Price
80 4-door notchback	$22650	—	—
80 Quattro 4-door notchback	26250	—	—

Dealer invoice, low price, and destination charge not available at time of publication.

Standard equipment:

80: 2.3-liter PFI 5-cylinder engine, 5-speed manual transmission, anti-lock 4-wheel disc brakes, power steering, driver-side air bag, air conditioning, cloth reclining front bucket seats with height adjustment, front and rear folding armrests, rear head restraints, tachometer, coolant temperature gauge, trip odometer, power windows and locks, cruise control, heated power mirrors, AM/FM cassette with diversity antenna, leather-wrapped steering wheel, seatback pockets, lighted right visor mirror, tinted glass, rear defogger, intermittent wipers, digital clock, 175/70TR14 tires. **80 Quattro** has permanent 4-wheel drive, sport seats, fog lights, alloy wheels.

Audi 80

Prices are accurate at time of publication; subject to manufacturer's change.

Optional equipment:

	Retail Price	Dealer Invoice	Low Price
Anti-theft alarm, 80	295	—	—
Power sunroof, 80 & 80 Quattro	855	—	—
Ski sack, Quattros	140	—	—
All Weather Pkg.	445	—	—
Heated front seats, heated front door locks, heated windshield washer nozzles, headlamp washers.			
Clearcoat or metallic paint	410	—	—
Compact disc changer (6 disc)	890	—	—

Audi 100

4-door notchback	$27700	—	—
S 4-door notchback	29900	—	—
CS 4-door notchback	32900	—	—
Destination charge	355	355	355

Dealer invoice and low price not available at time of publication.

Standard equipment:

100: 2.8-liter PFI 6-cylinder engine, 5-speed manual transmission, anti-lock 4-wheel disc brakes, power steering, driver-side air bag, tilt and telescoping steering column, velour reclining front bucket seats with height and lumbar adjustments, front and rear folding armrests, air conditioning, tachometer, oil temperature and pressure gauges, voltmeter, coolant temperature gauge, trip odometer, Auto Check System, power windows and locks, cruise control, heated power mirrors, power sunroof, AM/FM cassette with diversity antenna, wood trim, seatback pockets, leather-wrapped steering wheel, reading lamps, lighted visor mirrors, anti-theft alarm, tinted glass, rear defogger, intermittent wipers, analog clock, rear fog light, remote decklid release, floormats, 195/65HR15 tires. **S** adds: variable-assist power steering, 8-way power front bucket seats with manual lumbar adjusters, ski/storage sack, alloy wheels. **CS** adds: front fog lights, trip computer with outside temperature gauge, automatic climate control, remote locking system, driver's seat memory system, Bose music system.

Optional equipment:

4-speed automatic transmission	800	—	—
Leather seats, S & CS	1300	—	—
Metallic paint	470	—	—
Pearlescent paint, S & CS	935	—	—
All-Weather Pkg., S	445	—	—
CS	—	—	—
Heated front seats and windshield washer nozzles, heated front door locks, headlight washers.			
Voice-activated telephone, CS	—	—	—
CD player, CS	—	—	—

BMW 3-Series

BMW 325i 4-door

A new 325i bowed last summer as a 1992 model and returns this fall with some minor changes. It's offered for now only as a 4-door sedan, though convertibles based on the old design are still offered in 4-cylinder (318i) and 6-cylinder (325i) form. Compared with its predecessor, the new 325i sedan sits on a 5.1-inch longer wheelbase (106.3 inches). Length increases by 4.3 inches, to 174.5, and width by two. Despite the larger dimensions, interior volume expands only modestly. The new sedan uses a twin-cam version of the old 2.5-liter six rated at 189 horsepower, 21 more than before. A 5-speed manual transmission is standard, and the optional 4-speed overdrive automatic has economy, sport, and manual shift programs. A driver-side air bag and 4-wheel anti-lock disc brakes are standard. BMW's six feels somewhat weak until 3000 rpm, at which point the power unspools to the 6900-rpm redline and the car vaults ahead in a rush of acceleration. Some body roll accompanies fast turns, but the 325i feels lithe and—on dry roads—sure-footed. Poor grip on wet pavement allows the tail of this rear-drive sedan to slip sideways easily. The suspension soaks up imperfections while keeping the body from bobbing at high speeds. Inside, large analog gauges are unobstructed and the radio and climate controls are just a handspan from the steering wheel. The fabric upholstery

and unadorned vinyl door panels look a bit cheap in a
$28,000 car. Rear door openings that narrow on the bottom
hamper back-seat entry. Three in back is a real squeeze,
and the bottom of the front seatbacks snags shoes.

Specifications

	4-door notchback	2-door conv.
Wheelbase, in.	106.3	101.2
Overall length, in.	174.5	175.2
Overall width, in.	66.8	64.8
Overall height, in.	54.1	53.9
Curb weight, lbs.	3021	2990
Cargo vol., cu. ft.	15.2	11.0
Fuel capacity, gals.	17.2	16.4
Seating capacity	5	4
Front head room, in.	37.8	NA
Front leg room, max., in.	40.9	NA
Rear head room, in.	37.3	NA
Rear leg room, min., in.	34.1	NA

Powertrain layout: longitudinal front engine/rear-wheel drive or permanent 4WD.

Engines

	dohc I-4	ohc I-6	dohc I-6
Size, liters/cu. in.	1.8/110	2.5/152	2.5/152
Fuel delivery	PFI	PFI	PFI
Horsepower @ rpm	134 @ 6000	168 @ 5800	189 @ 5900
Torque (lbs./ft.) @ rpm	127 @ 4600	164 @ 4300	181 @ 4700
Availability	S[1]	S[2]	S[3]

EPA city/highway mpg

5-speed OD manual	20/26	17/24	18/26
4-speed OD automatic		18/23	18/25

1. 318i conv.　　2. 325i conv.　　3. 325i sedan.

Assembly point: Regensburg, Germany.

Prices

BMW 3-Series	Retail Price	Dealer Invoice	Low Price
318i 2-door convertible	$28870	—	—
325i 2-door convertible	36230	—	35230

	Retail Price	Dealer Invoice	Low Price
325i 4-door notchback	27990	—	—
Destination charge	375	375	375

Dealer invoice and low price not available at time of publication.

Standard equipment:

318i: 1.8-liter DOHC 16-valve PFI 4-cylinder engine, 5-speed manual transmission, power steering, anti-lock 4-wheel disc brakes, driver-side air bag, air conditioning, cloth or leatherette reclining bucket seats with height/tilt adjustments, power windows and locks, power mirrors, AM/FM cassette, power antenna, tinted glass, intermittent wipers, rear defogger, Service Interval Indicator, Active Check Control system, toolkit, 195/65R14 tires on alloy wheels. **325i convertible** adds: 2.5-liter DOHC 16-valve PFI 6-cylinder engine, variable-assist power steering, dual air conditioning controls, power locks, cruise control, leather upholstery, map lights, trip computer, premium sound system, 195/65HR14 tires on cross-spoke alloy wheels. **325i 4-door** adds to 318i: 2.5-liter DOHC 24-valve PFI V-6 engine, variable-assist power steering, dual air conditioning controls, power sunroof, 205/60R15 tires.

Optional equipment:

4-speed automatic transmission, convertibles	725	595	660
325i 4-door	800	655	728
Limited slip differential, 325i 4-door	510	NA	NA
Sport Pkg., 325i 4-door	NA	NA	NA
Sport seats, leather-wrapped steering wheel, sport suspension, cellular phone pre-wiring, cross-spoke alloy wheels.			
Comfort Pkg., 325i 4-door	NA	NA	NA
Front and rear armrests, tilt steering column, power driver's seat, cellular telephone pre-wiring.			
Metallic paint	435	355	395
Leather upholstery, 325i 4-door	1100	900	1000
Heated front seats, convertibles.	300	245	273
325i 4-door	350	285	318
On-board computer, 325i 4-door	410	335	373
Alarm system, convertibles	540	315	428
Power driver-seat, 325i 4-door	NA	NA	NA

BMW 5-Series

BMW trims the level of standard equipment slightly on the 525i, while adding more convenience features to the 535i. Both are 4-door sedans with inline-6-cylinder engines, but the 525i gets 189 horsepower from a twin-cam,

Prices are accurate at time of publication; subject to manufacturer's change.

1991 BMW 525i

24-valve 2.5-liter, while the 535i gets 208 from a single overhead-cam, 12-valve 3.4-liter. A limited-edition high-performance companion model, the M5, has a twin-cam 3.5 with 310 horsepower. A 5-speed manual transmission is standard (it's mandatory on the M5). A 4-speed overdrive automatic is otherwise optional, and later in the year is to get a shift interlock. On all models, central locking can now be engaged from the passenger's side as well as the driver's; the outside mirrors are no longer heated; the vent system gets a microfilter; and the fender-mounted radio antenna is replaced by a diversity antenna embedded in the rear window. Leather and wood trim, which is standard on the 535i, is a new option for the 525i. On the 535i, a remote-actuated anti-theft alarm is now standard; there's one-touch power down for all windows, not just the driver's; and a power adjustable steering wheel with memory is a new option. Few sedans can match the 5-Series' supple suspension, comfortable seats, precise steering, and power-ful brakes. The standard driver-side air bag and, on the 535i, optional traction control, are laudable features. But unless you prefer manual transmission or regularly spend hours at highway speeds, the Acura Legend is probably a better value than the 525i, and the Lexus LS 400 or Infiniti Q45 are likely to be more satisfying than the 535i in daily driving.

Specifications

	4-door notchback
Wheelbase, in.	108.7
Overall length, in.	185.8
Overall width, in.	68.9
Overall height, in.	55.6
Curb weight, lbs.	3484
Cargo vol., cu. ft.	16.2
Fuel capacity, gals.	21.1
Seating capacity	5
Front head room, in.	38.5
Front leg room, max., in.	42.0
Rear head room, in.	37.4
Rear leg room, min., in.	25.5

Powertrain layout: longitudinal front engine/rear-wheel drive.

Engines

	dohc I-6	ohc I-6	dohc I-6
Size, liters/cu. in.	2.5/152	3.4/209	3.5/216
Fuel delivery	PFI	PFI	PFI
Horsepower @ rpm	189 @ 5900	208 @ 5700	310 @ 6900
Torque (lbs./ft.) @ rpm	181 @ 4700	225 @ 4000	266 @ 4750
Availability	S[1]	S[2]	S[3]

EPA city/highway mpg

	dohc I-6	ohc I-6	dohc I-6
5-speed OD manual	17/25	15/23	12/23
4-speed OD automatic	17/25	16/22	

1. 525i.   2. 535i.   3. M5.

Assembly point: Dingolfing, Germany.

Prices

BMW 5-Series	Retail Price	Dealer Invoice	Low Price
525i 4-door notchback	$35600	NA	$34350
535i 4-door notchback	44350	NA	NA
1991 M5 5-door notchback	57600	47380	NA
Destination charge	375	375	375
Gas Guzzler Tax, 535i	1300	1300	1300
M5	3700	3700	3700

Prices are accurate at time of publication; subject to manufacturer's change.

Standard equipment:

525i: 2.5-liter DOHC 24-valve PFI 6-cylinder engine, 5-speed manual transmission, power steering, anti-lock 4-wheel disc brakes, driver's-side airbag, air conditioning with individual temperature controls, leather power front bucket seats, folding center armrests, rear armrest with storage, telescopic steering column, power windows and locks, heated power mirrors, fog lights, adjustable steering wheel, tinted glass, tachometer and coolant temperature gauge, rear defogger, seatback pockets, front and rear reading lights, dual LCD trip odometers, Service Interval Indicator, Active Check Control system, fuel economy indicator, trip computer, power sunroof, toolkit, 205/65R15 94H tires on alloy wheels. **535i** adds: 3.4-liter SOHC 12-valve engine, 5-speed manual or 4-speed automatic transmission, leather-wrapped steering wheel, automatic climate control, 225/60ZR15 tires. **M5** adds: 3.5-liter DOHC 24-valve 6-cylinder engine, close-ratio 5-speed manual transmission, upgraded suspension and brakes, self-leveling rear suspension, quicker-ratio steering, front sport seats, leather trim (on seats, door panels, center console and lower dashboard), 235/45ZR17 tires on special two-piece alloy wheels.

Optional equipment:	Retail Price	Dealer Invoice	Low Price
4-speed automatic transmission, 525i . . .	725	595	660
Leather upholstery, 525i	1200	985	1093
Limited-slip differential	465	380	423
ASC (Automatic Stability Control), 535i . .	1290	1055	1173
Heated front seats	300	245	273
CD changer	825	580	703
Alarm system	540	315	428
Cellular telephone	800	—	—
w/voice activation	1050	—	—

BMW 7-Series and 850i

Detail changes mark these premium rear-drive coupes and sedans. The 735i and 735iL sedans use a 208-horsepower 3.4-liter 6-cylinder engine. The "L" designation denotes a longer wheelbase and body. The 750iL sedan has the longer wheelbase and body, plus a 296-horsepower 5.0-liter V-12 that it shares with the 850i coupe. The coupe comes standard with a 6-speed manual transmission, but all sedans come with a 4-speed overdrive automatic transmission (optional on the coupe) that during the model year will get a shift interlock. New sedan features for 1992 include: an anti-theft alarm that unlocks the central locking system;

BMW 735i

one-touch power down for all windows, not just the driver's; a diversity radio antenna in the rear window; and a luggage net in the trunk. All 7- and 8-series cars now offer a power-adjusted steering wheel with memory and a microfiltered ventilation system. On the 735iL, a full-width manual adjustment for the position of the rear seat replaces individual power adjustments. The 750iL receives double pane insulated side-windows for better climate and noise insulation, and a power instead of manual rear sunshade. All these cars are extremely capable driving machines. The 735iL offers the same limousine-sized rear seating as the 750iL, but its smaller engine sacrifices some performance. The shorter 735i still has fine interior room along with remarkably alert acceleration, handling, and braking for a 3900-pound 6-cylinder sedan. The 850i coupe is no tire-smoking muscle car, but its engine is very smooth and provides plenty of power for effortless passing at freeway speeds. Trouble is, the least expensive among them costs more than $50,000, the 750iL goes for over $74,000, and the 850i starts at close to $80,000. BMW's own 535i provides performance similar to the 7-series sedans, while trading less cabin space for a smaller price tag. But as with the 5-Series cars, we must advise sedan shoppers in this bracket to also consider the Lexus LS 400 and Infiniti Q45, and those interested in the 850i coupe to look at the Lexus SC 400.

Prices are accurate at time of publication; subject to manufacturer's change.

Specifications

	735i 4-door notchback	735iL/750iL 4-door notchback	850i 2-door notchback
Wheelbase, in.	111.5	116.0	105.7
Overall length, in.	193.3	197.8	188.2
Overall width, in.	72.6	72.6	73.0
Overall height, in.	55.6	55.1	52.8
Curb weight, lbs.	3835	4015	4123
Cargo vol., cu. ft.	17.6	17.6	10.6
Fuel capacity, gals.	21.5	24.0	23.8
Seating capacity	5	5	4
Front head room, in.	38.3	38.3	37.3
Front leg room, max., in.	44.3	44.3	NA
Rear head room, in.	37.2	37.2	34.9
Rear leg room, min., in.	NA	32.8	NA

Powertrain layout: longitudinal front engine/rear-wheel drive.

Engines

	ohc I-6	ohc V-12
Size, liters/cu. in.	3.4/209	5.0/304
Fuel delivery	PFI	PFI
Horsepower @ rpm	208 @ 5700	296 @ 5200
Torque (lbs./ft.) @ rpm	225 @ 4000	332 @ 4100
Availability	S[1]	S[2]

EPA city/highway mpg

6-speed OD manual		12/19
4-speed OD automatic	15/21	12/18

1. 735i and 735iL.   2. 750iL and 850i.

Assembly point: Dingolfing, Germany.

Prices

BMW 7-Series	Retail Price	Dealer Invoice	Low Price
735i 4-door notchback	$52990	—	—
735iL 4-door notchback	56950	—	—
750iL 4-door notchback	76500	—	—
Destination charge	375	375	375
Gas Guzzler Tax, 735i, 735iL	1300	1300	1300
750iL	3000	3000	3000

Dealer invoice and low price not available at time of publication.

Standard equipment:

735i/735iL: 3.4-liter PFI 6-cylinder engine, 4-speed automatic transmission, anti-lock 4-wheel disc brakes, power steering, driver-side air bag, automatic climate control system with separate left/right adjustability, power front seats with driver's-side memory system, driver's seat lumbar support adjustment, power rear seats, leather (on seats, console, and door panels), door pockets, power windows and locks, cruise control, rear head restraints, rear armrest with storage, automatic dimming mirror, walnut trim, front and rear reading lamps, tinted glass, Service Interval Indicator, Active Check Control system, rear defogger, power sunroof, AM/FM cassette, toolkit, security alarm (735iL), 225/60ZR15 tires on alloy wheels. **750iL** adds: 5.0-liter PFI V-12, ASC + T traction control, heated front seats, cellular telephone, 6-disc CD changer, rear sunshade.

Optional equipment:	Retail Price	Dealer Invoice	Low Price
Limited-slip differential (NA 750iL)	465	380	—
ASC stability control, 735i, 735iL	1290	1055	—
EDC (Electronic Damping Control)	1470	1205	—
Heated front seats, 735i, 735iL	300	245	—
Heated rear seats, 750iL	300	245	—
CD changer, 735i, 735iL	825	580	—
Ski sack	180	150	—
Roll-up rear sunshade, 735iL	175	145	—
Remote alarm system, 735i	540	315	—
Cellular telephone, 735i, 735iL	800	—	—
w/voice activation	1050	—	—

BMW 850i

	Retail Price	Dealer Invoice	Low Price
2-door notchback	$77700	$62310	—
Destination charge	NC	NC	NC
Gas Guzzler Tax, w/automatic	3000	3000	3000
w/5-speed	3700	3700	3700

Low price not available at time of publication.

Standard equipment:

5.0-liter PFI V-12, 6-speed manual or 4-speed automatic transmission, anti-lock braking system, Automatic Stability Control, power steering, driver-side air bag, automatic climate control, power heated front seats, power head restraints and lumbar support adjustment, 3-position memory (for driver's seat, steering column and OS mirrors), leather trim (on seats, door panels, center console and lower dashboard), tilt/telescopic steering column, power windows, remote locking and alarm, AM/FM cassette with 6-disc CD player/changer, cellular telephone, power sunroof, cruise control, heated

Prices are accurate at time of publication; subject to manufacturer's change.

power mirrors, leather-wrapped steering wheel, first aid kit, tinted glass, Service Interval Indicator, Check Control, trip computer, tachometer, coolant temperature gauge, trip odometer, 235/50ZR16 tires with full-size spare.

Optional equipment:	Retail Price	Dealer Invoice	Low Price
Forged alloy wheels	1000	800	—
ASC + T traction control	1500	1200	—
EDC (Electronic Damping Control)	1470	1205	—

Buick Park Avenue/ Oldsmobile Ninety Eight

Buick Park Avenue

Availability of a supercharged engine and traction control are the major additions to these full-size front-drive luxury sedans. Both the Park Avenue and Ninety Eight were re-styled last year, and though the wheelbase was unchanged, they grew in length by eight inches, and cargo volume increased from 16.4 cubic feet to 20. The Park Avenue is offered in base and Ultra versions; the Ninety Eight comes in base, Elite, and Touring Sedan models. All except the Park Avenue Ultra come standard with a 170-horsepower 3.8-liter V-6 and electronically controlled 4-speed automatic transmission; the Ultra gets a new supercharged version of the 3.8 rated at 205 horsepower, which is optional in the Ninety Eight Touring Sedan. All have a driver-side air bag and anti-lock brakes as standard equipment, and can be ordered with the newly optional traction control, which reduces tire spin when accelerating on slippery surfaces. The base 3.8-liter V-6 and automatic provide smooth, fairly brisk acceleration. The supercharged engine is just as smooth, but noticeably stronger. Base models of both cars offer a cushy ride, but get bouncy over wavy surfaces and lean heavily in turns. The Park Avenue Ultra and Ninety Eight Touring Sedan come with firmer suspensions that offer better control with only a slight sacrifice in ride comfort; other Park Avenues and Ninety Eights can be ordered with optional "sport" suspensions that provide similar at-

Specifications

	4-door notchback
Wheelbase, in.	110.7
Overall length, in.	205.3
Overall width, in.	73.6
Overall height, in.	55.1
Curb weight, lbs.	3536
Cargo vol., cu. ft.	20.3
Fuel capacity, gals.	18.0
Seating capacity	6
Front head room, in.	38.8
Front leg room, max., in.	42.0
Rear head room, in.	37.8
Rear leg room, min., in.	41.6

Powertrain layout: transverse front engine/front-wheel drive.

Engines	ohv V-6	Supercharged ohv V-6
Size, liters/cu. in.	3.8/231	3.8/231
Fuel delivery	PFI	PFI
Horsepower @ rpm	170 @ 4800	205 @ 4400
Torque (lbs./ft.) @ rpm	220 @ 3200	260 @ 2800
Availability	S	S[1]

EPA city/highway mpg

4-speed OD automatic	18/27	17/27

1. Buick Park Avenue Ultra; opt. Ninety Eight Touring Sedan.

Assembly point: Wentzville, Mo.

Prices are accurate at time of publication; subject to manufacturer's change.

tributes. Four adults fit comfortably in all, with plenty of head and leg room; even six can ride without undue squeezing. Unfortunately, both Buick and Oldsmobile versions suffer the same weakness: poor control layout. Though the dash designs differ, each has its own confusing and hard-to-reach array of climate-control switches. While Park Avenue and Ninety Eight are worth considering, the Buick LeSabre and similar Olds Eighty Eight offer similar virtues at a lower cost.

Prices

Buick Park Avenue	Retail Price	Dealer Invoice	Low Price
4-door notchback	$25285	$21695	$23490
Ultra 4-door notchback	28780	24693	26737
Destination charge	600	600	600

Standard equipment:

3.8-liter PFI V-6, 4-speed automatic transmission, anti-lock brakes, variable-assist power steering, driver-side air bag, automatic level control, air conditioning, 55/45 cloth reclining front seat, storage armrest with cupholders, power driver's seat, power windows and locks, cruise control, AM/FM cassette, power mirrors, Pass-Key theft-deterrent system, intermittent wipers, tilt steering column, trip odometer, tinted glass, floormats, rear defogger, remote fuel door release, front and rear reading and courtesy lights, lighted right visor mirror, 215/70R15 tires on alloy wheels. **Ultra** adds: Supercharged 3.8-liter V-6 engine, automatic climate control with separate temperature controls, leather upholstery, rear head restraints, lighted left visor mirror, lighted mirrors for rear passengers, lower bodyside moldings, two-tone paint, power front seats with power recliners, leather-wrapped steering wheel.

Optional equipment:

Gran Touring Pkg., base	300	255	270
Base w/Pkg. SB/SC/SD	224	190	202
Base w/Pkg. SE	74	63	67
Ultra	166	141	149
Ultra w/Pkg. SB/SC/SD	86	73	77
Ultra w/Pkg. SE (credit)	(64)	(54)	(54)

Gran Touring suspension, 3.06 axle ratio, leather-wrapped steering wheel (base), 215/60R15 Goodyear Eagle GA tires on alloy wheels.

Popular Pkg. SB, base	684	581	616

Power passenger seat, power antenna, door edge guards, white-stripe tires, tachometer and analog gauges, oil level monitor, trunk net.

	Retail Price	Dealer Invoice	Low Price
Premium Pkg. SC, base	1084	921	976

Pkg. SB plus power seatback recliner, dual-control air conditioner, Concert Sound speakers, illuminated entry, Reminder Pkg.

| Luxury Pkg. SD, base . . . . | 1911 | 1624 | 1720 |

Pkg. SC plus cornering lamps, Twilight Sentinel, four-note horn, lamp monitors, power decklid pulldown, automatic locks with remote keyless entry, lighted left visor mirror, theft deterrent system, automatic day/night rearview mirror.

| Prestige Pkg. SE, base . . . . | 2572 | 2186 | 2315 |

Pkg. SD plus graphic equalizer, automatic day/night heated left outside mirror, memory seat and mirrors, self-sealing tires, trunk mat, rear seat climate controls.

| Popular Pkg. SB, Ultra . . . . | 270 | 230 | 243 |

Power antenna, door edge guards, white-stripe tires, oil level monitor, trunk net.

| Premium Pkg. SC, Ultra . . . . | 460 | 391 | 414 |

Pkg. SB plus Concert Sound speakers, illuminated entry, Reminder Pkg.

| Luxury Pkg. SD, Ultra . . . . | 1229 | 1045 | 1106 |

Pkg. SC plus cornering lamps, Twilight Sentinel, four-note horn, lamp monitors, power decklid pulldown, automatic locks with remote keyless entry, theft deterrent system, automatic day/night rearview mirror.

| Prestige Pkg. SE, Ultra . . . . | 1834 | 1559 | 1651 |

Pkg. SD plus graphic equalizer, automatic automatic day/night heated left outside mirror, memory seat and mirrors, self-sealing tires, trunk mat.

| AM/FM cassette w/EQ, w/Pkg. SB . . . . . | 220 | 187 | 198 |
| w/SC/SD . . . . | 150 | 128 | 135 |

Includes tape search/repeat, AM stereo, and Concert Sound speakers.

Bose music system, Ultra w/SB	793	674	714
Ultra w/SC/SD	723	615	651
Ultra w/SE	573	487	516
CD player w/EQ, w/SB	484	411	436
w/SC/SD	394	335	355
w/SE	264	224	238
Astroroof, base w/SB/SC	1408	1197	1267
Ultra w/SB/SC	1350	1148	1215
Base & Ultra w/SD/SE	1273	1082	1146
Trailering Pkg.	150	128	135
w/Gran Touring Pkg.	123	105	111
Leather/vinyl 55/45 seat, base	500	425	450
Electriclear heated windshield	250	213	225
Firemist paint	250	213	225
205/70R15 blackwall tires, w/SB/SC/SD (credit)	(76)	(64)	(64)
w/SE (credit)	(226)	(192)	(192)
215/70R15 blackwall tires, Ultra w/SB/SC/SD (credit)	(80)	(68)	(68)
Ultra w/SE (credit)	(230)	(196)	(196)

Prices are accurate at time of publication; subject to manufacturer's change.

	Retail Price	Dealer Invoice	Low Price
215/70R15 whitewall tires, Ultra w/o Pkgs .	80	68	72
Self-sealing tires, w/SB/SC/SD	150	128	135
Wire wheel covers	NC	NC	NC
Warranty enhancements for New York . . .	25	21	23
California emissions pkg.	100	85	90

Oldsmobile Ninety Eight

	Retail Price	Dealer Invoice	Low Price
Regency 4-door notchback	$24595	$21348	—
Regency Elite 4-door notchback	26195	22737	—
Touring Sedan 4-door notchback	28995	25168	—
Destination charge	600	600	600

Low price not available at time of publication.

Standard equipment:

Regency: 3.8-liter PFI V-6, 4-speed automatic transmission, anti-lock brakes, power steering, driver-side air bag, automatic climate control, cloth 55/45 reclining front seat, power driver's seat, cruise control, power windows and locks, power mirrors, AM/FM cassette, power antenna, remote fuel door and decklid releases, tilt steering column, automatic leveling, solar-control tinted glass, visor mirrors, intermittent wipers, rear defogger, floormats, wire wheel covers, 205/70R15 whitewall tires. **Regency Elite** adds: cornering lamps, power passenger seat, steering wheel touch controls, electrochromatic rearview mirror, lighted visor mirrors, alloy wheels. **Touring Sedan** adds: FE3 Touring Car suspension, variable-assist power steering, power front bucket seats with adjustable lumbar support and side bolsters, leather upholstery, console with storage, burl walnut trim, fog lamps, tachometer, coolant temperature and oil pressure gauges, voltmeter, Driver Information Center, cornering lamps, heated outside mirrors (electrochromatic driver-side), upgraded audio system with EQ, misc. lights, Remote Lock Control Pkg., steering wheel touch controls, leather-wrapped steering wheel, power decklid pulldown, Twilight Sentinel, 215/60R16 tires on alloy wheels.

Optional equipment:

	Retail Price	Dealer Invoice	Low Price
Supercharged 3.8-liter V-6 engine, Touring Sedan	1022	869	—
Traction control system	175	149	—
Option Pkg. 1SB, Regency	748	636	—

Reminder Pkg., electrochromatic rearview mirror, lighted visor mirrors, power passenger seat, steering wheel touch controls, cornering lamps.

Option Pkg. 1SC, Regency	1218	1035	—

Pkg. 1SB plus power decklid pull-down, Remote Accessory Control, Pkg., Twilight Sentinel, trunk net, heated electrochromatic driver-side outside mirror.

	Retail Price	Dealer Invoice	Low Price
Option Pkg. 1SB, Elite	470	400	—

Power decklid pull-down, Remote Accessory Control, Pkg., Twilight Sentinel, trunk net, heated electrochromatic driver-side outside mirror.

	Retail Price	Dealer Invoice	Low Price
Astroroof	1350	1148	—
Dual-control air conditioner	45	38	—
Heated windshield	250	213	—
FE3 Touring Car suspension, Regency . . .	384	326	—
Regency w/leather seats	330	281	—
Elite	253	215	—
Elite w/leather seats	199	169	—

Sport suspension, 3.06 axle ratio, high-capacity cooling, leather-wrapped steering wheel, 215/65R15 tires on alloy wheels.

	Retail Price	Dealer Invoice	Low Price
Computer Command Ride System, Regency & Elite	434	369	—
Regency & Elite w/leather seats	380	323	—
Wire wheel covers, Elite	NC	NC	NC
Alloy wheels, Regency	131	111	—
Cassette w/EQ, Regency & Elite	120	102	—
Cassette and CD player, Regency & Elite .	396	337	—
Cassette and CD player w/EQ, Regency & Elite Touring Sedan	516 396	439 337	—
Electronic instruments, Regency & Elite . .	449	382	—
Includes Driver Information Center.			
Glamour metallic paint, Regency & Elite . .	210	179	—
Towing Pkg.	150	128	—
Custom leather trim, Regency & Elite . . .	515	438	—
Heated seats, Touring Sedan	235	200	—
Accent stripe	45	38	—
205/70R15 blackwall touring tires, Regency & Elite	NC	NC	NC
Engine block heater	18	15	—
Warranty enhancements for New York state .	25	21	—
California emissions pkg.	100	85	—

Buick Regal

The Gran Sport sheds its options-group status and joins the Custom and Limited as a full-fledged Regal model. Anti-lock brakes are now standard on Limited and Gran Sport, optional on the Custom, but none offer an air bag. All Regals are front-wheel drive and available in 2- or 4-door body styles. Power door locks are standard across the line for 1992. A 140-horsepower 3.1-liter V-6 is standard

Prices are accurate at time of publication; subject to manufacturer's change.

Buick Regal Gran Sport 4-door

Specifications

	2-door notchback	4-door notchback
Wheelbase, in.	107.5	107.5
Overall length, in.	193.6	193.9
Overall width, in.	72.5	72.5
Overall height, in.	53.0	54.5
Curb weight, lbs.	3236	3320
Cargo vol., cu. ft.	15.6	15.8
Fuel capacity, gals.	16.5	16.5
Seating capacity	6	6
Front head room, in.	37.8	38.7
Front leg room, max., in.	42.3	42.4
Rear head room, in.	37.1	37.8
Rear leg room, min., in.	34.8	36.2

Powertrain layout: transverse front engine/front-wheel drive.

Engines	ohv V-6	ohv V-6
Size, liters/cu. in.	3.1/191	3.8/231
Fuel delivery	PFI	PFI
Horsepower @ rpm	140 @ 4400	170 @ 4800
Torque (lbs./ft.) @ rpm	185 @ 3200	220 @ 3200
Availability	S	O

EPA city/highway mpg

4-speed OD automatic	19/29	18/28

Assembly point: Oshawa, Ontario, Canada.

on Custom and Limited, a 170-horsepower 3.8-liter V-6 is standard on Gran Sport and optional on the others. A 4-speed overdrive automatic is the only transmission. The 3.1-liter V-6 is adequate for the job, but the 3.8 provides stronger acceleration, and though it growls a bit under hard throttle, it cruises quietly. Upshifts are smooth, but the automatic's downshifts aren't quite as quick as the electronically controlled unit in the Park Avenue. Gran Sport's firmer suspension provides taut handling and a well-controlled ride, but some testers find it a bit harsh. While rear-seat space is adequate for 6-footers, the bottom cushion is too unsubstantial for good long-distance comfort. Regal's analog instruments are crammed into a narrow horizontal channel on the dash, where they're difficult to read at a glance. Some are blocked by the steering wheel, and the fuel gauge actually is to the right of the car's center. So are the climate controls, though they consist of big, well-marked buttons. Power window switches are placed awkwardly on the driver's door, and outward visibility is compromised by wide front roof pillars.

Prices

Buick Regal	Retail Price	Dealer Invoice	Low Price
Custom 2-door notchback	$16610	$14417	$14617
Custom 4-door notchback	16865	14639	14839
Limited 2-door notchback	17790	15442	15642
Limited 4-door notchback	18110	15719	15919
Gran Sport 2-door notchback	18600	16145	16345
Gran Sport 4-door notchback	19300	16752	16952
Destination charge	505	505	505

Standard equipment:

Custom: 3.1-liter PFI V-6, 4-speed automatic transmission, power steering, 4-wheel disc brakes, air conditioning, door-mounted automatic front seatbelts, power locks, cloth reclining 55/45 front seat with storage armrest, tinted glass, intermittent wipers, left remote and right manual mirrors, visor mirrors, AM/FM radio, tilt steering column, 205/70R14 tires. **Limited** adds: anti-lock brakes, analog instrumentation, overhead console, reading lamps.

Prices are accurate at time of publication; subject to manufacturer's change.

Gran Sport adds: 3.8-liter PFI V-6, gran touring suspension, leather-wrapped steering wheel, cloth reclining bucket seats, console with armrest and cupholders, fog lights, 225/60R16 touring tires on alloy wheels.

Optional equipment:

	Retail Price	Dealer Invoice	Low Price
3.8-liter V-6	395	336	340
Anti-lock brakes	450	383	387
Popular Pkg. SB, Custom	475	404	409
Rear defogger, cruise control, floormats, 4-way manual seat adjuster.			
Premium Pkg. SC, Custom 2-door	935	795	804
Custom 4-door	1000	850	860
Pkg. SB plus cassette player, dual-control air conditioner, power windows.			
Luxury Pkg. SD, Custom 2-door	1503	1278	1293
Custom 4-door	1568	1333	1348
Pkg. SC plus power mirrors, power antenna, remote decklid release, 205/70R15 blackwall tires on alloy wheels.			
Prestige Pkg. SE, Custom 2-door	2070	1760	1780
Custom 4-door	2135	1815	1836
Pkg. SD plus lighted visor mirrors, power driver's seat, remote keyless entry, Concert Sound speakers.			
Popular Pkg. SB, Ltd. 2-door	520	442	447
Cruise control, rear defogger, 4-way manual seat adjuster, dual air conditioning controls, floormats.			
Premium Pkg. SC, Ltd. 2-door	1020	867	877
Ltd. 4-door	1085	922	933
Pkg. SB plus power windows, cassette player.			
Luxury Pkg. SD, Ltd 2-door	1573	1337	1353
Ltd 4-door	1638	1392	1409
Pkg. SC plus power mirrors, remote decklid release, Concert Sound speakers, 205/70R15 blackwall tires on alloy wheels.			
Prestige Pkg. SE, Ltd. 2-door	2195	1866	1888
Ltd. 4-door	2330	1981	2004
Pkg. SD plus lighted visor mirrors, power driver's seat, remote keyless entry, steering-wheel-mounted radio controls. 4-doors add door-mounted courtesy lights.			
Gran Sport Luxury Pkg. SD, 2-door	1228	1044	1056
4-door	1293	1099	1112
Power windows, cruise control, rear defogger, cassette player, Concert Sound speakers, power antenna, power mirrors, remote decklid release, dual air conditioning controls, floormats.			
Gran Sport Prestige Pkg. SE, 2-door	1875	1594	1613
4-door	1940	1649	1668
Pkg. SC plus power driver's seat, cassette player w/EQ, remote keyless entry, lighted visor mirrors.			

	Retail Price	Dealer Invoice	Low Price
Gran Touring Pkg., Custom w/SB/SC	755	642	649
Custom w/SD/SE	410	349	353
Ltd w/SB/SC	695	591	598
Ltd w/SD	350	298	301
Ltd w/SE	254	216	218

Gran Touring suspension, 225/60R16 tires on alloy wheels, leather-wrapped steering wheel (except Ltd. w/SE Pkg.), analog gauges with tachometer.

	Retail Price	Dealer Invoice	Low Price
Analog gauges & tachometer, Custom . . .	60	51	52
UX1 audio system, w/SB	290	247	249
Custom w/SC/SD/SE & Ltd. w/SC/SD . .	150	128	129
Gran Sport w/SD	150	128	129

Includes cassette player with tape search/repeat, AM stereo, and EQ.

	Retail Price	Dealer Invoice	Low Price
CD player, w/SB	414	352	356
Custom w/SC/SD/SE, Ltd. w/SC/SD, GS w/SD	274	233	236
Ltd. & GS w/SE	124	105	107
Power sunroof	695	591	598

Requires mirror reading lights.

	Retail Price	Dealer Invoice	Low Price
Steering-wheel-mounted radio controls,			
Gran Sport	29	25	25
Custom & Ltd	125	106	108
Power front seats w/SB/SC/SD	575	489	495
w/SE/	305	259	262
Reclining bucket seats, Custom	NC	NC	NC
Leather/vinyl 55/45 front seat, Ltd	500	425	430
Leather/vinyl bucket seats, Ltd. & GS . . .	500	425	430
Cloth Four Seater Pkg., Ltd	335	285	288
Gran Sport	240	204	206
Leather Four Seater Pkg., Ltd	835	710	718
Gran Sport	740	629	636
Front seat reading lights, Custom	30	26	26
Rear seat reading/courtesy lights, Custom			
4-door	25	21	22
Door courtesy lights, Gran Sport	70	60	60
Bodyside stripe, Custom & ltd. 2-doors . .	45	38	39
Styled steel wheels, Custom w/SB/SC . .	115	98	99
Wire wheel covers, w/SB/SC	240	204	206
w/SD/SE (credit)	(85)	(72)	(72)
14″ alloy wheels, w/SB/SC	295	251	254
205/70R14 whitewall tires, w/SA/SB/SC . .	76	65	65
205/70R15 whitewall tires, w/SA/SB/SC . .	96	82	83
w/SD/SE	76	65	65
Decklid luggage rack	115	98	99
Wide bodyside molding, Custom 2-door . .	70	60	60
Door edge guards, 2-doors	15	13	13
4-doors	25	21	22

Prices are accurate at time of publication; subject to manufacturer's change.

Buick Roadmaster/
Chevrolet Caprice/
Oldsmobile Custom Cruiser

Buick Roadmaster 4-door

Oldsmobile's Custom Cruiser comes only as a wagon, but Roadmaster and Caprice are available in 4-door sedan and wagon form. A 180-horsepower 5.7-liter V-8 is now standard on both wagon and sedan versions of the Buick Roadmaster, and optional on Custom Cruiser and Caprice wagons. It is not available on Caprice sedans. The standard engine on Custom Cruiser and Caprice is a 170-horsepower 5.0-liter V-8. All of these full-size, rear-wheel-drive vehicles come standard with anti-lock brakes and a driver-side air bag. Despite their big V-8s, none leap away from stoplights—primarily because of their heft. Sedans tip the scales at around 4000 pounds, while wagons weigh in at about 4400. Once all that mass is underway, however, there's decent throttle response and ample passing power. They all bound and float over wavy surfaces, but the Roadmaster sedan has a firmer, more controlled ride with less body lean than the Caprice sedan. Six adults can ride in the sedans, and wagons have a rear-facing third seat suitable for a couple of children. The Olds and Buick wagons also have a "vista roof," a fixed glass sunroof over the middle bench seat that brightens the interior. All these cars have convenient climate controls placed in the center of the dash, along with cup holders and plenty of interior storage space. Trunks are huge in the sedans, while wagons have middle and rear seats that fold to create a flat cargo area that can hold a 4×8 plywood sheet.

Specifications

	4-door notchback	5-door wagon
Wheelbase, in.	115.9	115.9
Overall length, in.	214.1	217.3
Overall width, in.	77.0	79.6
Overall height, in.	56.7	60.9
Curb weight, lbs.	3907	4354
Cargo vol., cu. ft.	20.4	92.7
Fuel capacity, gals.	23.0	22.0
Seating capacity	6	8
Front head room, in.	39.3	39.7
Front leg room, max., in.	42.2	42.2
Rear head room, in.	38.1	39.6
Rear leg room, min., in.	39.5	38.0

Powertrain layout: longitudinal front engine/rear-wheel drive.

Engines	ohv V-8	ohv V-8
Size, liters/cu. in.	5.0/305	5.7/350
Fuel delivery	TBI	TBI
Horsepower @ rpm	170 @ 4200	180 @ 4000
Torque (lbs./ft.) @ rpm	255 @ 2400	300 @ 2400
Availability	S[1]	S[2]

EPA city/highway mpg

4-speed OD automatic	17/26	16/25

1. Caprice, Custom Cruiser. 2. Roadmaster sedan and wgn., opt. Caprice wgn. and Custom Cruiser.

Assembly points: Willow Run, Mich.; Arlington, Tex.

Prices

Buick Roadmaster	Retail Price	Dealer Invoice	Low Price
4-door notchback	$21865	$18979	—
Limited 4-door notchback	24195	21001	—

Prices are accurate at time of publication; subject to manufacturer's change.

	Retail Price	Dealer Invoice	Low Price
Estate 5-door wagon	23040	19999	20449
Destination charge	555	555	555

Low price for sedans not available at time of publication.

Standard equipment:

Base: 5.7-liter TBI V-8 engine, 4-speed automatic transmission, anti-lock brakes, power steering, driver-side air bag, air conditioning, cloth 55/45 front seat with reclining backrests, center armrest, tachometer, coolant temperature and oil pressure gauges, voltmeter, trip odometer, power windows, left remote and right manual mirrors, AM/FM radio, instrument panel storage tray with cupholders, front seatback pockets, door pockets, tilt steering column, tinted glass, visor mirrors, intermittent wipers, door edge guards, 225/75R15 whitewall tires on alloy wheels. **Wagon** adds: rear-facing third seat, rear window wiper/washer, luggage rack, vista roof, woodgrain applique. **Limited** adds to base: leather-wrapped steering wheel, automatic climate control, power antenna, automatic door locks, front door courtesy and warning lights, reading lights and compass, power mirrors (heated left), lighted visor mirrors, cassette player, remote keyless entry, power driver and passenger seats w/power recliners, rear-seat armrest, variable-assist steering.

Optional equipment:

Premium Pkg. SC, wagon	565	480	497

Cruise control, power antenna, cassette, floormats, front storage armrest.

Luxury Pkg. SD, base sedan	727	618	640

Power driver's seat, power passenger seat recliner, lighted visor mirrors, cassette, power antenna.

Luxury Pkg. SD, wagon	1320	1122	1162

Pkg. SC plus automatic climate control, power driver's seat, front door courtesy and warning lights, lighted visor mirrors, reading lights and compass, cargo area cover.

Prestige Pkg. SE, base sedan	1685	1432	1483

Pkg. SD plus power passenger seat, automatic climate control, automatic power door locks, remote keyless entry system, heated power mirrors, door-mounted courtesy and warning lights, compass.

Prestige Pkg. SE, Limited	406	345	357

Power decklid pull-down, Twilight Sentinel, leather-wrapped steering wheel, cornering lamps, self-sealing tires.

Prestige Pkg. SE, wagon	2117	1799	1863

Luxury Pkg. plus cornering lamps, Twilight Sentinel, power mirrors, power passenger seat, remote keyless entry, power locks.

Rear defogger, wagon, w/o Pkg. SE	170	145	150
w/Pkg. SE	205	174	180

Includes heated outside mirrors with Pkg. SE.

	Retail Price	Dealer Invoice	Low Price
Trailer Towing Pkg., wagon	325	276	286

3.23 axle ratio, HD engine and transmission cooling, automatic level control, engine oil cooler; sedans add HD suspension and whitewall tires.

	Retail Price	Dealer Invoice	Low Price
Sedans w/o Prestige Pkg.	267	227	235
Limited w/Prestige Pkg.	117	99	103
Limited-slip differential	100	85	88
3.23 ratio, wagon	NC	NC	NC
3.08 ratio, sedans	NC	NC	NC
Solar glass windshield, sedans	50	43	44
Leather 55/45 seats, base sedan	760	646	669
Wagon	540	459	475
Limited w/o Prestige Pkg.	760	646	669
Limited w/Prestige Pkg.	710	604	625

Limited has front seat with storage armrests.

	Retail Price	Dealer Invoice	Low Price
AM/FM Cassette w/EQ, base sedan w/o SD or SE	325	276	286
Base sedan w/SD or SE; Limited	150	128	132
Wagon w/SC, SD or SE	185	157	163
AM/FM w/CD player, base sedan w/o SD or SE	569	484	501
Base sedan w/SD or SE, Limited	394	335	347
Wagon w/SC, SD or SE	429	365	378
Power antenna, base sedan & wagon . . .	85	72	75
Vinyl top	695	591	612
Wire wheel covers, sedans	240	204	211
Wagon	NC	NC	NC
Alloy wheels, sedans	325	276	286
Full-size spare tire, sedans	65	55	57
Self-sealing P235/70R15 tires, base sedan .	150	128	132
Vista cover, wagon	85	72	75
Third seat delete (credit), wagon	(215)	(183)	(183)
Warranty enhancement for New York	25	21	22
California emissions pkg	100	85	88

Chevrolet Caprice

	Retail Price	Dealer Invoice	Low Price
4-door notchback	$17300	$15016	$15416
Classic 4-door notchback	19300	16752	17152
5-door wagon	18700	16232	16632
Destination charge	555	555	555

Standard equipment:

5.0-liter TBI V-8 engine, 4-speed automatic transmission, anti-lock brakes, power steering, driver-side air bag, air conditioning, cloth bench seat with center armrest, tilt steering column, AM/FM radio, cargo net, visor mirrors,

Prices are accurate at time of publication; subject to manufacturer's change.

intermittent wipers, door pockets, left remote and right manual mirrors, visor mirrors, cup and coin holders, trunk cargo net, 215/75R15 tires; **wagon** has power vent windows, luggage rack, rear wiper/washer, 225/75R15 whitewall tires. **Classic** adds: power windows and locks, 55/45 front seat with recliners, Diagnostic System, front cornering lamps, rear armrest, alloy wheels.

Optional equipment:	Retail Price	Dealer Invoice	Low Price
5.7-liter V-8 engine, wagon	250	213	220
Preferred Group 1, base 4-door & wagon .	270	230	238
Cruise control, floormats.			
Preferred Group 2, base 4-door	998	848	878
Group 1 plus power windows and locks, power mirrors, remote decklid release.			
Preferred Group 2, base 4-door w/bench seat	1316	1119	1158
Base 4-door w/55/45 seat	1621	1378	1426
Group 2 plus AM/FM cassette, power antenna, front reading lamps, lighted right visor mirror, power driver's seat (with 55/45 seat).			
Preferred Group 1, Classic	838	712	737
AM/FM cassette, power driver's seat, cruise control, remote decklid release, floormats, lighted right visor mirror.			
Preferred Group 2, Classic	1891	1607	1664
w/LTZ Pkg	1603	1363	1411
Group 1 plus Delco/Bose sound system, power antenna, power passenger seat, remote keyless entry, Twilight Sentinel, front reading lamps with compass, power mirrors.			
Preferred Group 2, wagon w/bench seat . .	1178	1001	1037
Wagon w/55/45 seat	1483	1261	1305
Group 1 plus cassette player, power windows and locks, power driver's seat, power mirrors.			
Preferred Group 3, wagon w/bench seat . .	1505	1279	1324
Wagon w/55/45 seat	2115	1798	1861
Group 2 plus power passenger seat (with 55/45 seat), deluxe rear compartment decor, rear security cover, power antenna, front reading lamps with compass, lighted right visor mirror.			
LTZ Pkg., Classic	825	701	726
Sport suspension, heavy-duty frame and brakes, heavy-duty cooling, limited slip axle, leather-wrapped steering wheel, digital speedometer, analog gauges (oil pressure, coolant temperature, and voltmeter), remote keyless entry, power mirrors, remote decklid release, AM/FM cassette, power antenna, 235/70VR15 Eagle GA tires.			
Cloth 55/45 seat, base 4-door	223	190	196
Custom cloth 55/45 seat, wagon	300	255	264
Leather 55/45 seat	645	548	568
Limited-slip differential	140	119	123
w/V92 Trailering Pkg.	100	85	88

	Retail Price	Dealer Invoice	Low Price
V92 Trailering Pkg., 4-doors	220	187	194
w/LTZ Pkg	110	94	97
Wagon	171	145	150
HD cooling, engine oil cooler, performance axle ratio.			
Automatic leveling suspension, wagon . . .	175	149	154
Ride/Handling suspension	49	42	43
Rear defogger	170	145	150
w/heated mirrors	205	174	180
Cassette player	165	140	145
Delco/Bose cassette system, base w/Group 3	335	285	295
U1B CD player, base w/Group 3	561	477	494
Classic w/Group 2	226	192	199
U1C CD player, wagon w/o Option Group or			
w/Group 1	421	358	370
Wagon w/Group 2 or 3	256	218	225
Power locks, base	250	213	220
Wagon	325	276	286
Two-tone paint	141	120	124
Wire wheel covers, base & wagon	215	183	189
Classic (credit)	(61)	(52)	(52)
215/75R15 WSW tires	80	68	70
225/70R15 WSW tires	176	150	155
235/70VR15 WSW tires	90	77	79
Classic	111	94	98
Base w/P215 WSW tires	78	66	69
Classic w/P215 WSW tires	128	109	113
Base w/P225 WSW tires	89	76	78
Classic w/P225 WSW tires	139	118	122
Wagon w/225 WSW tires	NC	NC	NC
235 BSW tires, Classic w/wire wheel covers	103	88	91
235 BSW tires, Classic w/o wire wheels covers	153	130	135
235 WSW tires, Classic w/wire wheel covers	125	106	110
235 WSW tires, Classic w/wire wheel covers	175	149	154

Oldsmobile Custom Cruiser

5-door wagon	$20995	$18224	$18674
Destination charge	555	555	555

Standard equipment:

5.0-liter TBI V-8, 4-speed automatic transmission, anti-lock brakes, power steering, driver-side air bag, air conditioning, 55/45 cloth reclining front

Prices are accurate at time of publication; subject to manufacturer's change.

seat with armrest, rear-facing third seat, tinted glass, intermittent wipers, tilt steering column, tachometer, coolant temperature and oil pressure gauges, voltmeter, trip odometer, roof luggage rack, Vista Roof, remote mirrors, visor mirrors, AM/FM radio, 225/75R15 whitewall tires.

Optional equipment:	Retail Price	Dealer Invoice	Low Price
5.7-liter TBI V-8 engine	250	213	220
Limited-slip differential	100	85	88
Option Pkg. 1SB	1482	1260	1304
w/UX1 or U1C radio	1317	1119	1159
Cruise control, power windows and locks, cassette player, power driver's seat, power mirrors, floormats, door edge guards.			
Option Pkg. 1SC	2433	2068	2141
w/UX1 or U1C radio	2268	1928	1996
Pkg. 1SB plus , automatic leveling, power antenna, lighted visor mirrors, door courtesy lights, compass, Reminder Pkg., Remote Lock Control Pkg., power passenger seat.			
Option Pkg. 1SD	2733	2323	2405
w/UX1 or U1C radio	2568	2183	2260
Pkg. 1SC plus automatic climate control, cornering lamps, Twilight Sentinel.			
Rear defogger, w/Pkg. 1SA	170	145	150
w/o Pkg. 1SA (includes heated mirrors) .	205	174	180
Rear security cover	69	59	61
Alloy wheels	330	281	290
UX1 cassette player w/EQ	315	268	277
U1C CD player	421	358	370
Towing Pkg.	120	102	106
Custom leather trim	515	438	453
Engine block heater	18	15	16
Warranty enhancements for New York state .	25	21	22
California emissions pkg.	100	85	88

Cadillac Allante

Cadillac's flagship vehicle, the two-seat Allante luxury convertible, carries on for 1992 virtually unchanged from last year. At that time, it got a standard 200-watt Delco-Bose Gold Series audio system with cassette and CD player, a power latching system for the manually raised convertible top, and a traction control system. Anti-lock brakes and a driver-side air bag are standard. Allante also comes with speed-variable power-assisted steering, electronically controlled four-speed automatic, and a smaller (though rated

Cadillac Allante

Specifications

	2-door conv.
Wheelbase, in.	99.4
Overall length, in.	178.7
Overall width, in.	73.5
Overall height, in.	51.2
Curb weight, lbs.	3552
Cargo vol., cu. ft.	16.2
Fuel capacity, gals.	22.0
Seating capacity	2
Front head room, in.	37.2
Front leg room, max., in.	43.2
Rear head room, in.	—
Rear leg room, min., in.	—

Powertrain layout: transverse front engine/front-wheel drive.

Engines

	ohv V-8
Size, liters/cu. in.	4.5/273
Fuel delivery	PFI
Horsepower @ rpm	200 @ 4400
Torque (lbs./ft.) @ rpm	270 @ 3200
Availability	S

EPA city/highway mpg

4-speed OD automatic	15/22

Assembly points: Turin, Italy; Hamtramck, Mich.

Prices are accurate at time of publication; subject to manufacturer's change.

at the same 200 horsepower) 4.5-liter version of the 4.9-liter V-8 found in Cadillac's other front-drive cars. The convertible top features a glass rear window with defogger, as does the optional hardtop. Though it has become more and more competent over the years, its lofty price is hard to justify. Nevertheless, it combines spritely acceleration, a good ride/handling combination, and a full compliment of standard features, and wraps it all in an Italian-built convertible body with elegant styling.

Prices

Cadillac Allante	Retail Price	Dealer Invoice	Low Price
2-door convertible	$58470	$50352	—
2-door convertible w/hardtop	64090	55174	—
Price includes $1300 Gas Guzzler Tax.			
Destination charge	NC	NC	NC

Low price not available at time of publication.

Standard equipment:

4.5-liter PFI V-8, 4-speed automatic transmission, anti-lock 4-wheel disc brakes, power steering, driver-side air bag, Speed-Dependent Damping System, traction control, Recaro power bucket seats with Durosoft leather upholstery and position memory, automatic climate control, outside temperature readout, center console with armrest and storage, seatback pockets, Delco/Bose Symphony audio system with cassette and CD player, power antenna, intermittent wipers, cruise control, power windows and locks, rear defogger, heated power mirrors, Driver Information Center, remote fuel door and decklid releases, headlamp washers, illuminated entry, digital instruments (with hardtop; analog instruments may be substituted at no charge), lighted visor mirrors, automatic parking brake release, tinted glass, leather-wrapped steering wheel, tilt steering column, Twilight Sentinel, floormats, 225/55VR16 tires on forged alloy wheels.

Optional equipment:

Digital instrument cluster (std. w/hardtop) .	495	416	—
Pearl white paint, convertible	700	588	—
California emissions pkg.	100	84	—

Cadillac Brougham

Cadillac Brougham

The rear-drive Brougham adds 2000 pounds to its towing capacity this year and the available 5.7-liter V-8 escapes the federal gas-guzzler tax. Brougham is the longest car built in the U.S., and comes only as a 4-door sedan in a single price series. A 170-horsepower 5.0-liter V-8 is standard. Optional is a 185-horsepower 5.7 V-8. With the optional Trailer Towing Package, which includes the 5.7-liter engine, the Brougham can tow up to 7000 pounds. Anti-lock brakes are standard, but a driver-side air bag is unavailable. Despite having nearly 4300 pounds to move, Brougham's optional 5.7-liter V-8 provides brisk acceleration—noticeably better than the standard 5.0-liter V-8. On the highway, the 5.7 supplies sufficient power to climb hills effortlessly and overtake slow-moving vehicles safely, though we wish the transmission would kick down to passing gear more quickly. There's also a surprising amount of wind noise on the highway. Steering feel is very light and vague. The suspension is not as soft as in previous years, but it nonetheless permits wallowing on wavy or bumpy pavement and allows lots of body lean in turns. Door openings are tall and wide, making it easy to get in and out. Surprising is the limited amount of front leg room for tall drivers, though there's enough overall passenger room that six adults fit comfortably. Unfortunately, the soft seats provide little support on long trips. Instrumentation is limited to a horizontal speedometer and fuel gauge, while some controls, like the dash-mounted wiper switch, are difficult to operate. The trunk is large, but the spare tire takes up some usable space.

Specifications

	4-door notchback
Wheelbase, in.	121.5
Overall length, in.	221.0
Overall width, in.	76.5
Overall height, in.	57.4
Curb weight, lbs.	4277
Cargo vol., cu. ft.	19.6
Fuel capacity, gals.	25.0
Seating capacity	6
Front head room, in.	39.0
Front leg room, max., in.	42.0
Rear head room, in.	38.1
Rear leg room, min., in.	41.2

Powertrain layout: longitudinal front engine/rear-wheel drive.

Engines	ohv V-8	ohv V-8
Size, liters/cu. in.	5.0/305	5.7/350
Fuel delivery	TBI	TBI
Horsepower @ rpm	170 @ 4200	185 @ 3800
Torque (lbs./ft.) @ rpm	255 @ 2400	300 @ 2400
Availability	S	O
EPA city/highway mpg		
4-speed OD automatic	17/25	16/25

Assembly point: Arlington, Tex.

Prices

Cadillac Brougham	Retail Price	Dealer Invoice	Low Price
4-door notchback	$31740	$27233	$28767
Destination charge	600	600	600

Standard equipment:

5.0-liter TBI V-8, 4-speed automatic transmission, anti-lock braking system, power steering, door-mounted automatic front seatbelts, power 55/45 front seat with power recliners and storage armrest, automatic climate control, outside temperature readout, power windows and locks, illuminated entry, cruise control, power mirrors, AM/FM cassette with EQ, automatic level control, tilt/telescopic steering column, trip odometer, cornering lamps, automatic parking brakes release, tinted glass, intermittent wipers, rear defogger, right visor mirror, litter receptacle, padded vinyl roof, floormats, door edge guards, opera lamps, leather-wrapped steering wheel, 225/75R15 Uniroyal Royal Seal whitewall tires.

Optional equipment:

	Retail Price	Dealer Invoice	Low Price
5-7-liter V-8	250	210	223
Coachbuilder Pkg. (credit)	295	248	263
Includes 5.7-liter V-8; deletes vinyl roof, rear reading lights, front seatback assist straps, bodyside moldings, opera lights, closed-in rear window.			
Trailer Towing Pkg.	549	461	489
Includes 5.7-liter V-8.			
Option Pkg. B	325	273	289
Lighted visor mirrors, power decklid pulldown, Twilight Sentinel.			
Option Pkg. C	685	575	610
w/d'Elegance	360	302	320
Pkg. B plus remote fuel door release, theft-deterrent system.			
d'Elegance Pkg., w/cloth	1875	1575	1669
w/leather	2445	2054	2176
Upgraded seat trim, three overhead assist handles, lighted visor mirrors, Twilight Sentinel, power decklid pulldown.			
Gold Ornamentation Pkg.	395	332	352
Leather seating area	570	479	507
Automatic day/night mirror	110	92	98
Monotone Firemist paint	240	202	214
Primary Firemist paint	190	160	169
CD player	396	333	352
Wire wheel discs	445	374	396
Wire wheels	1000	840	890
California emissions pkg.	100	84	89

Cadillac De Ville and Fleetwood

Available traction control is the main addition to these premium front-drive coupes and sedans. De Ville and Fleetwood are both offered in 2- and 4-door body styles; the 4-doors ride a three-inch-longer wheelbase. Added late in the 1991 model year, the De Ville Touring Sedan returns

Prices are accurate at time of publication; subject to manufacturer's change.

Cadillac Sedan DeVille

Specifications

	2-door notchback	4-door notchback
Wheelbase, in.	110.8	113.8
Overall length, in.	205.1	208.0
Overall width, in.	73.4	73.4
Overall height, in.	54.4	55.0
Curb weight, lbs.	3519	3591
Cargo vol., cu. ft.	18.1	18.4
Fuel capacity, gals.	18.0	18.0
Seating capacity	6	6
Front head room, in.	39.2	39.3
Front leg room, max., in.	42.0	42.0
Rear head room, in.	37.9	38.1
Rear leg room, min., in.	40.3	43.6

Powertrain layout: transverse front engine/front-wheel drive.

Engines

	ohv V-8
Size, liters/cu. in.	4.9/300
Fuel delivery	PFI
Horsepower @ rpm	200 @ 4100
Torque (lbs./ft.) @ rpm	275 @ 3000
Availability	S

EPA city/highway mpg

4-speed OD automatic	16/25

Assembly point: Lake Orion, Mich.

with monotone exterior paint, firmer suspension, and walnut and leather interior trim. All models use a 200-horsepower 4.9-liter V-8 coupled to a 4-speed overdrive automatic transmission. The new traction control system limits wheelspin on acceleration at speeds under 30 mph. It's standard on Fleetwood and De Ville Touring Sedan and optional with the extra-cost Computer Command Ride System (CCR) on other De Villes. CCR, which varies suspension firmness according to vehicle speed, is standard on Fleetwood and the Touring Sedan and optional on other De Villes. Though slightly rough at idle, the V-8 delivers ample power for quick take-offs and easy passing on the open road. It's aided by the silky-smooth transmission's willingness to quickly drop down to a lower gear when more power is requested. The V-8 requires premium unleaded fuel. Handling and roadholding predictably favor conservative driving. The suspension lets these cars bounce and float too much at intermediate speeds, but the Computer Command Ride generally strikes a good balance between suppleness around town and firm control on the highway. Doors are tall and wide, allowing easy entry and exit to the huge cabin. The standard electronic instrument cluster displays ancillary readouts, including fuel level, on the lower part of the dash, where it's not readily visible.

Prices

Cadillac DeVille/Fleetwood	Retail Price	Dealer Invoice	Low Price
Coupe de Ville 2-door notchback	$31740	$27233	$28148
Sedan de Ville 4-door notchback	31740	27233	28148
De Ville Touring Sedan	35190	30193	—
Fleetwood 2-door notchback	36360	31197	32112
Fleetwood 4-door notchback	36360	31197	32112
Fleetwood Sixty Special 4-door notchback	39860	34200	35115
Destination charge	600	600	600

De Ville Touring Sedan low price not available at time of publication.

Standard equipment:

De Ville: 4.9-liter PFI V-8, 4-speed automatic transmission, anti-lock brakes, power steering, driver-side air bag, power 45/55 cloth reclining front seats with manual recliners, front storage armrest, automatic climate control, outside temperature readout, power windows, automatic power locks, heated

Prices are accurate at time of publication; subject to manufacturer's change.

power mirrors, cruise control, AM/FM cassette with EQ, power antenna, automatic level control, automatic parking brake release, Twilight Sentinel, automatic day/night mirror, solar-control glass, intermittent wipers, trip odometer, tilt steering column, remote decklid release, rear defogger, Fuel Data Center, Pass-Key theft-deterrent system, seatback pockets, door edge guards, litter receptacle, 205/70R15 whitewall tires on alloy wheels. **Touring Sedan** adds: Computer Command Ride System, traction control, larger front and rear stabilizer bars, sport suspension, 2.97:1 final drive ratio, walnut accents, leather seating area, power front seat recliners, leather-wrapped steering wheel, 215/60R16 Goodyear GA tires. **Fleetwood** adds: vinyl roof (4-door), cabriolet roof (2-door), fender skirts, remote fuel door release, front and rear lighted visor mirrors, floormats. **Sixty Special** adds: Ultrasoft leather upholstery, 22-way power heated front seats (includes 2-position memory, adjustable lumbar and side bolsters, and power head restraints).

Optional equipment:	Retail Price	Dealer Invoice	Low Price
Traction control, de Ville	175	147	156
Option Pkg. B, de Ville	356	299	317
Illuminated entry, lighted visor mirrors, power decklid pull-down, trunk mat.			
Option Pkg. C, de Ville	803	675	715
Pkg. B plus remote fuel door release, digital instruments, automatic day/night mirror, trumpet horn.			
Security Pkg.	295	248	263
Remote keyless entry, theft-deterrent system.			
Cold Weather Pkg.	369	310	328
Engine block heater, heated windshield.			
Custom Seating Pkg., Fleetwood	425	357	378
Memory seat, power front seat recliners.			
Touring Sedan Pkg. 1SC	NC	NC	NC
Power decklid pull-down, trunk mat, lighted visor mirrors, remote fuel door release, digital instruments, trumpet horn, remote keyless entry, theft deterrent system, Delco/Bose cassette system or CD player (Pkg. 1SD).			
Astroroof	1550	1302	1380
Coachbuilder Pkg., Sedan de Ville	1000	840	890
Computer Command Ride System, de Ville .	380	319	338
Gold Ornamentation Pkg.	395	332	352
HD Livery Pkg., Sedan de Ville	1000	840	890
Leather seating area (std. Sixty)	570	479	507
Delco/Bose audio system	576	484	513
w/CD player	872	732	776
Formal cabriolet roof, Coupe de Ville	925	777	823
Padded vinyl roof, Sedan de Ville	925	777	823
Full cabriolet roof, Coupe de Ville	1095	920	975
Phaeton roof, Sedan de Ville	1095	920	975
Wire wheel discs, de Ville	235	197	209
Fleetwood	NC	NC	NC
Lace alloy wheels, de Ville	235	197	209

Cadillac Eldorado and Seville

Cadillac Seville

The 4-door Seville and its 2-door sibling, the Eldorado, have been restyled for 1992. Both front-drivers are powered by a 200-horsepower 4.9-liter V-8 teamed with a 4-speed electronically controlled automatic transmission that gains a shift interlock. Wheelbase of the Eldorado remains at 108 inches, though length is up by nearly 11 inches; Seville's wheelbase stretches from 108 inches to 111, and length jumps more than a foot. Both gain about 2.5 inches in width. The Seville's longer wheelbase results in a 3.5-inch gain in rear leg room, and both models add rear-seat heater ducts and fan speed controls. Both also boast new interiors designed along the rounded-form theme that include digital instruments and wood inserts running the length of the dash and continuing into the doors. The sporty STS (Seville Touring Sedan) and Eldorado Touring Coupe return with standard analog gauges and leather seating surfaces, both of which are optional on the base models. A driver-side air bag and anti-lock brakes are again standard across the line. Neither model ever lacks for acceleration, and the transmission upshifts smoothly and downshifts without hesitation for passing. Cadillac's Computer Command Ride is a standard feature that automatically changes suspension firmness based on vehicle speed. The various settings are softer on base models, while the firmer suspensions on the STS and Touring Coupe feel more com-

Prices are accurate at time of publication; subject to manufacturer's change.

posed. Seville offers ample head room both front and rear, and even the Eldorado, with its shorter wheelbase, provides reasonable room in back. The only flaw in the otherwise conveniently laid-out new dashboards are climate-control push buttons hidden to the right of the steering wheel.

Specifications

	2-door notchback	4-door notchback
Wheelbase, in.	108.0	111.0
Overall length, in.	202.2	203.9
Overall width, in.	74.8	74.4
Overall height, in.	54.0	54.0
Curb weight, lbs.	3604	3648
Cargo vol., cu. ft.	15.3	14.4
Fuel capacity, gals.	18.8	18.8
Seating capacity	5	5
Front head room, in.	37.8	37.6
Front leg room, max., in.	42.6	42.8
Rear head room, in.	38.3	37.9
Rear leg room, min., in.	36.1	39.5

Powertrain layout: transverse front engine/front-wheel drive.

Engines	ohv V-8
Size, liters/cu. in.	4.9/300
Fuel delivery	PFI
Horsepower @ rpm	200 @ 4100
Torque (lbs./ft.) @ rpm	275 @ 3000
Availability	S

EPA city/highway mpg

4-speed OD automatic	16/25

Assembly point: Hamtramck, Mich.

Prices

Cadillac Eldorado	Retail Price	Dealer Invoice	Low Price
2-door notchback	$32470	$27859	—
Destination charge	600	600	600

Low price not available at time of publication.

Standard equipment:

4.9-liter PFI V-8, 4-speed automatic transmission, anti-lock 4-wheel disc brakes, power steering, driver-side air bag, Computer Command Ride System, automatic level control, cloth power front seats with manual recliners, center console with armrest and storage bins, automatic climate control, power windows and locks, cruise control, heated power mirrors, rear defogger, AM/FM cassette with EQ, power antenna, remote fuel door and decklid releases, power decklid pulldown, illuminated entry, Driver Information Center, lighted visor mirror (passenger), intermittent wipers, floormats, Pass-Key theft-deterrent system, tinted glass, leather-wrapped steering wheel, tilt steering column, Twilight Sentinel, trip odometer, 225/60R16 tires on alloy wheels.

Optional equipment:

	Retail Price	Dealer Invoice	Low Price
Option Pkg. B	181	152	—
Lighted visor mirrors, floormats, trunk mat, decklid liner, underhood lamp.			
Security Pkg.	480	403	—
Remote keyless entry, theft-deterrent system, automatic door locks, central door unlocking system.			
Seating Pkg.	340	286	—
Power front seat recliners, power lumbar supports, articulating front headrests; requires leather seats.			
Touring Coupe Pkg.	2100	1764	—
Uprated suspension, Eagle GA tires, leather seats with power recliners and lumbar support adjusters, Security Pkg.			
Astroroof	1550	1302	—
Heated windshield system	309	260	—
Leather seating area	650	546	—
Heated front seats	120	101	—
Sport interior	146	123	—
Automatic day/night mirror	110	92	—
Monotone Firemist paint	240	202	—
Gold/white diamond paint	240	202	—
Delco/Bose audio system, w/cassette & CD	972	816	—
225/60R16 tires	76	64	—
Striping	75	63	—
California emissions pkg.	100	84	—

Cadillac Seville

4-door notchback	$34975	$30009	—
STS 4-door notchback	37975	32583	—
Destination charge	600	600	600

Low price not available at time of publication.

Prices are accurate at time of publication; subject to manufacturer's change.

Standard equipment:

4.9-liter PFI V-8, 4-speed automatic transmission, anti-lock 4-wheel disc brakes, power steering, driver-side air bag, Computer Command Ride System, cloth power front seats with manual recliners, center console with armrest and storage bins, automatic climate control, power windows and locks, cruise control, heated power mirrors, rear defogger, AM/FM cassette with EQ, power antenna, remote fuel door and decklid releases, power decklid pulldown, illuminated entry, Driver Information Center, lighted visor mirror (passenger), intermittent wipers, Pass-Key theft-deterrent system, tinted glass, digital instrumentation, leather-wrapped steering wheel, tilt steering column, Twilight Sentinel, trip odometer, 225/60R16 whitewall tires. **STS** adds: Touring suspension, leather seats with power recliners, automatic locks with central unlocking and remote keyless entry, lighted visor mirror (driver), analog instruments with tachometer, full console, theft-deterrent system, floormats, trunk mat, 225/60R16 Eagle GA tires.

Optional equipment:	Retail Price	Dealer Invoice	Low Price
Option Pkg. B, base	181	152	—
Lighted visor mirrors, floormats, trunk mat, decklid liner, underhood lamp.			
Security Pkg.	480	403	—
Automatic locks with central unlocking and remote keyless entry, theft-deterrent system.			
Seating Pkg	340	286	—
Power front seat recliners with power lumbar supports, articulating front headrests; requires leather seats.			
Astroroof	1550	1302	—
Heated windshield system	309	260	—
Leather seating area, base	650	546	—
Heated front seats	120	101	—
Sport interior, base	146	123	—
Automatic day/night mirror	110	92	—
Monotone Firemist paint, base	240	202	—
Gold/white diamond paint	240	202	—
Delco/Bose audio system w/cassette & CD	972	816	—
Striping, base	75	63	—
California emissions pkg.	100	84	—

Chevrolet Astro/GMC Safari

Later this year, a more powerful extra-cost engine and a new rear-door configuration are due to join the options list of the Astro and its twin, the GMC Safari. These compact passenger and cargo vans are identical except for names,

Chevrolet Astro LT AWD Extended Length

trim designations, and the GMC's slightly higher base prices. Both are available as Extended-Length models that add 10 inches to the rear of the regular-length versions. All-wheel-drive models of both body lengths feature a permanently engaged 4WD system instead of the standard rear-wheel drive. A 150-horsepower 4.3-liter V-6 is standard, while a 200-horsepower H.P. (High-Performance) version is forthcoming. A 4-speed overdrive automatic is the only transmission. All Astro/Safari passenger vans have 4-wheel anti-lock brakes. Five-passenger seating is standard; seating for up to eight is optional. The new rear-door option will feature a one-piece glass liftgate with separately opening split panel doors below. The so-called Dutch doors make possible a newly optional wet-arm rear wiper/ washer and rear defogger. Astro/Safari is a smaller interpretation of the traditional van, so they ride and handle more like trucks; lighter-duty front-drive vans such as Chevy's own Lumina APV and Chrysler's minivan trio are more car-like. Four-wheel drive corrects the wet-weather traction problems of the 2WD Astro/Safari, but both have a high step-up into the front seat, making entry/exit difficult. Fuel mileage is poor; we averaged just 14.5 mpg during our most recent test of an AWD regular-length Astro. However, Astro and Safari are rated to tow up to 6000 lbs., far more than most minivans.

Prices are accurate at time of publication; subject to manufacturer's change.

Specifications

	5-door van	5-door van
Wheelbase, in.	111.0	111.0
Overall length, in.	176.8	186.8
Overall width, in.	77.5	77.5
Overall height, in.	73.7	73.7
Curb weight, lbs.	3909	3993
Cargo vol., cu. ft.	151.8	170.4
Fuel capacity, gals.	27.0	27.0
Seating capacity	8	8
Front head room, in.	39.2	39.2
Front leg room, max., in.	41.6	41.6
Rear head room, in.	37.9	37.9
Rear leg room, min., in.	36.5	36.5

Powertrain layout: longitudinal front engine/rear-wheel drive or permanent 4WD.

Engines

	ohv V-6	ohv V-6
Size, liters/cu. in.	4.3/262	4.3/262
Fuel delivery	TBI	TBI
Horsepower @ rpm	150 @ 4000	200 @ 4400
Torque (lbs./ft.) @ rpm	230 @ 2400	260 @ 3600
Availability	S	O[1]

EPA city/highway mpg

4-speed OD automatic	16/21	NA

1. 2WD models.

Assembly point: Baltimore, Md.

Prices

Chevrolet Astro/ GMC Safari Passenger Van	Retail Price	Dealer Invoice	Low Price
Astro CS SWB	$15185	$13636	$13886
Safari SWB	15404	13833	14083
Astro CS extended	15875	14256	14506
Safari XT	16094	14452	14702
Astro CS AWD SWB	17245	15486	15736
Safari AWD SWB	17484	15701	15951
Astro CS AWD extended	17885	16061	16311
Safari XT AWD	18104	16257	16507

SWB/XT denote short-wheelbase models.

	Retail Price	Dealer Invoice	Low Price
Destination charge	545	545	545

Standard equipment:

4.3-liter TBI V-6 engine, 4-speed automatic transmission, 4-wheel anti-lock brakes, coolant temperature and oil pressure gauges, voltmeter, trip odometer, tinted glass, intermittent wipers, AM radio (AM/FM on Safari), highback bucket seats, 5-passenger seating, rubber floor covering, remote fuel door release, 205/75R15 tires (SWB; extended have 215/75R15). AWD models have permanent 4-wheel drive.

Optional equipment:

	Retail Price	Dealer Invoice	Low Price
4.3-liter HP V-6	NA	NA	NA
Front air conditioning	845	718	744
Front & rear air conditioning	1368	1163	1204
Rear heater	205	174	180
Locking differential	252	214	222
7-passenger seating	1043	887	918
w/Sport Group 1 or CL	955	812	840
w/LT	852	724	750
w/Sport Group 2, Group 3 or 4	429	365	378
w/Sport Group 2, Group 3 or 4, and CL	315	268	277
w/Group 3 or 4 and LT or Group 5 (credit) .	(25)	(21)	(21)
8-passenger seating, w/Sport Group 1 or Group 1	369	314	325
w/Sport Group 1, Group 1 and CL	395	336	348
LT	877	745	772
w/Group 5 and CL (credit)	(429)	(365)	(365)
w/Group 5 and LT (credit)	(315)	(268)	(268)
Reclining seats w/armrests	245	208	216
Power driver's seat	240	204	211
CL Decor Group	1092	928	961
w/Sport Group 1	633	538	557
w/Sport Group 2	659	560	580

Air conditioning, rally wheels, AM/FM cassette, complete body glass, reclining front seats with armrests, power windows and locks, tilt steering column, cruise control, 8-passenger seating.

LT Decor Group	2848	2421	2506

CL Group plus roof console, roof rack, power mirrors, power driver's seat, 7-passenger seating, 205/75R15 tires (2WD SWB; others have 215/75R15 tires) on alloy wheels.

Sport Group 1, 2WD SWB	2140	1819	1883
2WD extended	2223	1890	1956

Air dam with fog lamps, FE3 sport suspension, sport steering wheel, wide bodyside moldings, specific exterior trim, 245/60R15 outlined white letter tires on rally wheels.

Prices are accurate at time of publication; subject to manufacturer's change.

	Retail Price	Dealer Invoice	Low Price
Sport Group 2, 2WD SWB	3821	3248	3362
2WD extended	3904	3318	3436
Preferred Group 2, CS & CL	1205	1024	1060
LT	1048	891	922
Preferred Group 3, CS	2202	1872	1938
CL	2228	1894	1961
LT	2308	1962	2031
Preferred Group 4, 2WD SWB CS	2982	2535	2624
2WD SWB CL	3008	2557	2647
2WD SWB LT	3088	2625	2717
2WD extended & AWD CS	2974	2528	2617
2WD extended & AWD CL	3000	2550	2640
2WD extended & AWD LT	3080	2618	2710
Preferred Group 5, 2WD SWB CS	4200	3570	3696
2WD SWB CL	3987	3389	3509
2WD SWB LT	3727	3168	3280
2WD extended & AWD CS	4192	3563	3689
2WD extended & AWD CL	3979	3382	3502
2WD extended & AWD LT	3719	3161	3273
FE3 sport suspension	469	399	413
w/CL or LT	377	320	332
w/Group 4 or 5	281	239	247
2WD extended	417	354	367
2WD extended w/CL or LT	325	276	286
2WD extended w/Group 4 or 5	237	201	209
Deluxe bumpers, CS	128	109	113
CL & LT	76	65	67
Luggage rack	126	107	111
Cold Climate Pkg	46	39	40
Rear door liftgate	NA	NA	NA
Roof console, CS	83	71	73
CL & LT	50	43	44
Stowage compartment	30	26	26
Convenience Group ZQ2	434	369	382
Power windows and locks.			
Power locks	223	190	196
Convenience Group ZQ3	383	326	337
Cruise control, tilt steering column.			
Engine oil cooler	135	115	119
HD radiator	56	48	49
HD radiator & transmission oil cooler	118	100	104
w/A/C	63	54	55
Complete body glass	157	133	138
Deep-tinted glass, CS & CL w/o body glass	161	137	142
CS & Cl w/body glass	290	247	255
Electronic instrumentation	195	166	172

	Retail Price	Dealer Invoice	Low Price
Auxiliary lighting	133	113	117
CS w/roof console	100	85	88
Deluxe outside mirrors	52	44	46
Power mirrors	150	128	132
w/Sport Group 1, Group 2 or 3	98	83	86
Deluxe two-tone paint	476	405	419
CL	251	213	221
Special two-tone paint	172	146	151
Custom two-tone paint	329	280	290
CL	104	88	92
AM/FM radio	151	128	133
AM/FM cassette	273	232	240
w/Sport Group 1, Group 2 or 3	122	104	107
AM/FM cassette w/EQ	423	360	372
w/Sport Group 1, Group 2 or 3	272	231	239
w/Sport Group 2, Group 4 or 5	150	128	132
AM/FM CD player, w/Group 1	557	473	490
w/Sport Group 1, Group 2 or 3	406	345	357
w/Sport Group 2, Group 4 or 5	284	241	250
205/75R15 WW tires	72	61	63
205/75R15 WL tires	96	82	84
215/75R15 WW tires, AWD SWB & extended	60	51	53
215/75R15 WL tires, AWD SWB & extended	88	75	77
WL denotes white letter; WW denotes whitewall.			
Trailering Special Equipment, HD	564	479	496
w/A/C	507	431	446
Trailering Special Equipment, LD	109	93	96
Alloy wheels	340	289	299
CL, LT, or w/sport suspension	248	211	218
Argent rally wheels	92	78	81
California emissions pkg.	100	85	88

Chevrolet Beretta/Corsica

Anti-lock brakes have been added as standard equipment to Chevy's compact, front-drive coupe and sedan. A driver-side air bag was made standard on both last year. Corsica drops the 5-door hatchback body style, and both get a more powerful standard engine; a new fuel injection system boosts output of the 2.2-liter 4-cylinder from 95 horsepower to 110. Beretta is offered in three trim levels: base, GT, and GTZ. Base models come standard with the 2.2-liter four.

Prices are accurate at time of publication; subject to manufacturer's change.

Chevrolet Beretta GT

A 140-horsepower 3.1-liter V-6 is again standard on GT and optional on base and GTZ Beretta models. GTZ comes standard with the 180-horsepower 16-valve 2.3-liter 4-cylinder Quad 4. The Quad 4 comes only with a 5-speed manual transmission; others offer an optional 3-speed automatic. Corsica comes in a single trim level, called LT, but an optional Z52 Sport Handling Package adds alloy wheels with larger tires, a sport steering wheel, and a sport suspension. The 2.2 is available with either a 5-speed manual or 3-speed automatic, but the optional 3.1-liter V-6 is only available this year with the automatic. Even with 15 more horsepower, the 4-cylinder engine won't be a fireball, and the conservative limits of the base suspension and tires on either car discourage even moderately aggressive driving. We recommend the optional V-6, even on the sporty Beretta GTZ—that car's standard Quad 4 is powerful, but concentrates that power at the high end of the rev range. Interiors of both cars were restyled last year. Though a vast improvement, they still aren't up to the tidy designs of most imports, and rear seat room is tight for taller riders. Overall, Corsica and Beretta are not as refined as some others in their respective classes, but they score points by offering an air bag, ABS, and a V-6 engine, along with frequent dealer discounts.

Specifications

	2-door notchback	4-door notchback
Wheelbase, in.	103.4	103.4
Overall length, in.	183.4	183.4
Overall width, in.	68.2	68.2
Overall height, in.	56.2	56.2
Curb weight, lbs.	2649	2638
Cargo vol., cu. ft.	13.4	13.5
Fuel capacity, gals.	15.6	15.6
Seating capacity	5	5
Front head room, in.	38.1	38.1
Front leg room, max., in.	43.4	43.4
Rear head room, in.	37.4	37.4
Rear leg room, min., in.	35.0	35.0

Powertrain layout: transverse front engine/front-wheel drive.

Engines

	ohv I-4	ohv V-6	dohc I-4
Size, liters/cu. in.	2.2/133	3.1/191	2.3/138
Fuel delivery	PFI	PFI	PFI
Horsepower @ rpm	110 @ 5200	140 @ 4200	180 @ 6200
Torque (lbs./ft.) @ rpm	130 @ 2800	185 @ 3200	160 @ 5200
Availability	S[1]	S[2]	S[3]

EPA city/highway mpg

5-speed OD manual	25/34	19/28	22/31
3-speed automatic	23/31	20/28	

1. Base Beretta, Corsica. 2. Beretta GT; opt. Corsica, Beretta GTZ. 3. Beretta GTZ.

Assembly point: Wilmington, Del.

Prices

Chevrolet Beretta

2-door notchback	$10999	$9877	$10177
GT 2-door notchback	12575	11292	11592
GTZ 2-door notchback	15590	14000	14300
Destination charge	475	475	475

Standard equipment:

2.2-liter PFI 4-cylinder engine, 5-speed manual transmission, anti-lock brakes, power steering, driver-side air bag, cloth reclining front bucket seats

Prices are accurate at time of publication; subject to manufacturer's change.

with 4-way manual driver's seat, remote manual mirrors, tinted glass, AM/FM radio, door pockets, 185/75R14 tires. **GT** adds: 3.1-liter PFI V-6, Level II sport suspension, floor console, tachometer, coolant temperature and oil pressure gauges, voltmeter, trip odometer, visor mirrors, 205/60R15 tires on alloy wheels. **GTZ** adds: 2.3-liter DOHC 16-valve PFI 4-cylinder engine, air conditioning, Level IV sport suspension, sport seats with driver-side lumbar support adjustment, aero lower body moldings, spoilers, leather-wrapped steering wheel, intermittent wipers, front reading lamps, 205/55R16 tires.

Optional equipment:

	Retail Price	Dealer Invoice	Low Price
3.1-liter V-6 engine, base	610	519	531
GTZ (credit)	(150)	(128)	(128)
GTZ requires 3-speed automatic transmission.			
3-speed automatic transmission	555	472	483
Air conditioning (std. GTZ)	805	684	700
Preferred Group 1, base	903	768	786
Air conditioning, intermittent wipers, floormats.			
Preferred Group 2, base	1258	1069	1094
Group 1 plus power locks, tilt steering column.			
Preferred Group 3, base	2018	1715	1756
Group 2 plus cassette player, power windows, console w/armrest, remote decklid release, cruise control.			
Preferred Group 1, GT	926	787	806
Air conditioning, intermittent wipers, reading lamps, floormats.			
Preferred Group 2, GT	1176	1000	1023
Group 1 plus power locks, tilt steering column.			
Preferred Group 3, GT	1981	1684	1723
Group 2 plus cassette player, remote decklid release, power windows, cruise control.			
Preferred Group 1, GTZ	388	330	338
Power locks, tilt steering column, floormats.			
Preferred Group 2, GTZ	1088	925	979
Group 1 plus cassette player, power windows, remote decklid release, cruise control.			
Convenience Pkg	223	190	201
Split folding rear seat, trunk cargo net, sunshade extensions, map lights, visor mirrors, full trunk trim.			
Floor console, base	60	51	54
Rear defogger	170	145	153
Power locks	210	179	189
Gauge Pkg. w/tachometer, base	139	118	125
Includes coolant temperature and oil pressure gauges, voltmeter, trip odometer.			
Front reading lamps, base & GT	23	20	21
Cassette player	140	119	126
CD player	396	337	356
Base & GT w/Group 3, GTZ w/Group 2 .	256	218	230

	Retail Price	Dealer Invoice	Low Price
Cruise control	225	191	203
Rear spoiler, GT	110	94	99
Tilt steering column	145	123	131
Removable sunroof	350	298	315
F41 sport suspension, base	49	42	44
195/70R14 tires, base	93	79	84
Remote decklid release	60	51	54
Power windows	275	234	248
Intermittent wipers	65	55	59
Decklid luggage rack	115	98	104
Front floormats	18	15	16
Rear floormats	15	13	14
California emissions pkg.	100	85	90

Chevrolet Corsica

LT 4-door notchback	$10999	$9877	$10177
Destination charge	475	475	475

Standard equipment:

2.2-liter PFI 4-cylinder engine, 5-speed manual transmission, anti-lock brakes, power steering, driver-side air bag, cloth reclining front bucket seats, coolant temperature gauge, AM/FM radio, remote mirrors, tinted glass, front door pockets, 185/75R14 tires.

Optional equipment:

3.1-liter V-6 (requires automatic)	610	519	531
3-speed automatic transmission	555	472	483
Air conditioning	805	684	700
Preferred Group 1	903	768	786
Air conditioning, intermittent wipers, floormats.			
Preferred Group 2	1298	1103	1129
Group 1 plus power locks, tilt steering column.			
Preferred Group 3	2123	1805	1847
Group 2 plus cassette player, power windows, console w/armrest, remote decklid release, cruise control.			
Comfort/Convenience Pkg.	223	190	194
Cargo net, 4-way passenger seat, sunshade extensions, visor mirrors, map lights, full trunk trim.			
Console w/armrest	60	51	52
Rear defogger	170	145	148
Power locks	250	213	218
Gauge Pkg. w/tachometer	139	118	121
Includes coolant temperature and oil pressure gauges, voltmeter, trip odometer.			

Prices are accurate at time of publication; subject to manufacturer's change.

	Retail Price	Dealer Invoice	Low Price
Cruise control	225	191	196
Tilt steering column	145	123	126
Z52 Sport Handling Pkg.	395	336	344
Level II sport suspension, bodyside moldings, 205/60R15 tires on alloy wheels.			
185/75R14 whitewall tires	68	58	59
Remote decklid release	60	51	52
Styled steel wheels	56	48	49
Power windows	340	289	296
Intermittent wipers	65	55	57
Cassette player	140	119	122
CD player	396	337	345
w/Preferred Group 3	256	218	223
Two-tone paint	123	105	107
Decklid luggage rack	115	98	100
Front floormats	18	15	16
Rear floormats	15	13	13
Engine block heater	20	17	17
California emissions pkg.	100	85	87

Chevrolet Camaro/ Pontiac Firebird

Chevrolet Camaro RS

Chevy's rear-drive pony car marks its 25th anniversary with a "Heritage Appearance" option, but is otherwise little changed as it awaits a 1993 redesign. Pontiac's version has likewise received few changes. Both cars are available in coupe and convertible form, and all come with a driver-side air bag. Anti-lock brakes are not available. Camaro is offered in two flavors: RS and Z28. Firebird comes in base, Formula, Trans Am, and GTA versions. Standard on Camaro RS is a 3.1-liter V-6 with 140 horsepower; optional is a 5.0-liter V-8 with 170. The Z28 comes with a 230-horsepower version of the 5.0 V-8 and Z28 coupes can be ordered with a 245-horsepower 5.7-liter V-8. The 5.7 must use a 4-speed overdrive automatic transmission; a 5-speed manual is standard with the other engines and the automatic is optional. On the Firebird side, a 140-horsepower 3.1-liter V-6 is again standard on the base coupe and convertible.

Specifications

	3-door hatchback	2-door conv.
Wheelbase, in.	101.1	101.1
Overall length, in.	192.6	192.6
Overall width, in.	72.4	72.4
Overall height, in.	50.4	50.3
Curb weight, lbs.	3103	3203
Cargo vol., cu. ft.	12.3	6.6
Fuel capacity, gals.	15.5	15.5
Seating capacity	4	4
Front head room, in.	37.0	37.2
Front leg room, max., in.	43.0	43.0
Rear head room, in.	34.7	36.8
Rear leg room, min., in.	28.9	28.3

Powertrain layout: longitudinal front engine/rear-wheel drive.

Engines

	ohv V-6	ohv V-8	ohv V-8	ohv V-8
Size, liters/cu. in.	3.1/191	5.0/305	5.0/305	5.7/350
Fuel delivery	PFI	TBI	PFI	PFI
Horsepower @ rpm	140 @ 4400	170 @ 4000	205 @ 4200	245 @ 4400
Torque (lbs./ft.) @ rpm	180 @ 3600	255 @ 2400	285 @ 3200	345 @ 3200
Availability	S[1]	S[2]	S[3]	S[4]

EPA city/highway mpg

5-speed OD manual	17/27	17/26	16/26	
4-speed OD automatic	18/27	17/26	16/25	17/25

1. Camaro RS, base Firebird.   2. Firebird Formula; opt., Camaro RS.   3. Camaro Z28, Firebird Trans Am.   4. Firebird GTA; opt., Camaro Z28.

Assembly point: Van Nuys, Calif.

Prices are accurate at time of publication; subject to manufacturer's change.

A 170-horsepower throttle-body-injected 5.0-liter V-8 is optional on the base model and standard on the Formula coupe. A tuned-port-injected version of the 5.0 rated at 205 horsepower is the standard engine for Trans Am coupes and ragtops. A 240-horsepower 5.7-liter V-8 is standard on the top-of-the line GTA model and is offered on all but the base Firebird and the convertibles. Optional on all but the base and soft-top models is a performance equipment group that boosts output of the tuned-port 5.0 to 230 horsepower. Like the Camaro, all can be equipped with either a 5-speed manual or 4-speed automatic except for those with the 5.7-liter V-8, which is available with automatic only. Extroverted styling and V-8 muscle are the major appeals of these two cars. Before you succumb, however, check with your insurance agent. A V-6 model will have the lowest premium, and while it can't match the acceleration of a V-8, it doesn't feel underpowered with the 5-speed. Other drawbacks common to all include a punishingly stiff ride, poor wet-road traction, and skimpy cargo room. Also, rattles and squeaks are frequent companions, especially in convertibles.

Prices

Chevrolet Camaro	Retail Price	Dealer Invoice	Low Price
RS 3-door hatchback	$12075	$10843	$11193
RS 2-door convertible	18055	16213	16563
Z28 3-door hatchback	16055	14417	14767
Z28 2-door convertible	21500	19307	19657
Destination charge	490	490	490

Standard equipment:

RS: 3.1-liter PFI V-6 engine, 5-speed manual transmission, power steering, driver-side air bag, AM/FM radio, left remote and right manual mirrors, cloth reclining front bucket seats, folding rear seat, rear shoulder belts, tilt steering column, intermittent wipers, tinted glass, Pass-Key theft deterrent system, power hatch pulldown, tachometer, coolant temperature and oil pressure gauges, voltmeter, 215/65R15 tires on alloy wheels. **Z28** adds: 5.0-liter TPI (PFI) V-8 engine, limited-slip differential, right visor mirror, fog lamps, 235/55ZR16 tires (coupe), 245/50ZR16 tires (convertible).

Optional equipment:

	Retail Price	Dealer Invoice	Low Price
5.0-liter TBI V-8, RS 3-door	369	314	332
5.7-liter TPI (PFI) V-8, Z28 3-door	300	255	270
4-speed automatic transmission	530	451	477
Performance axle ratio, w/o A/C	675	574	608
w/A/C	466	396	419
Includes performance exhaust.			
Air conditioning	830	706	747
Preferred Group 1, RS	1085	922	977
Air conditioning, AM/FM cassette, bodyside moldings, floormats.			
Preferred Group 2, RS 3-door	1937	1646	1743
RS conv.	1785	1517	1607
Group 1 plus power windows and locks, cruise control; 3-door adds power hatch release, cargo cover, front reading lamps.			
Preferred Group 1, Z28	925	786	833
Air conditioning, bodyside moldings, floormats.			
Preferred Group 2, Z28 3-door	1937	1646	1743
Z28 conv.	1785	1517	1607
Group 1 plus AM/FM cassette, power windows and locks, cruise control; 3-door adds power hatch release, cargo cover, front reading lamps.			
Preferred Group 3, Z28 3-door	2333	1983	2100
Z28 conv.	2181	1854	1963
Group 2 plus power driver's seat, power mirrors.			
Heritage Appearance Pkg	175	149	158
Striping, body-color grille, black hoodlamp pockets.			
Custom cloth bucket seats	327	278	294
Custom leather bucket seats	850	723	765
Power driver's seat	305	259	275
Cruise control	225	191	203
Rear defogger	170	145	153
Power windows	265	225	239
Power locks	210	179	189
Power hatch release	60	51	54
Rear window louvers	210	179	189
Cargo area cover	69	59	62
Power mirrors	91	77	82
Rearview mirror with reading lamps	23	20	21
Removable roof panels	895	761	806
235/55ZR16 tires, RS w/5.0	219	186	197
245/50ZR16 tires, Z28 3-door	400	340	360
Cassette player	160	136	144
CD player	396	337	356
w/Group 2 or 3	236	201	212
Delco/Bose AM/FM cassette system, RS			
3-doors	855	727	770
Z28 3-doors	1015	863	914
Front floormats	20	17	18

Prices are accurate at time of publication; subject to manufacturer's change.

	Retail Price	Dealer Invoice	Low Price
Bodyside moldings	60	51	54
Engine block heater	20	17	18
California emissions pkg.	100	85	90

Pontiac Firebird

	Retail Price	Dealer Invoice	Low Price
3-door hatchback	$12505	$11229	$11579
2-door convertible	19375	17399	—
Formula 3-door hatchback	16205	14552	14902
Trans Am (T/A) 3-door hatchback	18105	16258	16608
Trans Am (T/A) 2-door convertible	23875	21440	—
GTA 3-door hatchback	25880	23240	23590
Destination charge	490	490	490

Convertible low prices not available at time of publication.

Standard equipment:

3.1-liter PFI V-6, 4-speed automatic transmission, power steering, driver-side air bag, cloth reclining front bucket seats, tilt steering column, power hatch pulldown, AM/FM cassette, gauge cluster including tachometer, Pass-Key theft-deterrent system, 215/65R15 tires on alloy wheels. **Formula** adds: 5.0-liter PFI V-8, 5-speed manual transmission, WS6 sport suspension, air conditioning, leather-wrapped steering wheel, 245/50ZR15 tires on alloy wheels. **Trans Am** adds: 5.0-liter PFI V-8, F41 suspension, limited-slip differential, Aero Package, 215/60R16 tires on alloy wheels. **GTA** adds: 5.7-liter PFI V-8, 4-speed automatic transmission, four-wheel disc brakes, dual-converter exhaust, engine oil cooler, rear defogger, power windows and locks, tinted glass, cruise control, articulated bucket seats with inflatable lumbar support and thigh bolsters, floormats, upgraded upholstery, cargo cover, AM/FM cassette with EQ, power antenna, remote hatch release, power mirrors.

Optional equipment:

5.0-liter TBI V-8, base	369	314	323
Requires air conditioning.			
5.0-liter PFI V-8, Formula	745	633	652
GTA (credit)	(300)	(255)	(255)
Not available with hatch roof; requires limited-slip axle; models with manual transmission require Performance Enhancement Group and 245/50ZR16 tires.			
5.7-liter PFI V-8, Formula	1045	888	914
T/A	300	255	262
Not available with hatch roof; requires automatic transmission, Performance Enhancement Group, limited-slip axle and 245/50ZR16 tires.			

	Retail Price	Dealer Invoice	Low Price
5-speed manual transmission, GTA & base w/5.0 (credit)	(530)	(451)	(451)
4-speed automatic transmission, Formula & T/A	530	451	464
Air conditioning, base	830	706	726
Limited-slip axle, base & Formula	100	85	87
Performance Enhancement Group, Formula & T/A	444	377	388
GTA w/5.0 and automatic (credit)	(444)	(377)	(377)

Dual-converter exhaust, engine oil cooler, performance axle ratio, four-wheel disc brakes.

Option Pkg. 1SB, base w/V-6	413	366	377

Air conditioning, bodyside moldings, inside rearview mirror with floodlamp.

Option Pkg. 1SC, base w/V-6	804	706	726

Pkg. 1SB plus power windows and locks, remote hatch release, power mirrors.

Option Pkg. 1SB, base convertible w/V-6 .	390	347	357

Air conditioning, bodyside moldings.

Option Pkg. 1SC, base convertible w/V-6 .	721	635	653

Pkg. 1SB plus power windows and locks, power mirrors.

Option Pkg. 1SB, base w/V-8, Formula & T/A	223	200	206

Bodyside moldings, power windows and locks, inside rearview mirror with floodlamp.

Option Pkg. 1SC, base w/V-8, Formula . .	484	426	438
T/A	449	397	409

Pkg. 1SB plus 4-way manual seat adjuster (std. T/A), cruise control, remote hatch release, power mirrors.

Option Pkg. 1SB, base convertible w/V-8, T/A	225	201	—

Power windows and locks, bodyside moldings.

Option Pkg. 1SC, base convertible w/V-8 .	401	356	—
T/A	366	326	—

Pkg. 1SB plus cruise control, power mirrors, 4-way manual seat adjuster (std. T/A).

Value Option Pkg. R6A, base & Formula .	814	699	719

T-top roof, cassette player w/EQ.

Value Option Pkg. R6A, T/A convertible . .	680	581	598

Leather seats, cassette player w/EQ.

Cruise control, exc. GTA	225	191	197
Remote hatch release, exc. GTA	60	51	52
Rear defogger, exc. GTA	170	145	149
Locking hatch roof (T-tops)	914	777	799
Power mirrors, exc. GTA	91	77	79
Power locks, exc. GTA	210	179	184

Requires power windows.

Power windows, exc. GTA	280	238	245

Requires power locks.

Prices are accurate at time of publication; subject to manufacturer's change.

	Retail Price	Dealer Invoice	Low Price
Cassette player w/EQ, exc. GTA	150	128	131
CD player w/EQ, exc. GTA	376	320	329
GTA, others w/Pkg. R6A	226	192	198
Power antenna, exc. GTA	85	72	74
Cargo security screen, exc. GTA	69	59	60
Leather seats, GTA	475	404	415
T/A	780	663	682
4-way manual driver's seat, base & Formula .	35	30	31
Sport Appearance Pkg., base (std. convertible)	450	383	394
Trans Am fascias, fog lamps, aero side moldings.			
245/50ZR16 tires, T/A	313	266	274
Requires alloy wheels.			
Warranty enhancements for New York . . .	25	21	22
California emissions pkg.	100	85	87

Chevrolet Cavalier/ Pontiac Sunbird

Chevrolet Cavalier VL 2-door

Anti-lock brakes and more-powerful base engines are the primary changes to these aging front-drive subcompacts. Cavalier's VL- and RS-model 2-door coupes, 4-door sedans, and 5-door wagons return, as does the sporty Z24 coupe. The RS convertible is back and it's joined by a Z24 version, which returns after a two-year hiatus. A new fuel-injection system for the base 2.2-liter 4-cylinder engine gives it 15 more horsepower, now 110. It is standard on VL and RS models. The 3.1-liter V-6 standard on Z24 and optional on RS convertibles and wagons remains at 140 horsepower. A 5-speed manual or an optional 3-speed automatic are the transmission choices with either engine. Sunbird also gets a 15-horsepower boost for its base engine, but in this case it's a 2.0-liter four now with 111 horsepower. Sunbird is available in three trim levels: LE, SE, and GT. All come in 2- or 4-door versions except for the GT, which is a 2-door only. In addition, an SE convertible is offered. The 140-horse-

Specifications	2-door notchback	2-door conv.	4-door notchback	5-door wagon
Wheelbase, in.	101.3	101.3	101.3	101.3
Overall length, in.	182.3	182.3	182.3	181.1
Overall width, in.	66.3	66.3	66.3	66.3
Overall height, in.	51.3	52.0	52.9	52.8
Curb weight, lbs.	2436	2672	2444	2617
Cargo vol., cu. ft.	13.2	10.7	13.0	64.4
Fuel capacity, gals.	15.2	15.2	15.2	15.2
Seating capacity	5	4	5	5
Front head room, in.	37.8	37.8	39.1	38.9
Front leg room, max., in.	42.9	42.2	42.2	42.2
Rear head room, in.	36.1	37.3	37.4	38.5
Rear leg room, min., in.	31.2	32.0	33.3	32.5

Powertrain layout: transverse front engine/front-wheel drive.

Engines	ohc I-4	ohv I-4	ohv V-6
Size, liters/cu. in.	2.0/121	2.2/133	3.1/191
Fuel delivery	PFI	PFI	PFI
Horsepower @ rpm	111 @ 5200	110 @ 5200	140 @ 4200
Torque (lbs./ft.) @ rpm	125 @ 3600	130 @ 3200	185 @ 3200
Availability	S[1]	S[2]	S[3]

EPA city/highway mpg

5-speed OD manual	25/35	25/36	19/28
3-speed automatic	23/31	23/32	20/28

1. Sunbird LE, SE.   2. Cavalier VL, RS.   3. Cavalier Z24, Sunbird GT.

Assembly point: Lordstown, Ohio.

Prices are accurate at time of publication; subject to manufacturer's change.

power 3.1-liter V-6 is standard on GT, optional on SE, and not offered on LE. This year, the doors on all Cavaliers and Sunbirds lock when the automatic transmission is shifted into drive or, on cars with manual, when eight mph is reached; they must be unlocked manually. The brake pedal must now be applied before the automatic can be shifted from park. Convertibles continue with their standard power-operated top. Last year, Cavalier's dashboard was restyled, bringing controls that are easier to see and reach. Sunbird stuck with the old dash, but added a protruding control panel that put all radio and climate controls within arm's reach. Both, however, have a high cowl and low-mounted seats that make shorter drivers feel like they're sitting in a bathtub. While imports have jumped in price the past few years, Cavalier and Sunbird have inched higher by comparison. Neither car is as roomy or technically sophisticated as newer Japanese subcompacts, yet with standard ABS and available V-6 power, they offer good value for the money.

Prices

Chevrolet Cavalier	Retail Price	Dealer Invoice	Low Price
VL 2-door notchback	$8899	$8436	$8636
VL 4-door notchback	8999	8531	8731
VL 5-door wagon	10099	9574	9774
RS 2-door notchback	9999	9279	9479
RS 4-door notchback	10199	9465	9665
RS 5-door wagon	11199	10393	10593
RS 2-door convertible	15395	14287	NA
Z24 2-door notchback	12995	11670	11870
Z24 2-door convertible	18305	16438	NA
Destination charge	475	475	475

Convertible low prices not available at time of publication.

Standard equipment:

VL: 2.2-liter PFI 4-cylinder engine, 5-speed manual transmission (3-speed automatic on wagon), anti-lock brakes, power steering, door-mounted automatic front seatbelts, cloth reclining front bucket seats, tinted glass (wagon), power locks, floor console with armrest, door pockets (2-door), left remote mirror, 185/75R14 tires. **RS adds:** AM/FM radio, tinted glass, bodyside moldings; convertible has power windows. **Z24 adds:** 3.1-liter PFI

V-6, Level III sport suspension, 4-way driver's seat, seatback pockets, split folding rear seat, 205/60R15 Eagle GA tires on alloy wheels; convertible has power windows.

Optional equipment:

	Retail Price	Dealer Invoice	Low Price
3.1-liter V-6, wagons	610	519	531
Includes Level II performance suspension and 195/70R14 tires.			
3-speed automatic transmission (std. wagons)	495	421	431
Air conditioning	745	633	648
Preferred Group 1, VL 2- & 4-door	550	468	479
VL wagon	445	378	387
AM/FM radio, tinted glass (standard on wagon), left remote and right manual mirrors, floormats, bodyside moldings.			
Preferred Group 1, RS 2- & 4-door	1027	873	893
RS wagon	961	817	836
Air conditioning, split folding rear seat, intermittent wipers, left remote and right manual mirrors, floormats, remote decklid release (2- & 4-doors), reading lamp, visor mirrors.			
Preferred Group 2, RS 2-door	1877	1595	1633
RS 4-door	1942	1651	1690
RS wagon	1916	1629	1667
Group 1 plus cassette player, power windows, cruise control, tilt steering column, trunk cargo net (2- & 4-doors), roof luggage carrier (wagon).			
Preferred Group 1, RS convertible	854	726	743
Air conditioning, intermittent wipers, remote decklid release, floormats.			
Preferred Group 2, RS convertible	1394	1185	1213
Group 1 plus cassette player, cruise control, tilt steering column, trunk cargo net.			
Preferred Group 1, Z24	1023	870	890
Air conditioning, tilt steering column, intermittent wipers, floormats, dome reading lamp, remote decklid release.			
Preferred Group 2, Z24	1683	1431	1464
Group 1 plus power windows, cruise control, cassette player, trunk cargo net.			
Preferred Group 1, Z24 convertible	854	721	NA
Air conditioning, intermittent wipers, floormats, remote decklid release.			
Preferred Group 2, Z24 convertible	1394	1180	NA
Group 1 plus cassette player, cruise control, tilt steering column, trunk cargo net.			
Vinyl bucket seats, convertibles	75	64	65
Trunk cargo net	30	26	26
Luggage rack, 2- & 4-doors	115	98	100
Roof luggage carrier, wagons	115	98	100
Rear spoiler, Z24	110	94	96
Rear defogger	170	145	148
Dome reading lamp	24	20	21
Tinted glass (std. wagons)	105	89	95

Prices are accurate at time of publication; subject to manufacturer's change.

	Retail Price	Dealer Invoice	Low Price
Left remote & right manual mirrors	30	26	27
Visor mirrors	14	12	13
Z51 Performance Handling Pkg., RS	224	190	202
Tachometer and gauges, Level II sport suspension, trip odometer, 195/ 70R14 tires.			
Split folding rear seat, 2- & 4-doors	150	128	135
Wagons	50	43	45
Cruise control	225	191	203
Tilt steering column	145	123	131
Removable sunroof, Z24	350	298	315
205/60R15 OWL tires, Z24	98	83	88
Remote decklid release	11	9	10
Power windows, 2-doors	265	225	239
4-doors & wagons	330	281	297
Intermittent wipers	65	55	59
AM/FM radio, VL	332	282	299
AM/FM cassette, VL	472	401	425
VL w/Preferred Group 1, RS & Z24 . . .	140	119	126

Pontiac Sunbird

	Retail Price	Dealer Invoice	Low Price
LE 2-door notchback	$9620	$8927	$9127
LE 4-door notchback	9720	9020	9220
SE 2-door notchback	10380	9321	9521
SE 4-door notchback	10480	9411	9611
SE 2-door convertible	15345	13780	13980
GT 2-door notchback	12820	11512	11712
Destination charge	475	475	475

Standard equipment:

LE and **SE**: 2.0-liter PFI 4-cylinder engine, 5-speed manual transmission, anti-lock brakes, power steering, door-mounted automatic front seatbelts cloth reclining front bucket seats, power locks, illuminated entry system, AM/FM radio, 185/75R14 tires; **convertible** adds power windows, tinted glass. **GT** adds: 3.1-liter PFI V-6, dual sport suspension, front armrest, cassette player, dual mirrors, tachometer, fog lamps, rear spoiler, 195/ 65R15 touring tires on alloy wheels.

Optional equipment:

3.1-liter V-6, SE	585	497	509
Includes sport suspension; requires rally gauges and 195/70R14 tires.			
3-speed automatic transmission	495	421	431
Air conditioning	745	633	648
Requires tinted glass.			
Tinted glass, LE & SE	105	89	91

CONSUMER GUIDE®

	Retail Price	Dealer Invoice	Low Price
Option Pkg. 1SB, LE	903	768	786
SE	158	134	137

Tinted glass, left remote and right manual mirrors; LE adds air conditioning.

Option Pkg. 1SC, SE notchbacks	671	585	599

Pkg. 1SB plus air conditioning, tilt steering column, intermittent wipers, front armrest.

Option Pkg. 1SD, SE notchbacks	1135	980	1003

Pkg. 1SC plus cruise control, split folding rear seat, rally gauges, Lamp Group, remote decklid release.

Option Pkg. 1SB, SE convertible & GT . . .	955	812	831

Air conditioning, tilt steering column, intermittent wipers.

Option Pkg. 1SC, SE convertible	827	718	735

Pkg. 1SB plus Lamp Group, front armrest, rally gauges, cruise control, remote decklid release.

Option Pkg. 1SC, GT	1428	1214	1242

Pkg. 1SB plus cruise control, split folding rear seat, front armrest, Lamp Group, remote decklid release.

Value Option Pkg. R6A, LE, SE	258	223	228

Cassette player, crosslace wheel covers, 195/65R15 tires.

Value Option Pkg. R6B, SE 2-doors	790	683	699
SE 2-doors w/Pkg. 1SD	741	641	656
SE 4-door	720	623	638
SE 4-door w/Pkg. 1 SD	671	582	596

Pkg. R6A plus 3.1-liter V-6 and rally gauges with tachometer; 2-doors add rear spoiler.

Special Appearance Pkg., convertible	599	509	521
w/Pkg. R6A	386	328	336
w/Pkg. R6B	316	269	275

White convertible top, white vinyl interior, rear spoiler, 195/65R15 tires on white alloy wheels.

Dual sport mirrors, LE & SE	53	45	46
Front armrest, SE & GT	58	49	50
Cruise control, SE & GT	225	191	196
Remote decklid release, SE & GT	11	9	45
Rear defogger, exc. convertible	170	145	148
Power windows (NA LE), 2-doors	265	225	231
4-door	330	281	287

Requires front armrest.

Cassette player	170	145	148
CD player, SE & GT	396	337	345
SE w/Pkg. R6A or R6B	226	192	197
Rally gauges, SE	49	42	43
Rally gauges w/tachometer, SE	127	108	110
SE w/Pkg. 1SC or 1SD	78	66	68
Split folding rear seat, SE & GT	150	128	130

Prices are accurate at time of publication; subject to manufacturer's change.

	Retail Price	Dealer Invoice	Low Price
Decklid spoiler, LE & SE 2-doors	70	60	61
Tilt steering column	145	123	126
Removable glass sunroof, SE & GT	350	298	304
Intermittent wipers, SE & GT	65	55	57
White vinyl interior trim, convertible	75	64	65
Two-tone paint, SE	101	86	88
195/70R14 touring tires, LE	141	120	123
LE w/Pkg. R6A or R6B (credit)	(17)	(14)	(14)
Includes rear stabilizer bar, quicker steering ratio. Requires alloy wheels.			
195/65R15 touring tires, SE	158	134	137
Includes rear stabilizer bar, quicker steering ratio.			
14-inch alloy wheels, LE & SE	275	234	239
w/Pkg. R6A or R6B	220	187	191
Requires 14" touring tires.			
15-inch crosslace wheel covers, LE & SE .	55	47	48
Requires 195/65R15 touring tires.			
15-inch alloy wheels, LE & SE	275	234	239
w/Pkg. R6A or R6B	220	187	191

Chevrolet Corvette

Chevrolet Corvette coupe

A more powerful base engine and a traction control system are among the changes for this rear-drive two-seat sports car. Corvette returns in coupe and convertible form and as a coupe with the ultra-performance ZR-1 option. The new base V-8, called the LT-1, still displaces 5.7 liters, but now makes 300 horsepower, up from 245 last year. The ZR-1 option again brings the Lotus-developed 375-horsepower,

32-valve, twin-cam 5.7-liter LT5 V-8—but adds "ZR1" fender badges. Both engines come standard with a 6-speed manual transmission; a 4-speed overdrive automatic is optional with the LT1. The new traction system is called Acceleration Slip Regulation (ASR) and it's standard on all Corvettes. ASR automatically curtails engine power or applies rear brakes to maximize rear-wheel traction at any speed. A dash button can shut it off. Among other changes, Goodyear's new Eagle GS-C tires replace Eagle ZR Gatorbacks, and the optional Selective Ride Control gets new software designed to improve the ride quality. Anti-lock

Specifications

	3-door hatchback	2-door conv.
Wheelbase, in.	96.2	96.2
Overall length, in.	178.6	178.6
Overall width, in.	71.0[1]	71.0
Overall height, in.	46.7	46.4
Curb weight, lbs.	3223[2]	3263
Cargo vol., cu. ft.	12.6	6.6
Fuel capacity, gals.	20.0	20.0
Seating capacity	2	2
Front head room, in.	36.4	36.4
Front leg room, max., in.	42.6	42.6
Rear head room, in.	—	—
Rear leg room, min., in.	—	—

1. ZR-1, 73.2.　　2. ZR-1, 3465.

Powertrain layout: longitudinal front engine/rear-wheel drive.

Engines

	ohv V-8	dohc V-8
Size, liters/cu. in.	5.7/350	5.7/350
Fuel delivery	PFI	PFI
Horsepower @ rpm	300 @ 5000	375 @ 5800
Torque (lbs./ft.) @ rpm	330 @ 4000	370 @ 4800
Availability	S	S[1]

EPA city/highway mpg

6-speed OD manual	17/25	16/25
4-speed OD automatic	17/25	

1. ZR-1

Assembly point: Bowling Green, Ky.

Prices are accurate at time of publication; subject to manufacturer's change.

brakes and a driver-side air bag remain standard. Acceleration with the LT1 is the same rocket-launching experience it was before, but the engine now pulls strongly to 5500 rpm; last year's engine ran out of breath around 4500. The new ASR is a boon to safety, helping the rear tires maximize traction on wet surfaces. However, the instrument pod's mix of digital and analog gauges is still too gimmicky. And the Corvette is far from civilized, with a noisy, harsh ride, bellowing exhaust note, and a pit-like cockpit that's hard to climb into and see out of.

Prices

Chevrolet Corvette	Retail Price	Dealer Invoice	Low Price
3-door hatchback	$33635	$28522	$28922
2-door convertible	40145	34043	34443
Destination charge	550	550	550

Standard equipment:

5.7-liter PFI V-8, 6-speed manual or 4-speed automatic transmission, power steering, anti-lock 4-wheel disc brakes, driver-side air bag, Acceleration Slip Regulation, Pass-Key theft deterrent system, air conditioning, AM/FM cassette, power antenna, cruise control, rear defogger, leather-wrapped steering wheel, tinted glass, heated power mirrors, fog lamps, power windows and locks, intermittent wipers, 275/40ZR17 Goodyear Eagle GS-C tires on alloy wheels.

Optional equipment:

ZR-1 Special Performance Pkg.	31683	26297	NA
5.7-liter DOHC 32-valve PFI V-8, Selective Ride & Handling Pkg., heavy-duty brake system, leather power seats, low-tire-pressure warning, Delco/Bose Gold audio system with CD and cassette players, solar glass, 275/40ZR17 front and 315/35ZR17 rear tires.			
Leather seats	475	394	418
Arctic white leather seats	555	461	488
Leather sport seats	1100	913	968
Arctic white leather sport seats	1180	979	1038
Preferred Group 1	1333	1106	1173
Automatic climate control, Delco/Bose audio system, power driver's seat.			
Delco/Bose cassette system	823	683	724
Delco/Bose system w/cassette & CD player .	1219	1012	1073
w/Group 1	396	329	348
Automatic climate control	205	170	180

	Retail Price	Dealer Invoice	Low Price
Performance axle ratio	50	42	44
Luggage rack, convertible	140	116	123
Z07 Adjustable Handling Pkg.	2045	1697	1800
HD brakes, Bilstein Adjustable Ride Control System.			
FX3 Selective Ride Pkg.	1695	1407	1492
Low tire pressure warning indicator	325	270	286
Single removable roof panel	650	540	572
Dual removable roof panels	950	789	836
Removable hardtop, convertible	1995	1656	1756
Power seats, each	305	253	268
California emissions pkg.	100	83	88

Chevrolet Lumina/
Oldsmobile Cutlass Supreme/
Pontiac Grand Prix

Chevrolet Lumina Euro 3.4

For 1992, anti-lock brakes are available on all versions of GM's mid-size front-drive cars, though no air bags are offered. Lumina returns as a 2-door coupe in three models: base, upscale Euro, and sporty Z34. The 4-door sedan is back in base and Euro trim, and as a new model, the Euro 3.4. Over at Oldsmobile, the Cutlass Supreme features new

Prices are accurate at time of publication; subject to manufacturer's change.

front and rear styling, and the previously standard 2.3-liter Quad 4 is dropped. Two-door coupes and 4-door sedans return as S and International Series models. The SL changes from a model to an option group, but remains available on both body styles. The 2-door convertible—a Cutlass Supreme exclusive—continues in SL-level trim. Gone is the 2.3-liter 4-cylinder Quad 4. The Quad 4 has also been dropped from the Pontiac Grand Prix line, and all Grand Prix sedans get the front-end look of the top-line

Specifications	2-door notchback	4-door notchback	2-door conv.
Wheelbase, in.	107.5	107.5	107.5
Overall length, in.	198.3	198.3	192.3
Overall width, in.	71.7	71.0	71.0
Overall height, in.	53.3	53.6	54.3
Curb weight, lbs.	3115	3220	3602
Cargo vol., cu. ft.	15.5	15.7	12.1
Fuel capacity, gals.	16.5	16.5	16.5
Seating capacity	6	6	5
Front head room, in.	37.6	38.8	37.8
Front leg room, max., in.	42.4	42.4	42.3
Rear head room, in.	37.2	38.1	37.1
Rear leg room, min., in.	34.8	36.9	34.8

Powertrain layout: transverse front engine/front-wheel drive.

Engines	ohv I-4	ohv V-6	dohc V-6
Size, liters/cu. in.	2.5/151	3.1/191	3.4/207
Fuel delivery	TBI	PFI	PFI
Horsepower @ rpm	105 @ 4800	140 @ 4400	210 @ 5200
Torque (lbs./ft.) @ rpm	135 @ 3200	185 @ 3200	215 @ 4000
Availability	S[1]	S[2]	S[3]

EPA city/highway mpg

5-speed OD manual			17/27
3-speed automatic	21/28	19/27	
4-speed OD automatic		19/29	17/26

1. Base Lumina.   2. Lumina Euro; Cutlass S and conv.; Grand Prix LE, SE and GT.
3. Lumina Z34; Cutlass I-Series; Grand Prix STE.

Assembly points: Oshawa, Ontario, Canada; Doraville, Ga.; Fairfax, Kan.

STE. Replacing the Quad 4 as the base engine in the Grand Prix and Cutlass Supreme is a 140-horsepower 3.1-liter V-6. The Chevrolet Lumina retains its base 2.5-liter four, now rated at 105 horsepower. The 3.1 V-6 is optional on base models, standard on Euros. GM's double overhead-cam, 24-valve 210-horsepower 3.4-liter V-6 is optional on all versions of the Grand Prix and Cutlass Supreme, and standard on top-line Cutlass International Series and Grand Prix STE. It's also standard on Lumina Z34 and the new Euro 3.4 sedan. Only the 3.4-liter V-6 is available with a 5-speed manual transmission, except in the Grand Prix, where the 5-speed is standard with the 3.1 V-6, and in the Lumina Euro 3.4, which comes standard with a 4-speed automatic. All other powertrain combinations include a 3- or 4-speed automatic, and the latter is available as an option with the 3.4. Sportier versions of all these cars have suspensions that offer taut handling, but transmit some impact harshness through to the cabin. While we applaud the available ABS, the lack of an air bag puts them a step behind many competitors. The Ford Taurus is the most obvious of these, and GM's offerings don't quite match it in other areas either. However, GM's intermediates can be equipped with the high-performance 3.4-liter V-6 teamed with either a manual or automatic transmission, whereas Ford's Taurus SHO comes only with a 5-speed and is more expensive.

Prices

Chevrolet Lumina	Retail Price	Dealer Invoice	Low Price
2-door notchback	$13200	$11458	$11808
4-door notchback	13400	11631	11981
Euro 2-door notchback	15600	13541	13891
Euro 4-door notchback	15800	13714	14064
Z34 2-door notchback	18400	15971	NA
Destination charge	505	505	505

Z34 low price not available at time of publication.

Standard equipment:

2.5-liter TBI 4-cylinder engine, 3-speed automatic transmission, 4-wheel disc brakes, power steering, door-mounted automatic front seatbelts, cloth

Prices are accurate at time of publication; subject to manufacturer's change.

front bench seat with recliners, AM/FM radio, visor mirrors, tinted glass, left remote and right manual mirrors, intermittent wipers, 195/75R14 tires. **Euro** adds: 3.1-liter PFI V-6, anti-lock brakes, uprated suspension, air conditioning, decklid spoiler, front storage armrest, cargo net, 205/70R15 tires. **Z34** adds: 3.4-liter DOHC 24-valve PFI V-6, 5-speed manual transmission, four-way adjustable front bucket seats, remote mirrors, gauge package, sill moldings, cassette player, 225/60R16 tires on alloy wheels.

Optional equipment:	Retail Price	Dealer Invoice	Low Price
3.1-liter V-6, base	660	561	578
4-speed automatic transmission, base & Euro	200	170	175
Anti-lock brakes, base	450	383	394
Air conditioning, base	830	706	726
Preferred Group 1, base	1020	867	893
Air conditioning, tilt steering column, floormats.			
Preferred Group 2, base	1390	1182	1216
w/o luggage rack	1275	1084	1116
Group 1 plus cruise control, decklid luggage rack, cargo net.			
Preferred Group 3, base 2-door	1955	1662	1711
4-door	2060	1751	1803
w/o luggage rack, 2-door	1840	1564	1610
w/o luggage rack, 4-door	1945	1653	1702
Group 2 plus power windows and locks, remote decklid release, remote mirrors.			
Preferred Group 1, Euro	545	463	477
Cruise control, tilt steering column, tachometer and gauges, cargo net, floormats.			
Preferred Group 2, Euro 2-door	1250	1063	1094
Euro 4-door	1355	1152	1186
Group 1 plus cassette player, power windows and locks, remote decklid release, remote mirrors.			
3.4 Euro Sedan Pkg.	1885	1602	1649
3.4-liter DOHC PFI V-6 engine, 4-speed automatic transmission, bucket seats, 225/60R16 Eagle GT+4 tires on alloy wheels.			
Preferred Group 1, Z34	535	455	468
Power windows and locks, remote decklid release.			
Front storage armrest, base	50	43	44
Bucket seats & console	334	284	292
60/40 front seat	194	165	170
Custom cloth 60/40 front seat	234	199	205
w/front storage armrest	284	241	249
Power driver's seat	270	230	236
Cassette player	140	119	123
Delco/Bose audio system	475	404	416
Euro w/Group 2 & Z34	335	285	293
CD player	396	337	347
Euro w/Group 2 & Z34	256	218	224

	Retail Price	Dealer Invoice	Low Price
Cargo net	30	26	26
Rear defogger	170	145	149
Power locks, 2-doors	210	179	184
4-doors	250	213	219
Power windows, 2-doors	265	225	232
4-doors	330	281	289
Tachometer & gauges	100	85	88
Transmission oil cooler	75	64	66
Remote mirrors	30	26	26
Cruise control	225	191	197
Rear spoiler delete, Euro (credit)	(128)	(109)	(109)
Tilt steering column	145	123	127
195/75R14 whitewall tires, base	72	61	63
215/60R16 tires, Euro	112	95	98
Remote decklid release	60	51	53
Decklid luggage rack	115	98	101
Front floormats	25	21	22

Oldsmobile Cutlass Supreme

	Retail Price	Dealer Invoice	Low Price
S 2-door notchback	$15695	$13623	$13973
S 4-door notchback	15795	13710	14060
I Series 2-door notchback	21795	18918	19268
I Series 4-door notchback	21895	19005	19355
2-door convertible	21995	19092	NA
Destination charge	505	505	505

Standard equipment:

S: 3.1-liter PFI V-6 engine, 3-speed automatic transmission, 4-wheel disc brakes, power steering, door-mounted automatic front shoulder belts, air conditioning, cloth reclining front bucket seats, 4-way manual driver's seat, center console, trip odometer, AM/FM radio, tinted glass, 205/70R15 tires. **International Series** adds: 3.4-liter DOHC 24-valve PFI V-6, 5-speed manual transmission, anti-lock brakes, automatic climate control, articulated power front bucket seats, rear bucket seats (2-door), folding rear seat (4-door), cruise control, tachometer, coolant temperature and oil pressure gauges, voltmeter, intermittent wipers, Driver Information System, head-up display, Remote Lock Control Pkg., power mirrors, lighted right visor mirror, sill extensions, tilt steering column, leather-wrapped steering wheel, sport suspension, floormats, 225/60R16 tires. **Convertible** has SL equipment plus front bucket seats, sport suspension, remote outside mirrors.

Optional equipment:

3.1-liter PFI V-6 engine (credit), I-Series	(995)	(846)	(846)

Includes 4-speed automatic transmission.

Prices are accurate at time of publication; subject to manufacturer's change.

	Retail Price	Dealer Invoice	Low Price
3.4-liter DOHC V-6, S 2-door w/o BYP . . .	1285	1092	1105
S 2-door w/BYP	1083	921	931
S 4-door w/o BYP	1570	1335	1350
S 4-door w/BYP	1173	997	1009
5-speed manual transmission, S	NC	NC	NC
4-speed automatic transmission, S w/3.4 .	250	213	215
w/3.1	175	149	151
Anti-lock brakes (std. I Series)	450	383	387
Option Pkg. 1SB, S 2-door	1050	893	903

Tilt steering column, intermittent wipers, cruise control, Convenience Lamp & Mirror Group, rallye gauges, floormats, alloy wheels.

| Option Pkg. 1SB, S 4-door . . . . | 600 | 510 | 516 |

Tilt steering column, intermittent wipers, cruise control, Convenience Lamp & Mirror Group, floormats.

| Option Pkg. 1SC, base 2-door . . . . | 1797 | 1527 | 1545 |
| Base 4-door . . . . | 1452 | 1234 | 1249 |

Pkg. 1SB plus power mirrors, Remote Lock Control Pkg., power windows.

| Option Pkg. 1SD, base 2-door . . . . | 2662 | 2263 | 2289 |
| Base 4-door . . . . | 2317 | 1969 | 1993 |

Pkg. 1SC plus power driver's seat, automatic climate control system, steering wheel touch controls.

| BYP Sport Luxury Pkg., S 2-door . . . . . . | 628 | 534 | 540 |
| S 4-door . . . . | 988 | 840 | 850 |

4-speed automatic transmission with column shift, front bucket seats, cargo net, misc. lights, door pockets, dual remote mirrors, rallye gauges, cassette player, remote decklid release, fog lamps, 205/70R16 tires on alloy wheels.

| Option Pkg. 1SB, I Series 2-door . . . . . . | 545 | 463 | 469 |
| I Series 4-door . . . . | 610 | 519 | 525 |

Power windows, power driver's seat.

| Option Pkg. 1SB, conv. . . . . | 1057 | 898 | 909 |

Cruise control, tilt steering column, intermittent wipers, power mirrors, Remote Lock Control Pkg., rallye gauges, floormats.

| Option Pkg. 1SC, conv. . . . . | 1722 | 1464 | 1481 |

Pkg. 1SB plus power driver's seat, automatic climate control, steering wheel touch controls.

R7B Value Pkg., S 2-door w/1SB or 1SC . .	293	249	252
S 2-door w/1SD	128	109	110
S 4-door	653	555	562

BYP Sport Luxury Pkg., cassette player.

R7C Value Pkg., S 2-door w/o BYP	535	455	460
S 4-door w/o BYP	820	697	705
S 2-door w/BYP	333	283	286
S 4-door w/BYP	423	360	364

3.4-liter DOHC 24-valve PFI V-6 engine, 5-speed manual transmission.

| R7C Value Pkg. S 2-door w/o BYP . . . . . | 785 | 667 | 675 |
| S 4-door w/o BYP . . . . | 1070 | 910 | 920 |

	Retail Price	Dealer Invoice	Low Price
S 2-door w/BYP	583	496	501
S 4-door w/BYP	673	572	579

3.4-liter DOHC 24-valve PFI V-6 engine, 4-speed automatic transmission.

	Retail Price	Dealer Invoice	Low Price
55/45 front seat, base	NC	NC	NC
Split folding rear seat back, S	150	128	129
Power driver's seat, S	305	259	262
I-Series, convertible	270	230	232
Astroroof	695	591	598
Power locks, S 2-door	210	179	181
Base 4-door	250	213	215
Remote Lock Control Pkg., 2-door	395	336	340
4-door	435	370	374
Convertible	335	285	288
Power windows, 2-door	275	234	237
4-door	340	289	292
Tilt steering column, S	145	123	125
Cruise control, S	225	191	194
Rear defogger	170	145	146
Intermittent wipers, S	65	55	56
Automatic climate control, S	150	128	129
205/70R15 whitewall tires, S	76	65	65
Alloy wheels, S	285	242	245
Steering wheel touch controls, S w/o			
leather seats or R7B	410	349	353
w/leather seats & w/o R7B	320	272	275
w/o leather seats & w/R7B	245	208	211
w/leather seats & R7B	155	132	133
Convertible w/o leather seats	245	208	211
Convertible w/leather seats	155	132	133
Cassette player, S	165	140	142
Cassette player w/EQ, S w/Steering wheel			
touch controls	225	191	194
w/R7B & w/o Steering wheel touch controls	255	217	219
w/o Steering wheel touch controls & R7B .	420	357	361
I Series	225	191	194
Convertible w/o Steering wheel touch			
controls	130	111	112
Convertible w/Steering wheel touch			
controls	100	85	86
CD player, S w/Steering wheel touch controls	351	298	302
w/o Steering wheel touch controls & w/R7B	381	324	328
w/o Steering wheel touch controls & R7B .	546	464	470
I Series	351	298	302
Convertible w/o Steering wheel touch			
controls	256	218	220
Convertible w/Steering wheel touch			
controls	226	192	194

Prices are accurate at time of publication; subject to manufacturer's change.

	Retail Price	Dealer Invoice	Low Price
Power antenna, S	85	72	73
Custom leather trim, S	665	565	572
Convertible	515	438	443
I Series, Convertible w/1SC	425	361	366
Leather-wrapped steering wheel, S	90	77	77
Rallye gauges, S	165	140	142
Head-up instrument display, S	250	213	215
Convenience Lamp & Mirror Group, S	120	102	103
Front floormats	25	21	22
Rear floormats	20	17	17
Dual outside mirrors, S	77	65	66
Decklid luggage carrier	115	98	99
Bodyside moldings, S 2-door	60	51	52
HD cooling	125	106	108
Engine block heater	18	15	15
Warranty enhancements for New York state	25	21	22
California emissions pkg	100	85	86

Pontiac Grand Prix

	Retail Price	Dealer Invoice	Low Price
LE 4-door notchback	$14890	$13222	$13497
SE 2-door notchback	15390	13359	13634
SE 4-door notchback	16190	14053	14328
GT 2-door notchback	20340	17655	17930
STE 4-door notchback	21635	18779	19054
Destination charge	505	505	505

Standard equipment:

LE & SE: 3.1-liter PFI engine, 3-speed automatic transmission, power steering, 4-wheel disc brakes, air conditioning, door-mounted automatic front seatbelts, cloth 45/45 reclining front bucket seats, fog lights, AM/FM radio, 205/70R15 tires. **SE sedan** adds: 215/60R16 tires on alloy wheels. **GT** adds: 4-speed automatic transmission, anti-lock brakes, Y99 sport suspension, power articulating front seat, power windows and locks, cruise control, cassette player with EQ and Touch Control, 225/60R16 Eagle GT+4 tires on alloy wheels. **STE** adds: 3.4-liter V-6, Electronic Information Center, remote keyless entry.

Optional equipment:

3.4-liter V-6	995	846	875

Requires 225/60R16 tires on alloy wheels, dual exhausts, Y99 handling suspension, gauge cluster, bucket seats, transmission oil cooler.

5-speed manual transmission, SE 2-door, GT	(200)	(170)	(170)
4-speed automatic transmission, LE & SE	200	170	176

	Retail Price	Dealer Invoice	Low Price
Anti-lock brakes, LE & SE	450	383	396
Not available with 45/55 split seat or power sunroof.			
Option Pkg. 1SB, LE	175	157	162
SE	450	383	396
Intermittent wipers, tilt steering column, cruise control, illuminated entry.			
Option Pkg. 1SC, LE	540	474	491
Pkg. 1SB plus power windows and locks.			
Option Pkg. 1SC, SE 2-door	718	628	650
SE 4-door	1023	882	913
Pkg. 1SB plus power windows and locks, power driver's seat, power mirrors.			
Option Pkg. 1SD, SE 2-door	1084	939	972
SE 4-door	1389	1193	1235
Pkg. 1SC plus remote keyless entry, power antenna, lighted visor mirrors, remote decklid release.			
Option Pkg. 1SB, GT	841	715	740
Remote keyless entry, lighted visor mirrors, power antenna, Head-up instrument display, compass with trip computer and service reminder.			
Option Pkg. 1SB, STE	1145	973	1007
Leather seats, power sunroof.			
Value Option Pkg. R6A, LE	543	468	484
Rally gauges, tachometer, Custom Interior Trim Pkg., alloy wheels.			
Value Option Pkg. R6B, LE	488	421	436
Power driver's seat, Custom Interior Trim Pkg.			
Value Option Pkg. R6A, SE 2-door	818	701	726
SE 4-door	564	485	502
Sport Appearance Pkg., Custom Interior Trim Pkg.			
Value Option Pkg. R6B, SE 2-door	753	646	669
SE 4-door	774	663	686
Custom Interior Trim Pkg., rally gauges, tachometer, cassette w/EQ and 6 speakers.			
Value Option Pkg. R6C, SE 2-door	2228	1916	1983
R6B plus 3.4-liter V-6 engine, 4-speed automatic transmission, second gear start transmission switch, transmission oil cooler, dual exhausts, Y99 handling suspension, sport bucket seats, 225/60R16 tires on alloy wheels.			
Value Option Pkg. R6C, SE 4-door	1457	1259	1303
R6A plus 3.4-liter V-6 engine, 4-speed automatic transmission, second gear start transmission switch, transmission oil cooler, Y99 handling suspension, 225/60R16 tires.			
Remote decklid release, LE & SE	60	51	53
Rear defogger, SE, LE, & GT	170	145	150
Power sunroof, LE & SE	695	591	611
LE & SE w/Custom Interior Trim Pkg., GT, STE	670	570	589
Electronic compass, LE, SE & GT	285	242	251
Includes trip computer and service reminder.			

Prices are accurate at time of publication; subject to manufacturer's change.

	Retail Price	Dealer Invoice	Low Price
Head-up display, SE, GT, & STE	250	213	220
Remote keyless entry, LE, SE & GT	135	115	119
Power mirrors, LE & SE	78	66	69
Requires power windows.			
Tachometer & rally gauges, LE & SE	85	72	75
LE requires Pkg. 1SC.			
Power windows, SE 2-door	275	234	242
SE 4-door, LE	340	289	299
Power locks, SE 2-door	210	179	185
SE 4-door, LE	250	213	220
Convenience Group, LE & SE 4-door	450	383	396
Cruise control, intermittent wipers, tilt steering column, illuminated entry system.			
Custom Interior Trim Pkg., LE	383	326	337
SE 2-door	328	279	289
SE 4-door	324	275	285
Cargo net, leather-wrapped steering wheel, upgraded upholstery, reading lamps, rear seat pass-through, overhead console, covered visor mirrors, floormats.			
Aero Performance Pkg., SE 2-door, GT . .	2595	2206	2283
Aero skirts, wheel flares, wide bodyside applique, dual exhausts, 225/60R16 tires on alloy wheels; requires bucket seats, rally gauges, Y99 handling suspension.			
Cassette player, LE & SE	140	119	123
AM & FM stereo w/EQ, LE w/Pkg. 1SC, SE .	590	502	519
w/Custom Interior Trim Pkg	540	459	475
SE 2-door w/Custom Interior Trim Pkg. or Value Option Pkg. R6B or R6C	540	459	475
SE 4-door w/Custom Interior Trim Pkg.	540	459	475
CD player w/EQ, LE w/Pkg. 1SC, SE	816	694	718
w/Custom Interior Trim Pkg.	766	651	674
SE w/Custom Interior Trim & w/o R6B or R6C	766	651	674
SE w/Pkg. R6B or R6C, STE	226	192	199
Power antenna, exc. STE	85	72	75
Bucket seats & console, LE & SE	110	94	97
Requires rally gauges.			
Sport bucket seats & console, LE & SE . .	140	119	123
Requires rally gauges and custom trim.			
Power driver's seat, LE & SE	305	259	268
LE requires Pkg. 1SC.			
Leather trim, GT & STE	475	404	418
Sport Appearance Pkg., SE 2-door	690	587	607
SE 4-door w/Pkg. R6A or R6C	385	327	339
SE 4-door w/Custom Interior Trim	415	353	365
Aero skirts, bucket seats and console, rally gauges, dual exhausts, alloy wheels.			

	Retail Price	Dealer Invoice	Low Price
Y99 handling suspension, w/3.4	50	43	44
SE w/R6C	NC	NC	NC
SE requires Aero Performance Pkg.			
Dual exhausts, LE & SE	90	77	79
Second gear start transmission switch, w/3.4	25	21	22
Alloy wheels, LE & SE	275	234	242
215/60R16 tires, SE 2-door	112	95	99
Requires alloy wheels.			
225/60R16 tires, LE, SE 2-door	150	128	132
SE 4-door	48	41	42
225/50ZR16 tires, GT	209	178	184
Two-tone paint, LE, SE 2-door	105	89	92
Decklid luggage rack	115	98	101
Floormats, LE	45	38	40
Covered visor mirrors, LE	14	12	12
Transmission oil cooler, w/3.4	75	64	66

Chevrolet Lumina APV/ Oldsmobile Silhouette/ Pontiac Trans Sport

Chevrolet Lumina APV CL

More power and a new transmission are available for these front-drive minivans, and the Transport and Silhouette offer standard anti-lock brakes; Chevy says anti-lock brakes are on tap for its APV later in the model year. All are built with fiberglass-like composite exterior panels

Prices are accurate at time of publication; subject to manufacturer's change.

bonded to a steel frame. A sliding right-side door and a one-piece rear liftgate augment the two front doors. Lumina APV comes in base and CL trim; Pontiac Trans Sport is offered in SE and GT guise; and the Olds Silhouette has only one trim level. Seating capacity on all ranges from five to seven, and the standard powertrain is a 120-horsepower 3.1-liter V-6 coupled to a 3-speed automatic transmission, except on Trans Sport GT. Newly optional on all models (and standard on Trans Sport GT) is a 3.8 liter V-6 with 165 horsepower linked to a 4-speed overdrive automatic. Those equipped with the new powertrain can tow up to 3000 pounds, 1000 more than with the 3.1 V-6. Also new

Specifications

	4-door van
Wheelbase, in.	109.8
Overall length, in.	194.2
Overall width, in.	73.9
Overall height, in.	65.7
Curb weight, lbs.	3558
Cargo vol., cu. ft.	112.6
Fuel capacity, gals.	20.0
Seating capacity	7
Front head room, in.	35.7
Front leg room, max., in.	40.7
Rear head room, in.	35.6
Rear leg room, min., in.	33.1

Powertrain layout: transverse engine/front-wheel drive.

Engines	ohv V-6	ohv V-6
Size, liters/cu. in.	3.1/191	3.8/231
Fuel delivery	TBI	PFI
Horsepower @ rpm	120 @ 4400	165 @ 4300
Torque (lbs./ft.) @ rpm	175 @ 2200	220 @ 3200
Availability	S	O[1]

EPA city/highway mpg

3-speed automatic	18/23	
4-speed OD automatic		17/24

1. Std., Trans Sport GT.

Assembly point: Tarrytown, N.Y.

for 1992 are standard 15-inch tires (in place of 14s), available power mirrors, and later in the year, optional rear air conditioner and sunroof. The larger V-6 addresses one of APV's major shortfalls: a lack of power. Acceleration with the standard 3.1 is tepid if heavy cargo or several passengers are aboard. Another shortcoming is poor visibility caused by a long dash shelf, sloping nose, and a forest of front roof pillars. Hard-to-reach climate controls are a problem with all models, but otherwise, these minivans are very car-like. They corner with good control and ride well over most surfaces. Furthermore, the body resists dings and is impervious to rust, and the rear bucket seats are light and easy to remove.

Prices

Chevrolet Lumina APV	Retail Price	Dealer Invoice	Low Price
Passenger van	$15570	$13982	$14332
CL passenger van	17355	15585	15935
Destination charge	530	530	530

Standard equipment:

3.1-liter TBI V-6. 3-speed automatic transmission, power steering, four-way adjustable driver's seat, reclining front bucket seats, 3-passenger middle seat, tinted glass, left remote and right manual mirrors, AM/FM radio, rear wiper/washer, 205/70R14 tires. **CL** adds: air conditioning, tilt steering column, individual seats, misc. lights.

Optional equipment:

3.8-liter PFI V-6	619	526	545
Includes 4-speed automatic transmission.			
4-speed automatic transmission	200	170	176
Air conditioning, base	830	706	730
Front and rear air conditioning, base	1280	1088	1126
CL	450	383	396
Preferred Group 1, base	1070	910	942
Base w/6- or 7-passenger seating	1085	922	955
Air conditioning, tilt steering column, auxiliary lighting, floormats.			
Preferred Group 2, base w/5-pass. seating	2118	1800	1864
Base w/6- or 7-pass. seating	2133	1813	1877
Group 1 plus cassette player, power windows and locks, cruise control, power mirrors, cargo area net.			

Prices are accurate at time of publication; subject to manufacturer's change.

	Retail Price	Dealer Invoice	Low Price
Preferred Group 1, CL w/5-pass. seating .	1083	921	953
CL w/7-pass. seating	1098	933	966
Cassette player, power windows and locks, cruise control, power mirrors, floormats, cargo area net.			
6-passenger seating	510	434	449
Two front bucket seats and four modular rear seats.			
7-passenger seating, base	660	561	581
CL	425	361	374
Two front bucket seats and five modular rear seats.			
Trailering Pkg.	150	128	132
Luggage rack	145	123	128
Rear defogger	170	145	150
Deep-tinted glass	245	208	216
Auxiliary lighting	60	51	53
Power locks	300	255	264
Power windows	275	234	242
Power mirrors	78	66	69
Power driver's seat	270	230	238
Load leveling suspension	170	145	150
Cruise control	225	191	198
Tilt steering column	145	123	128
Two-tone paint	148	126	130
205/70R15 tires	35	30	31
Alloy wheels	275	234	242
Cassette player	140	119	123
CD player	396	337	348
Base w/Group 2, CL w/Group 1	256	218	225
Front floormats	20	17	18
Rear floormats, w/5-pass. seating	15	13	13
w/6- or 7-pass. seating	30	26	26
Engine block heater	20	17	18

Oldsmobile Silhouette

	Retail Price	Dealer Invoice	Low Price
4-door passenger van	$19095	$17147	$17497
Destination charge	530	530	530

Standard equipment:

3.1-liter TBI V-6, 3-speed automatic transmission, anti-lock brakes, power steering, air conditioning, cloth front bucket seats (4-way adjustable driver's seat), three middle and two rear modular seats, overhead console with compass, thermometer, and storage, power mirrors, tachometer, coolant temperature and oil pressure gauges, voltmeter, trip odometer, intermittent wipers, AM/FM radio, tilt steering column, solar-treated windshield, deep-tinted side and liftgate glass, 205/70R15 tires on alloy wheels.

Optional equipment:

	Retail Price	Dealer Invoice	Low Price
3.8-liter V-6 engine	800	680	708
Includes 4-speed automatic transmission.			
Option Pkg. 1SB	830	706	735
Power windows and locks, cruise control, cargo area net.			
Option Pkg. 1SC	1225	1041	1084
Pkg. 1SB plus power driver's seat, Remote Lock Control Pkg.			
6-passenger modular seating (credit)	(110)	(94)	(94)
Rear air conditioning	450	383	398
Power driver's seat	270	230	239
Rear defogger	170	145	150
Power windows	275	234	243
Power locks	300	255	266
Remote Lock Control Pkg.	125	106	111
Cruise control	225	191	199
FE3 Touring Car suspension	205	174	181
Sport suspension, automatic leveling, air inflation kit.			
Towing Pkg	355	302	314
205/70R15 self-sealing tires	150	128	133
Cassette player	140	119	124
CD player	396	337	350
Roof luggage carrier	145	123	128
Cargo area net	30	26	27
Custom leather trim, w/6-pass. seating	650	553	575
w/7-pass. seating	870	740	770
Engine block heater	18	15	16
Warranty enhancements for New York state	25	21	22
California emissions pkg.	100	85	89

Pontiac Trans Sport

SE van	$16225	$14570	$14920
GT van	20935	18800	19150
Destination charge	530	530	530

Standard equipment:

SE: 3.1-liter TBI V-6, 3-speed automatic transmission, anti-lock brakes, power steering, 5-passenger seating (reclining front bucket seats, middle bench seat), tinted glass, tachometer, coolant temperature and oil pressure gauges, voltmeter, trip odometer, AM/FM radio, door pockets, beverage holders, 205/70R15 tires. **GT** adds: 3.8-liter PFI V-6 engine, 4-speed automatic transmission, 6-passenger seating (two second row and two third row modular seats), air conditioning, power mirrors, pneumatic load leveling, deep-tint glass, cassette player, leather-wrapped steering wheel, Lamp Group, tilt steering column, cruise control, built-in inflator, 205/70R15 tires on alloy wheels.

Prices are accurate at time of publication; subject to manufacturer's change.

Optional equipment:

	Retail Price	Dealer Invoice	Low Price
3.8-liter V-6 engine, SE	819	696	725
Includes 4-speed automatic transmission.			
Air conditioning, SE	830	706	735
Front & rear air conditioning, SE	1280	1088	1134
GT	450	383	399
Requires 6- or 7-passenger seating, deep-tint glass, Lamp Group.			
Option Pkg. 1SB, SE	635	568	592
Air conditioning, cruise control, tilt steering column, Lamp Group, power locks.			
Option Pkg. 1SC, SE	835	740	771
Pkg. 1SB plus power windows.			
Option Pkg. 1SB, GT	345	308	321
Power windows and locks, power driver's seat.			
Value Option Pkg. R6A, SE	243	210	219
Remote keyless entry, power mirrors, 205/70R15 self-sealing tires.			
Value Option Pkg. R6B, SE	729	626	652
3.8-liter V-6 engine, 4-speed automatic transmission, remote keyless entry.			
Rear defogger	170	145	151
Deep-tint glass, SE	245	208	217
Cruise control, SE	225	191	199
Tilt steering column, SE	145	123	128
Luggage rack	145	123	128
Lamp Group, SE	60	51	53
Power mirrors, SE	48	41	43
Power locks	300	255	266
Power driver's seat	270	230	239
Power windows	275	234	244
Requires power locks.			
Remote keyless entry	135	115	120
Cassette player, SE	140	119	124
CD player w/EQ, SE	516	439	457
GT	376	320	333
6-passenger seating, SE	525	446	465
Two second row and two third row modular seats.			
7-passenger seating, SE	675	574	598
GT	110	94	97
Three second row and two third row modular seats.			
Trailer provisions, SE	320	272	283
GT	150	128	133
205/70R15 tires, SE	35	30	31
Self-sealing tires, SE	150	128	133
Alloy wheels, SE	275	234	244
Warranty enhancements for New York . . .	25	21	22
California emissions pkg.	100	85	89

Chevrolet S10 Blazer/ GMC Jimmy/ Oldsmobile Bravada

Chevrolet S10 Blazer 2WD 5-door

The GMC version of this compact sport-utility loses its "S15" prefix, and all but Chevy's Blazer gain a more potent optional engine. Four-wheel-drive models of Blazer and Jimmy can now be ordered with an electronic-shift transfer case; the Olds Bravada comes with permanently engaged 4WD. For 1992, 4-wheel anti-lock brakes that work both in 2- and 4-wheel drive are standard on all three. S10 Blazer and Jimmy are back in 3- and 5-door body styles, while the Bravada comes only as a 5-door. The only engine is a 4.3-liter V-6. In standard form, it's rated at 160 horsepower. A 200-horsepower "high-performance" variant is newly optional on the Jimmy and Bravada; Chevrolet has not announced plans to offer the HP 4.3 on the Blazer. A 5-speed manual transmission is standard and a 4-speed automatic optional on Blazer and Jimmy; the automatic is standard on the Bravada. With lots of torque at low engine speeds, even the standard 4.3 has strong around-town acceleration and good towing power. Blazer and Jimmy are available with rear-wheel drive or GM's Insta-Trac on-demand 4WD system, with automatic locking front

Prices are accurate at time of publication; subject to manufacturer's change.

hubs and shift-on-the-fly capability between 2WD and 4WD High. A luxury package with leather upholstery and a softer-riding suspension is optional on both versions. All now have round gauges in place of the previous "hockey-stick" instruments. These are appealing compact sport-utilities, but they've surrendered their sales leadership in the class to the newer Ford Explorer. However, compared to the Explorer, the ABS on Blazer, Bravada, and Jimmy works on all four wheels instead of just the rears, and it operates in 4WD instead of just in 2WD. But overall, none can match the smaller Jeep Cherokee for around-town nimbleness, nor the Explorer for all-round appeal.

Specifications	3-door wagon	5-door wagon
Wheelbase, in.	100.5	107.0
Overall length, in.	170.3	176.8
Overall width, in.	65.7	65.2
Overall height, in.	64.0	64.1
Curb weight, lbs.	2889	3583
Cargo vol., cu. ft.	62.7	74.3
Fuel capacity, gals.	20.0	20.0
Seating capacity	4	5-6
Front head room, in.	39.0	39.1
Front leg room, max., in.	42.5	42.5
Rear head room, in.	NA	38.8
Rear leg room, min., in.	NA	36.5

Powertrain layout: longitudinal front engine/rear-wheel drive or on-demand 4WD (permanent 4WD, Bravada).

Engines	ohv V-6	ohv V-6
Size, liters/cu. in.	4.3/262	4.3/262
Fuel delivery	TBI	PFI
Horsepower @ rpm	160 @ 4000	200 @ 4500
Torque (lbs./ft.) @ rpm	230 @ 2800	200 @ 3600
Availability	S	O
EPA city/highway mpg		
5-speed OD manual	16/20	NA
4-speed OD automatic	16/21	NA

Assembly points: Pontiac, Mich.; Shreveport, La.; Moraine, Ohio.

Prices

Chevrolet S10 Blazer/GMC Jimmy	Retail Price	Dealer Invoice	Low Price
S10 3-door wagon, 2WD	$14823	$13311	$13511
Jimmy 3-door wagon, 2WD	15022	13490	13690
S10 3-door wagon, 4WD	16583	14892	15092
Jimmy 3-door wagon, 4WD	16803	15089	15289
S10 5-door wagon, 2WD	15783	14173	14623
Jimmy 5-door wagon, 2WD	15982	14352	14802
S10 5-door wagon, 4WD	17953	16122	16572
Jimmy 5-door wagon, 4WD	18173	16319	16769
Destination charge	475	475	475

Standard equipment:

4.3-liter TBI V-6, 5-speed manual transmission, anti-lock brakes, power steering, tinted glass, coolant temperature and oil pressure gauges, voltmeter, AM radio (AM/FM on Jimmy), tow hooks (4WD), dual outside mirrors, front armrests, rubber floor covering, highback vinyl front bucket seats, 205/75R15 tires with full-size spare.

Optional equipment:

4-speed automatic transmission	890	757	783
Air conditioning	780	663	686
Optional axle ratio	44	37	39
Locking differential	252	214	222
Preferred Group 2, 2WD 3-door	1824	1550	1605
4WD 3-door	1792	1523	1577
Tahoe Preferred Group 2, 2WD 5-door	1354	1151	1192
4WD 5-door	945	803	832
Tahoe Preferred Group 3, 2WD 3-door	4070	3460	3582
4WD 3-door	4074	3463	3585
2WD 5-door	3775	3209	3322
4WD 5-door	3402	2892	2994
Tahoe LT Group, 2WD 5-door	4901	3120	4313
4WD 5-door	4829	3059	4250

Air conditioning, rear defogger, intermittent wipers, rear window wiper/washer, deep tinted glass, power windows and locks, leather seats, tilt steering column, cruise control, power mirrors, remote tailgate release, special paint, P205/75R15 all-season tires on alloy wheels (2WD; 4WD has P235/75R15 tires).

Sport Group, 2WD 3-door	271	230	238
4WD 3-door	303	258	267
2WD 5-door	682	580	600
4WD 5-door	744	632	655

Prices are accurate at time of publication; subject to manufacturer's change.

	Retail Price	Dealer Invoice	Low Price
Cloth reclining bucket seats, 3-door	74	63	65
5-door	345	293	304
Deluxe seat trim, w/folding rear seat	26	22	23
Leather seat trim, 3-door w/ folding rear seat	750	638	542
3-door w/o folding rear seat	475	404	343
w/Sport Group w/folding rear seat	700	595	506
Sport w/o folding rear seat	425	361	307
Folding rear seat	409	348	360
Air dam w/foglamps	115	98	101
HD battery	56	48	49
Spare wheel & tire carrier	159	135	140
Cold Climate Pkg.	179	152	158
3-door w/Sport Group, Group 2 or 3,			
5-door	109	93	96
Front console, 3-door	135	115	119
HD radiator	56	48	49
HD radiator & transmission oil cooler ...	118	100	104
w/A/C or LD Trailering Pkg.	63	54	55
Engine oil cooler	135	115	119
Driver Convenience Pkg. ZM7	204	173	180
Intermittent wipers, tilt steering column.			
Driver Convenience Pkg. ZM8	197	167	173
Rear defogger, remote tailgate release.			
Front floormats, 3-door	20	17	18
Deep-tinted glass	225	191	198
w/Group 2 or 3	81	69	71
w/light-tinted rear window	144	122	127
Electronic instrumentation	195	166	172
Luggage carrier	169	144	149
Power mirrors	83	71	73
Lighted visor mirrors, 3-door	75	64	66
3-door w/Group 2 or 3, 5-door	68	58	60
Wheel opening moldings, 3-door	43	37	38
3-door w/Group 2 or 3, 5-door	13	11	11
Operating Convenience Pkg., 3-door	367	312	323
5-door	542	461	477
Power windows and locks.			
Special two-tone paint	218	185	192
Deluxe two-tone paint	177	150	156
Custom Two-tone, 5-door	275	234	242
AM/FM radio	131	111	115
AM/FM cassette	253	215	223
w/Group 2	122	104	107
AM/FM cassette w/EQ	403	343	355
w/Group 2	272	231	239
w/Group 3	150	128	132

	Retail Price	Dealer Invoice	Low Price
AM/FM CD player	537	456	473
w/Group 2	406	345	357
w/Group 3	284	241	250
Shield Pkg.	75	64	66
HD shock absorbers	40	34	35
Electronic shift transfer case	123	105	108
Cruise control	238	202	209
Bodyside striping	55	47	48
HD front springs	63	54	55
Off-road suspension, 3-door	182	155	160
3-door w/Tahoe or Group 2 or 3	122	104	107
205/75R15 on/off-road WL tires	170	145	150
3-door w/Group 2 or 3, 5-door w/2-5	49	42	43
205/75R15 all-season WL tires	121	103	106
235/75R15 all-season WL tires, 5-door	296	252	260
w/Group 2 or 3	175	149	154
235/75R15 on/off road WL tires	345	293	304
w/Group 2 or 3	224	190	197
Trailering Special Equipment, HD	211	179	186
Trailering Special Equipment, LD	165	140	145
w/engine oil cooler	109	93	96
Wheel trim rings, 3-door	60	51	53
Rally wheels, 3-door	92	78	81
Alloy wheels	340	289	299
3-door w/Group 2 or 3, 5-door	248	211	218
3-door w/off-road suspension	284	241	250
5-door	284	241	250
Sliding side window, 3-door	257	218	226
Rear wiper/washer	125	106	110
California emissions pkg.	100	85	88

Oldsmobile Bravada

	Retail Price	Dealer Invoice	Low Price
5-door 4WD wagon	$24595	$22086	—
Destination charge	475	475	475

Low price not available at time of publication.

Standard equipment:

4.3-liter TBI V-6, 4-speed automatic transmission, permanent 4-wheel drive, anti-lock brakes, power steering, air conditioning, cloth reclining front bucket seats, center console with cupholders and electrical outlets, folding rear seat with armrest, cruise control, power windows, power locks with remote, power mirrors, rear wiper/washer, intermittent wipers, rear defogger, coolant temperature and oil pressure gauges, voltmeter, trip odometer, fog lights, lighted visor mirrors, remote tailgate release, roof luggage rack, AM/FM
Prices are accurate at time of publication; subject to manufacturer's change.

cassette w/EQ, leather-wrapped steering wheel, floormats, 235/75R15 tires on alloy wheels, full-size spare tire.

Optional equipment:	Retail Price	Dealer Invoice	Low Price
Custom leather trim	650	553	—
R7F Leather Pkg	504	428	—
Leather seats, electronic instruments, exterior spare tire carrier.			
R7F Leather Pkg	559	475	—
Leather seats, Towing Pkg.			
CD player	134	114	—
HD Towing Pkg.	409	348	—
Cold Climate Pkg.	90	77	—
Electronic instruments	195	166	—
Mud & snow tires	182	155	—
Exterior spare tire carrier	159	135	—
Warranty enhancements for New York state .	25	21	—
California emissions pkg.	100	85	—

Chrysler Imperial/
New Yorker Fifth Avenue

Chrysler Imperial

Revised front and rear styling gives the Fifth Avenue a slightly rounded nose and tail and a more distinct appearance from the related Imperial, which retains the straight-edge look for 1992. Included at the front of this year's Fifth Avenue are a new hood, grille, and headlamps. The Fifth Avenue rides the same front-drive chassis as the Imperial but is 4.4 inches shorter, at 198.6 inches overall. A 147-horsepower 3.3-liter V-6 engine remains standard on the Fifth Avenue and a 150-horsepower 3.8-liter V-6 continues as optional. Both engines mate to a 4-speed automatic transmission. The 3.8-liter engine is standard on the Imperial. Among new options for both models are a floor console with slots for cassette tapes and an automatically dimming electrochromatic rearview mirror. A driver-side air bag is standard on both models. Anti-lock brakes are standard on the Imperial and optional on the Fifth Avenue. These luxury sedans boast the usual array of power accessories in a cabin ripe with cushy upholstery, fake wood, and shiny

Specifications

	Imperial 4-door notchback	Fifth Ave. 4-door notchback
Wheelbase, in.	109.5	109.5
Overall length, in.	203.0	198.6
Overall width, in.	68.9	68.9
Overall height, in.	55.3	55.1
Curb weight, lbs.	3534	3425
Cargo vol., cu. ft.	16.7	16.5
Fuel capacity, gals.	16.0	16.0
Seating capacity	6	6
Front head room, in.	38.4	38.4
Front leg room, max., in.	43.0	43.0
Rear head room, in.	37.9	37.9
Rear leg room, min., in.	41.7	41.7

Powertrain layout: transverse front engine/front-wheel drive.

Engines	ohv V-6	ohv V-6
Size, liters/cu. in.	3.3/201	3.8/230
Fuel delivery	PFI	PFI
Horsepower @ rpm	147 @ 4800	150 @ 4400
Torque (lbs./ft.) @ rpm	183 @ 3600	203 @ 3200
Availability	S[1]	S[2]

EPA city/highway mpg

4-speed OD automatic	19/25	18/25

1. Fifth Ave.   2. Imperial; opt., Fifth Ave.

Assembly point: Belvidere, Ill.

Prices are accurate at time of publication; subject to manufacturer's change.

buttons. The driver-side air bag and the 4-wheel anti-lock disc brakes add some important functional items to the brew. But overall, Chrysler's flagships leave us unimpressed. The only thing of substance the Imperial and Fifth Avenue offer over the less-costly New Yorker Salon is more leg room and the larger 3.8-liter six. The 3.8 improves upon the 3.3's ample low-speed getaway and adequate passing response, but the automatic suffers sloppy gear changes and is reluctant to downshift for passing. The soft suspension delivers the worst of both worlds: lots of body lean and tire squeal in corners, yet poor bump absorption. Wide doors make for easy entry/exit, and there's ample leg room front and rear, but the body is too narrow to fit three across comfortably.

Prices

Chrysler Imperial	Retail Price	Dealer Invoice	Low Price
4-door notchback w/Pkg. 28A	$28453	$24241	$24766
w/Pkg. 28D	29478	25112	25637
Destination charge	610	610	610

Standard equipment:

3.8-liter PFI V-6, 4-speed automatic transmission, anti-lock 4-wheel disc brakes, power steering, driver-side air bag, automatic climate control, cloth 50/50 front seat with 8-way power adjustments and driver-side memory, power windows, speed-sensitive power locks, cruise control, heated power mirrors, AM/FM cassette with EQ, power antenna, power decklid pulldown, rear defogger, trip odometer, coolant temperature and oil pressure gauges, voltmeter, tilt steering column, leather-wrapped steering wheel, lighted visor mirrors, cornering lamps, tinted glass, floormats, bodyside moldings, remote decklid release, intermittent wipers, wire wheel covers, 195/75R14 whitewall tires. **Pkg. 28D** adds: Mark Cross leather trim, rear seat armrest cupholders, 8-way power front seats with driver-side seat and mirror memory.

Optional equipment:

Security Group	292	248	254
Security alarm, remote keyless entry and trunk release.			
Electronic Features Group	961	817	836
Overhead console with Vehicle Information Center, floor console, electronic instruments, automatic day/night mirror, Infinity RS audio system, wiring harness for cellular phone.			

	Retail Price	Dealer Invoice	Low Price
8-way power front seats	376	320	327
Includes driver's seat and mirror memory.			
Electronically controlled air suspension . . .	650	553	566
Extra cost paint	77	65	67
Conventional spare tire	85	72	74
California emissions pkg.	102	87	89

Chrysler New Yorker
Fifth Avenue

	Retail Price	Dealer Invoice	Low Price
4-door notchback w/Pkg. 26A (3.3)	$21874	$18933	$19333
w/Luxury Pkg. 28A (3.8)	22136	19156	19556
w/Luxury Pkg. 26B (3.3)	23096	19972	20372
w/Luxury Pkg. 28B (3.8)	23358	20194	20594
w/Luxury Pkg. 26C (3.3)	23673	20462	20862
w/Luxury Pkg. 28C (3.8)	23935	20684	21084
Destination charge	610	610	610

Standard equipment:

3.3- or 3.8-liter PFI V-6, 4-speed automatic transmission, power steering, driver-side air bag, air conditioning, 50/50 cloth front seat with folding armest, power driver's seat, power windows, speed-sensitive power locks, heated power mirrors, cruise control, tilt steering column, automatic load leveling, trip odometer, coolant temperature and oil pressure gauges, voltmeter, intermittent wipers, tinted glass, visor mirrors, bright bodyside moldings, AM/FM radio, landau vinyl roof, remote decklid release, 195/75R14 whitewall tires. **Pkgs. 26B/28B** add: wiring harness for cellular phone, automatic day/night rearview mirror, lighted visor mirrors, cornering lamps, illuminated entry, power front seats with driver-side memory, rear-seat armrest with cupholder, leather-wrapped steering wheel, wire wheel covers, floormats, floor console, cassette player, undercoating. **Pkgs. 26C/28C** add: leather seat trim.

Optional equipment:

Anti-lock 4-wheel disc brakes	899	764	782
Automatic climate control	292	248	254
Security Group	292	248	254
Security alarm, remote keyless entry and trunk release.			
Power Accessories Group	159	135	138
Power decklid pulldown, power antenna; requires Luxury Pkg.			
Electronic Features Group	1159	985	1008
Overhead console with Vehicle Information Center, electronic instruments; requires Luxury Pkg.			
AM/FM cassette w/EQ	428	364	372

Prices are accurate at time of publication; subject to manufacturer's change.

	Retail Price	Dealer Invoice	Low Price
Infinity RS Group	395	336	344
AM & FM Stereo w/cassette, EQ & 10 speakers; requires Luxury Pkg.			
Electronically controlled air suspension ...	650	553	566
Requires Luxury Pkg.			
Power sunroof	792	673	689
Alloy wheels	50	43	44
w/Pkgs. 26A/28A	278	236	242
Wire wheelcovers	228	194	198
Conventional spare tire	85	72	74
Extra cost paint	77	65	67
California emissions pkg.	102	87	89

Chrysler LeBaron

Chrysler LeBaron LX convertible

Anti-lock brakes and 16-inch cast-aluminum wheels are new options for the front-drive LeBaron convertible and coupe. Other 1992 changes on those two include standard rear shoulder belts for the ragtop (they already were standard on coupes); models with automatic transmission get a shift interlock; and models with the 5-speed manual won't start unless the clutch pedal is to the floor. The LeBaron 4-door sedan, which rides a longer front-drive chassis, came last year in a single price series with a Mitsubishi-made 141-horsepower 3.0-liter V-6 engine and 4-speed automatic transmission. This year there are base, LX, and Landau models. The V-6 and 4-speed automatic are standard on the LX and optional on the other two. A 100-horsepower

2.5-liter 4-cylinder and a 3-speed automatic are standard on the base and Landau. On the convertible and coupe, the 4-cylinder is standard on base models; the V-6 is standard on premium and GTC and optional on the base, and a 152-horsepower turbo four is optional on the GTC and base. The base four is lethargic, and while its turbocharged cousin is fast, neither is as smooth as the V-6, which delivers more than adequate acceleration. For anything above competent handling order the GTC, but its ride is choppy. Coupe and convertible back seats are small, but will carry adults.

Specifications

	2-door notchback	2-door conv.	4-door notchback
Wheelbase, in.	100.5	100.5	103.5
Overall length, in.	184.8	184.8	182.7
Overall width, in.	69.2	69.2	68.1
Overall height, in.	53.3	52.4	53.7
Curb weight, lbs.	2863	3010	2972
Cargo vol., cu. ft.	14.4	10.3	14.4
Fuel capacity, gals.	14.0	14.0	16.0
Seating capacity	5	4	6
Front head room, in.	37.6	38.3	38.4
Front leg room, max., in.	42.4	42.4	41.9
Rear head room, in.	36.3	37.0	37.9
Rear leg room, min., in.	33.0	33.0	38.3

Powertrain layout: transverse front engine/front-wheel drive.

Engines

	ohc I-4	Turbo ohc I-4	ohc V-6
Size, liters/cu. in.	2.5/153	2.5/153	3.0/181
Fuel delivery	TBI	PFI	PFI
Horsepower @ rpm	100 @ 4400	152 @ 4800	141 @ 5000
Torque (lbs./ft.) @ rpm	135 @ 2800	211 @ 2800	167 @ 3600
Availability	S	O	S[1]

EPA city/highway mpg

5-speed OD manual		21/27	20/28
3-speed automatic	23/27	20/25	21/26
4-speed OD automatic			20/27

1. LX, GTC.

Assembly points: Newark, Delaware; Toluca, Mexico.
Prices are accurate at time of publication; subject to manufacturer's change.

The sedan is a likable entry-level luxury compact, but it's basically a gussied up Dodge Spirit/Plymouth Acclaim, so look to our reports on those cars for more details. Nothing here measures up to the quality of Japanese rivals, but neither do the prices.

Prices

Chrysler LeBaron Coupe/ Convertible	Retail Price	Dealer Invoice	Low Price
2-door notchback	$13488	$11975	$12300
w/Pkg. 22C (2.5-liter)	13919	12341	12666
w/Pkg. 22D (2.5-liter)	15123	13364	13689
w/Pkg. 24C (Turbo)	14613	12931	13256
w/Pkg. 24D (Turbo)	15817	13954	14279
w/Pkg. 25A (3.0-liter/5-speed)	13625	12091	12416
w/Pkg. 25C (3.0-liter/5-speed)	14058	12457	12782
w/Pkg. 25D (3.0-liter/5-speed)	15260	13481	13806
w/Pkg. 26C (3.0-liter/4-speed automatic)	15260	13481	13806
w/Pkg. 26D (3.0-liter/4-speed automatic)	15910	14033	14358
LX 2-door notchback	16094	14242	14567
w/Pkg. 26D	16944	14964	15289
GTC 2-door notchback	16164	14303	14628
w/Pkg. 26G (3.0-liter/4-speed automatic)	16804	14847	15172
w/Pkg. 23H (Turbo/5-speed)	17932	15805	16130
w/Pkg. 24H (Turbo/3-speed automatic)	18324	16139	16464
2-door convertible	16734	14799	15124
w/Pkg. 22B (2.5-liter)	17565	15505	15830
w/Pkg. 22C (2.5-liter)	17783	15690	16015
w/Pkg. 24B (Turbo)	18259	16095	16420
w/Pkg. 24C (Turbo)	18477	16280	16605
w/Pkg. 25A (3.0-liter/5-speed)	16871	14915	15240
w/Pkg. 25B (3.0-liter/5-speed)	17702	15621	15946
w/Pkg. 25C (3.0-liter/5-speed)	17920	15807	16132
w/Pkg. 26B (3.0-liter/4-speed automatic)	18352	16174	16499
w/Pkg. 26C (3.0-liter/4-speed automatic)	18570	16359	16684
LX 2-door convertible	20130	17753	18078
GTC 2-door convertible	18985	16757	17582
w/Pkg. 26G (3.0-liter/4-speed automatic)	19625	17301	18126
w/Pkg. 23H (Turbo/5-speed)	21524	18915	19740
w/Pkg. 24H (Turbo/3-speed automatic)	21916	19248	20073
Destination charge	510	510	510

Standard equipment:

2.5-liter TBI 4-cylinder engine, 3-speed automatic transmission, power steering, driver-side air bag, cloth reclining front bucket seats, center console with storage, remote decklid release, rear defogger, tinted glass, trip odometer, coolant temperature gauge, voltmeter, dual remote mirrors, visor mirrors, AM/FM radio, power windows, intermittent wipers, 195/70R14 all-season tires. **Convertible** has power top. **LX** adds: 3.0-liter PFI V-6, 4-speed automatic transmission, air conditioning, power locks, tachometer, oil pressure gauge, heated power mirrors, leather-wrapped steering wheel, 60/40 split folding rear seat with armrest (notchback), cruise control, tilt steering column, 205/60R15 all-season tires. **GTC** adds: 5-speed manual transmission, Sport Handling Suspension, leather-wrapped sport steering wheel, remote trunk release, floormats, performance tires on alloy wheels. **Notchback Pkgs. 22C/24C/25C/26C:** air conditioning, cruise control, tilt steering wheel, remote trunk release, floormats. **22D/24D/25D/26D** adds: power driver's seat, power locks and mirrors, leather-wrapped steering wheel, Light Group, overhead console. **Convertible Pkgs. 22B/24B/25B/26B:** air conditioning. **22C/24C/25C/26C** adds: cruise control, tilt steering wheel, remote trunk release.

Optional equipment:	Retail Price	Dealer Invoice	Low Price
3.0-liter V-6, base	694	590	604
2.5-liter turbo, base	694	590	604
3-speed automatic, GTC	392	333	341
4-speed automatic, base	93	79	81
GTC	640	544	557
Anti-lock brakes	899	764	782
Deluxe Convenience Group, base	372	316	324
Cruise control, tilt steering column.			
Power Convenience Group, base	338	287	294
Power locks, heated power mirrors.			
Power driver's seat, base cars & GTC			
convertible	296	252	258
LX & GTC notchbacks	367	312	319
Sport Group, base notchback	NC	NC	NC
base convertible	100	85	87
Body-color grile, bodyside molding, lace wheel covers.			
Handling Group, LX	532	452	463
Sport Handling Pkg., 205/60R15 all-season tires on alloy wheels.			
Performance Group, GTC	188	160	164
Performance handling suspension, 205/55R16 all-season tires on alloy wheels.			
Light Group, convertibles, GTC notchback	196	167	171
Overhead console, GTC	265	225	231
Vinyl seats, base & GTC convertibles	102	87	89
Leather seats, LX & GTC notchbacks	1006	855	875
Includes power driver's seat.			
GTC convertible	1223	1040	1064
Electronic instruments, LX	305	259	265
Electronic Information Center, LX	678	576	590

Prices are accurate at time of publication; subject to manufacturer's change.

	Retail Price	Dealer Invoice	Low Price
Trip computer	93	79	81
Security alarm	149	127	130
Cassette player, base	155	132	135
AM & FM stereo/cassette	290	247	252
w/EQ and Infinity speakers	899	764	782
w/CD player	1348	1146	1173
Extra cost paint	77	65	67
195/70R14 whitewall tires, base	73	62	64
205/60R15 whitewall tires, LX	78	66	68
14″ alloy wheels, base	328	279	285
California emissions	102	87	89

Chrysler LeBaron Sedan

	Retail Price	Dealer Invoice	Low Price
4-door notchback	$13998	$12398	$12748
w/Pkg. 22U (2.5-liter/3-speed)	14613	12921	13271
w/Pkg. 26U (3.0-liter/3-speed)	15307	12988	13338
w/Pkg. 28U (3.0-liter/4-speed)	15400	13067	13417
LX 4-door notchback	15287	13520	13870
w/Pkg. 28U	15984	14112	14462
Landau 4-door notchback	15710	13688	14038
w/Pkg. 22L (2.5-liter/3-speed)	16369	14248	14598
w/Pkg. 28L (3.0-liter/4-speed)	16497	14357	14707
Destination charge	485	485	485

Standard equipment:

2.5-liter TBI 4-cylinder engine, 3-speed automatic transmission, power steering, driver-side air bag, rear defogger, tinted glass, trip odometer, coolant temperature and oil pressure gauges, voltmeter, dual remote mirrors, visor mirrors, 50/50 front seat w/armrest, floormats, narrow bodyside moldings, AM/FM, cruise control, tilt steering column, intermittent wipers, remote trunk and fuel door releases, 195/70R14 tires. **LX adds:** 3.0-liter PFI V-6, 4-speed automatic transmission, 205/60R15 all-season tires on alloy wheels. **Landau adds to base:** air conditioning, cassette player, vinyl roof. **Base Pkgs. 22U/26U/28U:** air conditioning, power windows and locks, power mirrors, 195/70R14 whitewall tires. **LX Pkg. 28U:** air conditioning, power windows and locks, power mirrors, cassette player. **Landau Pkg. 22L/28L:** power windows and locks, heated power mirrors, overhead console, lighted visor mirrors, illuminated entry, reading lamps, compass, leather-wrapped steering wheel, wire wheel covers.

Optional equipment:

Anti-lock 4-wheel disc brakes	899	764	787
4-speed electronic automatic, w/V-6	93	79	81
3.0-liter V-6, base & Landau	694	590	607

	Retail Price	Dealer Invoice	Low Price
Interior Convenience Group	400	340	350
Overhead console, reading lamps, compass, illuminated entry, lighted visor mirrors.			
Interior Illumination Group	195	166	171
Illuminated entry, lighted visor mirrors.			
Electronic Display Pkg, Landau	317	269	277
Electronic instruments, trip computer.			
Power Equipment Group, Landau	NC	NC	NC
Power windows and locks, heated power mirrors.			
Power driver's seat	296	252	259
Split folding rear seat, base & LX	61	52	53
Cassette player, base	155	132	136
Cassette w/Infinity speakers, base	430	366	376
LX	275	234	241
Landau	306	260	268
Cassette w/EQ & Infinity speakers, LX . . .	490	417	429
Landau	520	442	455
Leather-wrapped steering wheel	60	51	53
Wire wheel covers, Landau	228	194	200
Alloy wheels, base	255	217	223
Leather seats, Landau	668	568	585
Includes leather-wrapped steering wheel; requires Power Equipment Pkg. and power driver's seat.			
Conventional spare tire	95	81	83
Extra-cost paint	77	65	67

Dodge Caravan/ Plymouth Voyager/ Chrysler Town & Country

A driver-side air bag is now standard on all three Chrysler minivans. All-wheel drive, previously optional only on Caravan and Voyager, is available this year on the Town & Country as well. Anti-lock brakes are standard on the Town & Country, optional on Caravans and Voyagers with the 3.3-liter V-6. A new built-in child safety seat is optional on Caravans and Voyagers with 7-passenger seating. Town & Country is available for the first time without the wood-grain bodyside graphics, and lace-spoke gold-colored alloy wheels are a new option. Last year, all got a new interior and smoother exterior styling. Base SWB (short wheelbase) Caravans and Voyagers come with a 100-horsepower 2.5-

Prices are accurate at time of publication; subject to manufacturer's change.

Dodge Caravan SE

liter four and 5-speed manual transmission. Optional are
3.0-liter (147 horsepower) and 3.3-liter (150 horsepower)
V-6s, as are 3- and 4-speed automatics. Town & Country
comes standard with the 3.3 and 4-speed automatic. SWB
models ride a 112.3-inch wheelbase and are 178.1 inches
long. The Town & Country and long-wheelbase Grand versions of the Caravan and Voyager have a 119.3-inch wheelbase and 192.8-inch length. Town & Country comes loaded
with equipment, but offers nothing of substance that can't
be had for less money in an option-laden Grand LE version
of the Caravan or Voyager. All ride and drive much like
cars, which is a big part of their appeal. The seats are
comfortable, though they're not as easy to remove as the
lighter buckets in GM's front-drive minivans. But
Chrysler's minivans offer a combination of features (V-6,
air bag, ABS, AWD) unavailable elsewhere, keeping them
at the head of this class.

Specifications

	4-door van	4-door van
Wheelbase, in.	112.3	119.3
Overall length, in.	178.1	192.8
Overall width, in.	72.0	72.0
Overall height, in.	66.0	66.7
Curb weight, lbs.	3271	3644
Cargo vol., cu. ft.	123.1	148.4

	4-door van	4-door van
Fuel capacity, gals.	20.0[1]	20.0[1]
Seating capacity	7	7
Front head room, in.	39.1	39.1
Front leg room, max., in.	37.3	37.3
Rear head room, in.	38.5	38.4
Rear leg room, min., in.	37.6	37.7

1. 18.0, AWD.

Powertrain layout: transverse front engine/front-wheel drive or permanent 4WD.

Engines

	ohc I-4	ohc V-6	ohv V-6
Size, liters/cu. in.	2.5/153	3.0/181	3.3/201
Fuel delivery	TBI	PFI	PFI
Horsepower @ rpm	100 @ 4800	141 @ 5000	150 @ 4800
Torque (lbs./ft.) @ rpm	135 @ 2800	171 @ 2800	185 @ 3600
Availability	S[1]	S[2]	S[3]

EPA city/highway mpg

	ohc I-4	ohc V-6	ohv V-6
5-speed OD manual	20/28		
3-speed automatic	21/24	19/23	
4-speed OD automatic		18/24	17/23

1. Base Caravan/Voyager. 2. Caravan/Voyager LE. 3. Grand Caravan/Voyager, All-Wheel Drive models, and Town & Country.

Assembly points: Windsor, Ontario, Canada; St. Louis, Mo.

Prices

Dodge Caravan	Retail Price	Dealer Invoice	Low Price
Base SWB w/Pkg. 21S (2.5-liter/5-speed)	$13406	—	—
w/Pkg. 22S (2.5-liter/automatic 3)	13982	—	—
w/Pkg. 24S (3.0-liter/automatic 3)	14676	—	—
Base standard equipment.			
w/Pkg. 21T (2.5-liter/5-speed)	13619	—	—
w/Pkg. 22T (2.5-liter/automatic 3)	14195	—	—
w/Pkg. 24T (3.0-liter/automatic 3)	14889	—	—

21-24T add: air conditioning, dual-note horn, remote liftgate release, map and cargo area lights, bodyside moldings, storage drawer under front passenger seat.

Base Grand w/Pkg. 24E (3.0-liter/automatic 3)	17326	—	—

Base standard equipment plus: air conditioning, map and cargo area lights.

Prices are accurate at time of publication; subject to manufacturer's change.

	Retail Price	Dealer Invoice	Low Price
SE SWB w/Pkg. 22A (2.5-liter/automatic 3) .	15529	—	—
w/Pkg. 24A (3.0-liter/automatic 3)	16223	—	—
w/Pkg. 26A (3.0-liter/automatic 4)	16396	—	—
w/Pkg. 28A (3.3-liter/automatic 4)	16498	—	—
SE SWB AWD w/Pkg. 28A (3.3-liter/automatic 4)	18587	—	—
Grand SE w/Pkg. 28A (3.3-liter/automatic 4)	17511	—	—
Grand SE AWD w/Pkg. 28A (3.3-liter/automatic 4)	19511	—	—
SE standard equipment.			
w/Pkg. 22B (2.5-liter/automatic 3)	15742	—	—
w/Pkg. 24B (3.0-liter/automatic 3)	16436	—	—
w/Pkg. 26B (3.0-liter/automatic 4)	16609	—	—
w/Pkg. 28B (3.3-liter/automatic 4)	16711	—	—
SE SWB AWD w/Pkg. 28B (3.3-liter/automatic 4)	18800	—	—
Grand SE w/Pkg. 28B (3.3-liter/automatic 4)	17724	—	—
Grand SE AWD w/Pkg. 28B (3.3-liter/automatic 4)	19724	—	—
22-28B add: air conditioning, rear defogger, map and cargo area lights.			
w/Pkg. 22D (2.5-liter/automatic 3)	16881	—	—
w/Pkg. 24D (3.0-liter/automatic 3)	17575	—	—
w/Pkg. 26D (3.0-liter/automatic 4)	17748	—	—
w/Pkg. 28D (3.3-liter/automatic 4)	17850	—	—
SE SWB AWD w/Pkg. 28D (3.3-liter/automatic 4)	19939	—	—
Grand SE w/Pkg. 28D (3.3-liter/automatic 4)	18863	—	—
Grand SE AWD w/Pkg. 28D (3.3-liter/automatic 4)	20863	—	—
22-28D add to 22-28B: front console, cruise control, tilt steering column, added sound insulation, floormats, tachometer, oil pressure gauge, voltmeter, lighted visor mirrors, Light Group, power locks, styled steel wheels.			
LE SWB w/Pkg. 24J (3.0-liter/automatic 3) .	20072	—	—
w/Pkg. 26J (3.0-liter/automatic 4)	20245	—	—
w/Pkg. 28J (3.3-liter/automatic 4)	20347	—	—
LE SWB AWD w/Pkg. 28J (3.3-liter/automatic 4)	22347	—	—
Grand LE w/Pkg. 28J (3.3-liter/automatic 4) .	20965	—	—
Grand LE AWD w/Pkg. 28J (3.3-liter/automatic 4)	22965	—	—
LE standard equipment.			
w/Pkg. 24K (3.0-liter/automatic 3)	20651	—	—
w/Pkg. 26K (3.0-liter/automatic 3)	20824	—	—
w/Pkg. 28K (3.3-liter/automatic 4)	20926	—	—
LE SWB AWD w/Pkg. 28K (3.3-liter/automatic 4)	22926	—	—

CONSUMER GUIDE®

	Retail Price	Dealer Invoice	Low Price
Grand LE w/Pkg. 28K (3.3-liter/automatic 4)	21544	—	—
Grand LE AWD w/Pkg. 28K (3.3-liter/automatic 4)	23544	—	—

24-28K add: power driver's seat, power windows, Infinity I audio system, sunscreen glass, two-tone paint.

	Retail Price	Dealer Invoice	Low Price
w/Pkg. 24L (3.0-liter/automatic 3)	21283	—	—
w/Pkg. 26L (3.0-liter/automatic 4)	21456	—	—
w/Pkg. 28L (3.3-liter/automatic 4)	21558	—	—
LE SWB AWD w/Pkg. 28L (3.3-liter/automatic 4)	23558	—	—
Grand LE w/Pkg. 28L (3.3-liter/automatic 4)	22176	—	—
Grand LE AWD w/Pkg. 28L (3.3-liter/automatic 4)	24176	—	—

24-28L add to 24-28K: Woodgrain Decor Group (woodgrain appliques and moldings, luggage rack, 205/70R15 whitewall tires, wire wheel covers); deletes two-tone paint.

	Retail Price	Dealer Invoice	Low Price
w/ES Pkg. 24M (3.0-liter/automatic 3)	20788	—	—
w/ES Pkg. 26M (3.0-liter/automatic 4)	20961	—	—
w/ES Pkg. 28M (3.3-liter/automatic 4)	21063	—	—
LE SWB AWD w/ES Pkg. 28M (3.3-liter/automatic 4)	22858	—	—
Grand LE w/ES Pkg. 28M (3.3-liter/automatic 4)	21476	—	—
Grand LE AWD w/ES Pkg. 28M (3.3-liter/automatic 4)	23476	—	—

24-26M adds to 24-28K: ES Decor Group (body-color fascia and cladding, sport suspension, sunscreen glass, fog lights, 205/70R15 tires on alloy wheels), power driver's seat, power windows, Infinity I audio system; deletes two-tone paint.

	Retail Price	Dealer Invoice	Low Price
Destination charge	540	540	540

SWB denotes short wheelbase; AWD denotes All Wheel Drive.

Dealer invoice and low price not available at time of publication.

Engines and transmissions: 2.5-liter TBI four-cylinder with 5-speed manual or three-speed automatic; 3.0-liter PFI V-6 with three- or four-speed automatic; 3.3-liter PFI V-6 with four-speed automatic.

Standard equipment:

Base: driver-side air bag, power steering, 5-passenger seating (front bucket seats, 3-passenger middle bench seat), tinted glass, trip odometer, coolant temperature gauge, dual outside mirrors, visor mirrors, AM/FM radio, intermittent wipers, rear wiper/washer, 195/75R14 tires. **SE adds:** 7-passenger

Prices are accurate at time of publication; subject to manufacturer's change.

seating (2-passenger middle and 3-passenger rear bench seats), dual-note horn, power mirrors, remote liftgate release, rear trim panel storage and cup holders, striping, sport wheel covers. **LE** adds: front air conditioning, front storage console, overhead console with outside temperature readout and mini trip computer, rear defogger, power front windows, power quarter vent windows, power locks, remote fuel door release, tachometer, oil pressure gauge, voltmeter, illuminated entry, headlamp delay system, heated power mirrors, lighted visor mirrors, bodyside moldings, cruise control, tilt steering column, sport steering wheel, storage drawer under front passenger seat, floormats. **Grand** models have 3.3-liter PFI V-6, 4-speed automatic transmission (base has 3.0-liter PFI V-6, 3-speed automatic transmission), power mirrors, remote liftgate release, dual-note horn, storage drawer under front passenger seat, sport wheel covers, 205/70R15 tires. **All Wheel Drive** models have 3.3-liter PFI V-6, 4-speed automatic transmission, 7-passenger seating, power mirrors, 205/75R15 tires.

Optional equipment:

	Retail Price	Dealer Invoice	Low Price
3.0-liter V-6, 2WD SWB	694	590	638
3.3-liter V-6, SE/LE 2WD SWB	796	677	732
3-speed automatic transmission, base 2WD .	576	490	530
4-speed automatic transmission, SE/LE w/V-6	173	147	159
Anti-lock brakes, SWB SE w/3.3-liter V-6 .	687	584	632
SWB SE w/Trailer Towing Group, Sport Handling Group or 14″ whitewall tires, Grand SE	599	509	551
LE SWB w/J, K or L Pkgs.	687	584	632
LE SWB w/M Pkg. and 3.3-liter V-6 . . .	599	509	551
LE w/Trailer Tow Group, Sport Handling Group or 14″ whitewall tires	599	509	551
Grand SE & LE	599	509	551
Front air conditioning, base & SE	857	728	788
Air conditioning w/rear heater, base Grand .	699	594	643
Grand SE 28A/28B	699	594	643
Requires rear defogger.			
Grand SE 28A/28B w/Trailer Towing Group	636	541	585
Grand SE 28D	466	396	429
Grand SE 28D w/Trailer Towing Group .	404	343	372
Rear air conditioning, Grand LE	466	396	429
Grand LE w/Trailer Towing Group	571	485	525
Grand SE 2WD w/Trailer Towing Group .	509	433	468
Rear bench seat, base SWB	397	337	365
Includes trim panel storage area and cup holders.			
Seven-passenger seating w/integrated child seat, base SWB	597	507	549
SE & LE SWB, Grand	200	170	184

	Retail Price	Dealer Invoice	Low Price
Quad Command Seating, SE & LE	597	507	549
Two front and two middle bucket seats, 3-passenger rear bench seat.			
Converta-Bed 7-pass. seating, SE SWB, base/SE Grand	553	470	509
Leather trim, LE w/K, L or M Pkgs.	865	735	796
HD Trailer Towing Pkg., SE, LE w/J or K Pkgs.	557	473	512
LE w/L Pkg.	483	411	444
SE	443	377	408
Grand SE/LE	265	225	244
LE w/Pkgs. J or K and Sport Handling Group			
HD alternator, battery, flasher, radiator, and transmission oil cooler, trailer wiring harness; 2WD adds: HD suspension, sport wheel covers, 205/70R15 tires with conventional spare.			
Deluxe Convenience Pkg., base & SE . . .	372	316	342
Cruise control, tilt steering column.			
Power Convenience group, SE SWB w/A or B Pkgs. Grand SE	530	451	488
SE SWB w/D Pkg.	265	225	244
Power front windows, power locks.			
Sport Handling Group, SE SWB	207	176	190
Grand SE	93	79	86
LE SWB w/J, K or M Pkgs.	207	176	190
Grand LE w/J, K or M Pkgs.	93	79	86
HD brakes, rear sway bar, sport wheel covers, 205/70R15 tires.			
Rear defogger, base w/o Pkgs.	217	184	200
Base w/Pkgs. 22-28, SE	168	143	155
Base includes remote liftgate release w/Pkgs. 22-28.			
Power locks, base & SE	265	225	244
Sunscreen glass	414	352	381
Luggage rack	143	122	132
Cassette player	155	132	143
Infinity I audio system, SE/LE SWB, Grand SE/LE	461	392	424
Infinity II system, LE w/K, L or M Pkgs. .	214	182	197
HD suspension, 2WD	69	59	63
205/70R14 whitewall tires, 2WD SWB . . .	143	122	132
205/70R15 whitewall tires, SE/LE SWB, Grand w/Trailer Towing Pkg, Grand SE/LE	69	59	63
SE/LE	159	135	146
Conventional spare tire, 2WD	109	93	100
15" alloy wheels, SE	363	309	334
LE w/J or K Pkgs.	314	267	289
Requires Trailer Towing Pkg.			
LE w/L Pkg.	118	100	109
Styled steel wheels, SE	49	42	45
Extra-cost paint	77	65	71

Prices are accurate at time of publication; subject to manufacturer's change.

Plymouth Voyager

	Retail Price	Dealer Invoice	Low Price
Base SWB w/Pkg. 21S (2.5-liter/5-speed) .	$13406	—	—
w/Pkg. 22S (2.5-liter/automatic 3)	13982	—	—
w/Pkg. 24S (3.0-liter/automatic 3)	14676	—	—
Base standard equipment.			
w/Pkg. 21T (2.5-liter/5-speed)	13619	—	—
w/Pkg. 22T (2.5-liter/automatic 3)	14195	—	—
w/Pkg. 24T (3.0-liter/automatic 3)	14889	—	—

21-24T add: air conditioning, dual-note horn, remote liftgate release, map and cargo area lights, bodyside moldings, storage drawer under front passenger seat.

	Retail Price	Dealer Invoice	Low Price
Base Grand w/Pkg. 24E (3.0-liter/automatic 3)	17326	—	—

Base standard equipment plus: air conditioning, map and cargo area lights.

	Retail Price	Dealer Invoice	Low Price
SE SWB w/Pkg. 22A (2.5-liter/automatic 3) .	15529	—	—
w/Pkg. 24A (3.0-liter/automatic 3)	16223	—	—
w/Pkg. 26A (3.0-liter/automatic 4)	16396	—	—
w/Pkg. 28A (3.3-liter/automatic 4)	16498	—	—
SE SWB AWD w/Pkg. 28A (3.3-liter/automatic 4)	18587	—	—
Grand SE w/Pkg. 28A (3.3-liter/automatic 4)	17511	—	—
Grand SE AWD w/Pkg. 28A (3.3-liter/automatic 4)	19511	—	—
SE standard equipment.			
w/Pkg. 22B (2.5-liter/automatic 3)	15742	—	—
w/Pkg. 24B (3.0-liter/automatic 3)	16436	—	—
w/Pkg. 26B (3.0-liter/automatic 4)	16609	—	—
w/Pkg. 28A (3.3-liter/automatic 4)	16711	—	—
SE SWB AWD w/Pkg. 28B (3.3-liter/automatic 4)	18800	—	—
Grand SE w/Pkg. 28B (3.3-liter/automatic 4)	17724	—	—
Grand SE AWD w/Pkg. 28B (3.3-liter/automatic 4)	19724	—	—

22-28B add: air conditioning, rear defogger, map and cargo area lights.

	Retail Price	Dealer Invoice	Low Price
w/Pkg. 22D (2.5-liter/automatic 3)	16881	—	—
w/Pkg. 24D (3.0-liter/automatic 3)	17575	—	—
w/Pkg. 26D (3.0-liter/automatic 4)	17748	—	—
w/Pkg. 28D (3.3-liter/automatic 4)	17850	—	—
SE SWB AWD w/Pkg. 28D (3.3-liter/automatic 4)	19939	—	—
Grand SE w/Pkg. 28D (3.3-liter/automatic 4)	18863	—	—
Grand SE AWD w/Pkg. 28D (3.3-liter/automatic 4)	20863	—	—

22-28D add to 22-28B: front console, cruise control, tilt steering column, added sound insulation, floormats, tachometer, oil pressure gauge, voltmeter, lighted visor mirrors, Light Group, power locks.

	Retail Price	Dealer Invoice	Low Price
LE SWB w/Pkg. 24J (3.0-liter/automatic 3) .	20107	—	—
w/Pkg. 26J (3.0-liter/automatic 4)	20280	—	—
w/Pkg. 28J (3.3-liter/automatic 4)	20974	—	—

CONSUMER GUIDE®

	Retail Price	Dealer Invoice	Low Price
LE SWB AWD w/Pkg. 28J (3.3-liter/automatic 4)	22298	—	—
Grand LE w/Pkg. 28J (3.3-liter/automatic 4)	20916	—	—
Grand LE AWD w/Pkg. 28J (3.3-liter/automatic 4)	22916	—	—

LE standard equipment.

	Retail Price	Dealer Invoice	Low Price
w/Pkg. 24K (3.0-liter/automatic 3)	20513	—	—
w/Pkg. 26K (3.0-liter/automatic 4)	20686	—	—
w/Pkg. 28K (3.3-liter/automatic 4)	20806	—	—
LE SWB AWD w/Pkg. 28K (3.3-liter/automatic 4)	22877	—	—
Grand LE w/Pkg. 28K (3.3-liter/automatic 4)	21495	—	—
Grand LE AWD w/Pkg. 28K (3.3-liter/automatic 4)	23495	—	—

24-28K add: power driver's seat, power windows, Infinity I audio system, sunscreen glass, two-tone paint.

	Retail Price	Dealer Invoice	Low Price
w/Pkg. 24L (3.0-liter/automatic 3)	21194	—	—
w/Pkg. 26L (3.0-liter/automatic 4)	21367	—	—
w/Pkg. 28L (3.3-liter/automatic 4)	21469	—	—
LE SWB AWD w/Pkg. 28L (3.3-liter/automatic 4)	23558	—	—
Grand LE w/Pkg. 28L (3.3-liter/automatic 4)	22176	—	—
Grand LE AWD w/Pkg. 28L (3.3-liter/automatic 4)	24176	—	—

24-28L add to 24-28K: Woodgrain Decor Group (woodgrain appliques and moldings, luggage rack, 205/70R15 whitewall tires, wire wheel covers); deletes two-tone paint.

	Retail Price	Dealer Invoice	Low Price
LE SWB w/LX Pkg. 24M (3.0-liter/automatic 3)	20615	—	—
w/LX Pkg. 26M (3.0-liter/automatic 4)	20788	—	—
w/LX Pkg. 28M (3.3-liter/automatic 4)	20890	—	—
LE SWB AWD w/LX Pkg. 28M (3.3-liter/automatic 4)	24118	—	—

24-28M adds to 24-28K: LX Decor Group (body-color fascia and cladding, rear sway bar, fog lights, 205/70R15 tires on alloy wheels); deletes two-tone paint.

	Retail Price	Dealer Invoice	Low Price
Destination charge	540	540	540

SWB denotes short wheelbase; AWD denotes All Wheel Drive.

Dealer invoice and low price not available at time of publication.

Engines and transmissions: 2.5-liter TBI 4-cylinder with 5-speed manual or 3-speed automatic tranmission; 3.0-liter PFI V-6 with 3- or 4-speed automatic transmission; 3.3-liter PFI V-6 with 4-speed automatic transmission.

Prices are accurate at time of publication; subject to manufacturer's change.

Standard equipment:

Base: driver-side air bag, power steering, 5-passenger seating (front bucket seats, 3-passenger middle bench seat), tinted glass, trip odometer, coolant temperature gauge, dual outside mirrors, visor mirrors, AM/FM radio, intermittent wipers, rear wiper/washer, 195/75R14 tires. **SE** adds: 7-passenger seating (2-passenger middle and 3-passenger rear bench seats), dual-note horn, power mirrors, remote liftgate release, rear trim panel storage and cup holders, striping, sport wheel covers. **LE** adds: front air conditioning, front storage console, overhead console with outside temperature readout and mini trip computer, rear defogger, power front windows, power quarter vent windows, power locks, remote fuel door release, tachometer, oil pressure gauge, voltmeter, illuminated entry, headlamp delay system, heated power mirrors, lighted visor mirrors, bodyside moldings, cruise control, tilt steering column, sport steering wheel, storage drawer under front passenger seat, floormats. **Grand** models have 3.3-liter PFI V-6, 4-speed automatic transmission (base has 3.0-liter PFI V-6, 3-speed automatic transmission), power mirrors, remote liftgate release, dual-note horn, storage drawer under front passenger seat, sport wheel covers, 205/70R15 tires. **All Wheel Drive** models have 3.3-liter V-6, 4-speed automatic transmission, 7-passenger seating, power mirrors, 205/75R15 tires.

Optional equipment:

	Retail Price	Dealer Invoice	Low Price
Anti-lock brakes, SWB SE w/3.3-liter V-6 .	687	584	632
SWB SE w/Trailer Towing Group, Sport Handling Group or 14″ whitewall tires, Grand SE .	599	509	551
LE SWB w/J, K, or L Pkgs.	687	584	632
LE SWB w/M Pkg. and 3.3-liter V-6 . . .	599	509	551
LE w/Trailer Towing Group, Sport Handling Group or 14″ whitewall tires . .	599	509	551
Grand SE & LE	599	509	551
Front air conditioning, base & SE	857	728	788
Air conditioning w/rear heater, base Grand .	699	594	643
Grand SE 28A/28B	699	594	643
Requires rear defogger.			
Grand SE 28A/28B w/Trailer Towing Group	636	541	585
Grand SE 28D	466	396	429
Grand SE 28D w/Trailer Towing Group .	404	343	372
Rear air conditioning, Grand LE	466	396	429
Grand LE w/Trailer Towing Group	571	485	525
Grand SE 2WD w/Trailer Towing Group .	509	433	468
Rear bench seat, base SWB	397	337	365
Includes rear trim panel storage area and cup holders.			
Seven-passenger seating w/integrated child seat, Base SWB	597	507	549
SE & LE Grand	200	170	184
Quad Command Seating, SE & LE	597	507	549
Two front and two middle bucket seats, 3-passenger rear bench seat.			

	Retail Price	Dealer Invoice	Low Price
Converta-Bed 7-pass. seating, SE SWB, base/SE Grand	553	470	509
Leather trim, LE w/K, L, or M Pkgs.	865	735	796
HD Trailer Tow Pkg., SE SWB	557	473	512
SE & LE w/L Pkg.	483	411	444
SE SWB w/Sport Handling Group	443	377	408
LE w/J or K Pkg. & Sport Handling Group	443	377	408
Grand SE/LE	443	377	408

HD alternator, battery, flasher, radiator, and transmission oil cooler, trailer wiring harness, HD suspension (2WD), sport wheel covers, 205/70R15 tires with conventional spare.

	Retail Price	Dealer Invoice	Low Price
Deluxe Convenience Pkg., base & SE	372	316	342

Cruise control, tilt steering column.

	Retail Price	Dealer Invoice	Low Price
Power Convenience Pkg., SE SWB w/A or B Pkgs, Grand SE	530	451	488
SE w/D Pkg.	265	225	244

Power front windows, power locks.

	Retail Price	Dealer Invoice	Low Price
Sport Handling Pkg., SE SWB	207	176	190
Grand SE, Grand LE w/J, K, or M Pkgs	93	79	86
LE SWB w/J, K, or M Pkgs.	207	176	190

HD brakes, rear sway bar, sport wheel covers, 205/70R15 tires.

	Retail Price	Dealer Invoice	Low Price
Rear defogger, base w/o Pkgs.	217	184	200
Base w/Pkgs. 22-28, SE	168	143	155

Base includes remote liftgate release w/Pkgs. 22-28.

	Retail Price	Dealer Invoice	Low Price
Power locks, base & SE	265	225	244
Sunscreen glass	414	352	381
Luggage rack	143	122	132
Cassette player	155	132	143
Infinity I audio system, SE/LE	461	392	424
Infinity II system, SE/LE w/K, L, or M Pkgs.	214	182	197
HD suspension, 2WD	69	59	63
205/70R14 whitewall tires, 2WD SWB	143	122	132
205/70R15 whitewall tires, SE/LE	69	59	63
w/Trailer Towing Pkg., Grand SE/LE	159	135	146
Conventional spare tire, 2WD	109	93	100
15″ alloy wheels, SE	363	309	334
LE w/J or K Pkgs.	314	267	289

Requires Trailer Towing Pkg.

	Retail Price	Dealer Invoice	Low Price
LE w/L Pkg.	118	100	109
Styled steel wheels, SE	49	42	45
Extra-cost paint	77	65	71
California emissions pkg.	102	87	94

Chrysler Town & Country

	Retail Price	Dealer Invoice	Low Price
4-door van w/Pkg. 28X	$24621	$22036	$22386
w/Pkg. 28Y	24621	22036	22386

Prices are accurate at time of publication; subject to manufacturer's change.

	Retail Price	Dealer Invoice	Low Price
4WD 4-door van w/Pkg. 28X	26516	23704	24054
Pkg. 28Y	26516	23704	24054
Destination charge	540	540	540

Standard equipment:

3.3-liter PFI V-6, 4-speed automatic transmission, anti-lock brakes, power steering, driver-side air bag, air conditioning, 7-passenger seating (reclining front bucket seats, 2-passenger middle and 3-passenger rear bench seats), power driver's seat, leather upholstery, power front door and rear quarter vent windows, power locks, forward storage console, overhead console (with compass, outside temperature readout, and front and rear reading lights), rear defogger, cruise control, tilt steering column, remote fuel door release, tinted windshield and front door glass, sunscreen glass (other windows), leather-wrapped steering wheel, electronic instruments (tachometer, coolant temperature and oil pressure gauges, trip odometer), floormats, luggage rack, power mirrors, lighted visor mirrors, remote liftgate release, Infinity I AM/FM cassette, rear wiper/washer, imitation woodgrain exterior applique, 205/70R15 tires on alloy wheels. (4WD has full-time four-wheel drive.) **Pkg. 28Y** substitutes gold stripe and gold painted alloy wheels for woodgrain exterior applique.

Optional equipment:

Rear air conditioning, 2WD	466	396	408
Includes rear heater.			
Cloth & leather seat trim	NC	NC	NC
Quad Command 7-passenger seating	NC	NC	NC
Four bucket seats in front and middle rows, rear bench seat.			
Extra cost paint w/Pkg. 28X	77	65	67
Whitewall tires w/Pkg. 28X	69	59	60
Alloy wheels, gold painted, ...	363	309	318
California emissions pkg.	102	87	89

Dodge/Plymouth Colt and Eagle Summit

The Colt is made in Japan by Mitsubishi, which sells a similar model as the Mirage (see separate report). It's offered in identical 3-door form in base and up-level GL versions under the Dodge and Plymouth banners, and Eagle dealers sell Summit-badged base and ES models in 3- and 4-door body styles. The only engine offered in Colt/Summit

Dodge Colt GL

is a 92-horsepower 1.5-liter 4-cylinder. A 4-speed manual transmission is standard on the base models. A 5-speed manual is standard on upper-line models, and a 3-speed automatic is optional on all. For 1992, base Colts lose their optional wheel trim rings and GLs lose their optional alloy wheels. Cloth-faced seats are optional in place of vinyl ones on the base model in the only change to these slow-selling subcompacts. Production of the 4-door Summit was recently moved from Japan to Diamond-Star Motors, the Chrysler-Mitsubishi joint venture plant in Illinois. Entry-level transportation at reasonable cost is the mission of Colt and Summit, and they deliver. With the 4-speed gear box and manual steering, the base models are really barebones. The high-line models add a few amenities such as cigarette lighter and dual outside mirrors. Colt/Summit pluses include competent road manners and a comfortable ride. Handling and roadholding fall short of sporty, however, even in GL and ES models with their wider tires. Front-seat room is fine for a subcompact, though rear-seat head room is scarce for those over 5-foot-10. Usable trunk space in 4-door Summits is above average for the class. Acceleration and fuel economy suffer with the optional automatic transmission, so stick with manual shift to get the most performance at the least cost. Overall, Colt and Summit are well-rounded subcompacts at an attractive price. They're built better than most domestic competitors, but lack the high level of refinement and assembly quality enjoyed by such rivals as the Honda Civic, Nissan Sentra, or Toyota Corolla.

Prices are accurate at time of publication; subject to manufacturer's change.

Specifications

	3-door hatchback	4-door notchback
Wheelbase, in.	93.9	96.7
Overall length, in.	158.7	170.1
Overall width, in.	65.7	65.7
Overall height, in.	51.9	52.8
Curb weight, lbs.	2205	2271
Cargo vol., cu. ft.	34.7	10.3
Fuel capacity, gals.	13.2	13.2
Seating capacity	5	5
Front head room, in.	38.3	39.1
Front leg room, max., in.	41.9	41.9
Rear head room, in.	36.9	37.5
Rear leg room, min., in.	32.5	34.3

Powertrain layout: transverse front engine/front-wheel drive.

Engines

	ohc I-4
Size, liters/cu. in.	1.5/90
Fuel delivery	PFI
Horsepower @ rpm	92 @ 6000
Torque (lbs./ft.) @ rpm	93 @ 3000
Availability	S

EPA city/highway mpg

4-speed OD manual	31/36
5-speed OD manual	29/35
3-speed automatic	28/31
4-speed OD automatic	26/32

Assembly points: Normal, Ill.; Mizushima, Japan.

Prices

Dodge/Plymouth Colt	Retail Price	Dealer Invoice	Low Price
3-door hatchback, w/Pkg. 21A (4-speed)	$7302	$6933	$7133
w/Pkg. 24A (automatic)	7915	7460	7660
Base standard equipment.			
w/Pkg. 21B (4-speed)	7368	6990	7190
w/Pkg. 24B (automatic)	7981	7517	7717
Pkg. A adds: rear defogger.			
w/Pkg. 21C (4-speed)	7648	7230	7430

	Retail Price	Dealer Invoice	Low Price
w/Pkg. 24C (automatic)	8261	7758	7958
Pkg. B plus tinted glass, AM/FM stereo.			
w/Pkg. 21D (4-speed)	7772	7337	7537
w/Pkg. 24D (automatic)	8386	7864	8064
Pkg. C plus rear shelf, fabric seats.			
GL 3-door hatchback, w/Pkg. 23G (5-speed)	8122	7682	7882
ES standard equipment.			
w/Pkg. 23G (5-speed)	8468	7979	8179
w/Pkg. 24G (automatic)	8976	8416	8616
23/24G adds: rear defogger, tinted glass, AM/FM stereo.			
w/Pkg. 23H (5-speed)	8936	8382	8582
w/Pkg. 24H (automatic)	9444	8819	9019
Pkg. H adds: cassette player, air conditioning, power steering, intermittent wipers.			
w/Pkg. 23K (5-speed)	9123	8542	8742
w/Pkg. 24K (automatic)	9631	8979	9179
Pkg. K adds: digital clock, rear wiper/washer.			

Standard equipment:

3-door: 1.5-liter PFI 4-cylinder engine, 4-speed manual or 3-speed automatic transmission, motorized front shoulder belts, vinyl reclining front bucket seats, split folding rear seat, coolant temperature gauge, trip odometer, left manual mirror, locking fuel door, 155/80R13 tires. **GL 3-door** adds: 5-speed manual or 3-speed automatic transmission, cloth upholstery, cigar lighter, remote mirrors, 175/70R13 tires.

Optional equipment:

3-speed automatic transmission	613	527	530
GL 3-door	508	437	439
Air conditioning	753	625	651
AM/FM radio	217	180	188

Eagle Summit

3-door hatchback, w/Pkg. 21A (4-speed) .	$7302	$6933	$7133
w/Pkg. 24A (automatic)	7915	7460	7660
Base standard equipment.			
w/Pkg. 21B (4-speed)	7368	6990	7190
w/Pkg. 24B (automatic)	7981	7517	7717
Pkg. A adds: rear defogger.			
w/Pkg. 21C (4-speed)	7648	7230	7430
w/Pkg. 24C (automatic)	8261	7758	7958
Pkg. B plus tinted glass, AM/FM stereo.			
w/Pkg. 21D (4-speed)	7772	7337	7537
w/Pkg. 24D (automatic)	8386	7864	8064
Pkg. C plus rear shelf, fabric seats.			

Prices are accurate at time of publication; subject to manufacturer's change.

	Retail Price	Dealer Invoice	Low Price
ES 3-door hatchback, w/Pkg. 23G (5-speed)	8122	7682	7882
ES standard equipment.			
w/Pkg. 23G (5-speed)	8468	7979	8179
w/Pkg. 24G (automatic)	8976	8416	8616
23/24G adds: rear defogger, tinted glass, AM/FM stereo.			
w/Pkg. 23H (5-speed)	8936	8382	8582
w/Pkg. 24H (automatic)	9444	8819	9019
Pkg. H adds: cassette player, air conditioning, power steering, intermittent wipers.			
w/Pkg. 23K (5-speed)	9123	8542	8742
w/Pkg. 24K (automatic)	9631	8979	9179
Pkg. K adds: digital clock, rear wiper/washer.			
4-door notchback, 5-speed	8981	8481	8681
4-door notchback, automatic	9668	9072	9272
Base 4-door standard equipment.			
4-door w/Pkg. 21B (5-speed)	9736	9131	9331
4-door w/Pkg. 22B (automatic)	10423	9721	9044
B Pkg. adds: remote fuel door and decklid releases, visor mirrors, intermittent wipers, rear defogger, upgraded trunk trim.			
4-door w/Pkg. 21C (5-speed)	10489	9778	9978
4-door w/Pkg. 22C (automatic)	11176	10369	10569
C Pkg. adds: power steering, digital clock, AM/FM radio, power mirrors.			
4-door w/Pkg. 21D (5-speed)	10704	9963	10163
4-door w/Pkg. 22D (automatic)	11391	10554	10754
D Pkg. adds: cassette player; D Pkgs. do not include power mirrors.			
ES 4-door, 5-speed	9998	9368	9568
ES 4-door, automatic	10685	9959	10159
ES 4-door standard equipment.			
ES 4-door w/Pkg. 21F (5-speed)	11427	10596	10796
ES 4-door w/Pkg. 22F (automatic)	12114	11187	11387
F Pkg. adds: AM/FM radio, cruise control, intermittent wipers.			
Destination charge	343	343	343

Standard equipment:

3-door: 1.5-liter PFI 4-cylinder engine, 4-speed manual or 3-speed automatic transmission, motorized front shoulder belts, vinyl reclining front bucket seats, split folding rear seat, coolant temperature gauge, trip odometer, left manual mirror, locking fuel door, 155/80R13 tires; **4-door** has 5-speed manual or 4-speed automatic transmission, cloth upholstery, fixed rear seat, tinted glass. **ES 3-door** adds: 5-speed manual or 3-speed automatic transmission, cloth upholstery, cigar lighter, remote mirrors, 175/70R13 tires; **4-door** has 5-speed manual or 4-speed automatic transmission, power steering, tachometer, power mirrors, digital clock, remote fuel door and decklid releases, rear defogger, dual-note horn, visor mirrors, velour upholstery, driver-seat height adjustment, split folding rear seat, tilt/telescopic steering column, intermittent wipers.

Optional equipment:	Retail Price	Dealer Invoice	Low Price
3-speed automatic transmission, base 3-door	613	527	530
ES 3-door	508	437	439
4-speed automatic transmission, 4-doors	687	591	594
Power steering, 4-doors	259	223	224
Air conditioning	753	625	651
Rear defogger, 4-doors	66	57	57
Cruise control & intermittent wipers, 4-doors	208	179	180
Power windows and locks, 4-doors	435	374	376
AM/FM radio, 3-doors	217	180	188
4-doors	300	258	260
AM/FM cassette, 4-doors	167	144	144
Requires AM/FM stereo.			
Alloy wheels, 4-doors	275	237	238

Dodge Daytona

Dodge Daytona ES

Dodge's front-drive sports coupe gets a fresh front and rear look and anti-lock brakes as a new option. Plus, a new high-performance model, the IROC R/T, will supplant the Shelby-badged Daytona variant. The R/T will join base, ES, and "regular" IROC models. Styling changes include a new nose with exposed aero headlamps, full-width tail-lamps, and new outer door panels and side window openings. ES and IROC models also get new ground-effects lower-body trim. Standard in the base and ES is a naturally aspirated 100-horsepower 2.5-liter 4-cylinder engine. A tur-bocharged version with 152 horsepower is optional only on

Prices are accurate at time of publication; subject to manufacturer's change.

the IROC version. A Mitsubishi-made 141-horsepower 3.0-liter V-6 is standard on the IROC and optional on the base and ES. At mid-year, Dodge's 224-horsepower 2.2-liter Turbo III 4-cylinder finds a second home in the Daytona IROC R/T, which will have a production run of only 800 or so units. This engine debuted last year in the Spirit R/T compact sport sedan. A 5-speed manual transmission is standard with all engines and mandatory with the Turbo III; automatics are optional elsewhere. ABS is a new option for all models and include rear discs for the base and ES

Specifications

	3-door hatchback
Wheelbase, in.	97.2
Overall length, in.	179.8
Overall width, in.	69.3
Overall height, in.	51.8
Curb weight, lbs.	2779
Cargo vol., cu. ft.	33.0
Fuel capacity, gals.	14.0
Seating capacity	4
Front head room, in.	37.1
Front leg room, max., in.	42.5
Rear head room, in.	34.3
Rear leg room, min., in.	30.0

Powertrain layout: transverse front engine/front-wheel drive.

Engines	ohc I-4	Turbo ohc I-4	ohc V-6	Turbo dohc I-4
Size, liters/cu. in.	2.5/153	2.5/153	3.0/181	2.2/135
Fuel delivery	TBI	PFI	PFI	PFI
Horsepower @ rpm	100 @ 4800	152 @ 4800	141 @ 5000	224 @ 6000
Torque (lbs./ft.) @ rpm	135 @ 2800	210 @ 2000	171 @ 2800	217 @ 2800
Availability	S[1]	O	S[2]	S[3]

EPA city/highway mpg

5-speed OD manual	23/31	21/27	19/28	19/27
3-speed automatic	23/27	18/24		
4-speed OD automatic			20/27	

1. Base Daytona, ES.   2. IROC.   3. IROC R/T.

Assembly points: St. Louis, Mo.; Sterling Heights, Mich.

models (rear discs are standard on the IROCs). A driver-side air bag remains standard on all models. Budget-minded sports-coupe buyers should give Daytona a look. The most satisfying versions have the V-6. It's more powerful than the base 2.5, delivers more linear performance than the turbos, and is quietest of all. Daytona gives imports an edge in refinement and assembly quality, but makes up for it with lower prices.

Prices

Dodge Daytona	Retail Price	Dealer Invoice	Low Price
3-door hatchback w/Pkg. 21A	$10469	—	—
w/Pkg. 22A (2.5-liter/automatic)	11026	—	—
Standard equipment.			
w/Pkg. 21B (2.5-liter/5-speed)	11597	—	—
w/Pkg. 22B (2.5-liter/automatic)	12154	—	—
w/Pkg. 25B (3.0-liter/5-speed)	12291	—	—
w/Pkg. 26B (3.0-liter/automatic)	12931	—	—
ES 3-door hatchback w/Pkg. 21A	11510	—	—
w/Pkg. 22A (2.5-liter/automatic)	12067	—	—
w/Pkg. 25A (3.0-liter/5-speed)	12204	—	—
w/Pkg. 26A (3.0-liter/automatic)	12844	—	—
ES standard equipment.			
w/Pkg. 21B (2.5-liter/5-speed)	12638	—	—
w/Pkg. 22B (2.5-liter/automatic)	13195	—	—
w/Pkg. 25B (3.0-liter/5-speed)	13332	—	—
w/Pkg. 26B (3.0-liter/automatic)	13972	—	—
IROC 3-door hatchback w/Pkg. 25A	12805	—	—
IROC standard equipment.			
w/Pkg. 23B (Turbo/5-speed)	14098	—	—
w/Pkg. 24B (Turbo/automatic)	14490	—	—
w/Pkg. 25B (3.0-liter/5-speed)	13933	—	—
w/Pkg. 26B (3.0-liter/automatic)	14573	—	—
Destination charge	499	499	499

Dealer invoice and low price not available at time of publication.

Standard equipment:

2.5-liter TBI 4-cylinder engine, 5-speed manual transmission, power steering, driver-side air bag, cloth reclining front bucket seats, split folding rear seat, tachometer, coolant temperature and oil pressure gauges, voltmeter, trip odometer, intermittent wipers, tinted glass, console with armrest and storage, remote fuel door and hatch releases, time-delay headlamp system, remote manual mirrors, visor mirrors, AM/FM radio, 185/70R14 tires. **ES**

Prices are accurate at time of publication; subject to manufacturer's change.

adds: fog lamps, sill extensions, rear spoiler, Message Center, tonneau cover, 205/60HR15 tires on alloy wheels. **IROC** adds: 3.0-liter PFI V-6, 4-wheel disc brakes, Maximum Performance Suspension, leather-wrapped steering wheel, 205/55VR16 tires on alloy wheels. **Pkgs. 21-26B** add: air conditioning, rear defogger, floormats, Light Group, power locks, heated power mirrors, cassette player, remote hatch release, cruise control, tilt steering column.

Optional equipment:	Retail Price	Dealer Invoice	Low Price
Anti-lock brakes, ES & IROC	899	764	773
Value Group, base & ES	630	536	542
Light Group, power locks, cassette player, cruise control, tilt steering.			
V-6 Performance Group, ES	1007	856	866
3.0-liter V-6, 4-wheel disc brakes, Performance Handling Suspension, leather-wrapped steering wheel.			
Premium Light Group, ES & IROC	196	167	169
Illuminated entry, lighted visor mirrors.			
Sport Group, base	345	293	297
Spoiler, 205/60R15 tires, stripes, sport wheelcovers.			
Overhead console, ES & IROC	265	225	228
Includes compass, outside temperature readout, dome and map lights, storage for sunglasses and garage door transmitter.			
Infinity audio system, ES & IROC	493	419	424
w/EQ	706	600	607
CD player, w/Infinity systems	449	382	386
Power driver's seat (6-way), base & ES . .	296	252	255
Power cloth driver's seat (12-way), ES & IROC	751	638	646
w/leather upholstery	1402	1192	1206
Requires V-6 Performance Pkg. and power windows.			
Security alarm, ES & IROC	149	127	128
Rear defogger	209	178	180
Rear window sun louver, ES & IROC	214	182	184
Removable sunroof	405	344	348
Power windows	265	225	228
Rear wiper/washer	129	110	111
Alloy wheels, base	328	279	282

Dodge Dynasty/
Chrysler New Yorker Salon

Dodge's mid-size Dynasty sedan receives few changes for 1992, while Chrysler's more luxurious New Yorker Salon version gets new rounded front and rear styling and an optional landau vinyl roof cap. The landau roof cap reap-

Dodge Dynasty

pears after a one-year absence and is available in four colors. Salon's softer front and rear appearance is similar to that of the full-size Chrysler Fifth Avenue. Also joining Salon's options list for 1992 are an electrochromatic rearview mirror and a floor console with cassette storage. An overhead lamp module with storage pocket is a new standard item. Dynasty and Salon are built off the same frontdrive platform as the larger Chrysler New Yorker Fifth Avenue and the Imperial, though Chrysler stretches the wheelbase from 104.5 inches to 109.5 for those more expensive models. Dynasty is offered in base and LE versions; Salon comes in only one trim level. Dynasty base models come standard with a 2.5-liter 4-cylinder with 100 horsepower, while a Mitsubishi-made 3.0-liter V-6 with 141 comes with the LE, and a Chrysler-manufactured 147-horsepower 3.3-liter V-6 is optional on both. Salon comes with the 3.3-liter V-6. Both have standard driver-side air bags, and offer anti-lock brakes as an option on V-6-powered models. They are smooth and fairly quiet, but unexciting. However, these well-designed family sedans offer plenty of room and adequate engine performance—as long as you get one of the V-6s. Those with the V-6 come with Chrysler's Ultradrive 4-speed automatic, which tends to vibrate during shifting and emits an annoying whistling sound. Any hint of spirited cornering brings on tire-squealing body lean, and while the ride is smooth, there's too much bouncing and pitching at speed. Generous head and leg room allows four adults to ride in comfort. Putting three abreast

Prices are accurate at time of publication; subject to manufacturer's change.

in front or back is a squeeze, however, because the interior is rather narrow. Note that the Dodge Dynasty is the same car as the Salon and it can be equipped virtually identically to a Salon at a lower price.

Specifications

	4-door notchback
Wheelbase, in.	104.5
Overall length, in.	192.0
Overall width, in.	68.9
Overall height, in.	53.6
Curb weight, lbs.	3026
Cargo vol., cu. ft.	16.5
Fuel capacity, gals.	16.0
Seating capacity	6
Front head room, in.	38.3
Front leg room, max., in.	41.9
Rear head room, in.	37.8
Rear leg room, min., in.	38.1

Powertrain layout: transverse front engine/front-wheel drive.

Engines	ohc I-4	ohc V-6	ohv V-6
Size, liters/cu. in.	2.5/153	3.0/181	3.3/201
Fuel delivery	TBI	PFI	PFI
Horsepower @ rpm	100 @ 4800	141 @ 5000	147 @ 4800
Torque (lbs./ft.) @ rpm	135 @ 2800	171 @ 2400	183 @ 3600
Availability	S[1]	S[2]	S[3]

EPA city/highway mpg

	ohc I-4	ohc V-6	ohv V-6
3-speed automatic	22/28		
4-speed OD automatic		20/27	19/25

1. Base Dynasty.   2. Dynasty LE.   3. New Yorker Salon.

Assembly point: Belvidere, Ill.

Prices

Dodge Dynasty	Retail Price	Dealer Invoice	Low Price
4-door notchback w/Pkg. 22A (2.5)	$14277	$12355	$12705
w/Pkg. 24A (3.0)	15064	13024	13374
w/Pkg. 26A (3.3)	15064	13024	13374

	Retail Price	Dealer Invoice	Low Price
w/Pkg. 22B (2.5)	15181	13124	13474
w/Pkg. 24B (3.0)	15968	13792	14142
w/Pkg. 26B (3.3)	15968	13792	14142
w/Pkg. 22C (2.5)	15363	13279	13629
w/Pkg. 24C (3.0)	16150	13948	14298
w/Pkg. 26C (3.3)	16150	13948	14298
LE 4-door notchback w/Pkg. 24A (3.0) . .	15767	13622	13972
w/Pkg. 26A (3.3)	15767	13622	13972
w/Pkg. 26C (3.3)	17093	14749	15099
w/Pkg. 26D (3.3)	18267	15747	16097
Destination charge	565	565	565

Engines and transmissions: 2.5-liter TBI 4-cylinder engine with 3-speed automatic transmission; 3.0- or 3.3-liter V-6 with 4-speed automatic transmission. **Other equipment, base:** power steering, driver-side air bag, cloth front bench seat with armrest, rear defogger, tinted glass, intermittent wipers, trip odometer, coolant temperature and oil pressure gauges, voltmeter, remote mirrors, visor mirrors, AM/FM radio, remote decklid release, 195/75R14 tires. **LE adds:** Message Center, 50/50 split front seat armrest with cup holders, rear seat armrest, premium wheel covers. **Base Pkgs. 22B/24B/26B:** air conditioning, 195/75R14 whitewall tires. **Base Pkgs. 22C/24C/26C: Pkgs. 22B/24B/26B** plus front console, cruise control, tilt steering column, power locks, cassette player, floormats, Message Center, undercoating, striping. **LE Pkg. 26C: Base Pkgs. 22C/24C/26C** plus: heated power mirrors, power windows; deletes striping. **LE Pkg. 26D: LE Pkg. 26C** plus: rear armrest with cup holders, illuminated entry, lighted vanity mirrors, automatic day/night rearview mirror, power front seats, leather-wrapped steering wheel, wire harness for cellular phone, wire wheel covers.

Optional equipment:

3.0- or 3.3-liter V-6, base	694	590	602
4-speed automatic transmission, base w/V-6	93	79	81
Anti-lock 4-wheel disc brakes (V-6 req.) . .	899	764	780
Deluxe Convenience Group, LE	372	316	323
Cruise control, tilt steering column.			
Power Convenience Pkg., base	384	326	333
Power windows, heated power mirrors.			
Security Group	292	248	253
LE	277	235	240
Security alarm, remote keyless entry.			
Power Accessories Pkg., LE	159	135	138
Power decklid pulldown, power antenna.			
Power locks	331	281	287
Cassette player	155	132	134
w/EQ	273	232	237
Infinity RS audio system, LE	668	568	579

Prices are accurate at time of publication; subject to manufacturer's change.

	Retail Price	Dealer Invoice	Low Price
Power driver's seat (6-way), LE	296	252	257
Power front seats (8-way) w/memory, LE .	396	337	344
50/50 front seat, base	372	316	323
Leather 50/50 seat, LE w/Pkg. 26D	590	502	512
Power sunroof, LE	792	673	687
Automatic load leveling suspension, LE . .	225	191	195
195/75R14 whitewall tires	73	62	63
Wire wheel covers	228	194	198
Alloy wheels, LE	278	236	241
w/Pkg. 26D	50	43	43
Conventional spare tire	85	72	74
Pearl coat/clearcoat paint	77	65	67

Chrysler New Yorker Salon

	Retail Price	Dealer Invoice	Low Price
4-door notchback	$18849	$16282	$16682
w/Popular Pkg. 26C	19569	16894	17294
w/Popular Pkg. 26D	20854	17986	18386
Destination charge	565	565	565

Standard equipment:

3.3-liter PFI V-6, 4-speed automatic transmission, power steering, driver-side air bag, air conditioning, cloth 50/50 front seat with armrest, rear defogger, heated power mirrors, power windows, tinted glass, trip odometer, coolant temperature and oil pressure gauges, voltmeter, visor mirrors, bright wide lower bodyside moldings, AM/FM radio, remote decklid release, intermittent wipers, 195/75R14 whitewall tires. **Pkg. 26C** adds: cruise control, tilt steering column, power locks, cassette player, floor console, floormats, whitewall tires. **Pkg. 26D** adds: wiring harness for cellular phone, illuminated entry, lighted visor mirrors, automatic day/night mirror, power front seats, leather-wrapped steering wheel, rear armrest with cupholder, wire wheel covers.

Optional equipment:

Anti-lock 4-wheel disc brakes	899	764	787
Deluxe Convenience Group	372	316	326
Cruise control, tilt steering column.			
Security Pkg.	292	248	256
Security alarm, keyless remote entry; requires Popular Pkg.			
Power Accessories Pkg.	159	135	139
Power decklid pulldown, power antenna; requires Popular Pkg. 26D.			
Power locks	331	281	290
Cassette player	155	132	136
Cassette player w/EQ	273	232	239
Requires Popular Pkg.			

	Retail Price	Dealer Invoice	Low Price
Infinity RS Group	668	568	585
AM & FM Stereo w/cassette, EQ, 10 speakers; requires Pkg. 26D.			
Leather seat trim	590	502	516
Requires Pkg. 26D			
Power driver's seat (6-way)	296	252	259
Requires Popular Pkg.			
Power front seats (8-way)	396	337	347
Includes driver's seat and mirror memory system; requires Pkg. 26D.			
Power sunroof	792	673	693
Requires Pkg. 26D.			
Landau vinyl roof	325	276	284
Requires Popular Pkg.			
Automatic load leveling suspension	225	191	197
Requires Popular Pkg.			
Wire wheel covers	228	194	200
Requires Popular Pkg.			
Alloy wheels	50	43	44
Requires Pkg. 26D			
195/75R14 whitewall tires	73	62	64
Conventional spare tire	85	72	74
Extra cost paint	77	65	67
California emissions pkg.	102	87	89

Eagle Premier/Dodge Monaco

Dodge Monaco ES

The mid-size front-drive Dodge Monaco and Eagle Premier are virtual clones, and both continue basically unchanged for 1992, which will be their last year. AMC and the French automaker Renault designed these sedans, which are built in a Canadian plant and still use a 150-horsepower 3.0-liter

Renault V-6 hitched to a 4-speed automatic transmission. Premier returns in LX, ES, and sporty ES Limited models. LX and ES this year get a new grille and taillamps much like those given the ES Limited for 1991. Anti-lock brakes are standard on ES Limited, optional on LX and ES. A driver-side air bag is not offered. Monaco is offered in LE and ES trim. Anti-lock brakes are optional on both, though a driver-side air bag is not offered. The ES has as standard several items that are optional on the LE, including a touring suspension, air conditioning, 4-wheel disc brakes, and a stereo radio/cassette system. Both can be fitted with 15-inch tires in place of the base 14 inchers. The smooth V-6 teams with a precise-shifting automatic transmission

Specifications

	4-door notchback
Wheelbase, in.	106.0
Overall length, in.	192.8
Overall width, in.	70.0
Overall height, in.	54.7
Curb weight, lbs.	3039
Cargo vol., cu. ft.	17.0
Fuel capacity, gals.	16.0
Seating capacity	5
Front head room, in.	38.5
Front leg room, max., in.	43.8
Rear head room, in.	37.5
Rear leg room, min., in.	39.4

Powertrain layout: longitudinal front engine/front-wheel drive.

Engines	ohc V-6
Size, liters/cu. in.	3.0/180
Fuel delivery	PFI
Horsepower @ rpm	150 @ 5000
Torque (lbs./ft.) @ rpm	171 @ 3600
Availability	S

EPA city/highway mpg	
4-speed OD automatic	18/26

Assembly point: Bramalea, Ontario, Canada.

to deliver ample power. A firm, but pliant and well-controlled ride is the rule. Supportive seats and plenty of room for five highlight the airy cabin. The trunk is spacious. Some controls are quirky, however. Slide levers and buttons that operate the headlamps, wipers, and climate system are on flimsy-feeling plastic pods mounted adjacent to the steering wheel. They are easy to reach, but some are illogical in their operation. Overall, Premier and Monaco are sound cars, and moribund sales and frequent dealer discounts mean these two are attractively priced for their size and level of equipment. But low resale value and imminent demise makes them questionable investments.

Prices

Eagle Premier	Retail Price	Dealer Invoice	Low Price
LX 4-door notchback w/Pkg. 24A	$15716	$13609	$13734
LX standard equipment.			
w/Pkg. 24B	16227	14043	14168
24B adds: cruise control, tilt steering column, cassette player.			
w/Pkg. 24C	16516	14289	14414
24C adds to 24B: power windows and locks, lighted visor mirrors.			
w/Pkg. 24D	17514	15137	15262
24D adds to 24C: illuminated keyless entry, remote decklid and fuel door releases, power driver's seat, premium audio system, trip computer.			
ES 4-door notchback w/Pkg. 24E	18057	15598	15723
ES standard equipment.			
w/Pkg. 24F	18243	15757	15882
24F adds to 24E: power windows, power driver's seat, illuminated keyless entry, remote decklid and fuel door releases.			
w/pkg. 24G	18524	15995	16120
24G adds to 24F: premium audio system.			
ES Limited 4-door notchback	20212	17430	17555
Destination charge	500	500	500

Standard equipment:

LX: 3.0-liter PFI V-6, 4-speed automatic transmission, 4-wheel disc brakes, power steering, motorized front shoulder belts, automatic air conditioning, cloth 45/45 front seat, full-length console with armrest, rear armrest, door pockets, rear defogger, tachometer, coolant temperature and oil pressure gauges, trip odometer, tinted glass, heated power mirrors, AM/FM radio, intermittent wipers, floormats, 195/70R14 tires. **ES** adds: power locks, lower body cladding, lighted visor mirrors, cassette player, trip computer, leather-wrapped steering wheel, cruise control, tilt steering column, 205/

Prices are accurate at time of publication; subject to manufacturer's change.

60R15 tires on polycast wheels. **ES Limited** adds: anti-lock brakes, monochrome exterior treatment, leather upholstery, power front seats, keyless illuminated entry, remote fuel door and decklid releases, power windows, premium audio system with EQ, 205/60HR15 tires on alloy wheels with conventional spare.

Optional equipment:

	Retail Price	Dealer Invoice	Low Price
Anti-lock brakes, LX & ES	799	679	683
Fabric upholstery, ES Ltd. (credit)	(296)	(252)	(252)
Deletes power passenger seat.			
Power locks, LX w/Pkg. 24B	240	204	205
Power Group, LX w/Pkg. 24C	309	263	264
Keyless illuminated entry, remote decklid and fuel door releases.			
Power driver's seat, LX w/Pkg. 24C	296	252	253
Premium audio system, LX w/Pkg. 24C,			
ES w/Pkg. 24F	381	324	326
Cassette player, EQ, Jensen speakers, power antenna.			
Cruise control, LX w/Pkg. 24A	224	190	192
Requires tilt steering column.			
Tilt steering column, LX w/Pkg. 24A	148	126	127
Requires cruise control.			
Luggage rack, LX, ES w/Pkg. 24F	117	99	100
Conventional spare tire, LX & ES	95	81	81
Alloy wheels & 205/60R15 tires, LX	523	445	447
Alloy wheels, ES	301	256	257
California emissions	102	87	87

Dodge Monaco

LE 4-door notchback	$14354	$12451	$12576
w/Pkg. 24K	15934	13794	13919
w/Pkg. 24L	16690	14437	14562
ES 4-door notchback	17203	14873	14998
w/Pkg. 24P	18383	15876	16001
w/Pkg. 24R	18951	16358	16483
Destination charge	500	500	500

Standard equipment:

LE: 3.0-liter PFI V-6, 4-speed automatic transmission, motorized front shoulder belts, power steering, cloth reclining bucket seats, console with cupholder, overhead console with reading lights, rear defogger, tinted glass, coolant temperature and oil pressure gauges, tachometer, trip odometer, intermittent wipers, dual remote mirrors, folding rear center armrest, right visor mirror, AM/FM radio, 195/70R14 tires. **Pkg. 24K** adds: automatic climate control, cruise control, tilt steering column, power locks and windows. **Pkg. 24 L** adds to 24K: heated power mirrors, floormats, power driver's seat, cassette player, remote fuel door and decklid releases, polycast wheels. **ES** adds:

4-wheel disc brakes, automatic temperature control air conditioning, touring suspension, remote fuel door and decklid releases, heated power mirrors, lighted visor mirrors, AM/FM cassette with six Jensen speakers, leather-wrapped steering wheel, two-tone paint, 205/70R14 tires on alloy wheels. **Pkg. 24P** adds: cruise control, tilt steering column, floormats, illuminated and keyless entry, power locks and windows, power driver's seat, remote fuel door and decklid releases, 205/60R15 tires on alloy wheels. **Pkg. 24R** adds to 24P: premium audio system, trip computer.

Optional equipment:	Retail Price	Dealer Invoice	Low Price
Anti-lock brakes	799	679	683
Cassette player, LE	239	203	204
Premium AM/FM cassette w/EQ	381	324	326
AM/FM cassette, LE	239	203	204
Power driver's seat	296	252	253
Leather seats, ES w/24R	891	757	762
Alloy wheels, LE w/24K	523	445	447
w/Pkg. 24L	419	356	358
Decklid luggage rack	117	99	100
Conventional spare tire	95	81	81
California emissions pkg.	102	87	87

Ford Aerostar

Ford Aerostar Eddie Bauer 4WD Extended Length

A driver-side air bag is standard as the major change for this minivan. Aerostar joins the Chrysler minivans and the Toyota Previa as the only vehicles in this class with this safety feature. In addition, the Aerostar has a new

Prices are accurate at time of publication; subject to manufacturer's change.

dashboard with redesigned headlamp and climate-system controls. The shift lever on automatic transmission models moves from the floor to the steering column and the brakes must be applied to shift out of park. Outside, the nose has a new grille and flush-mounted aero headlamps. Aerostar is mechanically unchanged. Sharing a 118.9-inch wheel base is a regular-length body (174.9 inches) and an extended version that grafts 15.4 inches onto the tail for an additional 29 cubic feet of cargo space. Both are available with rear-wheel drive or permanently engaged 4-wheel-drive. Two V-6 engines return: a 145-horsepower 3.0-liter

Specifications

	4-door van	4-door van
Wheelbase, in.	118.9	118.9
Overall length, in.	174.9	190.3
Overall width, in.	71.7	72.0
Overall height, in.	72.9	74.0
Curb weight, lbs.	3374	3478
Cargo vol., cu. ft.	139.3	167.7
Fuel capacity, gals.	21.0	21.0
Seating capacity	7	7
Front head room, in.	39.5	39.5
Front leg room, max., in.	41.4	41.4
Rear head room, in.	38.8	38.7
Rear leg room, min., in.	39.5	40.5

Powertrain layout: longitudinal front engine/rear-wheel drive or permanent 4-wheel drive.

Engines

	ohv V-6	ohv V-6
Size, liters/cu. in.	3.0/182	4.0/245
Fuel delivery	PFI	PFI
Horsepower @ rpm	145 @ 4800	155 @ 4200
Torque (lbs./ft.) @ rpm	165 @ 3600	215 @ 2400
Availability	S	S[1]

EPA city/highway mpg

5-speed OD manual	17/23	
4-speed OD automatic	17/22	16/21

1. Aerostar 4WD; optional Aerostar extended length 2WD.

Assembly point: St. Louis, Mo.

is standard on 2WD models; a 155-horsepower 4.0-liter is standard on 4WD versions and optional on extended 2WD Aerostars. Rear anti-lock brakes are standard. Aerostar is more truck-like than the majority of minivans, but the air bag and attractive new dash are two car-like touches we like. Still, if you're looking at a minivan to replace the family station wagon, look to something like the Caravan/Voyager, Chevrolet Lumina APV, or other lighter-duty van. Aerostar, like the Chevrolet Astro/GMC Safari, is better suited to heavy work like hauling hefty payloads or towing trailers.

Prices

Ford Aerostar Wagon	Retail Price	Dealer Invoice	Low Price
XL regular length (RL), 2WD	$13739	$12290	$12590
XL extended, 2WD	15531	13867	14167
XL regular length, 4WD	16978	15140	15440
XL extended, 4WD	17966	16010	16310
XL Plus regular, 2WD	15235	13607	13907
XL Plus extended, 4WD	16420	14650	14950
XL Plus regular, 2WD	18014	16052	16352
XL Plus extended, 4WD	19002	16922	17222
XLT regular length, 2WD	17944	15990	16290
XLT extended, 2WD	18621	16587	16887
XLT regular length, 4WD	20119	17905	18205
XLT extended, 4WD	21086	18756	19056
Eddie Bauer regular length, 2WD	21636	19240	21936
Eddie Bauer extended, 2WD	22604	20091	20391
Eddie Bauer regular length, 4WD	23414	20804	21104
Eddie Bauer extended, 4WD	24381	21655	21955
Destination charge	535	535	535

Standard equipment:

XL: 3.0-liter PFI V-6 with 5-speed manual transmission (2WD; 4WD models have 4.0-liter V-6 with 4-speed automatic transmission), cloth and vinyl front bucket seats, 3-passenger middle bench seat, tinted glass, dual outside mirrors, rear wiper/washer, intermittent wipers, remote fuel door release, AM/FM radio, visor mirrors, 215/70R14 tires. **XLT** adds: front air conditioning, cloth front captain's chairs, 2-passenger middle and 3-passenger rear bench seats, underseat storage bin, dual-note horn, two-tone paint, upgraded upholstery and trim, liftgate convenience net, Light Group, leather-wrapped steering wheel. **Eddie Bauer** adds: high-capacity air conditioning/rear heater, rear seat/bed, upgraded upholstery, luggage rack, rear defogger,

Prices are accurate at time of publication; subject to manufacturer's change.

overhead console, electronic instruments, trip computer, autolamp system, automatic day/night rearview mirror, Super Sound System, floormats, forged alloy wheels.

Optional equipment:	Retail Price	Dealer Invoice	Low Price
4.0-liter V-6, 2WD	300	255	263
4-speed automatic transmission, 2WD . . .	750	638	656
Limited-slip axle	252	215	221
Optional axle ratio	38	32	33
XL Plus Pkg. 401A, 2WD & Ext. 4WD . . .	734	624	642
7-passenger seating with front captain's chairs, air conditioning, privacy glass, cruise control, tilt steering column.			
XL Value Pkg. 402A, 2WD	NC	NC	NC
Air conditioning.			
XLT Pkg. 403A, XLT	391	332	342
Privacy glass, rear defogger, power windows and locks, power mirrors, cassette player.			
Eddie Bauer Pkg. 405A	426	362	373
Privacy glass, power windows and locks, power mirrors, floor console with storage and cupholders.			
7-passenger seating	346	294	303
w/front captain's chairs	1043	886	913
w/front captain's chairs & seat/bed, XL .	1595	1356	1396
w/Pkg. 401A or 403A	552	470	483
w/four captain's chairs	598	508	523
Front captain's chairs, XL	644	547	564
4 captain's chairs & seat/bed, XLT w/Pkg.			
403A	622	529	544
Eddie Bauer w/Pkg. 405A	NC	NC	NC
w/leather upholstery	848	720	742
Front air conditioning, XL	857	729	750
High-capacity/rear heater	1433	1218	1254
High-capacity/rear heater, w/any pkg. . .	576	489	504
Floor console w/storage & cupholders . . .	174	148	152
Floor console delete (credit)	(61)	(52)	(52)
Rear defogger	168	143	147
Electronics Group, w/Pkg. 401A	923	785	808
XLT w/Pkg. 403A	813	691	711
Overhead console, electronic instruments, Super Sound System.			
Exterior Appearance Group	615	522	538
w/Pkg. 401A	213	181	186
w/Pkg. 403A	94	80	82
XLT w/o privacy glass & pwr. conv. group	513	436	449
Light Group, XL & XL Plus	159	135	139
Luggage rack (std. Eddie Bauer)	143	121	125
Swing-lock mirrors (NA Eddie Bauer)	52	45	46
Bodyside molding	63	54	55

CONSUMER GUIDE®

	Retail Price	Dealer Invoice	Low Price
Power Convenience Group, XL & XL Plus .	538	457	471
w/Exterior Appearance Pkg.	485	413	424
Power windows and locks, power mirrors.			
Cruise control & tilt steering column, XL .	371	315	325
Sport Appearance Pkg., w/Pkg. 402A . . .	1096	932	959
w/Pkg. 401A	1067	907	934
XLT	984	836	861
Trailer Towing Pkg.	282	239	247
Underseat storage bin, XL	37	31	32
Forged alloy wheels, XL	363	309	318
XLT or w/Exterior Appearance Group . .	324	276	284
AM/FM cassette	122	104	107
AM/FM delete (credit)	(183)	(155)	(155)
Engine block heater	33	28	29
215/70R14SL WSW all-season tires	84	72	74
215/75R14SL WSW all-season tires	84	72	74
California emissions pkg.	100	85	88

Ford Escort/Mercury Tracer

Ford Escort LX-E 4-door

The Escort gets the 4-door notchback sedan body previously exclusive to its Mercury Tracer cousin. The new notchback comes in LX trim and as a new model, the LX-E. The LX-E shares with the Escort GT and Tracer LTS a 127-horsepower Mazda 1.8-liter 4-cylinder engine, as well 4-wheel disc brakes and a sport suspension. Three-door hatchback ver-

Prices are accurate at time of publication; subject to manufacturer's change.

sions of the subcompact Escort are back in Pony, LX, and GT trim, while the 5-door hatchback and 5-door station wagon return in LX form. Besides the LTS sedan, the Tracer comes as a sedan and wagon in base trim. The Pony and LX Escorts and base Tracers continue with an 88-horsepower Ford 1.9-liter four. A 5-speed manual transmission is standard and a 4-speed overdrive automatic is optional with both engines. Power windows are a new option for all Escorts except the 3-doors, and the Pony Comfort Group, added as a running change during the 1991 model year, makes air conditioning and power steering available for the first time on the entry-level model. Escort and Tracer

Specifications	3-door hatchback	5-door hatchback	4-door notchback	5-door wagon
Wheelbase, in.	98.4	98.4	98.4	98.4
Overall length, in.	170.0	170.0	170.9	171.3
Overall width, in.	66.7	66.7	66.7	66.7
Overall height, in.	52.5	52.5	52.7	53.6
Curb weight, lbs.	2312	2355	2364	2411
Cargo vol., cu. ft.	35.2	36.0	12.1	66.9
Fuel capacity, gals.	11.9	11.9	11.9	11.9
Seating capacity	5	5	5	5
Front head room, in. . . .	38.4	38.4	38.4	38.4
Front leg room, max., in. .	41.7	41.7	41.7	41.7
Rear head room, in.	37.6	37.6	37.4	38.5
Rear leg room, min., in. . .	34.6	34.6	34.6	34.6

Powertrain layout: transverse front engine/front-wheel drive.

Engines	ohc I-4	dohc I-4
Size, liters/cu. in.	1.9/114	1.8/109
Fuel delivery	PFI	PFI
Horsepower @ rpm	88 @ 4400	127 @ 6500
Torque (lbs./ft.) @ rpm	108 @ 3800	114 @ 4500
Availability	S[1]	S[2]

EPA city/highway mpg

5-speed OD manual	30/37	26/31
4-speed OD automatic	25/35	23/30
1. Escort Pony and LX, base Tracer. 2. Escort GT and LX-E, Tracer LTS.		

Assembly points: Wayne, Mich.; Hermosillo, Mexico.

use the front-drive platform and other key mechanical components from the Mazda Protege. The current Escort is a much better car than the original version. It has adequate acceleration with the base engine and is quite lively with the Mazda 1.8-liter engine. Fuel economy is good with either. Assembly quality is above average, the interiors have adequate room for four adults, and cargo volume is good for this class in the hatchbacks and wagons.

Prices

Ford Escort	Retail Price	Dealer Invoice	Low Price
Pony 3-door hatchback	$8355	$7723	$8023
LX 3-door hatchback	9055	8197	8497
GT 3-door hatchback	11871	10685	10985
LX 4-door notchback	9795	8838	—
LX-E 4-door notchback	11933	10740	—
LX 5-door hatchback	9483	8559	8859
LX 5-door wagon	10067	9080	9380
Destination charge	375	375	375

Low price on 4-door notchbacks not available at time of publication.

Standard equipment:

Pony: 1.9-liter PFI 4-cylinder engine, 5-speed manual transmission, motorized front shoulder belts, cloth and vinyl reclining bucket seats, one-piece folding rear seatback, tinted glass, coolant temperature gauge, trip odometer, intermittent wipers, cargo cover, door pockets, right visor mirror, 175/70R13 tires. **LX adds:** upgraded upholstery, 60/40 split rear seatback, console storage bin and cupholders, AM/FM radio, bodyside molding, full wheel covers. **Sedan adds:** tachometer, intermittent wipers, 175/65R14 tires. **GT/LX-E adds:** 1.8-liter DOHC 16-valve engine, power steering, 4-wheel disc brakes, sport suspension, tachometer, cloth sport seats, AM/FM cassette, Light Group, lighted visor mirrors, removable cupholder tray, remote fuel door and hatch releases, power mirrors, variable-intermittent wipers, fog lights (except sedan), rear spoiler, rocker panel cladding, 185/60HR15 tires on alloy wheels. **Sedan** has 185/60R14 tires.

Optional equipment:

4-speed automatic transmission	732	622	641
Air conditioning, LX & GT	759	645	664
Power steering, LX	261	222	228
Pony Comfort Group	841	715	736
Air conditioning, power steering.			

Prices are accurate at time of publication; subject to manufacturer's change.

	Retail Price	Dealer Invoice	Low Price
Preferred Pkg. 320A, LX	248	210	217
Power steering, Light/Convenience Group, rear defogger.			
Preferred Pkg. 325A, LX-E	554	471	485
Rear defogger, air conditioning, tilt steering column, cruise control.			
Preferred Pkg. 330A, GT	554	471	485
Air conditioning, rear defogger, Luxury Convenience Group.			
Cayman Decor Group, GT	274	233	240
Clearcoat paint, specific alloy wheels, leather-wrapped steering wheel, Cayman-colored accents on seats, doors and floormats.			
Rear defogger	170	144	149
Light/Convenience Group, LX	317	269	277
Light Group, power mirrors, remote fuel door and hatch releases, removable tray with cup holders.			
Light Group/Removable Cupholder Tray . .	118	100	103
Removable cupholder tray, dual map, cargo area, underhood and ignition key lights, headlights-on warning chime, illuminated visor mirrors.			
Luxury Convenience Group, LX 3- and 5-door,			
wagon	428	364	375
4-door & GT	369	314	323
Tilt steering column, cruise control, tachometer, power locks.			
Power Equipment Group, 4-door, Wagon			
w/Luxury Convenience Group	296	252	259
Wagon w/o Luxury Convenience Group . .	355	302	311
Power windows and locks, tachometer.			
Power mirrors	98	83	86
Power moonroof, LX, LX-E, GT	549	466	480
Remote duel door/liftgate releases	101	86	88
AM/FM radio, Pony	312	265	273
AM/FM cassette, Pony	467	397	409
LX	155	132	136
Premium sound system	138	117	121
Radio delete (credit), LX	(312)	(265)	(265)
LX-E & GT (credit)	(467)	(397)	(397)
Wagon Group	250	212	219
Luggage rack, rear wiper/washer.			
Clearcoat paint	91	77	80
Engine block heater	20	17	18
California emissions pkg.	72	61	63

Mercury Tracer

	Retail Price	Dealer Invoice	Low Price
4-door notchback	$9773	$8828	$9128
5-door wagon	10794	9737	10037
LTS 4-door notchback	12023	10831	11131
Destination charge	375	375	375

Standard equipment:

1.9-liter PFI 4-cylinder engine, 5-speed manual transmission, motorized front shoulder belts, cloth reclining front bucket seats, 60/40 split rear seatback, AM/FM radio, tachometer, coolant temperature gauge, right seatback pocket, tinted glass, 175/70R13 tires. **Wagon** adds: power steering, variable intermittent wipers, remote fuel door release, power mirrors, rear defogger, cargo cover, rear wiper/washer, 175/65R14 tires, full wheel covers. **LTS** adds: 1.8-liter DOHC 16-valve engine, 4-wheel disc brakes, sport suspension, tilt steering column, AM/FM cassette, remote decklid release, Light Group, driver's seat tilt adjustment, cruise control, center console with removable tray, leather-wrapped steering wheel, 185/60R14 82H tires on alloy wheels.

Optional equipment:	Retail Price	Dealer Invoice	Low Price
4-speed automatic transmission	732	622	641
Requires power steering.			
Power steering, base 4-door	261	222	228
Air conditioning	759	645	664
Requires power steering.			
Preferred Pkg. 572A, base 4-door	543	460	475
Wagon	116	98	102
Power steering, intermittent wipers, remote fuel door and decklid releases, power mirrors, rear defogger, Light Group, full wheel covers.			
Preferred Pkg. 573A, base 4-door	1234	1046	1080
Wagon	657	557	575
Pkg. 572A plus air conditioning, driver's seat tilt adjustment, tilt steering column.			
Rear defogger, base	170	144	149
Remote fuel door release, base	41	35	36
Remote decklid release, base	60	51	53
Driver's seat tilt adjustment, base	37	31	32
Light Group, base	116	98	102
Tilt steering column, base	145	123	127
Cruise control, base	224	191	196
Power windows	330	281	289
Power mirrors, base 4-door	98	83	86
Power locks	205	174	179
Intermittent wipers, base 4-door	65	55	57
Luggage rack, wagon	115	97	101
Cassette player, base	155	132	136
Premium sound system	138	117	121
Requires cassette player.			
Power moonroof (NA wagon)	549	466	480
AM/FM delete, base (credit)	(312)	(265)	(265)
AM/FM cassette delete, LTS (credit)	(467)	(397)	(397)
175/65R14 tires, base 4-door	132	112	116
Engine block heater	20	17	18

Prices are accurate at time of publication; subject to manufacturer's change.

Ford Explorer/Mazda Navajo

Ford Explorer Eddie Bauer 5-door

The Explorer sport-utility—the best selling vehicle in its class—enters its second model year with minor equipment changes. The Explorer comes in 3- and 5-door body styles, while the Mazda Navajo comes only as a 3-door. The Navajo is built for Mazda by Ford and is identical to the Explorer except for minor appearance differences and interior trim. The only engine for all models is a 4.0-liter V-6. Ford says the V-6 produces 145 horsepower with a 5-speed manual transmission and 160 with the optional 4-speed overdrive automatic. Mazda says it makes 155 horsepower in the Navajo with either transmission. All are available with rear-wheel drive or Touch-Drive, a part-time 4-wheel-drive system with automatic locking front hubs and shift on the fly. The standard anti-lock rear brakes operate in 2WD only. On the Explorer, Sport and XLT versions get a standard rear wiper/washer and deep-tinted privacy glass for 5-door models is supposed to be added as an option during the year. At Mazda, there are two trim levels this year—DX and LX—instead of one. Explorer leaped to the head of the sport-utility sales race within months of its introduction as an early 1991 model—and with good reason. Roomy and versatile, with a strong, responsive engine and civilized on-road manners, it strikes a good balance between car-like accommodations and truck-like toughness. We especially like the 5-door model. The ride can be a bit bouncy on wavy surfaces, but a high level of overall comfort is due in large measure to having one of the longest wheelbases in the compact 4 × 4 class. Test drive Explorer before buying anything else in this class.

Specifications

	3-door wagon	5-door wagon
Wheelbase, in.	102.1	111.9
Overall length, in.	174.4	184.3
Overall width, in.	70.2	70.2
Overall height, in.	67.5	67.3
Curb weight, lbs.	3854	4046
Cargo vol., cu. ft.	69.4	81.6
Fuel capacity, gals.	19.0	19.0
Seating capacity	4	6
Front head room, in.	39.9	39.9
Front leg room, max., in.	42.4	42.4
Rear head room, in.	39.0	39.1
Rear leg room, min., in.	35.6	36.6

Powertrain layout: longitudinal front engine/rear-wheel drive or on-demand 4-wheel drive.

Engines

	ohv V-6
Size, liters/cu. in.	4.0/245
Fuel delivery	PFI
Horsepower @ rpm	160 @ 4400[1]
Torque (lbs./ft.) @ rpm	225 @ 2400
Availability	S

EPA city/highway mpg

5-speed OD manual	17/21
4-speed OD automatic	15/19

1. 145 @ 3800 with manual trans.

Assembly point: Louisville, Ky.

Prices

Ford Explorer	Retail Price	Dealer Invoice	Low Price
XL 3-door wagon, 2WD	$15854	$14192	$14542
XL 3-door wagon, 4WD	17644	15766	16116

Prices are accurate at time of publication; subject to manufacturer's change.

	Retail Price	Dealer Invoice	Low Price
Sport 3-door wagon, 2WD	17000	15200	15550
Sport 3-door wagon, 4WD	18731	16723	17073
Eddie Bauer 3-door wagon, 2WD	20428	18217	18567
Eddie Bauer 3-door wagon, 4WD	22159	19740	20090
XL 5-door wagon, 2WD	16692	14929	15679
XL 5-door wagon, 4WD	18505	16524	17274
XLT 5-door wagon, 2WD	18647	16649	17399
XLT 5-door wagon, 4WD	20401	18193	18943
Eddie Bauer 5-door wagon, 2WD	21798	19422	20172
Eddie Bauer 5-door wagon, 4WD	23553	20967	21717
Destination charge	485	485	485

Standard equipment:

XL: 4.0-liter PFI V-6, 5-speed manual transmission, anti-lock rear brakes, power steering, Touch Drive electronic shift (4WD), knitted vinyl front bucket seats, split folding rear seat, tinted glass, flip-open opera windows (3-door), intermittent wipers, dual outside mirrors, carpet, load floor tiedown hooks, rear seat heat duct, tachometer, coolant temperature gauge, trip odometer, AM/FM radio, 225/70R15 tires with full-size spare. **Sport** adds: rear quarter privacy glass (2-door adds rear window privacy glass), rear wiper/washer, rear defogger, Light Group, map light, load floor tiedown net, cargo area cover, leather- wrapped steering wheel, lighted visor mirrors, alloy wheels. **XLT** adds: cloth captain's chairs, floor console, power mirrors, upgraded door panels with pockets, power windows and locks, cruise control, tilt steering column, full privacy glass (4-door; 2-door has rear window privacy glass), floormats. **Eddie Bauer** adds to Sport: premium captain's chairs, floor console, power mirrors, power windows and locks, cruise control, tilt steering column, roof rack, upgraded door panels with pockets, floormats, garment bag, duffle bag, Ford Care maintenance and warranty program.

Optional equipment:

4-speed automatic transmission	890	757	788
Limited-slip rear axle	252	215	223
Air conditioning	780	663	690
w/manual transmission	NC	NC	NC
Preferred Pkg. 931A, Sport 2-door	602	512	533
Air conditioning, power windows and locks, power mirrors, cloth captain's chairs, outlined white letter tires.			
Preferred Pkg. 932A, Eddie Bauer 2-door .	NC	NC	NC
Air conditioning, premium cassette player.			
Preferred Pkg. 941A, XLT w/automatic ...	435	370	385
XLT w/5-speed	NC	NC	NC
Air conditioning, striping, premium cassette player.			
Preferred Pkg. 942A, Eddie Bauer	480	408	425
Air conditioning, premium cassette player.			

	Retail Price	Dealer Invoice	Low Price
Cloth captain's chairs, XL, Sport	274	233	242
Cloth 60/40 split bench seat, XL 5-door . .	232	197	205
XLT (credit)	(43)	(36)	(36)
Cloth sport bucket seats, Sport	1022	869	904
XLT	956	813	846
XLT, Sport w/captain's chairs	748	635	662
Leather sport seats, XLT	1434	1219	1269
XLT	1368	1163	1211
XLT, Sport w/captain's chairs	1160	986	1027
Eddie Bauer w/automatic transmission .	412	350	365
Eddie Bauer w/manual transmission . . .	NC	NC	NC
Super engine cooling	56	48	50
Privacy glass	226	192	200
Manual locking hubs, 4WD (credit)	(104)	(88)	(88)
Light Group	29	25	26
Bodyside molding	121	103	107
Power Equipment Group, Sport	620	527	549
Luggage rack	126	107	112
w/manual transmission	NC	NC	NC
Tilt-up air roof	250	213	221
Cruise control & tilt steering column	383	325	339
w/manual transmission	NC	NC	NC
Alloy wheels, XL 2WD	326	277	289
XL 4WD	265	225	235
Sport	NC	NC	NC
XLT/Eddie Bauer	NC	NC	NC
Deluxe wheels w/trim rings, 2WD	61	52	54
Trailer Towing Pkg.	106	90	94
Rear defogger & wiper/washer	279	237	247
AM/FM cassette	122	104	108
Premium AM/FM cassette	200	170	177
w/manual transmission	NC	NC	NC
Ford JBL Audio System	688	585	609
Upgrade from premium cassette	488	415	432
Ford JBL Audio System w/CD player	983	835	870
Upgrade from premium cassette	783	665	693
Cargo area cover	80	68	71
Engine block heater	33	28	29
Deluxe tape stripe, 5-door	55	47	49
Deluxe two-tone paint	122	104	108
All-terrain tires	228	194	202
Floormats	46	39	41

Mazda Navajo

DX 3-door 2WD wagon	$15795	—	—
LX 3-door 2WD wagon	17495	—	—

Prices are accurate at time of publication; subject to manufacturer's change.

	Retail Price	Dealer Invoice	Low Price
DX 3-door 4WD wagon	17595	—	—
LX 3-door 4WD wagon	19295	—	—
Destination charge	490	490	490

Dealer invoice and low price not available at time of publication.

Standard equipment:

DX: 4.0-liter PFI V-6, 5-speed manual transmission, anti-lock rear brakes, power steering, cloth reclining front bucket seats, split folding rear seat, intermittent wipers, tinted glass, power mirrors, AM/FM radio, skid plates, 225/70R15 tires. **LX** adds: power windows and locks, privacy glass, upgraded upholstery, bodyside moldings, alloy wheels.

Optional equipment:

4-speed automatic transmission, LX	870	740	785
DX Special Pkg.	595	—	—
Air conditioning, cassette player, floor console with armrest, bodyside moldings, 235/75R15 all-terrain tires.			
LX Leather Pkg.	3770	NA	NA
Automatic transmission, leather upholstery, LX Premium Pkg., Towing Pkg., luggage rack, power driver's seat; requires LX Premium Pkg.			
LX Premium Pkg., w/5-speed	1100	—	—
w/automatic	1400	—	—
Air conditioning, cassette player, removable glass moonroof, cruise control, tilt steering column, sport front seats with power lumbar and adjustable side bolsters, rear defogger and wiper/washer, console with armrest, floormats, 235/75R15 all-terrain tires.			
Towing Pkg., LX	325	—	—
Performance axle, upgraded engine cooling, trailer wiring harness, limited-slip differential; requires automatic transmission.			
Luggage rack, LX	125	107	113
Florrmats, DX	65	—	—
California emissions pkg.	100	—	—

Ford Festiva

A new appearance option package leads the short list of changes to Ford's front-drive mini-compact. Festiva is a 3-door hatchback designed by Mazda and built for Ford by Kia Motors in South Korea. It comes in L and GL trim, both with a 63-horsepower 1.3-liter 4-cylinder engine and a 5-speed manual transmission. A 3-speed automatic is

Ford Festiva GL

Specifications

	3-door hatchback
Wheelbase, in.	90.2
Overall length, in.	140.5
Overall width, in.	63.2
Overall height, in.	55.3
Curb weight, lbs.	1797
Cargo vol., cu. ft.	26.5
Fuel capacity, gals.	10.0
Seating capacity	4
Front head room, in.	38.6
Front leg room, max., in.	40.6
Rear head room, in.	37.4
Rear leg room, min., in.	35.7

Powertrain layout: transverse front engine/front-wheel drive.

Engines

	ohc I-4
Size, liters/cu. in.	1.3/81
Fuel delivery	PFI
Horsepower @ rpm	63 @ 5000
Torque (lbs./ft.) @ rpm	73 @ 3000
Availability	S

EPA city/highway mpg

5-speed OD manual	35/41
3-speed automatic	31/33

Assembly point: Seoul, South Korea.

Prices are accurate at time of publication; subject to manufacturer's change.

optional only on the GL. The GL this year gets standard alloy wheels. The GL previously was available with power steering, but that option is dropped for 1992, along with the L model's optional rear wiper. New for the Festiva is the Sport Appearance Package. It includes cloth trim on the seats and doors, a rear spoiler, and a choice of six different tape-stripe graphics. As one of the lightest cars sold in the U.S., Festiva needs only a tiny 1.3-liter engine that returns great fuel economy. However, the engine is short of power and too noisy at higher speeds. We're sorry to see the optional power steering axed because the manual steering is heavy at parking speeds. In corners, the body leans mightily and the front tires squeal and plow because of the tall design, forward weight bias, and skinny 12-inch tires. There's adequate room for adults up front, not enough in the rear. Cargo room behind the back seat is minimal and even with the rear seatback folded it's mediocre. With its low price and high fuel economy, Festiva is economical around-town transportation, but look for something more substantial if you do a lot of highway driving.

Prices

Ford Festiva	Retail Price	Dealer Invoice	Low Price
L 3-door hatchback	$6941	$6540	$6741
GL 3-door hatchback	7980	7504	7742
Destination charge	295	295	295

Standard equipment:

L: 1.3-liter PFI 4-cylinder engine, 5-speed manual transmission, motorized front shoulder belts, cloth and vinyl reclining front bucket seats, folding rear seatback, coolant temperature gauge, locking fuel door, bodyside molding, 145SR12 tires. **GL** adds: AM/FM radio, rear wiper/washer, cargo cover, door pockets, right outside mirror, 165/70SR12 tires on alloy wheels.

Optional equipment:

3-speed automatic transmission, GL	515	437	451
Air conditioning, GL	863	734	755
Rear defogger	170	144	149
AM/FM radio, L	312	265	273
AM/FM cassette, L	467	397	409
GL	155	132	136
Flip-up air roof	243	206	213

	Retail Price	Dealer Invoice	Low Price
Sports Appearance Pkg	341	290	298

Sport cloth seat and door trim, rear spoiler, tape stripes.

California emissions	72	61	63

Ford Mustang

Ford Mustang GT 3-door

An optional 4-way power driver's seat is a new option for Ford's "pony-car" and color-keyed body moldings and bumper rub strips are added to the LX model. The Mustang is otherwise the same as last year. Base LX models come in 2-door coupe, 3-door hatchback, and 2-door convertible styling with a 105-horsepower 2.3-liter 4-cylinder engine. The LX 5.0L shares with the Mustang GT a 5.0-liter V-8 rated at 225 horsepower. The LX 5.0L comes in all three body styles, the GT only in the 3-door and convertible body styles. A 5-speed manual transmission is standard with both engines and a 4-speed overdrive automatic is optional. The LX 5.0L uses the GT's sport suspension, alloy wheels, and 16-inch tires, but lacks its aero-body flares and spoilers. A driver-side air bag is standard on all. The current Mustang design dates to the 1979 model year, though there have been major styling and mechanical changes since. It is expected to get fresh sheetmetal for 1993 to answer a

Prices are accurate at time of publication; subject to manufacturer's change.

redesign of the Chevrolet Camaro and Pontiac Firebird. These are the only affordable survivors of an era in which rear-wheel drive and V-8 engines ruled. Four-cylinder Mustangs have adequate power, but V-8 LXs and GTs outsell them 2-to-1, so it's clear what the attraction is here. A V-8 Mustang, with its abundant power at all speeds, is indeed the best of this breed—if you can live with its drawbacks. They include: a jarring ride; terrible traction on wet surfaces due to its rear-drive design and wide tires; poor fuel economy; and braking ability that doesn't match the engine's ability to accelerate.

Specifications

	2-door notchback	3-door hatchback	2-door conv.
Wheelbase, in.	100.5	100.5	100.5
Overall length, in.	179.6	179.6	179.6
Overall width, in.	68.3	68.3	68.3
Overall height, in.	52.1	52.1	52.1
Curb weight, lbs.	2775	2834	2996
Cargo vol., cu. ft.	10.0	30.0	6.4
Fuel capacity, gals.	15.4	15.4	15.4
Seating capacity	4	4	4
Front head room, in.	37.0	37.0	37.6
Front leg room, max., in.	41.7	41.7	41.7
Rear head room, in.	35.9	35.7	37.0
Rear leg room, min., in.	30.7	30.7	30.7

Powertrain layout: longitudinal front engine/rear-wheel drive.

Engines	ohc I-4	ohv V-8
Size, liters/cu. in.	2.3/140	5.0/302
Fuel delivery	PFI	PFI
Horsepower @ rpm	105 @ 4600	225 @ 4200
Torque (lbs./ft.) @ rpm	135 @ 2600	300 @ 3200
Availability	S[1]	S[2]

EPA city/highway mpg		
5-speed OD manual	22/30	17/24
4-speed OD automatic	21/28	18/25

1. LX.   2. LX 5.0L, GT.

Assembly point: Dearborn, Mich.

Prices

Ford Mustang

	Retail Price	Dealer Invoice	Low Price
LX 2-door notchback	$10215	$9261	$9511
LX 3-door hatchback	10721	9712	9962
LX 2-door convertible	16899	15210	15460
LX 5.0L 2-door notchback	13422	12116	12516
LX 5.0L 3-door hatchback	14207	12814	13214
LX 5.0L 2-door convertible	19644	17653	18053
GT 3-door hatchback	15243	13736	14136
GT 2-door convertible	20199	18147	18547
Destination charge	440	440	440

Standard equipment:

LX: 2.3-liter PFI 4-cylinder engine, 5-speed manual transmission, variable-assist power steering, driver-side air bag, cloth reclining front bucket seats, split folding rear seat (hatchback), tachometer, coolant temperature and oil pressure gauges, voltmeter, trip odometer, remote mirrors, cargo arear cover (hatchback), console with amrest, intermittent wipers, tinted glass, visor mirrors, AM/FM radio, 195/75R14 tires; convertibles have power windows, locks, and mirrors. **LX 5.0L** adds: 5.0-liter PFI V-8 with dual exhaust, Traction-Lok axle, handling suspension, articulated sport seats with power lumbar adjustment, leather-wrapped steering wheel, lighted visor mirrors, 225/55ZR16 all-season performance tires on alloy wheels. **GT** adds: front air dam with fog lamps, rear spoiler, sill extensions; tires are not all-season, but all-season tread may be substituted at no charge.

Optional equipment:

4-speed automatic transmission	595	506	536
Air conditioning	817	695	735
Preferred Pkg. 240A, LX exc. conv.	276	235	248
LX conv.	122	104	110

Power windows and locks, power mirrors, remote decklid/hatch release, cruise control, cassette player, styled road wheels.

Preferred Pkg. 245A, LX 5.0L	551	469	496
V-8 conv.	NC	NC	NC

Power windows and locks, power mirrors, remote decklid/hatch release, cruise control, cassette player with premium sound.

Preferred Pkg. 249A, GT exc. conv.	1367	1163	1230
GT conv.	763	650	687

Power windows and locks, power mirrors, remote decklid/hatch release, cruise control, cassette player with premium sound, air conditioning, trunk cargo net, front floormats.

Convenience Group	99	84	89

Trunk cargo net, front floormats.

Prices are accurate at time of publication; subject to manufacturer's change.

	Retail Price	Dealer Invoice	Low Price
Leather upholstery, LX 5.0L & GT	523	445	471
Rear defogger, exc. conv.	170	144	153
Premium sound system	168	143	151
Premium sound w/graphic EQ	307	261	276
Graphic EQ	139	118	125
Requires Premium Sound Package.			
V-8s with Preferred Pkg. 245A/249A ..	139	118	125
Cassette player	155	132	140
Power Equipment Group (std. conv.)	604	513	544
Power windows and locks, power mirrors, remote decklid/hatch release.			
Power driver's seat	183	155	165
Flip-up air roof, hatchbacks	355	302	320
Cruise control	224	191	202
Illuminated visor mirrors	100	85	90
Titanium lower accent treatment, GT	159	135	143
Alloy wheels, LX	401	341	361
w/Pkg. 240A	208	177	187
Styled road wheels, LX	193	164	174
Clearcoat paint	91	78	82
Vinyl seat trim, LX	76	64	68
Engine block heater	20	17	18
California emissions pkg.	100	85	90

Ford Probe

Ford Probe LX

A new Sport Option Package for the LX model is the major change for this front-drive 3-door coupe. Probe's exterior and interior were designed by Ford, but the car borrows its platform and most mechanical features from the Mazda MX-6. Both are built at Mazda's plant in Michigan. The base Probe GL returns with a 110-horsepower 2.2-liter 4-cylinder engine. The GT comes with a turbocharged version of the 2.2 and the LX with a 3.0-liter V-6, both rated at 145 horsepower. Mazda builds the 4-cylinder engines, Ford makes the V-6. A 5-speed manual transmission is standard with all engines and a 4-speed overdrive automatic is optional. Anti-lock brakes are optional on the LX and GT. The LX's new Sport Option Package includes a rear spoiler and 205/60HR15 tires on new alloy wheels. Both the LX and GT lose some previously standard equipment to the options list, including a rear defogger; intermittent wipers;

Specifications

	3-door hatchback
Wheelbase, in.	99.0
Overall length, in.	177.0
Overall width, in.	67.9
Overall height, in.	51.8
Curb weight, lbs.	2730
Cargo vol., cu. ft.	41.9
Fuel capacity, gals.	15.1
Seating capacity	4
Front head room, in.	37.3
Front leg room, max., in.	42.5
Rear head room, in.	35.0
Rear leg room, min., in.	29.9

Powertrain layout: transverse front engine/front-wheel drive.

Engines	ohc I-4	Turbo ohc I-4	ohv V-6
Size, liters/cu. in.	2.2/133	2.2/133	3.0/182
Fuel delivery	PFI	PFI	PFI
Horsepower @ rpm	110 @ 4700	145 @ 4300	145 @ 4800
Torque (lbs./ft.) @ rpm	130 @ 3000	190 @ 3500	165 @ 3400
Availability	S[1]	S[2]	S[3]
EPA city/highway mpg			
5-speed OD manual	24/31	21/27	19/26
4-speed OD automatic	21/28	19/25	18/24

1. GL.   2. GT.   3. LX.

Assembly point: Flat Rock, Mich.

Prices are accurate at time of publication; subject to manufacturer's change.

power mirrors; tinted glass; and a tilt steering column. GL and LX models gain body-colored side moldings and monotone fascia/bumper covers. Introduced as a 1989 model, Probe is scheduled to be redesigned for 1993 and will remain a 3-door hatchback based on Mazda mechanicals. The LX is our favorite Probe. The V-6 has satisfying acceleration and works better with automatic transmission than the 4-cylinder engines, though the automatic shifts harshly with all three engines. The sports coupe market is extremely competitive and the Probe's 3-year-old styling no longer turns heads like it did at first. That means Ford dealers should be willing to cut their prices.

Prices

Ford Probe	Retail Price	Dealer Invoice	Low Price
GL 3-door hatchback	$12257	$11074	$11374
LX 3-door hatchback	13257	11964	12264
GT 3-door hatchback	14857	13388	13688
Destination charge	330	330	330

Standard equipment:

GL: 2.2-liter PFI 4-cylinder engine, 5-speed manual transmission, power steering, motorized front shoulder belts, cloth reclining front bucket seats with driver's-seat height adjustment, split folding rear seat, tachometer, coolant temperature and oil pressure gauges, ammeter, trip odometer, tinted backlight and quarter windows, right visor mirror, cargo area cover, center console, left remote and right manual mirrors, AM/FM radio, 185/70R14 tires. **LX** adds: 3.0-liter PFI V-6, 4-wheel disc brakes, full console with armrest and storage, overhead console with map light, door pockets, driver's adjustable lumbar support and side bolsters, lighted visor mirrors, remote fuel door and hatch releases, 195/70R154 tires. **GT** adds: 2.2-liter turbocharged engine, handling suspension, automatic adjusting suspension, front air dam with foglamps, rear spoiler, sill extensions, visor mirrors, 205/60VR15 tires on alloy wheels.

Optional equipment:

4-speed automatic transmission	732	622	633
Anti-lock brakes, LX & GT	595	506	515
Air conditioning, GL w/o tinted glass	937	796	811
Others	817	695	707
Automatic climate control, LX & GT	1000	850	865

	Retail Price	Dealer Invoice	Low Price
Preferred Pkg. 251A, GL	308	261	266
Tinted glass, tilt steering column and instrument cluster, rear defogger, power mirrors, intermittent wipers, Light Group.			
Preferred Pkg. 253A, LX	1842	1565	1593
Pkg. 261A, GT	1397	1187	1208
Air conditioning, power windows and locks, cruise control, cassette player with premium sound and power antenna, illuminated entry, lighted visor mirror, walk-in passenger seat, rear wiper/washer, cargo tiedown net.			
Sport Option Pkg., LX	445	378	385
Rear spoiler, 205/60HR15 tires on alloy wheels.			
Convenience Group I, GL	213	181	184
Power mirrors, intermittent wipers, Light Group.			
Convenience Group II, LX & GT	323	275	279
GL	188	160	163
Walk-in passenger seat, rear wiper/washer, cargo tiedown net.			
Rear defogger, GL	170	144	147
Illuminated entry, LX & GT	82	69	71
Electronic instruments	463	394	400
Includes Vehicle Maintenance Monitor, overhead console with maplights.			
Tinted glass, GL	120	102	104
Power locks	210	178	182
Power driver's seat, LX & GT	305	259	264
Leather seats, LX & GT	523	445	452
Power windows and locks, LX & GT	485	413	420
Cassette player	372	316	322
Cassette & CD players	1080	918	934
LX & GT w/Pkg. 253A/261A	709	602	613
Optional audio systems include premium sound and power antenna.			
Radio delete (credit), GL	(245)	(208)	(208)
Flip-up air roof	355	302	307
Tilt steering column & instrument cluster . .	205	174	177
Cruise control	224	191	202
Trip computer, LX & GT	215	182	194
Alloy wheels & 195/70HR14 tires, GL . . .	313	266	282
w/205/60HR15 tires, LX	376	319	338

Ford Taurus/Mercury Sable

Ford Motor Company's front-drive intermediates are re-styled and have a new dashboard with an optional passenger-side air bag. Most sheetmetal on the Taurus and Sable is new for 1992, yet the differences are hardly obvious. Interior dimensions and the wheelbase are unchanged, but the 4-door sedans are about 3.5 inches longer and the 5-door

Prices are accurate at time of publication; subject to manufacturer's change.

Ford Taurus LX

wagons about 1.2 inches longer. The 2.5-liter 4-cylinder engine has been dropped from the Taurus line, leaving a choice of 3.0- and 3.8-liter V-6s, both rated at 140 horsepower for Taurus and Sable. A 4-speed overdrive automatic is the only transmission available with these engines. The high-performance Taurus SHO keeps its Yamaha-built 220-horsepower 3.0 V-6 and 5-speed manual transmission. The new passenger-side air bag, optional on all models, joins the standard driver-side air bag. The electronic gauge cluster has been dropped as a Taurus option but remains available on the Sable. The optional Insta-Clear heated windshield has been dropped from both. Anti-lock brakes remain standard on the SHO and optional on the others. Solid, roomy, and pleasant to drive, Taurus and Sable remain excellent choices among mid-size cars. No other cars in this class are available with both passenger- and driver-side air bags. Some competitors, including the Honda Accord, don't make anti-lock brakes available on all models. The 3.0-liter V-6 has adequate performance and the 3.8-liter V-6 gives stronger acceleration and passing power by virtue of having more torque. Neither engine is a fuel miser. The Taurus L starts at nearly $15,000 and the Sable GS at more than $16,000—considerably more than a few years ago—but both models should be carrying rebates, low-rate financing, or other incentives that will reduce selling prices.

Specifications

	4-door notchback	5-door wagon
Wheelbase, in.	106.0	106.0
Overall length, in.	192.0	193.1
Overall width, in.	71.2	71.2
Overall height, in.	54.1	55.5
Curb weight, lbs.	3131	3294
Cargo vol., cu. ft.	17.9	81.1
Fuel capacity, gals.	16.0	16.0
Seating capacity	6	8
Front head room, in.	38.3	38.6
Front leg room, max., in.	41.7	41.7
Rear head room, in.	37.6	38.1
Rear leg room, min., in.	37.5	36.7

Powertrain layout: transverse front engine/front-wheel drive.

Engines	ohv V-6	ohv V-6	dohc V-6
Size, liters/cu. in.	3.0/182	3.8/232	3.0/182
Fuel delivery	PFI	PFI	PFI
Horsepower @ rpm	140 @ 4800	140 @ 3800	220 @ 6200
Torque (lbs./ft.) @ rpm	160 @ 3000	215 @ 2200	200 @ 4800
Availability	S[1]	O[2]	S[3]

EPA city/highway mpg

5-speed OD manual			18/26
4-speed OD automatic	20/29	18/28	

1. Taurus L, GL, LX sdn.   2. Std., Taurus LX wgn.   3. Taurus SHO.

Assembly points: Atlanta, Ga.; Chicago, Ill.

Prices

Ford Taurus	Retail Price	Dealer Invoice	Low Price
L 4-door notchback	$14980	$12908	$13283
GL 4-door notchback	15280	13163	13538
LX 4-door notchback	17775	15282	15657
SHO 4-door notchback	23889	20438	20813
L 5-door wagon	16013	13786	14161
GL 5-door wagon	16290	14022	14397
LX 5-door wagon	19464	16718	17093
Destination charge	490	490	490

Prices are accurate at time of publication; subject to manufacturer's change.

Standard equipment:

L: 3.0-liter PFI V-6, 4-speed automatic transmission, power steering, driver-side air bag, cloth reclining split bench seat with dual center armrests, tilt steering column, power mirrors, tinted glass, intermittent wipers, cup/coin holder, door pockets, AM/FM radio, 205/70R14 tires. **GL** adds: visor mirrors, striping. **LX** adds: (3.8-liter V-6 on wagon), air conditioning, power windows and locks, power driver's seat, power front lumbar supports, variable-assist power steering, remote fuel door and decklid releases, tachometer, diagnostic alert lights, automatic parking brake release, automatic on/off headlamps, cornering lamps, bodyside cladding, Convenience Kit (vinyl pouch with fluorescent lantern, tire pressure gauge, gloves, poncho, shop towel, distress flag, headlamp bulb), Light Group, cargo tiedown net, 205/65R15 tires on alloy wheels. **SHO** deletes automatic parking brake release and remote fuel door and decklid releases. **SHO** adds: 3.0-liter DOHC 24-valve V-6 with dual exhaust, anti-lock 4-wheel disc brakes, foglamps, front bucket seats with console, high-level audio system, power antenna, leather-wrapped steering wheel, rear defogger, cruise control, floormats, 215/60VR16 tires on alloy wheels.

Optional equipment:

	Retail Price	Dealer Invoice	Low Price
3.8-liter V-6 (std. LX wgn, NA on L)	555	472	488
Anti-lock brakes (std. SHO)	595	506	524
Passenger-side air bag	488	415	429
Manual air conditioning, L & GL	841	715	740
Automatic air conditioning, LX & SHO . . .	183	155	161
Preferred Pkg. 203A (L Plus), L	686	582	604
Air conditioning, rear defogger.			
Preferred Pkg. 204A, GL	2023	1720	1780
Air conditioning, rear defogger, power windows and locks, power driver's seat, remote fuel door release, remote decklid release (4-door), Light Group, cassette player, cruise control, floormats, deluxe wheel covers, cargo tiedown net.			
Preferred Pkg. 208B, LX 4-door	454	386	400
LX wagon	655	557	576
Rear defogger, cruise control, cassette player, power antenna, keyless entry, leather-wrapped steering wheel, floormats. Wagons add: cargo area cover, picnic table load floor extension, rear wiper/washer.			
Preferred Pkg. 211A, SHO	219	186	193
Keyless entry, automatic climate control.			
Luxury Convenience Group, LX	1407	1196	1238
Power front seats, power moonroof, Ford JBL audio system.			
Bucket seats w/console, GL	NC	NC	NC
Leather bucket seats w/console, GL	618	526	544
LX & SHO	515	437	453
Leather split bench seat, LX	515	437	453
AM/FM cassette (std. SHO)	171	145	150
Power antenna, LX	102	87	90

	Retail Price	Dealer Invoice	Low Price
High-level audio system, GL & LX	502	427	442
GL w/204A & 208B	332	282	292
CD player, (NA L)	491	418	432
Ford JBL audio system, L Plus, GL, LX & SHO	526	447	463
Cargo area cover, wagons	66	56	58
Cargo tiedown net (NA L)	44	37	39
Rear defogger	170	144	150
Remote fuel door & decklid release, 4-doors	101	86	89
Keyless entry, LX & SHO	146	124	128
Light Group	59	50	52
Picnic table load floor extension, GL &			
LX wagons	90	77	79
Power locks	257	219	226
Requires power windows.			
Power windows	356	303	313
Power moonroof, LX & SHO	776	659	683
Rear-facing third seat, wagons	155	132	136
Power seats, each	305	259	268
Cruise control	224	191	197
Leather-wrapped steering wheel, LX & SHO .	96	82	84
HD suspension (NA SHO)	26	22	23
Rear wiper/washer, wagons	135	115	119
Alloy wheels, GL	389	331	342
w/Pkg. 204A	239	203	210
205/65R15 tires w/wheelcovers, GL	150	128	132
Conventional spare tire (NA SHO)	73	62	64
HD battery (NA SHO)	27	23	24
Engine block heater	20	17	18
Rubber floor covering, L	27	23	24
Front floormats	33	28	29
Front & rear floormats	45	38	40
California emissions pkg.	100	85	88

Mercury Sable

	Retail Price	Dealer Invoice	Low Price
GS 4-door notchback	$16418	$14146	$14521
LS 4-door notchback	17368	14953	15328
GS 5-door wagon	17396	14977	15352
LS 5-door wagon	18395	15826	16201
Destination charge	490	490	490

Standard equipment:

3.0-liter PFI V-6, 4-speed automatic transmission, power steering, driver-side air bag, air conditioning, cloth reclining 50/50 front seat with armrests, tinted glass, intermittent wipers, tachometer, coolant temperature gauge,

Prices are accurate at time of publication; subject to manufacturer's change.

trip odometer, power mirrors, tilt steering column, AM/FM radio, slide-out cupholders and coin holder, front door pockets, rear armrest (4-door), covered package tray storage bin (4-door), visor mirrors, cargo net, 205/70R14 tires; wagon has 60/40 folding rear seat, tiedown hooks, luggage rack. **LS** adds: power windows, automatic parking brake release, remote fuel door and decklid releases, Light Group, bodyside cladding, power lumbar supports, seatback pockets, lighted visor mirrors.

Optional equipment:

	Retail Price	Dealer Invoice	Low Price
3.8-liter V-6	555	472	488
3.0-liter V-6, wagons (credit)	(555)	(472)	(472)
Passenger-side air bag	488	415	429
Anti-lock 4-wheel disc brakes	595	506	524
Automatic climate control, LS	183	155	161
Preferred Pkg. 450A, GS	838	713	737
Power windows and locks, cruise control, rear defogger.			
Preferred Pkg. 451A, GS	1258	1069	1107
Pkg. 450A plus power driver's seat, cassette player, Light Group, floormats, alloy wheels.			
Preferred Pkg. 461A, LS	1398	1189	1230
3.8-liter V-6, power driver's seat, leather-wrapped steering wheel, cruise control, rear defogger, cassette player with premium sound, power antenna, power locks, floormats, alloy wheels.			
Preferred Pkg. 462A, LS	2186	1859	1924
Pkg. 461A plus keyless entry, electronic instruments, Autolamp system, automatic climate control, High Level Audio System.			
Autolamp system, LS	73	62	64
Cargo area cover, wagons	66	56	58
Rear defogger	170	144	150
Extended-range fuel tank	46	39	40
Electronic instruments, LS	351	299	309
Includes extended-range fuel tank.			
Keyless entry, LS	228	194	201
Includes illuminated entry; requires Power Lock Group.			
Light Group, GS	59	50	52
Power Lock Group, GS	358	305	315
LS	257	219	226
Power locks, remote fuel door and decklid releases.			
Power moonroof, LS	776	659	683
Cassette player	171	145	150
High Level Audio System, GS (450A),			
LS (462A)	502	427	442
GS w/Pkg. 451A	332	282	292
LS w/Pkg. 461A	163	139	143
CD player	491	418	432
Requires High Level Audio System.			
Ford JBL sound system, 4-doors	526	447	463
High Level Audio System or CD player.			

	Retail Price	Dealer Invoice	Low Price
Premium sound system	168	143	148
Power antenna	102	87	90
AM/FM radio delete (credit)	(206)	(175)	(175)
Rear-facing third seat, wagons	155	132	136
Power front seats, each	305	259	268
Bucket seats w/console, GS	NC	NC	NC
Leather seat trim, LS	515	437	453
Vinyl seat trim, GS wagon	37	31	33
Cruise control	224	191	197
Leather-wrapped steering wheel	96	82	84
Requires cruise control.			
HD suspension	26	22	23
Rear wiper/washer, wagons	135	115	119
Requires rear defogger.			
Power windows, GS	356	303	313
Requires rear defogger.			
Picnic tray, wagons	90	77	79
Conventional spare tire	73	62	64
Alloy wheels	270	229	238

Geo Metro

Geo Metro 3-door

Revised front and rear styling and a new instrument panel
are changes for these front-drive minicompacts. The Metro
3-door hatchback comes in fuel-miser XFi trim, base trim,
and in top-line LSi guise. A 5-door hatchback, available
as a base or LSi model, adds four inches to the wheelbase
and body of the 3-door. A convertible rides the chassis of

Prices are accurate at time of publication; subject to manufacturer's change.

the 3-door, but has seats for two instead of four. All use a 1.0-liter 3-cylinder engine, rated at 52 horsepower in base and LSi Metros and 49 in the XFi. A 5-speed manual transmission is standard; a 3-speed automatic is optional on all but XFi. The convertible has a standard driver-side air bag and manual folding cloth top. The hatchbacks have automatic front seat belts. Built by Suzuki, the Metro is sold by Chevrolet dealers. Metro's forte is fuel economy: We averaged 38.5 mpg primarily from rush-hour commuting with a 5-speed 3-door. The hatchbacks are the lightest cars sold in America and weight-savings are evident in frail-feeling fenders and doors, thin interior panels, even the tiny wheels

Specifications	3-door hatchback	5-door hatchback	2-door conv.
Wheelbase, in.	89.2	93.1	89.2
Overall length, in.	147.4	151.4	147.4
Overall width, in.	62.0	62.0	62.7
Overall height, in.	52.4	53.5	52.0
Curb weight, lbs.	1650	1694	1753
Cargo vol., cu. ft.	29.1	31.4	6.4
Fuel capacity, gals.	10.6	10.6	10.6
Seating capacity	4	4	2
Front head room, in.	37.8	38.8	39.6
Front leg room, max., in.	42.5	42.5	42.4
Rear head room, in.	36.5	38.0	—
Rear leg room, min., in.	29.8	32.6	—

Powertrain layout: transverse front engine/front-wheel drive.

Engines	ohc I-3
Size, liters/cu. in.	1.0/61
Fuel delivery	TBI
Horsepower @ rpm	52 @ 5700[1]
Torque (lbs./ft.) @ rpm	56 @ 3300
Availability	S

EPA city/highway mpg	
5-speed OD manual	53/58
3-speed automatic	36/39

1. XFi 49 hp.

Assembly points: Kosai, Japan; Ingersoll, Ontario, Canada.

and tires. Manual-transmission Metro hatchbacks have fairly lively acceleration, but models with automatic and the heavier convertible lose some fuel economy and acceleration. The cabin is cramped for adults of more than average height, and road, wind, and engine noise are excessive. We would give strong consideration to this car—along with the similarly sized Ford Festiva and Subaru Justy—only if low prices and high fuel economy were our top priorities.

Prices

Geo Metro	Retail Price	Dealer Invoice	Low Price
XFi 3-door hatchback	$6999	$6474	$6674
Base 3-door hatchback	6999	6474	6674
Base 5-door hatchback	7399	6844	7044
LSi 3-door hatchback	8199	7584	7784
LSi 5-door hatchback	8599	7954	8154
LSi 2-door convertible	9999	9249	9550
Destination charge, hatchbacks	265	265	265
Convertible	255	255	255

Standard equipment:

XFi: 1.0-liter TBI 3-cylinder engine, 5-speed manual transmission, cloth and vinyl reclining front bucket seats, one-piece folding rear seatback, rear shoulder belts, intermittent wipers, left door pocket, 145/80R12 tires. **Base** adds: left remote and right manual mirrors, intermittent wipers, bodyside moldings, wheel covers. **LSi** adds: composite headlamps, full cloth upholstery, tachometer, trip odometer, center console, door pockets, split folding rear seatback, wheel covers, cargo security cover, remote hatch release, rear defogger, visor mirrors; **convertible** has driver-side air bag, 165/65R13 tires.

Optional equipment:

3-speed automatic transmission	495	436	443
Air conditioning	720	634	644
Preferred Group 2, hatchbacks . . . . AM/FM radio.	301	265	269
Preferred Group 3, base & LSi hatchbacks . Group 2 plus air conditioning.	1021	898	914
Preferred Group 2, convertible . . . . 3-speed automatic transmission.	495	436	443
Rear defogger, XFi & base	150	132	134

Prices are accurate at time of publication; subject to manufacturer's change.

	Retail Price	Dealer Invoice	Low Price
Rear wiper/washer, hatchbacks	125	110	112
AM/FM radio, convertible	301	265	269
AM/FM cassette, hatchbacks w/Group 2 or 3	140	123	125
Convertible	441	388	395
Front and rear floormats	25	22	22
Front only	15	13	13
Bodyside moldings, XFi	50	44	45
Cargo security cover, XFi & base	50	44	45
Dual outside mirrors, XFi	20	18	18

Geo Prizm

Geo Prizm LSi

The subcompact, front-drive Prizm, which is derived from
the Toyota Corolla, comes only as a 4-door notchback sedan
for 1992. The 5-door hatchback has been dropped. The flagship of Chevy's Geo line of captive imports, Prizm is built
alongside the Corolla at a General Motors-Toyota plant in
California. Base and sporty GSi models return, with LSi
option packages available to dress up the base versions.
The base Prizm has a 102-horsepower 1.6-liter 4-cylinder
engine and the sporty GSi a 130-horsepower version of this
engine, plus 4-wheel disc brakes and larger wheels and
tires. A 5-speed manual is standard; a 3-speed automatic
is optional with the 102-horsepower engine and a 4-speed
automatic is optional with the 130-horsepower version. The
Prizm shares with the Corolla a sound design, good assem-

bly quality, and a reputation for reliability. We can see no difference in quality between Prizms made in California and Corollas built in Japan. Prizm starts at $10,125—hardly cheap for a subcompact—and resale value of the Geo brand doesn't match Toyota's. Even so, there's good value here and Chevy dealers should be discounting prices. Prizm has good fuel economy and a supple ride for a small sedan. The base engine provides adequate acceleration and the GSi's 130-horsepower engine gives the Prizm frisky performance. The Prizm is the best small car sold by Chevrolet, thanks mainly to its Toyota heritage.

Specifications

	4-door notchback
Wheelbase, in.	95.7
Overall length, in.	170.7
Overall width, in.	65.2
Overall height, in.	52.4
Curb weight, lbs.	2435
Cargo vol., cu. ft.	12.0
Fuel capacity, gals.	13.2
Seating capacity	5
Front head room, in.	38.3
Front leg room, max., in.	40.9
Rear head room, in.	36.1
Rear leg room, min., in.	31.6

Powertrain layout: transverse front engine/front-wheel drive.

Engines

	dohc l-4	dohc l-4
Size, liters/cu. in.	1.6/97	1.6/97
Fuel delivery	PFI	PFI
Horsepower @ rpm	102 @ 5800	130 @ 6800
Torque (lbs./ft.) @ rpm	101 @ 4800	105 @ 6000
Availability	S[1]	S[2]

EPA city/highway mpg

5-speed OD manual	28/33	25/31
3-speed automatic	25/29	
4-speed OD automatic		23/30

1. Base Prizm.   2. GSi.

Assembly point: Fremont, Calif.

Prices are accurate at time of publication; subject to manufacturer's change.

Prices

Geo Prizm	Retail Price	Dealer Invoice	Low Price
4-door notchback	$10125	$9366	$9566
GSi 4-door notchback	13770	12737	12937
Destination charge	345	345	345

Standard equipment:

1.6-liter DOHC PFI 4-cylinder engine, 5-speed manual transmission, door-mounted automatic front shoulder belts, cloth reclining front bucket seats, tinted glass, door pockets, cup holders, left remote mirror, remote fuel door release, bodyside molding, 155/80R13 tires. **GSi** adds: higher-output engine, 4-wheel disc brakes, power steering, uprated suspension, air conditioning, tilt steering column, driver-seat height adjustment, split folding rear seat, tachometer and oil pressure gauge, rear spoiler, left remote and right manual mirrors, remote decklid release, rear defogger, AM/FM radio, visor mirrors, floormats, 185/60HR14 tires on alloy wheels.

Optional equipment:

3-speed automatic transmission, base & LSi	495	421	433
4-speed automatic transmission, GSi	775	659	678
Air conditioning (std. GSi)	745	633	652
Preferred Group 2, base	760	646	665
AM/FM radio, power steering, left remote and right manual mirrors, full wheel covers, 175/70SR13 tires.			
Preferred Group 3, base	1785	1517	1562
Group 2 air conditioning, power locks, remote decklid release.			
LSi Group 1, base	2628	2234	2300
Air conditioning, AM/FM radio, power steering, tachometer, power locks, tilt steering column, remote decklid release, rear defogger, cargo area lamp, full wheel covers, body-colored bumpers, custom interior, map pockets, dual outside mirrors (left remote), dual visor mirrors, split folding rear seat, 175/70SR13 tires.			
LSi Preferred Group 2, base	3143	2672	2750
Group 1 items plus power windows, cruise control, intermittent wipers.			
Preferred Group 2, GSi	735	625	643
Power windows and locks, cruise control, intermittent wipers.			
Rear defogger	105	89	92
Power sunroof	530	451	464
AM/FM cassette	140	119	123
Floormats	40	34	35
California emissions pkg.	70	60	61

Geo Storm

Geo Storm GSi

New front and rear styling and a larger standard engine for the top-line model are the changes for 1992. Storm comes as a 2+2 3-door fastback in base and sporty GSi guise, and as a 3-door hatchback with the rear roof squared off to create more back-seat head room. The latter comes only in base trim and has rear windows that can be removed for an open-air feeling. Four mini headlamps highlight the new nose and the stern sports new taillamps. On the GSi, round fog lamps replace rectangular lamps, and there's a new wing-type rear spoiler. The GSi trades its 1.6-liter 4-cylinder engine for a 1.8-liter four and gains 10 horsepower to 140. All others have a 95-horsepower 1.6-liter engine. With both engines, a 5-speed manual transmission is standard. A 3-speed automatic is optional with the 1.6-liter and a 4-speed automatic with the 1.8-liter. A driver-side air bag is standard on all models. Storm is built by Isuzu and sold through Chevrolet's Geo outlets. Isuzu is partly owned by General Motors and sells its own version of this car as the Impulse. The base engine's harsh mechanical voice is accompanied by only adequate acceleration. The GSi isn't much more muffled, but at least it packs a stronger punch. All models have nimble handling. While the firm ride can turn harsh on rough roads, Storm still absorbs bumps better than most sports coupes. Low slung seats add a sports-car flavor, but the fixed steering column

Prices are accurate at time of publication; subject to manufacturer's change.

is set too high for some drivers to be comfortable. Storm prices aren't dirt-cheap, though this car is well-equipped in standard form and there aren't many big-ticket options.

Specifications

	3-door hatchback	2+2 3-door hatchback
Wheelbase, in.	96.5	96.5
Overall length, in.	164.0	164.0
Overall width, in.	66.7	66.7
Overall height, in.	51.7	51.1
Curb weight, lbs.	2292	2357
Cargo vol., cu. ft.	11.0	11.7
Fuel capacity, gals.	12.4	12.4
Seating capacity	4	4
Front head room, in.	37.5	37.5
Front leg room, max., in.	43.8	43.8
Rear head room, in.	31.9	36.2
Rear leg room, min., in.	30.4	30.4

Powertrain layout: transverse front engine/front-wheel drive.

Engines

	ohc I-4	dohc I-4
Size, liters/cu. in.	1.6/97	1.8/110
Fuel delivery	PFI	PFI
Horsepower @ rpm	95 @ 5800	140 @ 6400
Torque (lbs./ft.) @ rpm	97 @ 4800	120 @ 4600
Availability	S[1]	S[2]

EPA city/highway mpg

5-speed OD manual	30/36	23/31
3-speed automatic	24/31	
4-speed OD automatic		22/30

1. Base Storm.   2. GSi.

Assembly point: Fujisawa, Japan.

Prices

Geo Storm	Retail Price	Dealer Invoice	Low Price
3-door 2+2 hatchback	$11330	$10254	$10654
3-door hatchback	12100	10950	11350

	Retail Price	Dealer Invoice	Low Price
GSi 3-door 2 + 2 hatchback	13300	12037	12437
Destination charge	325	325	325

Standard equipment:

1.6-liter 12-valve PFI 4-cylinder engine, 5-speed manual transmission, power steering, driver-side air bag, cloth and vinyl reclining front bucket seats, one-piece folding rear seatback, AM/FM radio, rear defogger, remote mirrors, tachometer, tinted glass, door pockets, visor mirror, cargo security cover (except 2 + 2), remote hatch release, 185/60HR14 tires. **GSi** adds: 1.8-liter PFI DOHC engine, sport suspension, faster steering ratio, contoured front seats with bolsters, rocker extensions, rear spoiler, oil pressure gauge, fog lamps, 205/50VR15 tires on alloy wheels.

Optional equipment:

Air conditioning	745	633	652
Preferred Group 2, base	545	463	477
3-speed automatic transmission.			
Preferred Group 2, GSi	745	633	652
4-speed automatic transmission.			
Preferred Group 3, base	335	285	293
Alloy wheels.			
Preferred Group 4, base	880	748	770
Group 3 plus 3-speed automatic transmission.			
Cargo security cover, base	50	43	44
AM/FM cassette	140	119	123
Floormats	30	26	26
California emissions pkg.	70	60	61

Geo Tracker

Built in Canada from a Suzuki design, the Tracker returns as a 2-door convertible with a removable fabric top and as a 2-door wagon with a full metal roof. Suzuki sells its own version as the Sidekick, but adds a 4-door hard-top wagon to the mix. All Trackers use an 80-horsepower 1.6-liter 4-cylinder engine. A 5-speed manual transmission is standard and a 3-speed automatic is optional. The base convertible remains the only Tracker without 4-wheel drive. Other models come with on-demand, part-time 4WD (not for use on dry pavement) with a floor-mounted transfer case lever. Base 4 × 4s have manual locking front hubs; LSi versions come with automatic locking hubs. All models have rear

Prices are accurate at time of publication; subject to manufacturer's change.

Geo Tracker LSi convertible

anti-lock brakes that work in 2WD only. Tracker and its Sidekick cousin are among the most likeable mini 4 × 4s—but that doesn't mean we recommend them or any of their ilk as daily transportation. They're better viewed as low-speed runabouts or budget off-road vehicles. Tracker's engine has adequate power with manual transmission, but staying abreast of traffic with the automatic requires flooring the throttle. The ride is choppy, there's lots of engine, wind, and road noise, and interior room is sparse. In turns, copious body lean brought on by the tall, narrow body warns the driver to slow down. Tracker feels more modern than the Jeep Wrangler and is attractively priced, but consider any of these 4 × 4s only if you can live within their obvious limitations.

Specifications

	2-door wagon
Wheelbase, in.	86.6
Overall length, in.	142.5
Overall width, in.	64.2
Overall height, in.	65.6
Curb weight, lbs.	2189[1]
Cargo vol., cu. ft.	31.9
Fuel capacity, gals.	11.1
Seating capacity	4

	2-door wagon
Front head room, in.	39.5
Front leg room, max., in.	42.1
Rear head room, in.	38.3
Rear leg room, min., in.	31.6

1. Conv.; 2387, hard top.

Powertrain layout: longitudinal front engine/rear-wheel drive or on-demand 4WD.

Engines

	ohc I-4
Size, liters/cu. in.	1.6/97
Fuel delivery	TBI
Horsepower @ rpm	80 @ 5400
Torque (lbs./ft.) @ rpm	94 @ 3000
Availability	S

EPA city/highway mpg

5-speed OD manual	25/27
3-speed automatic	23/24

Assembly point: Ingersoll, Ontario, Canada.

Prices

Geo Tracker	Retail Price	Dealer Invoice	Low Price
2-door convertible, 2WD	$9695	$9162	$9362
3-door wagon, 4WD	11900	11246	11446
LSi 3-door wagon, 4WD	13200	12474	12674
2-door convertible, 4WD	11500	10868	11068
LSi 2-door convertible, 4WD	12600	11907	12107
Destination charge	280	280	280

Standard equipment:

1.6-liter TBI 4-cylinder engine, 5-speed manual transmission, anti-lock rear brakes, cloth reclining front bucket seats, folding rear bench seat (4WD), rear shoulder belts, tachometer and trip odometer (4WD), coolant temperature gauge, door pockets, assist straps, dual outside mirrors, tow hooks, rear defogger (except convertible), 195/75R15 tires (2WD), 205/75R15 all-terrain tires (4WD). **LSi** adds: automatic locking front hubs, tinted glass, upgraded seats, spare tire cover, rear bucket seats, intermittent wipers, rear wiper/washer, styled wheels.

Prices are accurate at time of publication; subject to manufacturer's change.

Optional equipment:	Retail Price	Dealer Invoice	Low Price
3-speed automatic transmission	565	497	506
Air conditioning	745	656	667
Power steering	275	242	246
Tilt steering column	115	101	103
Preferred Group 2, base	302	266	270
AM/FM radio.			
Preferred Group 3, base	1047	921	937
Group 2 plus air conditioning.			
Preferred Group 2, LSi	139	122	124
AM/FM cassette.			
Preferred Group 3, LSi	884	778	791
Group 2 plus air conditioning.			
AM/FM cassette, base w/Group 2 or 3 . . .	139	122	124
Rear seat, 2WD	445	392	398
Transfer case shield, 4WD	75	66	67
Trailering special equipment	109	96	98
Trailer hitch, wiring harness.			
Alloy wheels	335	295	300
Floormats, base	28	25	25
Bodyside moldings, base hardtop	59	52	53
Convertibles	85	75	76

Honda Accord

Honda Accord EX 4-door

Still America's best-selling car line, the front-drive Accord gains a driver-side air bag as standard equipment. Last year's leather-trimmed SE 4-door has been dropped, but the top-line EX sedan gets more horsepower, while all EX models receive anti-lock brakes as standard. Returning are a 2-door coupe and 4-door sedan in DX, LX, and EX trim, and a 5-door wagon in LX and EX guise. A driver-side air bag was standard last year in the wagon. Only the EX models have anti-lock brakes and that feature includes rear disc brakes instead of drums. EX sedans also gain 10 horsepower by switching to the 140-horsepower 2.2-liter 4-cylinder engine used last year in the EX wagon. Other Accords retain a 125-horsepower version. All models come with a 5-speed manual standard and a 4-speed automatic optional. Refined and roomy, with a sensible control layout and capable road manners, the Accord is an impressive car. Add Honda's outstanding assembly quality, high resale value, and now a standard driver-side air bag, and this is

Specifications

	2-door notchback	4-door notchback	5-door wagon
Wheelbase, in.	107.1	107.1	107.1
Overall length, in.	184.8	184.8	186.0
Overall width, in.	67.9	67.9	67.9
Overall height, in.	53.9	54.7	55.1
Curb weight, lbs.	2738	2773	3122
Cargo vol., cu. ft.	14.4	14.4	64.6
Fuel capacity, gals.	17.0	17.0	17.0
Seating capacity	5	5	5
Front head room, in.	38.8	38.9	39.0
Front leg room, max., in.	42.9	42.6	42.7
Rear head room, in.	36.5	37.5	37.6
Rear leg room, min., in.	32.3	34.3	34.1

Powertrain layout: transverse front engine/front-wheel drive.

Engines

	ohc I-4	ohc I-4
Size, liters/cu. in.	2.2/132	2.2/132
Fuel delivery	PFI	PFI
Horsepower @ rpm	125 @ 5200	140 @ 5600
Torque (lbs./ft.) @ rpm	137 @ 4000	142 @ 4500
Availability	S	S[1]

EPA city/highway mpg

5-speed OD manual	24/30	24/30
4-speed OD automatic	22/29	22/29

1. EX.

Assembly points: Marysville, Ohio; Saitama, Japan.

Prices are accurate at time of publication; subject to manufacturer's change.

an excellent choice in a mid-size car. We especially like the low cowl design and airy greenhouse, which combine for excellent visibility. The suspension is fairly taut for a family car, but it returns good control over bumps and dips and helps Accord feel composed in turns. Among the few sour notes, anti-lock brakes aren't available on the less-expensive Accords (rivals such as the Ford Taurus make them available on all models), and the automatic transmission tends to shift harshly. However, the Accord has many more pluses than minuses and Honda dealers are discounting their prices.

Prices

Honda Accord	Retail Price	Dealer Invoice	Low Price
DX 2-door notchback, 5-speed	$13025	—	—
DX 2-door notchback, automatic	13775	—	—
LX 2-door notchback, 5-speed	15625	—	—
LX 2-door notchback, automatic	16375	—	—
EX 2-door notchback, 5-speed	18045	—	—
EX 2-door notchback, automatic	18795	—	—
DX 4-door notchback, 5-speed	13225	—	—
DX 4-door notchback, automatic	13975	—	—
LX 4-door notchback, 5-speed	15825	—	—
LX 4-door notchback, automatic	16575	—	—
EX 4-door notchback, 5-speed	18245	—	—
EX 4-door notchback, automatic	18995	—	—
LX 5-door wagon, 5-speed	17450	—	—
LX 5-door wagon, automatic	18200	—	—
EX 5-door wagon, 5-speed	19900	—	—
EX 5-door wagon, automatic	20650	—	—
Destination charge	290	290	290

Dealer invoice and low price not available at time of publication.

Standard equipment:

DX: 2.2-liter SOHC 16-valve PFI 4-cylinder engine, 5-speed manual or 4-speed automatic transmission, power steering, driver-side air bag, cloth reclining front bucket seats, folding rear seatback, tachometer, coolant temperature gauge, trip odometer, tinted glass, tilt steering column, intermittent wipers, rear defogger, remote fuel door and decklid releases, door pockets, maintenance interval indicator, 185/70R14 87S tires. **LX** adds: air conditioning, cruise control, power windows and locks, power mirrors, AM/FM cassette, power antenna, rear armrest, beverage holder; wagon has cargo cover, 195/60R15 87H tires. **EX** adds: 140-horsepower engine, driver-seat lumbar support adjuster, front spoiler, power sunroof, sport suspension, upgraded audio system, 195/60R15 tires on alloy wheels; wagon adds remote keyless entry.

OPTIONS are available as dealer-installed accessories.

Honda Civic

Honda Civic VX 3-door

Civic has been redesigned for 1992 and all models have a standard driver-side air bag. The 5-door wagons are gone, but front-drive 3-door hatchbacks and 4-door sedans are back. Wheelbases are longer by three inches on hatchbacks and nearly five on sedans. Sedans include DX and mid-level LX models powered by a 1.5-liter 4-cylinder with 102 horsepower. The EX 4-door comes with a 1.6-liter four with 125 horsepower and anti-lock brakes. Power steering is now standard on all 4-doors. Hatchbacks include a base CX with a 70-horsepower 1.5-liter engine; a high-fuel-economy VX with 92 horsepower; and a DX with 102 horsepower. The sporty Si hatchback has the 125-horsepower 1.6-liter engine. A 5-speed manual transmission is standard on all Civics. The DX is the only hatchback available with automatic transmission; the 4-speed automatic is optional on all sedans. The new Civics are impressive cars with no serious vices and several key virtues. The air bag is a safety

Prices are accurate at time of publication; subject to manufacturer's change.

plus among subcompacts, as are the EX's anti-lock brakes. Passenger room has increased with the longer wheelbases; in fact, Civic sedans now have about the same interior space as 1986-89 Accords. While acceleration is not greatly improved, the automatic transmission shifts much more smoothly. Higher prices make top-line Civics about as costly as low-end Accords, though that's partly offset by Honda's strong resale values and reputation for reliability. (Hatchback prices weren't announced in time for this issue.) The new Civics keep Honda among the leaders in the sub-compact segment.

Specifications

	3-door hatchback	4-door notchback
Wheelbase, in.	101.2	103.1
Overall length, in.	160.4	173.0
Overall width, in.	66.6	67.0
Overall height, in.	53.0	54.1
Curb weight, lbs.	2094	2275
Cargo vol., cu. ft.	11.9	12.4
Fuel capacity, gals.	11.9	11.9
Seating capacity	5	5
Front head room, in.	38.6	39.1
Front leg room, max., in.	42.5	42.5
Rear head room, in.	36.5	37.1
Rear leg room, min., in.	28.1	30.3

Powertrain layout: transverse front engine/front-wheel drive.

Engines

	ohc I-4	ohc I-4	ohc I-4	ohc I-4
Size, liters/cu. in.	1.5/91	1.5/91	1.5/91	1.6/97
Fuel delivery	PFI	PFI	PFI	PFI
Horsepower @ rpm	70 @ 5000	92 @ 5500	102 @ 5900	125 @ 6600
Torque (lbs./ft.) @ rpm	91 @ 2000	97 @ 4500	98 @ 5000	106 @ 5200
Availability	S[1]	S[2]	S[3]	S[4]

EPA city/highway mpg

5-speed OD manual	42/48	48/55	35/40	29/36
4-speed OD automatic			30/37	27/34

1. CX.   2. VX.   3. DX, LX.   4. EX, Si.

Assembly points: East Liberty, Ohio; Alliston, Ontario, Canada; Suzuka, Japan.

Prices

Honda Civic	Retail Price	Dealer Invoice	Low Price
CX 3-door hatchback, 5-speed	NA	NA	NA
DX 3-door hatchback, 5-speed	NA	NA	NA
DX 3-door hatchback, automatic	NA	NA	NA
VX 3-door hatchback, 5-speed	NA	NA	NA
Si 3-door hatchback, 5-speed	NA	NA	NA
DX 4-door notchback, 5-speed	10555	NA	NA
DX 4-door notchback, automatic	11305	NA	NA
LX 4-door notchback, 5-speed	11385	NA	NA
LX 4-door notchback, automatic	12135	NA	NA
EX 4-door notchback, 5-speed	13575	NA	NA
EX 4-door notchback, automatic	14325	NA	NA
Destination charge	290	290	290

Civic hatchback and dealer invoice and low price not available at time of publication.

Standard equipment:

1.5-liter PFI 8-valve 70-bhp 4-cylinder engine, 5-speed manual transmission, driver-side air bag, reclining front bucket seats, 50/50 split folding rear seatback, remote fuel door and hatch releases, tinted glass, rear defogger, 165/70R13 tires. **DX** adds: 1.5-liter PFI 16-valave 102-bhp engine, 5-speed manual or 4-speed automatic transmission, power steering (sedans; hatchbacks with automatic transmission only), motorized front shoulder belts (4-door), rear wiper/washer (hatchback), tilt steering column, cargo cover (hatchback), intermittent wipers, bodyside moldings, 175/70R13 tires. **VX** adds to CX: 1.5-liter PFI 16-valve 92-bhp engine, tachomter, alloy wheels. **Si** adds: 1.6-liter PFI 16-valve 125-bhp engine, 4-wheel disc brakes, power steering, dual power mirrors, power moonroof, digital clock, tachometer, sport seats, cruise control, wheel covers, 185/60R14 tires. **LX** adds to DX 4-door: power mirrors, power windows and locks, cruise control, digital clock, tachometer, front armrest, wheel covers. **EX** adds: 1.6-liter PFI 16-valve 125-bhp engine, anti-lock brakes, power moonroof, upgraded interior trim, 175/65R14 tires.

OPTIONS are available as dealer-installed accessories.

Honda Prelude

The Prelude, Honda's front-drive sports coupe, has been redesigned for 1992 and is markedly different in appearance from the 1988-91 design. Wheelbase is fractionally shorter, overall length some three inches trimmer, and

Prices are accurate at time of publication; subject to manufacturer's change.

Honda Prelude S

Specifications

	2-door notchback
Wheelbase, in.	100.4
Overall length, in.	174.8
Overall width, in.	69.5
Overall height, in.	50.8
Curb weight, lbs.	2764
Cargo vol., cu. ft.	7.9
Fuel capacity, gals.	15.9
Seating capacity	4
Front head room, in.	38.0
Front leg room, max., in.	44.2
Rear head room, in.	35.1
Rear leg room, min., in.	28.1

Powertrain layout: transverse front engine/front-wheel drive.

Engines

	ohc I-4	dohc I-4
Size, liters/cu. in.	2.2/132	2.3/138
Fuel delivery	PFI	PFI
Horsepower @ rpm	135 @ 5200	160 @ 5800
Torque (lbs./ft.) @ rpm	142 @ 4000	156 @ 4500
Availability	S[1]	S[2]

EPA city/highway mpg

	ohc I-4	dohc I-4
5-speed OD manual	23/29	22/26
4-speed OD automatic	22/28	22/26

1. S   2. Si.

Assembly point: Sayama, Japan.

width two inches greater. The base Prelude S has a 2.2-liter 4-cylinder engine with 135 horsepower. The Si uses a new 2.3-liter four with 160 horsepower—20 more than last year's Si. The Prelude Si 4WS has the 160-horsepower engine and 4-wheel-steering. This year's 4WS system is electronically rather than mechanically controlled. A 5-speed manual transmission is standard and a 4-speed automatic is optional on all models. All Preludes come with a driver-side air bag for the first time, and exclusive to the Si 4WS is a standard passenger-side air bag. Anti-lock brakes are standard on Si models, but aren't offered on the S. For all its changes, Prelude still puts finesse ahead of features. We applaud the air bag, but the new dashboard, designed to accommodate the 4WS model's passenger-side air bag, moves the glove box far back on the center console, where it's hard for front-seaters to get at. Fuel and temperature gauges are vacuum-fluorescent dials positioned halfway across the car; they're hard to read except at night. On the bright side, this year's larger engines deliver stronger performance without a penalty in fuel economy. Prelude is now one of the most expensive cars in its class. Some rivals are not only faster and flashier but cost less, too.

Prices

Honda Prelude	Retail Price	Dealer Invoice	Low Price
S 2-door notchback, 5-speed	$16250	—	—
S 2-door notchback, automatic	17000	—	—
Si 2-door notchback, 5-speed	19250	—	—
Si 2-door notchback, automatic	20000	—	—
Si 4WS 2-door notchback, 5-speed	21750	—	—
Si 4WS 2-door notchback, automatic	2320	—	—
Destination charge	290	290	290

Dealer invoice and low price not available at time of publication.

Standard equipment:

S: 2.2-liter PFI 16-valve 135-bhp 4-cylinder engine, 5-speed manual or 4-speed automatic transmission, 4-wheel disc brakes, variable-assist power steering, driver-side air bag, cloth reclining front bucket seats, power moonroof, power mirrors, AM/FM cassette with power antenna, remote fuel door and decklid releases, rear defogger, intermittent wipers, power mirrors, cruise control, tilt steering column, digital clock, tachometer, visor miroors,

Prices are accurate at time of publication; subject to manufacturer's change.

folding rear seatback, 185/60R14 tires. **Si** adds: 2.3-liter DOHC PFI 16-valve 160-bhp 4-cylinder engine, anti-lock brakes, air conditioning, power locks, driver-seat height and lumbar support adjusters, 205/60R14 tires on alloy wheels. **4WS** adds: 4-wheel steering, passenger-side air bag.

OPTIONS are available as dealer-installed accessories.

Hyundai Elantra

Hyundai Elantra

Elantra debuts for 1992 and is slotted between the low-buck subcompact Excel and the compact Sonata in both size and price. Hyundai pitches it as a "high-end" subcompact intended to do battle with the Toyota Corolla, Nissan Sentra, Ford Escort, and others. Available only as a 4-door notchback, the front-drive Elantra comes in base and fancier GLS trim. Both come with a 113-horsepower 1.6-liter 4-cylinder engine and standard 5-speed manual transmission. Order the optional 4-speed automatic and horsepower drops to 105. Elantras with the 5-speed exhibit spirited performance around town and in highway passing. We haven't tested one with the automatic, but expect our enthusiasm to be dimmed somewhat because automatics tend to sap a lot of energy from small, high-revving 4-cylinder engines. In its favor, Elantra's engine is relatively smooth, though it's never really quiet. Hard acceleration produces a loud growl and the engine buzzes at 60 mph. Elantra's suspension is biased toward a smooth ride. As a result, the car grows bouncy over wavy surfaces and leans heavily in corners. Inside, head room is adequate all around, though tall drivers might wish for more rearward seat travel. Visibility is good in all directions, and the gauges and controls are well laid out except that the radio is mounted too low in the center of the dashboard. While the Elantra rates no better than average overall, both models are better equipped than most comparably priced competitors.

Specifications

	4-door notchback
Wheelbase, in.	98.4
Overall length, in.	171.6
Overall width, in.	65.9
Overall height, in.	54.5
Curb weight, lbs.	2452
Cargo vol., cu. ft.	11.3
Fuel capacity, gals.	13.7
Seating capacity	5
Front head room, in.	38.4
Front leg room, max., in.	42.6
Rear head room, in.	37.6
Rear leg room, min., in.	33.4

Powertrain layout: transverse front engine/front-wheel drive.

Engines

	dohc I-4
Size, liters/cu. in.	1.6/97
Fuel delivery	PFI
Horsepower @ rpm	113 @ 6000[1]
Torque (lbs./ft.) @ rpm	102 @ 5000
Availability	S

EPA city/highway mpg

5-speed OD manual	22/29
4-speed OD automatic	22/29

1. 105 w/automatic trans.

Assembly point: Ulfan, South Korea.

Prices

Hyundai Elantra	Retail Price	Dealer Invoice	Low Price
4-door notchback, 5-speed	$8995	$8074	—
4-door notchback, automatic	9645	8657	—

Prices are accurate at time of publication; subject to manufacturer's change.

	Retail Price	Dealer Invoice	Low Price
GLS 4-door notchback, 5-speed	9999	8771	—
GLS 4-door notchback, automatic	10649	9354	—
Destination charge	380	380	380

Low price not available at time of publication.

Standard equipment:

1.6-liter DOHC 16-valve PFI 4-cylinder engine, 5-speed manual or 4-speed automatic transmission, power steering, motorized front shoulder belts, cloth reclining front bucket seats, center console, digital clock, remote fuel door and decklid releases, rear defogger, variable-intermittent wipers, tinted glass, dual outside mirrors, 175/65R14 tires. **GLS** adds: 6-way adjustable driver's seat, split folding rear seat, upgraded upholstery, power mirrors, front map pockets, tachomter, coolant temperature gauge, trip odometer, power windows and locks, tilt steering column, AM/FM cassette, 185/60HR14 tires.

Optional equipment:

Option Pkg. 1, base	335	256	—
AM/FM cassette.			
Option Pkg. 2, base	1130	905	—
Pkg. 1 plus air conditioning.			
Option Pkg. 3, base	810	644	—
Pkg. 1 plus sunroof.			
Option Pkg. 4, base	1605	1293	—
Pkg. 2 plus sunroof.			
Option Pkg. 5, base	1550	1246	—
Upgraded cassette radio, air conditioning, tilt steering column, cruise control.			
Option Pkg. 6, base	2425	1960	—
Pkg. 5 plus air conditioning, sunroof, upgraded cassette radio, 185/60HR14 tires on alloy wheels.			
Option Pkg. 7, GLS	920	745	—
Upgraded AM/FM cassette, air conditioning.			
Option Pkg. 8, GLS	1715	1394	—
Pkg. 7 plus sunroof, alloy wheels.			
Option Pkg. 9, GLS	2140	1729	—
Pkg. 8 plus cruise control, high-level cassette radio.			
Option Pkg. 10, GLS	1345	1080	—
Pkg. 7 plus cruise control, high-level cassette radio.			
Option Pkg., 11, GLS	1130	916	—
Pkg. 7 plus cruise control.			
Floormats	56	37	—
Front armrest	102	62	—

	Retail Price	Dealer Invoice	Low Price
Door edge guards	34	21	—
Mud guards, front	38	23	—
Mud guards, front & rear	76	46	—
Security system	190	117	—
Sunroof wind deflector	50	23	—

Hyundai Excel/Scoupe

1991 Hyundai Excel GS 3-door

The subcompact Excel and similar Scoupe return for 1992 with only minor trim changes. The Excel comes in 3-door hatchback and 4-door sedan styling, while the sportier Scoupe comes in 2-door notchback styling. They're built on the same front-drive platform and share an 81-horsepower 1.5-liter 4-cylinder engine. The Scoupe differs from the Excel in its styling, suspension calibrated by Lotus of England, different interior design, and shorter final-drive ratio designed to produce quicker acceleration. A 4-speed manual is standard on base Excels; a 5-speed manual is standard on GS and GL Excels and the base and LS Scoupes. A 4-speed automatic is optional on all. An identical version of the Excel hatchback is sold as the Mitsubishi Precis. The Excel and Scoupe are similar in that both have tepid acceleration, especially with automatic transmission. That's easier to accept in the economy-car Excel, but hardly a selling point for a sports coupe like the Scoupe. On both

Prices are accurate at time of publication; subject to manufacturer's change.

the suspension favors ride comfort over handling, though the Scoupe is more crisp and responsive. With either the Excel or Scoupe, rear head room is sufficient for medium-size adults, but leg room is tight unless the front seats are well forward. Good visibility and convenient controls make for a comfortable driving position. Low price remains the main appeal for both these cars. They offer more features at lower cost than most competitors. Neither is close to being best in class for performance, accommodations, or reliability. Shoppers with a small budget should keep them in mind.

Specifications

	2-door notchback	3-door hatchback	4-door notchback
Wheelbase, in.	93.8	93.8	93.8
Overall length, in.	165.9	161.4	168.3
Overall width, in.	64.0	63.3	63.3
Overall height, in.	50.0	54.5	54.5
Curb weight, lbs.	2119	2040	2202
Cargo vol., cu. ft.	9.3	37.9	11.4
Fuel capacity, gals.	11.9	11.9	11.9
Seating capacity	4	5	5
Front head room, in.	38.1	37.8	37.8
Front leg room, max., in.	42.8	41.7	41.7
Rear head room, in.	43.4	37.6	37.6
Rear leg room, min., in.	29.4	33.1	33.1

Powertrain layout: transverse front engine/front-wheel drive.

Engines

	ohc I-4
Size, liters/cu. in.	1.5/90
Fuel delivery	PFI
Horsepower @ rpm	81 @ 5500
Torque (lbs./ft.) @ rpm	91 @ 3000
Availability	S

EPA city/highway mpg

4-speed OD manual	30/36
5-speed OD manual	29/36
4-speed OD automatic	27/32

Assembly point: Ulfan, South Korea.

Prices

Hyundai Excel	Retail Price	Dealer Invoice	Low Price
3-door hatchback, 4-speed	$6595	$6121	$6321
3-door hatchback, automatic	7220	6701	7001
GS 3-door hatchback, 5-speed	7599	6821	7121
GS 3-door hatchback, automatic	8174	7337	7637
4-door notchback, 4-speed	7695	7142	7442
4-door notchback, automatic	8329	7722	8022
GL 4-door notchback, 5-speed	8499	7629	7929
GL 4-door notchback, automatic	9024	8100	8400
Destination charge	380	380	380

Standard equipment:

1.5-liter PFI 4-cylinder engine, 4-speed manual or 4-speed automatic transmission, door-mounted front shoulder belts, cloth and vinyl reclining front bucket seats, 60/40 folding rear seatback (3-door), dual outside mirrors, trip odometer, center bodyside molding, rear defogger, locking fuel door, intermittent wipers, cargo cover (3-door), 155/80R13 tires. **GL** adds: 5-speed manual or 4-speed automatic transmission, power steering (with automatic), full cloth upholstery, 60/40 folding rear seatback, tinted glass, digital clock, door pockets, remote fuel door and decklid/hatch releases, AM/FM cassette player, right visor mirror, large console with cassette storage. **GS** adds: tachometer, driver's-seat lumbar support and cushion height adjustments, 175/70R13 tires.

Optional equipment:

Option Pkg. 1, base	310	237	267
AM/FM cassette.			
Option Pkg. 2, base	570	462	503
Pkg. 1 plus power steering.			
Option Pkg. 3, base	1415	1152	1252
Pkg. 2 plus air conditioning, tinted glass.			
Option Pkg. 4, base	1155	927	1016
Air conditioning, tinted glass, AM/FM cassette player.			
Option Pkg. 5, GS & GL 5-speed	795	649	704
Air conditioning.			
Option Pkg. 6, GS & GL	1055	874	941
Air conditioning, power steering.			
Option Pkg. 7, GL 5-speed	425	347	377
Sunroof.			
Option Pkg. 8, GS & GL	1480	1221	1318
Air conditioning, sunroof, power steering.			
Option Pkg. 9, GS & GL	260	225	237
Power steering.			

Prices are accurate at time of publication; subject to manufacturer's change.

	Retail Price	Dealer Invoice	Low Price
Option Pkg. 10, GS 5-speed	725	592	642
Sunroof, alloy wheels.			
Option Pkg. 11, GL automatic	685	572	613
Sunroof, power steering.			
Option Pkg. 12, GS automatic	985	817	879
Pkg. 10 plus power steering.			
Sunroof air deflector	50	23	36
Floormats	56	37	45
Door edge guards	21	13	17
4-door	34	21	27
Console armrest	102	62	80
Mud guards, rear	38	23	30

Hyundai Scoupe

	Retail Price	Dealer Invoice	Low Price
2-door notchback, 5-speed	$8799	$7898	$8398
2-door notchback, automatic	9374	8420	8920
LS 2-door notchback, 5-speed	9999	8771	9271
LS 2-door notchback, automatic	10574	9293	9793
Destination charge	380	380	380

Standard equipment:

1.5-liter PFI 4-cylinder engine, 5-speed manual or 4-speed automatic transmission, door-mounted front shoulder belts, cloth reclining front bucket seats, 60/40 folding rear seatback, tachometer, trip odometer, remote outside mirrors, tinted glass, intermittent wipers, remote fuel door and decklid releases, digital clock, cargo tiedowns, door pockets, 175/70R13 tires. **LS** adds: power steering, power windows and mirrors, 6-way driver's seat, AM/FM cassette, rear spoiler, cupholder, 185/60HR14 tires.

Optional equipment:

Option Pkg. 1, base	850	699	756
AM/FM cassette player, power steering, sunroof.			
Option Pkg. 2, base	2370	1931	2098
Pkg. 1 plus air conditioning, high-level cassette radio, 185/60HR14 tires on alloy wheels.			
Option Pkg. 3, base	595	484	526
AM/FM cassette, power steering.			
Option Pkg. 4, base	1650	1356	1466
Pkg. 1 plus air conditioning.			
Option Pkg. 5, base	1790	1471	1591
Pkg. 3 plus air conditioning, 185/60HR14 tires on alloy wheels·			
Option Pkg. 6, base	1390	1141	1235
Pkg. 3 plus air conditioning.			
Option Pkg. 7, LS	795	657	708
Air conditioning.			

CONSUMER GUIDE®

	Retail Price	Dealer Invoice	Low Price
Option Pkg. 8, LS	1375	1136	1225
Pkg. 7 plus alloy wheels, sunroof.			
Option Pkg. 9, LS	1780	1456	1579
Pkg. 8 plus cruise control, high-level cassette radio.			
Security system	318	197	251
Console armrest	102	62	80
Floormats	56	35	44
Door edge guards	21	13	17

Hyundai Sonata

Hyundai Sonata

A 128-horsepower 2.0-liter 4-cylinder is the new standard engine for this front-drive 4-door sedan. It replaces a 2.4-liter four that made 116 horsepower. A 142-horsepower 3.0-liter V-6 remains optional on both the base and GLS models. The Sonata, a compact, has a new grille, different taillamps, and other exterior changes for 1992 and GLS models equipped with the V-6 can now be ordered with optional anti-lock brakes. A 5-speed manual transmission is standard on both models. A 4-speed automatic is optional with the 4-cylinder and mandatory with the V-6. Though Hyundai is based in Korea, all Sonatas sold in North America are now built in Quebec, Canada. Compared to the previous 4-cylinder, the new 2.0-liter has more top-end horsepower but less mid-range torque. As a result, acceleration with the 5-speed feels more spirited, while automatic Sonatas

Prices are accurate at time of publication; subject to manufacturer's change.

are a bit lazier off the line. You'll give up some fuel economy with the V-6, but it makes the Sonata noticeably quicker. The new Sonata seems a touch quieter than previous models, though the new 4-cylinder is rather loud and coarse under throttle. The newly optional anti-lock brakes should cure the premature wheel-locking we experienced on one of last year's models under sudden braking—especially in the wet. The interior has ample room for four adults and the trunk has generous cargo space for a compact. Hyundai's assembly quality seems to be moving closer to the Japanese, though it's not as good from what we can tell. Sonata's price, however, makes it competitive in its class.

Specifications

	4-door notchback
Wheelbase, in.	104.3
Overall length, in.	184.3
Overall width, in.	68.9
Overall height, in.	55.4
Curb weight, lbs.	2723
Cargo vol., cu. ft.	14.0
Fuel capacity, gals.	15.8
Seating capacity	5
Front head room, in.	38.5
Front leg room, max., in.	42.4
Rear head room, in.	37.4
Rear leg room, min., in.	37.5

Powertrain layout: transverse front engine/front-wheel drive.

Engines

	dohc I-4	ohc V-6
Size, liters/cu. in.	2.0/122	3.0/181
Fuel delivery	PFI	PFI
Horsepower @ rpm	128 @ 6000	142 @ 5000
Torque (lbs./ft.) @ rpm	121 @ 5000	168 @ 2500
Availability	S	O

EPA city/highway mpg

5-speed OD manual	20/27	
4-speed OD automatic	20/27	18/24

Assembly point: Bromont, Quebec, Canada.

CONSUMER GUIDE®

Prices

Hyundai Sonata	Retail Price	Dealer Invoice	Low Price
4-door notchback, 5-speed	$11150	$9895	$10393
4-door notchback, automatic	11900	10629	11125
4-door notchback w/V-6, automatic	12690	11314	11854
GLS 4-door notchback, 5-speed	13995	12142	12907
GLS 4-door notchback, automatic	14745	12876	13640
GLS 4-door notchback w/V-6, automatic . .	15535	13561	14368
Destination charge	380	380	380

Standard equipment:

2.4-liter PFI 4-cylinder or 3.0-liter PFI V-6 engine, 5-speed manual or 4-speed automatic transmission, power steering, motorized front shoulder belts, cloth reclining front bucket seats, driver's-seat height adjustment, center console, tachometer, trip odometer, AM/FM cassette, tilt steering column, digital clock, remote fuel door and decklid releases, rear defogger, door pockets, remote outside mirrors, bodyside molding, tinted glass, intermittent wipers, visor mirrors, 195/70R14 tires. **GLS** adds: air conditioning, power windows and locks, cruise control, upgraded audio system, power antenna, 6-way driver's seat, oil pressure gauge, voltmeter, power mirrors, 60/40 folding rear seatback, console with storage, lighted right visor mirror, seatback pockets, 205/60HR15 tires.

Optional equipment:

Option Pkg. 1, base	850	694	762
Air conditioning.			
Option Pkg. 2, base	3505	2860	3143
Pkg. 1 plus AM/FM cassette player, Alloy Wheel Pkg. (includes 205/60HR15 tires), Power Pkg. (includes power windows and locks, power mirrors, power antenna, cruise control), sunroof.			
Option Pkg. 3, base	2010	1640	1802
Pkg. 1 plus upgraded cassette radio, Power Pkg.			
Option Pkg. 4, base	1690	1379	1516
Pkg. 1 plus upgraded cassette radio, sunroof.			
Option Pkg. 5, base	2530	2064	2269
Pkg. 4 plus Power Pkg., upgraded cassette radio.			
Option Pkg. 6, base	1690	1379	1516
Pkg. 1 plus Power Pkg.			
Option Pkg. 7, GLS	520	424	466
Anti-lock brakes.			
Option Pkg. 8, GLS	1020	832	915
Pkg. 7 plus upgraded cassette radio.			
Option Pkg. 9, GLS	1170	988	1066
Pkg. 7 plus Leather Pkg.			

Prices are accurate at time of publication; subject to manufacturer's change.

	Retail Price	Dealer Invoice	Low Price
Option Pkg. 10, GLS V-6	1915	1596	1734
Pkg. 9 plus CD player.			
Option Pkg. 11, GLS V-6	2765	2333	2518
Pkg. 10 plus anti-lock brakes.			
Option Pkg. 12, GLS V-6	1350	1145	1232
Pkg. 7 plus high-level cassette radio.			
Option Pkg. 13, GLS	1670	1396	1514
Pkg. 9 plus high-level cassette radio.			
Security system	350	225	284
Floormats	65	42	53
Front armrest	125	85	104
Door edge guards	42	26	34
Mud guards	90	56	72
Alarm system	350	225	284
Sunroof wind deflector	50	25	37

Infiniti G20

Infiniti G20

Introduced to the U.S. market last year as the first rung on Nissan's upscale Infiniti ladder, the G20 gets one standard equipment change for its second season. The power door locks have been revised so that one turn of the key in either front door unlocks that door and a second turn unlocks the other doors. All-season tires are a no-cost option for 1992. The G20 is a compact 4-door sedan with front-wheel drive and a 140-horsepower twin-cam 2.0-liter 4-cylinder engine. A 5-speed manual transmission is standard and a 4-speed overdrive automatic is optional. An air bag is not available, but the G20 comes with 4-wheel anti-lock disc brakes. It feels liveliest with the manual transmission, but can be quick with the automatic if you use a heavy throttle foot. The engine grows excessively loud around 4000 rpm, however, and in normal 30-50-mph driving, the automatic tends to shift too much, as if it's undecided about which gear it should be in. In turns, the G20 is nimble, with little body lean and tenacious grip. The down side is a stiff ride. No tar strip goes unnoticed, and big bumps

Specifications

	4-door notchback
Wheelbase, in.	100.4
Overall length, in.	175.0
Overall width, in.	66.7
Overall height, in.	54.9
Curb weight, lbs.	2535
Cargo vol., cu. ft.	14.1
Fuel capacity, gals.	15.9
Seating capacity	5
Front head room, in.	38.8
Front leg room, max., in.	42.0
Rear head room, in.	37.3
Rear leg room, min., in.	32.2

Powertrain layout: transverse front engine/front-wheel drive.

Engines

	dohc I-4
Size, liters/cu. in.	2.0/122
Fuel delivery	PFI
Horsepower @ rpm	140 @ 6400
Torque (lbs./ft.) @ rpm	132 @ 4800
Availability	S

EPA city/highway mpg

5-speed OD manual	24/32
4-speed OD automatic	22/29

Assembly point: Oppama, Japan.

Prices are accurate at time of publication; subject to manufacturer's change.

send a jolt through the body. Four adults ride in comfort in the G20, though the narrow rear doors force some twisting and turning to get in or out. A quieter engine that works better with automatic transmission would make the G20 a more appealing car. Even with the 4-cylinder engine, the G20 merits consideration as a "near-luxury" sedan.

Prices

Infiniti G20	Retail Price	Dealer Invoice	Low Price
4-door notchback, 5-speed	$18300	$14640	—
4-door notchback, automatic	19200	15360	—
Destination charge	385	385	385

Low price not available at time of publication.

Standard equipment:

2.0-liter DOHC 16-valve PFI 4-cylinder engine, 5-speed manual or 4-speed automatic transmission, anti-lock 4-wheel disc brakes, power steering, motorized front shoulder belts, automatic climate control, cloth reclining front bucket seats, tachometer, coolant temperature gauge, trip odometer, power windows and locks, power mirrors, power AM/FM cassette, power antenna, leather-wrapped steering wheel, remote fuel door and decklid releases, tinted glass, anti-theft device, 195/60HR14 tires on alloy wheels.

Optional equipment:

Leather seating surfaces	1000	800	—
Power glass sunroof	900	720	—

Infiniti M30

The M30 is a carryover from 1991 save for a new power door lock system. Two-door coupe and convertible body styles are back, both powered by a 162-horsepower 3.0-liter V-6 driving the rear wheels through a 4-speed overdrive automatic transmission. All Infinitis receive a power door lock system with 2-stage "select logic" operation. A first turn of the key in either door unlocks that door; a second turn unlocks the other door. The convertible, a conversion performed by American Sunroof Corporation in California, features a standard power top that automatically latches/

Infiniti M30 coupe

Specifications

	2-door notchback	2-door conv.
Wheelbase, in.	103.0	103.0
Overall length, in.	188.8	188.8
Overall width, in.	66.5	66.5
Overall height, in.	54.3	54.3
Curb weight, lbs.	3333	NA
Cargo vol., cu. ft.	11.6	12.3
Fuel capacity, gals.	17.2	17.2
Seating capacity	5	4
Front head room, in.	36.8	35.0
Front leg room, max., in.	42.2	42.2
Rear head room, in.	35.7	35.2
Rear leg room, min., in.	30.2	30.2

Powertrain layout: longitudinal front engine/rear-wheel drive.

Engines

	ohc V-6
Size, liters/cu. in.	3.0/181
Fuel delivery	PFI
Horsepower @ rpm	162 @ 5200
Torque (lbs./ft.) @ rpm	180 @ 3600
Availability	S

EPA city/highway mpg

4-speed OD automatic	19/25

Assembly point: Oppama, Japan.

Prices are accurate at time of publication; subject to manufacturer's change.

unlatches at the windshield header and also raises/lowers the side windows at the same time. Anti-lock brakes and a driver-side air bag are standard on both models. Acceleration is more than adequate, with smooth, timely shifts from the transmission. Ride quality is another mixed bag. In the Comfort mode, the standard Sonar Suspension II allows too much nose-bobbing. Switch to the firmer Sport mode and the ride gets jittery. Drivers over 6-feet tall may have trouble fitting in the coupe because there's too little head room beneath the power sunroof. The convertible has adequate head room, but the top has wide rear "pillars" and slim rear side windows that restrict over-the-shoulder vision. In either version, rear leg room is inadequate unless the front seats are moved well forward. We're not enthused enough about either M30 model to recommend them over other cars in the same price range.

Prices

Infiniti M30	Retail Price	Dealer Invoice	Low Price
2-door notchback	$25000	$20000	—
2-door convertible	33000	26400	NA
Destination charge	385	385	385

Low price not available at time of publication.

Standard equipment:

3.0-liter PFI V-6, 4-speed automatic transmission, 4-wheel anti-lock disc brakes, power steering, limited-slip differential, driver-side air bag, cruise control, automatic climate control, Nissan/Bose AM/FM cassette with power antenna, leather upholstery, power sunroof, tinted glass, power windows and locks, power driver's seat, tilt steering column, power mirrors, remote fuel door and decklid releases, intermittent wipers, front and rear folding armrests, theft deterrent system, 215/60HR15 tires on alloy wheels.

Infiniti Q45

Infiniti's top-line sedan returns for its third year with newly optional high-performance all-season tires and a revised power door lock system. The Q45 is a rear-drive 4-door notchback with a 4.5-liter twin-cam V-8 of 278 horsepower.

Infiniti Q45

Specifications

	4-door notchback
Wheelbase, in.	113.2
Overall length, in.	199.8
Overall width, in.	71.9
Overall height, in.	56.3
Curb weight, lbs.	3950
Cargo vol., cu. ft.	14.8
Fuel capacity, gals.	22.5
Seating capacity	5
Front head room, in.	38.2
Front leg room, max., in.	43.9
Rear head room, in.	36.3
Rear leg room, min., in.	32.0

Powertrain layout: longitudinal front engine/rear-wheel drive.

Engines

	dohc V-8
Size, liters/cu. in.	4.5/274
Fuel delivery	PFI
Horsepower @ rpm	278 @ 6000
Torque (lbs./ft.) @ rpm	292 @ 4000
Availability	S

EPA city/highway mpg

4-speed OD automatic	16/22

Assembly point: Tochigi, Japan.

Prices are accurate at time of publication; subject to manufacturer's change.

A 4-speed overdrive automatic is the only transmission. The Q45 has three major options: Full-Active Suspension (priced as a separate model at $5000 additional); Traction Control (not available on the Full-Active model); and a Touring Package with alloy wheels, rear spoiler, and Nissan's "Super HICAS" 4-wheel steering. Full-Active Suspension replaces conventional shock absorbers with a computer-controlled hydraulic actuator at each wheel. It counteracts body lean in corners, nose lift in hard acceleration, nose dive in braking, and fore/aft pitch over wavy surfaces. With the new power locks, a first turn from either front passenger door locks or unlocks that door; turning the key a second time locks/unlocks remaining doors. A driver-side air bag and anti-lock brakes are standard. Where the rival Lexus LS 400 is cushy and luxurious, the Q45 is more like a European sport sedan. It has a firmer ride than the Lexus and more athletic handling ability. You'll hear more exhaust and road noise in the Q45, though neither is intrusive. Clear analog gauges and simple controls in a cabin devoid of wood trim reinforce Q45's sport-oriented message. Both the Q45 and LS 400 are excellent cars. We recommend you try both to see which fits your driving style best.

Prices

Infiniti Q45	Retail Price	Dealer Invoice	Low Price
4-door notchback	$42000	$33800	—
w/Full-Active Suspension	47000	38020	—
Destination charge	385	385	385

Low price not available at time of publication.

Standard equipment:

4.5-liter DOHC 32-valve V-8, 4-speed automatic transmission, 4-wheel anti-lock disc brakes, power steering, limited-slip differential, driver-side air bag, cruise control, automatic climate control, leather reclining front bucket seats (wool is available at no charge), Nissan/Bose AM/FM cassette, power antenna, power sunroof, tinted glass, power windows and locks, power driver's seat with 2-position memory (memory includes tilt/telescopic steering column), power passenger seat, heated power mirrors, remote fuel door and decklid releases, intermittent wipers, front and rear folding armrests, theft deterrent system, 215/65VR15 tires on alloy wheels.

CONSUMER GUIDE®

Optional equipment:

	Retail Price	Dealer Invoice	Low Price
Touring Pkg.	2800	2240	—

Touring Pkg.   2800   2240   —
Super HICAS 4-wheel steering, rear spoiler, forged alloy wheels.
Traction control   1500   1200   —
Not available with Full-Active Suspension.

Isuzu Rodeo

1991 Isuzu Rodeo 5-door

Rodeo carries on for 1992 virtually unchanged. It is offered
only as a 5-door wagon in several levels of trim and equipment. The price-leader 2-wheel-drive S has Isuzu's 120-horse-
power 2.6-liter 4-cylinder engine and a 5-speed manual
transmission. Optional is a 3.1-liter General Motors V-6,
also rated at 120 horsepower. The V-6 is standard on the
4WD S as well as on the 2WD and 4WD versions of the
mid-range XS and top-shelf LS models. Optional for all
Rodeos except the 2WD S is a 4-speed overdrive automatic.
Rodeo 4×4s employ a part-time, on-demand 4WD system
that's not for use on dry pavement. Automatic-locking front
hubs are standard except on the 4WD S, which has manual
hubs. All Rodeos have 4-wheel power disc brakes with rear
anti-lock control that works in 2WD only. We tested both
2- and 4-wheel-drive LS models and came away impressed.

Prices are accurate at time of publication; subject to manufacturer's change.

The V-6 is no powerhouse, but runs smoothly and quietly once up to speed. Rodeo also rides smoothly, largely due to its relatively long 108.7-inch wheelbase. Inside, driver and front passenger are treated well, with adequate head and leg room and a comfortable driving position. We wish the Rodeo had a more convenient 4WD system. Unlike the "shift-on-the-fly" of most competitors, the 4WD Rodeo, even with its automatic locking hubs, has to be stopped before 4WD can be engaged and backed up before it can be disengaged.

Specifications

	5-door wagon
Wheelbase, in.	108.7
Overall length, in.	176.4
Overall width, in.	66.5
Overall height, in.	65.4
Curb weight, lbs.	3490
Cargo vol., cu. ft.	74.9
Fuel capacity, gals.	21.9
Seating capacity	5
Front head room, in.	38.2
Front leg room, max., in.	42.5
Rear head room, in.	37.8
Rear leg room, min., in.	36.1

Powertrain layout: longitudinal front engine/rear-wheel drive or on-demand 4WD.

Engines	ohc I-4	ohv V-6
Size, liters/cu. in.	2.6/156	3.1/191
Fuel delivery	PFI	TBI
Horsepower @ rpm	120 @ 5000	120 @ 4400
Torque (lbs./ft.) @ rpm	146 @ 2600	165 @ 2800
Availability	S	O

EPA city/highway mpg		
5-speed OD manual	18/22	15/19
4-speed OD automatic		14/18

Assembly point: Lafayette, Ind.

Prices

Isuzu Rodeo

	Retail Price	Dealer Invoice	Low Price
S 2WD 5-door wagon, 5-speed . . . . . . $	12919	—	—
S V6 2WD 5-door wagon, 5-speed	13859	—	—
XS V6 2WD 5-door wagon, 5-speed	14779	—	—
XS V6 2WD 5-door wagon, automatic . . .	15669	—	—
LS 2WD 5-door wagon, 5-speed	16089	—	—
LS 2WD 5-door wagon, automatic	16979	—	—
S V6 4WD 5-door wagon, 5-speed	15549	—	—
XS 4WD 5-door wagon, 5-speed	17529	—	—
XS 4WD 5-door wagon, automatic	18629	—	—
LS 4WD 5-door wagon, 5-speed	17849	—	—
LS 4WD 5-door wagon, automatic	18949	—	—
Destination charge	319	319	319

Dealer invoice and low price not available at time of publication.

Standard equipment:

S: 2.6-liter PFI 4-cylinder engine (2WD), 3.1-liter TBI V-6 (4WD), 5-speed manual transmission, anti-lock rear brakes, manual locking front hubs (4WD), power steering (4WD), front bench seat, folding rear seat, coolant temperature gauge, trip odometer, 225/75R15 tires. **S V6** adds: 3.1-liter V-6, power steering, reclining front bucket seats. **XS** adds: 5-speed manual or 4-speed automatic transmission, automatic locking front hubs (4WD), AM/FM radio, 31.0×10.5R tires on alloy wheels (4WD), outside spare tire carrier with cover. **LS** adds: split folding rear seat, cassette player, velour upholstery, map and courtesy lights, intermittent wipers, rear wiper/washer, tilt steering column, cargo net, right visor mirror, leather-wrapped steering wheel, 225/75R15 tires on steel wheels.

Optional equipment:

Air conditioning	800	680	—
Power steering, S 2WD	325	275	—
10.5R tires on alloy wheels, S 4WD	1295	NA	—
w/limited slip differential, S 4WD	1535	NA	—
LS 4WD	825	NA	—
Includes outside spare tire with cover.			
Rear wiper/washer, S	165	NA	—
Convenience Pkg., LS	975	828	—
Power windows and locks, cruise control, sunroof.			
Outside spare tire cover with cover	225	191	—
Two-tone paint, LS	180	153	—
Brush/grille guard	405	285	—
AM/FM radio, S	210	147	—

Prices are accurate at time of publication; subject to manufacturer's change.

	Retail Price	Dealer Invoice	Low Price
AM/FM cassette, S . . . . , ...	575	400	—
XS	365	253	—
CD player, LS	535	375	—
Cassette & CD player, XS	975	NA	—
Hood protector	65	45	—
Bosch light bar	320	225	—
Huron Aero luggage rack	185	130	—
Yakima luggage rack	220	155	—
Trim rings, S V6	75	52	—
Floormats	55	39	—
Lockable center console, S V6 & XS	110	NA	—
LS	85	NA	—

Jaguar Sedan and XJS

1991 Jaguar Sovereign

Jaguar's sedan accounts for 80 percent of the company's sales, but the V-12-powered XJS coupe and convertible get most of the attention for 1992. The changes to the XJS include a black grille, two ovoid headlamps instead of four rectangular lamps, a redesigned roof, a new instrument panel, tilt instead of telescoping steering wheel, and a 6-speaker stereo system. The coupe and convertible retain last year's 262-horsepower 5.3-liter V-12 engine and 3-speed automatic transmission. Anti-lock brakes and a driver-side air bag are standard on both XJS models. Sedans are virtual carryovers from 1991 except that the top-line Vanden Plas Majestic, first introduced in 1990, returns after a one-year hiatus. The model line is now comprised of base,

Sovereign, Vanden Plas, and Vanden Plas Majestic. All sedans have a 223-horsepower 4.0-liter inline-6-cylinder engine and 4-speed automatic transmission. Anti-lock brakes are standard on the Jaguar sedans, but an air bag isn't offered. Though Jaguar has significantly improved its quality over the past several years, its cars lag behind most competitors in performance and value. Prices have increased nearly $5000 from a year ago, which means that the base sedan is still more expensive than a Lexus LS 400. As a result, these sedans appeal primarily to those who covet traditional British luxury and Jaguar's distinct pedigree.

Specifications

	XJS 2-door notchback	XJS 2-door conv.	4-door notchback
Wheelbase, in.	102.0	102.0	113.0
Overall length, in.	191.7	191.7	196.4
Overall width, in.	70.6	70.6	78.9
Overall height, in.	47.8	47.8	54.3
Curb weight, lbs.	4015	4190	3935
Cargo vol., cu. ft.	10.6	NA	15.1
Fuel capacity, gals.	24.0	21.6	23.2
Seating capacity	4	2	5
Front head room, in.	36.1	36.1	36.6
Front leg room, max., in.	41.3	41.3	41.7
Rear head room, in.	33.4	NA	36.5
Rear leg room, min., in.	23.4	NA	33.1

Powertrain layout: longitudinal front engine/rear-wheel drive.

Engines

	dohc I-6	ohc V-12
Size, liters/cu. in.	4.0/243	5.3/326
Fuel delivery	PFI	PFI
Horsepower @ rpm	223 @ 4750	262 @ 5000
Torque (lbs./ft.) @ rpm	278 @ 3650	290 @ 3000
Availability	S[1]	S[2]

EPA city/highway mpg

3-speed automatic		13/18
4-speed OD automatic	17/22	

1. Sedans   2. XJS.

Assembly point: Coventry, England.

Prices are accurate at time of publication; subject to manufacturer's change.

Prices

Jaguar Sedan

	Retail Price	Dealer Invoice	Low Price
4-door notchback	$44500	—	—
Sovereign 4-door notchback	49500	—	—
Vanden Plas 4-door notchback	54500	—	—
Vanden Plas Majestic 4-door notchback . .	59500	—	—
Destination charge	525	525	525

Dealer invoice and low price not available at time of publication.

Standard equipment:

4.0-liter DOHC 24-valve PFI 6-cylinder engine, 4-speed automatic transmission, anti-lock 4-wheel disc brakes, power steering, motorized front shoulder belts, power front bucket seats, leather seat facings, automatic climate control, power windows and locks, cruise control, heated power mirrors, heated door locks and windshield washer nozzles, trip computer, adjustable steering wheel, remote fuel door and decklid releases, rear defogger, AM/FM cassette with CB channel 19 monitor, folding rear armrest, lighted visor mirrors, seatback pockets, console with storage, map light, 205/70VR15 tires on alloy wheels. **Sovereign** adds: hydraulic leveling, power sunroof, burl walnut inlays, rear head restraints. **Vanden Plas** adds: limited-slip differential, headlight washers with heated nozzles, footwell rugs, heated front seats, folding burl walnut picnic tables on front seatbacks, leather on seatbacks and borders, storage in rear armrest, rear reading lights, fog lights. **Majestic** adds: Black Cherry mica metallic paint, Cream leather interior, alarm system.

Jaguar XJS

	Retail Price	Dealer Invoice	Low Price
2-door notchback	$53000	—	—
2-door convertible	63600	—	—
Destination charge	525	525	525

Dealer invoice and low price not available at time of publication.

Standard equipment:

5.3-liter PFI V-12, 3-speed automatic transmission, anti-lock 4-wheel disc brakes, limited-slip differential, power steering, driver's-side airbag, automatic climate control, full leather interior, heated reclining front bucket seats with power lumbar, power windows and locks, heated power mirrors, cruise control, trip computer, tinted glass, intermittent wipers, tachometer, coolant temperature and oil pressure gauges, AM/FM cassette with power antenna, rear defogger, leather-wrapped steering wheel, tilt steering column, heated windshield washer nozzles, fog lights, Pirelli P600 235/60VR15 or Goodyear NCTS 235/60ZR15 tires on alloy wheels.

CONSUMER GUIDE®

Jeep Cherokee

Jeep Cherokee Limited 5-door

These sport-utility vehicles get new comfort and convenience features for 1992 but are otherwise reruns. Jeep's big news will come in spring 1992 with the Grand Cherokee, a new, larger upscale model that will be sold alongside the present Cherokee. For 1992, Cherokee returns in 3- and 5-door styling, both available with 2- or 4-wheel drive. Base models have a 130-horsepower 2.5-liter 4-cylinder engine. Sport, Laredo, Limited, and Briarwood models come with a 190-horsepower 4.0-liter 6-cylinder that's optional on the base version. Standard on the base 4×4 is Command-Trac, a part-time 4WD system with shift-on-the-fly capability. The Limited and Briarwood are offered only in the 5-door body style with a 4-speed automatic transmission and Selec-Trac 4WD, a full-time system that can be used on smooth, dry pavement. The 4-speed automatic and Selec-Trac are optional on Sport, Laredo, and 6-cylinder base models. Anti-lock brakes are optional on 6-cylinder/automatic Cherokees with Selec-Trac. Jeep's ABS works on all four wheels and in 2WD and 4WD. The 4-cylinder has adequate power with the 5-speed, but it's sluggish and unresponsive with automatic. The 4.0-liter six provides brisk acceleration with either transmission. Cherokee remains attractive for its convenient 4WD systems (both of which have full shift-on-the-fly), ample passenger and cargo room, commendable off-road capabilities, and civilized on-road manners.

Prices are accurate at time of publication; subject to manufacturer's change.

Specifications

	3-door wagon	5-door wagon
Wheelbase, in.	101.4	101.4
Overall length, in.	168.8	168.8
Overall width, in.	70.5	70.5
Overall height, in.	63.3	63.3
Curb weight, lbs.	2985	3028
Cargo vol., cu. ft.	71.8	71.8
Fuel capacity, gals.	20.0	20.0
Seating capacity	5	5
Front head room, in.	38.3	38.3
Front leg room, max., in.	41.0	41.0
Rear head room, in.	38.0	38.0
Rear leg room, min., in.	35.3	35.3

Powertrain layout: longitudinal front engine/rear-wheel drive or on-demand 4WD.

Engines

	ohv I-4	ohv I-6
Size, liters/cu. in.	2.5/150	4.0/242
Fuel delivery	PFI	PFI
Horsepower @ rpm	130 @ 5250	190 @ 4750
Torque (lbs./ft.) @ rpm	149 @ 3000	225 @ 4000
Availability	S	O

EPA city/highway mpg

5-speed OD manual	19/23	17/21
4-speed OD automatic		15/19

Assembly point: Toledo, Ohio.

Prices

Jeep Cherokee	Retail Price	Dealer Invoice	Low Price
3-door 2WD, Pkg. 23A (2.5/5-speed)	$14346	$12919	$13169
3-door 2WD, 25A (4.0/5-speed)	14458	13015	13265
3-door 2WD, 26A (4.0/automatic)	15223	13665	13915
3-door 4WD, 23A (2.5/5-speed)	15832	14227	14477
3-door 4WD, 25A (4.0/5-speed)	15944	14322	14572
3-door 4WD, 26A (4.0/automatic)	16709	14973	15223
5-door 2WD, 23A (2.5/5-speed)	15357	13809	14259

	Retail Price	Dealer Invoice	Low Price
5-door 2WD, 25A (4.0/5-speed)	15469	13904	14354
5-door 2WD, 26A (4.0/automatic)	16234	14555	15005
5-door 4WD, 23A (2.5/5-speed)	16842	15116	15566
5-door 4WD, 25A (4.0/5-speed)	16954	15211	15661
5-door 4WD, 26A (4.0/automatic)	17719	15861	16311
Base standard equipment.			
Sport 3-door 2WD, 25C (5-speed)	14449	12995	13245
Sport 3-door 2WD, 26C (automatic)	15326	13741	13991
Sport 3-door 4WD, 25C (5-speed)	15935	14303	14553
Sport 3-door 4WD, 26C (automatic)	16812	15048	15298
Sport 5-door 2WD, 25C (5-speed)	15460	13885	14135
Sport 5-door 2WD, 26C (automatic)	16337	14630	14880
Sport 5-door 4WD, 25C (5-speed)	16945	15192	15442
Sport 5-door 4WD, 26C (automatic)	17822	15937	16187
Sport standard equipment.			
Sport 3-door 2WD, 25D (5-speed)	15663	14027	14277
Sport 3-door 2WD, 26D (automatic)	16540	14772	15022
Sport 3-door 4WD, 25D (5-speed)	16674	14917	15167
Sport 3-door 4WD, 26D (automatic)	17551	15662	15912
Sport 5-door 2WD, 25D (5-speed)	17149	15335	15785
Sport 5-door 2WD, 26D (automatic)	18026	16080	16530
Sport 5-door 4WD, 25D (5-speed)	18159	16224	16674
Sport 5-door 4WD, 26D (automatic)	19036	16969	17419
Pkg. 25D/26D: air conditioning, cassette player, console with armrest, tachometer and gauges, spare tire cover, tilt steering column, dual remote mirrors, intermittent wipers.			
Laredo 5-door 2WD, 25J (5-speed)	17255	15411	15861
Laredo 5-door 2WD, 26J (automatic) . . .	18132	16156	16606
Laredo 3-door 4WD, 25J (5-speed)	17730	15829	NA
Laredo 3-door 4WD, 26J (automatic) . . .	18607	16574	NA
Laredo 5-door 4WD, 25J (5-speed)	18740	16717	NA
Laredo 5-door 4WD, 26J (automatic) . . .	19617	17463	NA
Laredo standard equipment.			
Laredo 5-door 2WD, 25K (5-speed)	18846	16763	17213
Laredo 5-door 2WD, 26K (automatic) . . .	19723	17508	17958
Laredo 3-door 4WD, 25K (5-speed)	19176	17058	17308
Laredo 3-door 4WD, 26K (automatic) . . .	20053	17803	18053
Laredo 5-door 4WD, 25K (5-speed)	20331	18070	18520
Laredo 5-door 4WD, 26K (automatic) . . .	21208	18815	19265
Pkg. 25K/26K: air conditioning, power windows, power locks with keyless entry, cassette player with premium speakers, cruise control, tilt steering column.			
Limited 5-door 4WD	25334	22589	23039
Briarwood 5-door 4WD	24799	22118	22568
Destination charge	485	485	485

Prices are accurate at time of publication; subject to manufacturer's change.

Standard equipment:

2.5-liter PFI 4-cylinder or 4.0-liter PFI 6-cylinder engine, 5-speed manual or 4-speed automatic transmission, power steering, vinyl front bucket seats, folding rear seat, mini console, AM/FM radio, digital clock, tinted glass, 195/75R15 tires; 4WD system is Command-Trac part-time. **Sport** adds: 4.0-liter 6-cylinder engine, hockey-stick-style armrests, cargo tiedown hooks, 225/75R15 outlined white letter all-terrain tires on alloy wheels. **Laredo** adds: reclining front bucket seats, fabric upholstery, skid strips, console with armrest and storage, upgraded sound insulation, tachometer, coolant temperature and oil pressure gauges, voltmeter, trip odometer, front vent windows, swing-out rear quarter windows (3-door), dual-note horn, headlamp delay system, misc. lights, dual outside mirrors, roof rack, spare tire cover, intermittent wipers, rear wiper/washer, floormats, 215/75R15 outlined white letter tires on alloy wheels. **Limited** adds: 4-speed automatic transmission, Selec-Trac transfer case, air conditioning, leather upholstery, power front seats, power windows, power locks with illuminated keyless entry system, lighted visor mirrors, cruise control, rear defogger, fog lamps, deep-tinted rear glass, power mirrors, cassette player, AM/FM cassette, power antenna, tilt steering column, leather-wrapped steering wheel, 225/70R15 Eagle GA tires. **Briarwood** adds: power mirrors, bright trim, wood-grain exterior applique, 215/75R15 tires on crosswire alloy wheels; deletes deep-tinted rear glass.

Optional equipment:	Retail Price	Dealer Invoice	Low Price
Anti-lock brakes	500	425	438
Requires 4.0-liter engine.			
Trac-Lok rear differential	285	242	249
Air conditioning, base, Sport, & Laredo . .	836	711	732
Selec-Trac, base, Sport, & Laredo 4WD . . .	394	335	345
Fabric seats, base & Sport	137	116	120
Console w/armrest, base & Sport	147	125	129
Rear defogger, base & Sport	161	137	141
Cassette player, base, Sport & Laredo . . .	201	171	176
Premium speakers, Laredo	174	148	152
Roof rack, base & Sport	139	118	122
Tilt steering column, base, Sport & Laredo .	132	112	116
Base & Sport require intermittent wipers.			
Spare tire cover, Sport	46	39	40
Rear wiper/washer, base & Sport	147	125	129
Deep-tinted glass, base & Sport 3-door . .	333	283	291
Gauge Group w/Tachometer, Sport	139	118	122
Front vent windows, base & Sport	91	77	80
HD Alternator & Battery Group, base, Sport			
& Laredo	135	115	118
Base, Sport & Laredo w/defogger	63	54	55
Intermittent wipers, base & Sport	61	52	53
Fog lamps, Laredo	110	94	96

	Retail Price	Dealer Invoice	Low Price
Overhead console (NA base & Sport)	203	173	178
Illuminated entry, Laredo	171	145	150
Includes lighted visor mirrors; requires Power Window & Lock Group.			
Power Window & Lock Group, Sport & Laredo			
3-door	437	371	382
Sport & Laredo 5-door	582	495	509
Dual outside mirrors, base & Sport	77	65	67
Power mirrors, Laredo	100	85	88
Power front seats, Laredo	416	354	364
Security alarm, Laredo	320	272	280
Limited & Briarwood	149	127	130
Includes illuminated entry; requires Power Window & Lock Group.			
Light Group, base & Sport	145	123	127
Cargo area cover (NA base & Sport)	72	61	63
Skid Plate Group, 4WD models	144	122	126
Cruise control, base, Sport, & Laredo . . .	230	196	201
Base and Sport require intermittent wipers.			
Trailer Tow Pkg.	358	304	313
4WD models w/Off-Road Pkg.	242	206	212
Off-Road Pkg. (4WD only), base	982	835	859
Sport	552	469	483
Laredo	579	492	507
Manual sunroof, Laredo	357	303	312
Limited & Briarwood	154	131	135
215/75R15 tires, base	93	79	81
215/75R15 OWL tires, base	359	305	314
225/75R15 OWL tires, base	405	344	354
Laredo	46	39	40
225/70R15 OWL Eagle GA tires, Briarwood .	72	61	63
4 styled steel wheels, base	103	88	90
5 styled steel wheels, base	129	110	113
4 alloy wheels, base	348	296	305
5 alloy wheels, base	432	367	378
Leather-wrapped steering wheel, Sport &			
Laredo	48	41	42

Jeep Wrangler

Wrangler, Jeep's pint-sized sport-utility vehicle, has had a standard rollbar (Jeep calls it a "sportbar") mounted to the frame behind the front seats since it was introduced for the 1987 model year. This year the rollbar has been extended to the rear of the cargo area, where it serves as the anchor point for new 3-point rear seatbelts. The combina-

Prices are accurate at time of publication; subject to manufacturer's change.

Jeep Wrangler Sahara

tion lap-shoulder belts replace lap belts for the two rear seating positions. The Sahara option package, which gives Wrangler a desert motif, has a broader color palette for 1992, including two new low-gloss exterior colors (sand and sage green) and a new dark green interior color. Wrangler comes in price-leader S and base models. In addition to the Sahara option group, there are also Islander and Renegade packages. A 123-horsepower 2.5-liter 4-cylinder engine is standard on all models. A 180-horsepower 4.0-liter 6-cylinder engine is included with Renegade equipment and optional on other Wranglers except the S. All versions have an on-demand, part-time 4-wheel-drive system. The Wrangler's image as a rugged, go-anywhere vehicle makes it attractive to some buyers, but we find too many compromises in comfort and performance to make this our everyday transportation. Truck-like ride and handling, excessive noise, a cramped interior with poor ergonomics, and mediocre fuel economy are good reasons to look elsewhere.

Specifications	2-door w/hard top	2-door w/soft top
Wheelbase, in.	93.4	93.4
Overall length, in.	153.0	153.0
Overall width, in.	66.0	66.0
Overall height, in.	69.6	72.0

CONSUMER GUIDE®

	2-door w/hard top	2-door w/soft top
Curb weight, lbs.	NA	2935
Cargo vol., cu. ft.	43.2	43.2
Fuel capacity, gals.	15.0[1]	15.0[1]
Seating capacity	4	4
Front head room, in.	40.2	41.4
Front leg room, max., in.	39.4	39.4
Rear head room, In.	40.5	40.3
Rear leg room, min., in.	35.0	35.0

1. 20.0 gal. on Wrangler Sahara and Renegade.

Powertrain layout: longitudinal front engine/rear-wheel drive with on-demand 4WD.

Engines

	ohv I-4	ohv I-6
Size, liters/cu. in.	2.5/150	4.0/242
Fuel delivery	PFI	PFI
Horsepower @ rpm	123 @ 5250	180 @ 4750
Torque (lbs./ft.) @ rpm	139 @ 3250	220 @ 4000
Availability	S	O

EPA city/highway mpg

	ohv I-4	ohv I-6
5-speed OD manual	18/20	17/21
3-speed automatic		15/16

Assembly point: Brampton, Ontario, Canada.

Prices

Jeep Wrangler	Retail Price	Dealer Invoice	Low Price
S soft top, 23A	$10393	$9890	$10190
Base soft top	12839	11523	11823
Destination charge	485	485	485

Standard equipment:

S: 2.5-liter PFI 4-cylinder engine, 5-speed manual transmission, vinyl front bucket seats, tachometer, coolant temperature and oil pressure gauges, voltmeter, trip odometer, tinted windshield, fuel tank skid plate, swingaway outside spare tire carrier, 205/75R15 tires. Base adds: reclining front seats, fold-and-tumble rear seat, right outside mirror, AM/FM radio, 215/75R15 all-terrain tires on 6-spoke steel wheels.

Prices are accurate at time of publication; subject to manufacturer's change.

Optional equipment:

	Retail Price	Dealer Invoice	Low Price
4.0-liter 6-cylinder engine (NA S)	612	520	532
3-speed automatic transmission (NA S) . .	573	487	499
Requires 4.0-liter engine and tilt steering column.			
Air conditioning (NA S)	878	746	764
Requires 4.0-liter engine, power steering, carpet.			
Power steering, S, Base, & Islander	300	255	261
Rear Trac-Lok differential (NA S)	278	236	242
Reclining front seats, S	75	64	65
Requires rear seat.			
Cloth seats, Islander	107	91	93
Rear seat, S	455	387	396
Requires carpet and reclining front seats.			
Carpet, S & Base	137	116	119
Hardtop, w/regular tinted glass	755	642	657
w/deep-tinted glass	923	785	803
S Pkg. 23B	1030	876	896
Rear bumperettes, carpeting, right-side mirror, reclining front bucket seats, folding rear seat.			
Base Pkg. D	973	827	847
Carpeting, power steering, Convenience Group, extra-capacity fuel tank, tilt steering column, full-size spare tire. Requires 4.0-liter engine.			
Base Pkg. E (Islander)	1350	1148	1175
Islander Decor Group (exterior graphics, color-keyed fender flares and bodyside steps), vinyl spare tire cover, map pocket, carpeting, 4.0-liter engine, 215/75R15 OWL all-terrain tires.			
Base Pkg. F (Islander)	2204	1873	1917
Pkg. E plus, extra-capacity fuel tank, power steering, tilt steering column, full-size spare tire.			
Base Pkg. G (Sahara)	2499	2124	2174
Includes Sahara Decor Group (black exterior trim, fog lights, vinyl spare tire cover, exterior graphics, color-keyed fender flares and bodyside steps, cloth upholstery, map pockets, leather-wrapped steering wheel, carpeting, floormats, Convenience Group, power steering, extra-capacity fuel tank, HD battery and alternator, 4.0-liter engine.			
Base Pkg. H (Sahara)	3004	2553	2613
Pkg. G plus tilt steering column, full-size spare tire, AM/FM cassette.			
Base Pkg. J (Renegade)	4266	3626	3711
Sahara items plus Renegade Decor Group (unique lower body panels and fascias, color-keyed bumpers w/step pads, exterior graphics), 29-9.5R15LT OWL all-terrain tires on alloy wheels. Tilt steering column required with automatic transmission.			
Base Pkg. K (Renegade)	4864	4134	4232
Pkg. J plus tilt steering column, AM/FM cassette, sound bar.			
Convenience Group, S, Base, & Islander .	233	198	203
S, Base, & Islander w/tilt steering column	170	145	148
Intermittent wipers, center console with cup holders, misc. lights.			

	Retail Price	Dealer Invoice	Low Price
HD Alternator & Battery Group, S, Base, & Islander	135	115	117
Right outside mirror, S	27	23	23
Rear defogger for hardtop	164	139	143
Off-Road Pkg., Base	129	110	112
HD shock absorbers, draw bar, tow hooks.			
Sound bar (NA S)	204	173	177
AM/FM radio, S	270	230	235
AM/FM cassette, S	534	454	465
Except S	264	224	230
Tilt steering column, S, Base, & Islander	193	164	168
Sahara & Renegade	130	111	113
5 215/75R15 OWL Wrangler tires, S	272	231	237
Base & Sahara	228	194	198
Base & Sahara w/Pkg. D	117	99	102
5 225/75R15 OWL Wrangler tires, S	463	394	403
Base & Sahara	419	356	365
Base & Sahara w/Pkg. D	308	262	268
Islander	319	271	278
Islander w/Pkg. D	190	162	165
Alloy wheels (std. Renegade)	339	288	295
Metallic paint, Base, Islander, & Renegade	173	147	151
Rear bumperettes, S	36	31	31
Extra-capacity fuel tank, Base, S, & Islander	62	53	54
California emissions pkg.	128	109	111

Lexus ES 300

The ES 300 replaces the ES 250 as the entry-level Lexus. As before, it is based on the Toyota Camry, which also is redesigned for 1992. The change in model designation reflects a change in engine displacement; the previous 2.5-liter twin-cam V-6 is enlarged to 3.0 liters, with a resulting jump in horsepower from 156 to 185. It's the same engine offered in the new V-6 Camrys. The ES 300 comes only as a front-wheel-drive 4-door sedan with standard 5-speed manual transmission or optional 4-speed automatic. It rides the same 103.1-inch wheelbase as the Camry, but has different styling and is longer by nearly five inches, wider by three, and taller by one. Anti-lock brakes and a driver-side air bag are standard. The engine emits a subdued growl when worked hard but otherwise purrs quietly, and there is little wind or tire noise at highway speeds. Driven

Prices are accurate at time of publication; subject to manufacturer's change.

Lexus ES 300

hard along twisty stretches, the ES 300 feels soft, exhibiting moderate body roll and a bit of bouncing up front. But overall, it rides smoothly and grips well. Head clearance for 6-footers is marginal beneath the power moonroof, though it's fine without that option. Long-legged drivers may wish for more rearward seat travel, but the driving position is relatively high for a good view out and adaptable with the power driver's seat and tilt wheel. Though the ES 300 shares some features with the Camry, it has enough differences to justify its higher price. Beware that a full load of options gets it close to $30,000.

Specifications

	4-door notchback
Wheelbase, in.	103.1
Overall length, in.	187.8
Overall width, in.	70.0
Overall height, in.	53.9
Curb weight, lbs.	3362
Cargo vol., cu. ft.	14.3
Fuel capacity, gals.	18.5
Seating capacity	5
Front head room, in.	37.8
Front leg room, max., in.	43.5

	4-door notchback
Rear head room, in.	36.6
Rear leg room, min., in.	33.1

Powertrain layout: transverse front engine/front-wheel drive.

Engines

	dohc V-6
Size, liters/cu. in.	3.0/181
Fuel delivery	PFI
Horsepower @ rpm	185 @ 5200
Torque (lbs./ft.) @ rpm	195 @ 4400
Availability	S

EPA city/highway mpg

5-speed OD manual	19/26
4-speed OD automatic	17/24

Assembly point: Tsutsumi, Japan.

Prices

Lexus ES 300	Retail Price	Dealer Invoice	Low Price
4-door notchback, 5-speed	$25250	$20705	—
4-door notchback, automatic	26150	21443	—
Destination charge	350	350	350

Low price not available at time of publication.

Standard equipment:

3.0-liter PFI V-6, 5-speed manual or 4-speed automatic transmission, anti-lock 4-wheel disc brakes, variable-assist power steering, driver-side air bag, tilt steering column, air conditioning, cruise control, power windows and locks, AM/FM cassette, cloth reclining front bucket seats, folding rear seat-back, remote keyless entry system, theft deterrent system, 205/65R15 Eagle GA tires on alloy wheels.

Optional equipment:

Leather Pkg.	1200	960	—
Heated front seats	300	240	—
Moonroof	900	720	—
CD player	700	525	—
Remote 6-CD auto changer	900	675	—

Prices are accurate at time of publication; subject to manufacturer's change.

Lexus LS 400

Lexus LS 400

The car that proved Japan could successfully compete with established Europeans in the premium sedan category is a virtual rerun for its third season. Lexus' rear-drive LS 400 flagship carries a 4.0-liter 250-horsepower V-8 and 4-speed automatic transmission. Numerous standard features include anti-lock brakes, driver-side air bag, tilt/telescoping steering column, automatic climate control system, and walnut interior trim. The limited options list includes air suspension, tilt/slide power moonroof, leather interior, and traction control (with heated front seats included). The LS 400 is powerful, quiet, composed, and elegant, possessing a level of refinement previously reserved for cars costing much more. We timed an LS 400 at 8.1 seconds from 0-60 mph, a commendable showing. There's no gas guzzler tax, but the V-8 requires premium unleaded fuel and we averaged 19.6 mpg in a mix of city and highway driving. The LS 400 rides with reassuring stability at high speed, yet is supple enough to absorb tar strips and bumps with little or no reaction. The interior is elegant, comfortable, and generally accommodating. An electronic gauge cluster simulates round analog gauges with luminescent readouts. Tall drivers have plenty of room up front, and though there's sufficient leg room in back, there is little space under the front seat to slide your feet. The middle rear passenger must straddle the large driveline hump. While the LS 400's base price has increased $7200 in two years, this car continues to be one of our favorites.

Specifications

	4-door notchback
Wheelbase, in.	110.8
Overall length, in.	196.7
Overall width, in.	71.7
Overall height, in.	55.3
Curb weight, lbs.	3759
Cargo vol., cu. ft.	14.4
Fuel capacity, gals.	22.5
Seating capacity	5
Front head room, in.	38.6
Front leg room, max., in.	43.8
Rear head room, in.	36.8
Rear leg room, min., in.	34.3

Powertrain layout: longitudinal front engine/rear-wheel drive.

Engines

	dohc V-8
Size, liters/cu. in.	4.0/242
Fuel delivery	PFI
Horsepower @ rpm	250 @ 5600
Torque (lbs./ft.) @ rpm	260 @ 4400
Availability	S

EPA city/highway mpg

4-speed OD automatic	18/23

Assembly point: Tahara, Japan.

Prices

Lexus LS 400	Retail Price	Dealer Invoice	Low Price
4-door notchback	$42200	$33760	—
Destination charge	350	350	350

Low price not available at time of publication.

Standard equipment:

4.0-liter DOHC 32-valve PFI V-8, 4-speed automatic transmission, anti-lock braking system, 4-wheel disc brakes, power steering, driver-side air bag, automatic climate control, leather upholstery, reclining front bucket seats, power windows and locks, remote entry, cruise control, power mirrors, *Prices are accurate at time of publication; subject to manufacturer's change.*

tachometer, trip odometer, coolant temperature gauge, tilt/telescopic steering column, AM/FM cassette, intermittent wipers, tool kit, first aid kit, 205/65VR15 tires on alloy wheels.

Optional equipment:

	Retail Price	Dealer Invoice	Low Price
Moonroof	1000	800	923
Traction control & heated front seats	1700	1360	1569
Electronic air suspension	1500	1200	1385
Requires all-season tires and moonroof.			
Memory system	800	640	738
Lexus/Nakamichi audio system	1000	750	897
Requires CD changer.			
Remote 6-CD auto-changer	900	675	808
All-season tires	NC	NC	NC

Lexus SC 300/400

Lexus SC 400

The rear-drive SC 400 2-door coupe went on sale in June 1991 carrying the same 250-horsepower 4.0-liter V-8 and 4-speed automatic as the Lexus LS 400 sedan, though on a shorter chassis. It was joined in the fall by the SC 300. The new entry shares the SC 400's 2 + 2 notchback body, but with slightly different front-end styling, fewer standard features, and a 225-horsepower 3.0-liter inline 6-cylinder engine. A 5-speed manual transmission is standard and a

4-speed automatic is optional. The Lexus coupes are 5.6 inches shorter, 1.2 inches narrower, and 2.9 inches lower than the LS 400 sedan, and ride a wheelbase 4.9 inches shorter. Anti-lock brakes and a driver-side air bag are standard on both coupes. Major options include traction control and a power moonroof. The SC 400 blasts to 60 mph almost a second faster than the LS 400 sedan: 7.3 seconds in our test. While we haven't yet driven an SC 300, we'd expect performance to be almost as good. Road, wind, and engine noise aren't quite as muted as in the sedan, though the SC 400 is still highly refined. Body roll in tight turns is

Specifications

	2-door notchback
Wheelbase, in.	105.9
Overall length, in.	191.1
Overall width, in.	70.5
Overall height, in.	52.4
Curb weight, lbs.	3494[1]
Cargo vol., cu. ft.	9.3
Fuel capacity, gals.	20.6
Seating capacity	4
Front head room, in.	38.3
Front leg room, max., in.	44.1
Rear head room, in.	36.1
Rear leg room, min., in.	27.2

1. SC 300; 3575 lbs., SC 400.

Powertrain layout: longitudinal front engine/rear-wheel drive.

Engines

	dohc I-6	dohc V-8
Size, liters/cu. in.	3.0/183	4.0/242
Fuel delivery	PFI	PFI
Horsepower @ rpm	225 @ 6000	250 @ 5600
Torque (lbs./ft.) @ rpm	210 @ 4800	260 @ 4400
Availability	S[1]	S[2]
EPA city/highway mpg		
5-speed OD manual	NA	
4-speed OD automatic	18/22	18/22

1. SC 300.   2. SC 400.

Assembly point: Tsutsumi, Japan.

Prices are accurate at time of publication; subject to manufacturer's change.

barely evident, and the ride is supple, though not quite as lush as that of the LS 400. With 6-footers up front, the seats will likely be pushed back far enough back to almost eliminate rear leg room. Taller drivers may find head room to be limited, particularly with the optional moonroof. The trunk is small for a car of this size. The dashboard is similar to the sedan's, with attractive gauges and easy-to-use controls. We're highly impressed with the SC 400 and find it an attractive alternative to the more expensive German luxury coupes.

Prices

Lexus SC 300/400	Retail Price	Dealer Invoice	Low Price
300 2-door notchback, 5-speed	$31100	—	—
300 2-door notchback, automatic	32000	—	—
400 2-door notchback	37500	30000	—
Destination charge	350	350	350

Low prices and 300 invoice prices not available at time of publication.

Standard equipment:

300: 3.0-liter DOHC PFI V-6 engine, 5-speed manual or 4-speed automatic transmission, 4-wheel anti-lock disc brakes, variable-assist power steering, driver-side air bag, automatic climate control, tinted glass, power front seats, power tilt/telescoping steering wheel, rear defogger, heated power mirrors, power windows and door locks, remote keyless entry system, cruise control, tachometer, 7-speaker AM/FM cassette, power antenna, full size spare, 215/60VR15 Eagle GSD tires on alloy wheels. **400** adds: 4.0-liter DOHC PFI V-8 engine, 4-speed automatic transmission, leather upholstery, power front seats with driver-side memory system, 225/55VR16 Eagle GSD tires.

Optional equipment:

Traction control system	1600	1280	—
Includes heated front seats.			
Remote CD player w/auto changer	900	675	—
Lexus/Nakamichi premium sound system .	1000	750	—
Requires CD player.			
Leather seats, 300	1700	NA	—
Includes memory system.			
Rear spoiler, 400	300	240	—
Power moonroof	900	720	—
Heated front seats, 300	300	NA	—

Lincoln Continental

1991 Lincoln Continental Signature Series

A passenger-side air bag is standard for 1992 as the major change for the Continental, Lincoln's front-drive luxury sedan. The Continental started the 1990 model year with a standard passenger-side air bag. A shortage of propellent to inflate air bags forced Lincoln to drop it during the second half of the model year. A driver-side air bag has been standard since 1989. Among other changes for this year, a new transmission shift interlock requires the brakes be applied to shift out of park and most body panels are now made of corrosion-resistant 2-sided galvanized steel. The Continental comes in base Executive Series and plusher Signature Series price levels, both with a 160-horse-power 3.8-liter V-6 engine and a 4-speed automatic transmission with electronic shift controls. The Continental has adequate acceleration but lacks the brisk, refined performance we expect of cars this expensive. The engine responds slowly to the throttle and sounds rough and coarse in acceleration. The spacious interior has room for four adults to stretch out, and you can squeeze in as many as six. The roomy trunk has a flat floor that's wide and long, and a low, bumper-height opening that eases loading and unloading. Despite the standard dual air bags and other commendable features, the Continental lacks the overall performance and value of some competing luxury sedans in the same price range, including the Cadillac De Ville and Seville.

Prices are accurate at time of publication; subject to manufacturer's change.

Specifications

	4-door notchback
Wheelbase, in.	109.0
Overall length, in.	205.1
Overall width, in.	72.7
Overall height, in.	55.6
Curb weight, lbs.	3628
Cargo vol., cu. ft.	19.1
Fuel capacity, gals.	18.4
Seating capacity	6
Front head room, in.	38.7
Front leg room, max., in.	41.7
Rear head room, in.	38.4
Rear leg room, min., in.	39.2

Powertrain layout: transverse front engine/front-wheel drive.

Engines

	ohv V-6
Size, liters/cu. in.	3.8/232
Fuel delivery	PFI
Horsepower @ rpm	160 @ 4000
Torque (lbs./ft.) @ rpm	225 @ 3000
Availability	S

EPA city/highway mpg

4-speed OD automatic	17/25

Assembly point: Wixom, Mich.

Prices

Lincoln Continental	Retail Price	Dealer Invoice	Low Price
Executive 4-door notchback	$32263	$27446	$28046
Signature Series 4-door notchback	34253	29118	29718
Destination charge	590	590	590

Standard equipment:

3.8-liter PFI V-6, 4-speed automatic transmission, anti-lock 4-wheel disc brakes, power steering, driver- and passenger-side air bag, automatic climate control, 50/50 leather front seat (cloth is available at no cost), power driver's seat with power recliner, tilt steering column, cruise control, automatic parking brake release, rear defogger, heated power mirrors, power windows

CONSUMER GUIDE®

and locks, remote fuel door and decklid releases, AM/FM cassette, power antenna, tinted glass, intermittent wipers, cornering lamps, electronic instruments, coolant temperature and oil pressure gauges, voltmeter, trip odometer, trip computer, service interval reminder, door pockets, right visor mirror, front floormats, 205/70R15 tires. **Signature Series** adds: power passenger seat with power recliner, keyless illuminated entry, Autolamp system, automatic dimmer, power decklid pulldown, lighted visor mirrors, leather-wrapped steering wheel, alloy wheels.

Optional equipment:	Retail Price	Dealer Invoice	Low Price
Anti-theft alarm system	295	248	260
Comfort/Convenience Group, base	828	696	729
Power passenger seat with power recliner, Autolamp system, automatic dimmer, lighted visor mirrors, power decklid pulldown, rear floormats.			
Special Value Pkg. 952A, base	NC	NC	NC
Comfort/Convenience Group, keyless illuminated entry, leather-wrapped steering wheel, alloy wheels.			
Overhead Console Group	361	303	318
Includes compass and automatic day/night mirror; base requires Comfort/Convenience Group; not available with power moonroof.			
Keyless illuminated entry, base	306	257	269
Requires Comfort/Convenience Group.			
Power moonroof	1550	1303	1364
Base requires Comfort/Convenience Group.			
CD player	617	519	543
Requires Ford JBL audio system.			
Ford JBL audio system	577	484	508
Base requires Comfort/Convenience Group.			
Leather-wrapped steering wheel, base . . .	120	101	106
Cellular telephone	459	386	404
Insta-Clear heated windshield	309	259	272
Base requires Comfort/Convenience Group.			
Alloy wheels, base	556	467	489
Engine block heater	61	51	54
California emissions pkg.	100	84	88

Lincoln Mark VII

Lincoln's rear-drive luxury coupe gets only minor trim changes for its final season under the Mark VII label. It is scheduled to be redesigned for 1993 and renamed Mark VIII. The Mark VIII will be powered by Ford Motor Company's 4.6-liter overhead-camshaft V-8. For 1992 it returns in Bill Blass Designer Series and sportier LSC trim levels.

Prices are accurate at time of publication; subject to manufacturer's change.

1991 Lincoln Mark VII LSC

Specifications

	2-door notchback
Wheelbase, in.	108.5
Overall length, in.	202.8
Overall width, in.	70.9
Overall height, in.	54.2
Curb weight, lbs.	3782
Cargo vol., cu. ft.	14.2
Fuel capacity, gals.	21.0
Seating capacity	5
Front head room, in.	37.8
Front leg room, max., in.	42.0
Rear head room, in.	37.1
Rear leg room, min., in.	36.9

Powertrain layout: longitudinal front engine/rear-wheel drive.

Engines

	ohv V-8
Size, liters/cu. in.	5.0/302
Fuel delivery	PFI
Horsepower @ rpm	225 @ 4200
Torque (lbs./ft.) @ rpm	300 @ 3200
Availability	S

EPA city/highway mpg

4-speed OD automatic	17/24

Assembly point: Wixom, Mich.

They share a 225-horsepower 5.0-liter overhead-valve V-8 and 4-speed automatic transmission. A driver-side air bag and anti-lock brakes are standard on both. Both models have potent acceleration and capable anti-lock brakes. However, the firm suspension gives them a stiff, harsh ride over bumps and the wide tires have poor traction in rain and snow. Like most coupes, the Mark VII has little rear seat room. The well-shaped, comfortable front seats have adequate room. The Mark VII was introduced as a 1984 model and has become nearly invisible in the luxury coupe market the past few years. That's bad news for Lincoln, but good news for consumers. Dealers should be anxious to find a prospective buyer. Prospective buyers should encourage dealers to offer big discounts, which are likely, given the Mark VII's slow sales.

Prices

Lincoln Mark VII	Retail Price	Dealer Invoice	Low Price
Bill Blass 2-door notchback	$32032	$27252	$27702
LSC 2-door notchback	32156	27356	27806
Destination charge	590	590	590

Standard equipment:

Bill Blass: 5.0-liter PFI V-8, 4-speed automatic transmission, anti-lock 4-wheel disc brakes, power steering, driver-side air bag, automatic climate control, power front bucket seats, leather upholstery (cloth may be substituted at no cost), keyless illuminated entry, power windows and locks, heated power mirrors, overhead console with compass and thermometer, cruise control, power decklid pulldown, Autolamp system, automatic dimmer, rear defogger, tinted glass, AM/FM cassette, power antenna, remote fuel door and decklid releases, cornering lamps, electronic instruments, trip odometer, intermittent wipers, tilt steering column, trip computer, center console with armrest, storage, and cupholder, lighted visor mirrors, 225/60R16 tires on alloy wheels. **LSC** adds: articulated sport seats, analog instruments including tachometer and coolant temperature gauge, fog lights.

Optional equipment:

Anti-theft alarm system	295	248	217
Traction-Lok axle	101	85	74
Special Edition Pkg.	680	571	500
Includes unique BBS wheels with dark titanium wheel spiders.			
Automatic day/night mirror	111	93	81

Prices are accurate at time of publication; subject to manufacturer's change.

	Retail Price	Dealer Invoice	Low Price
Power moonroof	1550	1303	1140
CD player	299	251	220
Requires Ford JBL audio system.			
Ford JBL audio system	576	484	424
Cellular telephone	459	386	338
Engine block heater	61	51	45
California emissions pkg.	100	84	74

Lincoln Town Car

Lincoln Town Car Cartier Designer Series

A front passenger-side air bag is standard this year on the Town Car, Lincoln's rear-drive luxury sedan. A driver-side air bag has been standard since 1990. A passenger-side air bag was standard at the start of the 1990 model year, but a shortage of propellent resulted in it being dropped. Other major changes for 1992 will arrive later in the model year. They include a new electronically controlled automatic transmission, a shift interlock that requires the brakes be applied to shift out of park, and an optional trunk-mounted compact disc changer. The Town Car was restyled for 1990 and last year it received a new engine, a 4.6-liter V-8 engine with overhead camshafts instead of the overhead valves usually found on American V-8s. The standard version of the 4.6-liter engine is rated at 190 horsepower. Optional dual exhausts boost horsepower to 210. Anti-lock brakes are standard and a traction-control system, called Traction Assist, is optional. The 4.6-liter V-8 gives the heavy Town

Car much livelier acceleration from low speeds and stronger passing ability than the old 5.0-liter overhead-valve V-8. The new engine is also quieter, smoother, and more economical. We reached nearly 25 mpg in highway cruising, a pipe dream with the old V-8. However, in urban rush-hour driving, we recorded less than 14 mpg. Bountiful interior space is one of the Town Car's best features. There's ample head room all around and generous leg room except in the middle front position, where occupants find their knees pressed into the dashboard. Lincoln has greatly improved the Town Car's performance and safety features the past two years. It's a better choice than the rival Cadillac Brougham in a full-size, rear-drive American luxury car.

Specifications

	4-door notchback
Wheelbase, in.	117.4
Overall length, in.	218.8
Overall width, in.	76.9
Overall height, in.	56.9
Curb weight, lbs.	4024
Cargo vol., cu. ft.	22.3
Fuel capacity, gals.	20.0
Seating capacity	6
Front head room, in.	39.0
Front leg room, max., in.	42.5
Rear head room, in.	38.1
Rear leg room, min., in.	42.8

Powertrain layout: longitudinal front engine/rear-wheel drive.

Engines

	ohc V-8
Size, liters/cu. in.	4.6/281
Fuel delivery	PFI
Horsepower @ rpm	190 @ 4200[1]
Torque (lbs./ft.) @ rpm	260 @ 3200[2]
Availability	S

EPA city/highway mpg

4-speed OD automatic	17/23

1. 210 @ 4600 with dual exhaust.   2. 270 @ 3400 with dual exhaust.

Assembly point: Wixom, Mich.

Prices are accurate at time of publication; subject to manufacturer's change.

Prices

Lincoln Town Car	Retail Price	Dealer Invoice	Low Price
Executive 4-door notchback	$31211	$26577	$27577
Signature Series 4-door notchback	34252	29132	30132
Cartier Designer Series 4-door notchback .	36340	30885	31885
Destination charge	590	590	590

Standard equipment:

4.6-liter PFI V-8, 4-speed automatic transmission, 4-wheel anti-lock disc brakes, power steering, driver- and passenger-side air bags, automatic climate control, 50/50 front seat with folding armrests, power driver's seat, rear armrest, power windows and locks, tilt steering column, cruise control, automatic parking brake release, heated power mirrors, rear defogger, AM/FM cassette, power antenna, tinted glass, remote fuel door release, cornering lamps, intermittent wipers, coolant temperature gauge, front floormats, 215/70R15 whitewall tires. **Signature Series** adds: power passenger seat, electronic instruments, keyless illuminated entry, power decklid pulldown, leather-wrapped steering wheel, Autolamp system, automatic dimmer, lighted visor mirrors, seatback pockets. **Cartier Designer Series** adds: cloth and leather seat with position memory and power lumbar support, power recliners, Ford JBL audio system.

Optional equipment:

Traction Assist	222	187	200
Dual exhaust system	83	69	75
Leather seat trim (std. Cartier)	570	479	513
Anti-theft alarm system	295	248	266
Base requires keyless illuminated entry.			
Comfort/Convenience Group, base	658	553	592
Autolamp system, automatic dimmer, power passenger seat, power decklid pulldown, lighted visor mirrors.			
Electronic instrumentation, base	249	209	224
Keyless illuminated entry, base	225	189	203
Requires Comfort/Convenience Group.			
Programmable memory seat	548	460	493
Automatic day/night mirror	111	93	100
Base requires Comfort/Convenience Group.			
Power moonroof	1550	1303	1395
Base requires Comfort/Convenience Group.			
CD player	833	700	750
Base requires Comfort/Convenience Group; base and Signature require Ford JBL audio system.			
Ford JBL audio system, base & Signature .	576	484	518
Leather-wrapped steering wheel, base . . .	120	101	108

CONSUMER GUIDE®

	Retail Price	Dealer Invoice	Low Price
Padded vinyl roof	800	672	720
Insta-Clear heated windshield	309	259	278

Base requires electronic instruments and Comfort/Convenience Group.

Heavy-Duty Pkg.	770	647	693
High altitude	688	578	619

3.55 Traction-Lok axle, dual exhaust, HD cooling, transmission oil and and steering fluid coolers, uprated suspension, full-size spare tire, HD alternator and battery, steel wheels.

Dual exhaust	83	69	75
Trailer Tow III Pkg.	417	351	375
High altitude	335	281	302

3.55 axle ratio, dual exhaust, HD cooling, transmission oil and and steering fluid coolers, uprated suspension, full-size spare tire, trailer wiring harness, etc.

Livery Pkg.	417	351	375
High altitude	335	281	302

Same as Heavy Duty Pkg. but with standard cooling system.

Alloy wheels, Executive	556	467	500
Cellular telephone	459	386	413
Engine block heater	61	51	55
California emissions pkg.	100	84	90

Mazda Miata

Mazda Miata

Mazda has little reason to mess with its successful roadster, so mechanical and appearance changes for 1992 are limited to convenience items. A remote trunk release joins the standard equipment roster, a power antenna has been

Prices are accurate at time of publication; subject to manufacturer's change.

added to the "B" option package, the optional hardtop gets an electric rear-window defogger, and color choices have been broadened to include bright yellow and black. Miata is a rear-drive 2-seater that comes in a single trim level. A Special Edition model with leather upholstery and British racing green paint isn't returning after a limited run of 4000 units for 1991. The Miata's engine is a dual-cam 1.6-liter 4-cylinder that makes 116 horsepower with the standard 5-speed manual transmission and 105 with the optional 4-speed automatic. Standard equipment includes a driver-side air bag and a manual folding convertible top. Anti-lock brakes are optional. Acceleration is energetic

Specifications

	2-door conv.
Wheelbase, in.	89.2
Overall length, in.	155.4
Overall width, in.	65.9
Overall height, in.	48.2
Curb weight, lbs.	2216
Cargo vol., cu. ft.	3.6
Fuel capacity, gals.	11.9
Seating capacity	2
Front head room, in.	37.1
Front leg room, max., in.	42.7
Rear head room, in.	—
Rear leg room, min., in.	—

Powertrain layout: longitudinal front engine/rear-wheel drive.

Engines

	dohc I-4
Size, liters/cu. in.	1.6/97
Fuel delivery	PFI
Horsepower @ rpm	116 @ 6500[1]
Torque (lbs./ft.) @ rpm	100 @ 5500
Availability	S[2]

EPA city/highway mpg

5-speed OD manual	24/30
4-speed OD automatic	23/28

1. 105 @ 6000 with automatic.   2. 100 @ 4000 with automatic.

Assembly point: Hiroshima, Japan.

with the manual transmission, decidedly more subdued with the automatic, but neither engine makes a lot of low-end power. For such a fine-handling sports car, the Miata offers a compliant ride that won't jar your teeth the way some other sports cars are apt to do. The standard 4-wheel disc brakes are powerful enough, but we find them prone to early rear-wheel locking during panic stops. We recommend the optional anti-lock brakes. The cabin is fairly roomy for a car of this size, but the trunk is minuscule—not unusual for a 2-seater. Overall, Miata remains one of our favorites. It's still the best bargain among sports cars.

Prices

Mazda Miata	Retail Price	Dealer Invoice	Low Price
2-door convertible	$14800	NA	NA
Destination charge	350	350	350

Dealer invoice and low price not available at time of publication.

Standard equipment:

1.6-liter DOHC 16-valve PFI 4-cylinder engine, 5-speed manual transmission, 4-wheel disc brakes, driver-side air bag, cloth reclining bucket seats, tachometer, coolant temperature gauge, trip odometer, intermittent wipers, remote decklid release, 185/60R14 tires.

Optional equipment:

4-speed automatic transmission	750	NA	NA
Anti-lock brakes	900	765	900
Requires Pkg. B.			
Air conditioning	830	NA	NA
Detachable hardtop	1500	NA	NA
Includes rear defogger; requires Option Pkg. A or B.			
Option Pkg. A	1370	1151	1370
Power steering, alloy wheels, leather-wrapped steering wheel, AM/FM cassette.			
Option Pkg. B	2040	NA	NA
Pkg. A plus power windows, cruise control, headrest speakers, power antenna.			
Limited-slip differential	250	200	250
CD player	600	480	600
Requires Option Pkg. B.			
Floormats	65	NA	NA
California emissions pkg.	70	NA	NA

Prices are accurate at time of publication; subject to manufacturer's change.

Mazda MPV

Mazda MPV

Eight-passenger seating and a power moonroof are new options for Mazda's minivan. The MPV (Multi-Purpose Vehicle) returns in a single body length with rear-wheel drive or optional 4-wheel drive. Seats for five are standard; seats for seven or eight are optional. Standard on 2WD versions is a 2.6-liter 4-cylinder engine with 121 horsepower. A V-6 with 155-horsepower—up five from last year—is optional on 2WD models and standard on 4WD MPVs. A 4-speed overdrive automatic is the only transmission offered. Rear-wheel anti-lock brakes are standard across the line. MPV has a swing-open rear side door rather than the more common sliding door. Compact dimensions, good visibility, and a well-controlled suspension make MPV maneuverable and car-like to drive. However, models with the 4-cylinder engine and 4WD have only leisurely acceleration because there's too much weight for too little engine (4WD adds nearly 500 pounds to the curb weight). The 4WD and rear-drive versions with the V-6 also have a healthy thirst for fuel. The interior has a well-designed dashboard and easy-to-reach controls. The swing-open rear side door requires less muscle to open than most sliding side doors, but makes entry or loading cargo difficult in tight parking spaces. There's little cargo space with all seats in place, and unlike some minivans that have light, easy-to-remove rear seats,

MPV's are bolted to the floor. On balance, however, the MPV is a well-designed minivan that should serve well as a family vehicle.

Specifications

	4-door van	4WD 4-door van
Wheelbase, in.	110.4	110.4
Overall length, in.	175.8	175.8
Overall width, in.	71.9	72.3
Overall height, in.	68.1	70.8
Curb weight, lbs.	3459	3948
Cargo vol., cu. ft.	37.5	37.5
Fuel capacity, gals.	15.9[1]	19.8
Seating capacity	8	8
Front head room, in.	40.0	40.0
Front leg room, max., in.	40.6	40.6
Rear head room, in.	39.0	39.0
Rear leg room, min., in.	34.8	34.8

1. 19.6 gals., V-6.

Powertrain layout: longitudinal front engine/rear-wheel drive or on-demand 4WD.

Engines

	ohc I-4	ohc V-6
Size, liters/cu. in.	2.6/159	3.0/180
Fuel delivery	PFI	PFI
Horsepower @ rpm	121 @ 4600	155 @ 5000
Torque (lbs./ft.) @ rpm	149 @ 3500	169 @ 4000
Availability	S	O[1]

EPA city/highway mpg

4-speed OD automatic	18/24	17/22

1. Std. 4WD.

Assembly point: Hiroshima, Japan.

Prices

Mazda MPV	Retail Price	Dealer Invoice	Low Price
Wagon, 5-pass., 2.6	$15165	—	—
Wagon, 7-pass., 2.6	16585	—	—

Prices are accurate at time of publication; subject to manufacturer's change.

	Retail Price	Dealer Invoice	Low Price
Wagon, 7-pass., 3.0	17365	—	—
4WD wagon, 7-pass., 3.0	20135	—	—
Destination charge	400	400	400

Dealer invoice and low price not available at time of publication.

Standard equipment:

5-passenger: 2.6-liter PFI 4-cylinder engine, 4-speed automatic transmission, anti-lock rear brakes, power steering, reclining front bucket seats, 3-passenger middle bench seat, remote mirrors, tachometer, coolant temperature gauge, trip odometer, intermittent wipers, rear defogger and wiper/washer, tinted glass, door pockets, remote fuel door release, tilt steering column, AM/FM cassette, 205/70R14 tires. **7-passenger:** 2.6-liter 4-cylinder or 3.0-liter PFI V-6, two-passenger middle and 3-passenger rear bench seats, power mirrors. 4WD has selectable 4WD, 215/65R15 tires on alloy wheels.

Optional equipment:

Single air conditioning	859	704	791
Dual air conditioning (3.0 req.)	1497	1228	1380
Touring Pkg.	570	NA	NA
Eight-passenger seating, beverage holders, outboard armrests.			
Cold Pkg.	298	256	281
HD battery, larger windshield washer solvent reservoir, rear heater.			
Value Pkg. A, 2WD	1050	NA	NA
Power windows and locks, cruise control, privacy glass, cruise control.			
Value Pkg. B, 2WD V6	1695	NA	NA
Pkg. A plus 16-inch tires on alloy wheels, color-keyed exterior treatment.			
Value Pkg. C, 4WD	1250	NA	NA
Pkg. A plus color-keyed exterior treatment.			
Luxury Pkg. (Option Pkg. D), 2WD V6 . . .	3895	NA	NA
4WD	3450	NA	NA
Value Pkg. B (2WD), Value Pkg. C (4WD), leather seating, leather-wrapped steering wheel, color-keyed bodyside moldings, two-tone paint, lace alloy wheels; requires dual air conditioning.			
CD player, 2WD V6	699	559	637
Requires Value Pkg. B or C, or Luxury Pkg.			
Power monroof, 2WD V6	995	NA	NA
Requires Value Pkg. B or C or Luxury Pkg.			
Two-tone paint, 2WD	251	206	231
Towing Pkg., 2WD V6	498	428	469
4WD	398	342	375
Transmission oil cooler, HD radiator and fan, conventional spare, automatic load leveling (2WD).			
Alloy wheels, 2WD	NA	NA	NA
California emissions pkg.	70	NA	NA

Mazda MX-3

Mazda MX-3 GS

Mazda's new front-drive MX-3 joins the sports coupe fray
and attempts to one-up Japanese rivals such as the Nissan
NX 1600/2000, Geo Storm, and Toyota Paseo by offering a
V-6 engine. A 3-door hatchback coupe, the MX-3 is based
on the subcompact Mazda 323 platform. Its 96.3-inch
wheelbase and 165.7-inch overall length are almost identical to the Geo Storm's. MX-3 comes in two versions. The
base model has an 88-horsepower 1.6-liter 4-cylinder engine. The upscale GS comes with the industry's smallest
V-6 engine, a new 1.8-liter 24-valve, twin-cam unit packing
130 horsepower. Both engines come with a 5-speed manual
transmission standard and a 4-speed automatic optional.
Anti-lock brakes are optional only on the GS. We haven't
driven a base MX-3 with the 4-cylinder engine, but since
it weighs about 100 pounds more than a 323 hatchback
and offers only six additional horsepower, we'd expect acceleration to be adequate but hardly sporting. The GS, however, is a different story. The eager V-6 revs to its 7000-rpm
redline with the smoothness of an electric motor. We clocked
a GS at 8.9 seconds to 60 mph, which puts it near the top
of this class in acceleration. The GS rides well over patchy
pavement and bumpy roads, especially for a sports coupe
that offers such agile handling. Inside, head and hip room
might be tight for larger drivers, and the rear seat is no
place for even medium-size adults. The MX-3 is a worthy
addition to the growing ranks of sports coupes.

Prices are accurate at time of publication; subject to manufacturer's change.

Specifications

	3-door hatchback
Wheelbase, in.	96.3
Overall length, in.	165.7
Overall width, in.	66.7
Overall height, in.	51.6
Curb weight, lbs.	2332[1]
Cargo vol., cu. ft.	36.6
Fuel capacity, gals.	13.2
Seating capacity	4
Front head room, in.	38.2
Front leg room, max., in.	42.6
Rear head room, in.	33.9
Rear leg room, min., in.	31.1

1. Base model; 2541 lbs., GS.

Powertrain layout: transverse front engine/front-wheel drive.

Engines

	ohc I-4	dohc V-6
Size, liters/cu. in.	1.6/97	1.8/113
Fuel delivery	PFI	PFI
Horsepower @ rpm	88 @ 5000	130 @ 6500
Torque (lbs./ft.) @ rpm	98 @ 4000	115 @ 4500
Availability	S	S[1]

EPA city/highway mpg

	ohc I-4	dohc V-6
5-speed OD manual	29/35	23/28
4-speed OD automatic	25/32	20/27

1. GS.

Assembly point: Hiroshima, Japan.

Prices

Mazda MX-3	Retail Price	Dealer Invoice	Low Price
3-door hatchback	$11000	—	—
GS 3-door hatchback	13800	—	—
Destination charge	350	350	350

Dealer invoice and low price not available at time of publication.

Standard equipment:

1.6-liter PFI 16-valve 4-cylinder engine, 5-speed manual transmission, cloth reclining front bucket seats, power steering, tachometer, coolant temperature gauge, variable-intermittent wipers, rear defogger, folding rear seat, power mirrors, tinted glass, remote fuel door and hatch releases, rear cargo cover, wheel covers, 185/65R14 tires. **GS** adds: 1.8-liter DOHC 24-valve V-6, 4-wheel disc brakes, rear wiper/washer, front and rear spoilers, tilt steering column, 205/55R15 tires on alloy wheels.

Optional equipment:	Retail Price	Dealer Invoice	Low Price
Anti-lock brakes, GS	900	—	—
4-speed automatic transmission	700	—	—
Air conditioning	830	—	—
Power Pkg., base	300	—	—
Power windows and locks.			
Power Pkg., GS	500	—	—
Power windows and locks, cruise control.			
Power sunroof, GS	560	—	—
AM/FM cassette	450	—	—
CD player, GS	520	—	—
Alloy wheels, base	425	—	—
Armrest	65	—	—
Floormats	70	—	—
California emissions pkg.	70	—	—

Mazda 323/Protege

Mazda's front-drive subcompacts are unchanged for 1992. The 323 is a 3-door hatchback and Protege a 4-door notch-back sedan. Protege's 98.4-inch wheelbase is longer than the 323's by two inches and its overall length of 171.5 inches is longer by about eight. The Protege's basic design is used for the Ford Escort and Mercury Tracer. The 323 comes in base and SE trim, Protege in DX and LX guise. A Protege with permanently engaged 4-wheel drive was discontinued midway through the 1991 model run. The 323 uses an 82-horsepower 1.6-liter 4-cylinder engine. Protege DX carries a 1.8-liter four with 103 horsepower. The top-of-the-line Protege LX has a twin-cam version of the 1.8 rated at 125 horsepower. The 323 and Protege are solid, competitive entries in the subcompact field. The standout in Mazda's small-car line is the Protege LX, a roomy sedan with com-

Prices are accurate at time of publication; subject to manufacturer's change.

Mazda 323

mendable handling, good fuel economy, and a firm, stable ride. Its 125-horsepower engine supplies lively acceleration with manual transmission, and better-than-average quickness for this class when coupled to the automatic. DX versions have similar attributes, but with a moderate drop in acceleration and handling, and also in features and price. The 323 hatchback has less interior space than the Protege, but still has adequate rear head and leg room. While the 323 and Protege DX don't match the road manners of the Protege LX, they offer good value for the money.

Specifications

	323 3-door hatchback	Protege 4-door notchback
Wheelbase, in.	96.5	98.4
Overall length, in.	163.6	171.5
Overall width, in.	65.7	65.9
Overall height, in.	54.3	54.1
Curb weight, lbs.	2238	2359
Cargo vol., cu. ft.	15.8	12.8
Fuel capacity, gals.	13.2	14.5
Seating capacity	5	5
Front head room, in.	38.6	38.4
Front leg room, max., in.	42.2	42.2
Rear head room, in.	37.6	37.1
Rear leg room, min., in.	34.2	34.6

Powertrain layout: transverse front engine/front-wheel drive.

Engines	ohc I-4	323 3-door hatchback ohc I-4	Protege 4-door notchback dohc I-4
Size, liters/cu. in.	1.6/97	1.8/112	1.8/112
Fuel delivery	PFI	PFI	PFI
Horsepower @ rpm	82 @ 5000	103 @ 5500	125 @ 6500
Torque (lbs./ft.) @ rpm	92 @ 2500	111 @ 4000	114 @ 4500
Availability	S[1]	S[2]	S[3]
EPA city/highway mpg			
5-speed OD manual	29/37	28/36	25/30
4-speed OD automatic	26/33	24/31	24/29

1. 323.   2. Protege DX.   3. Protege LX.

Assembly point: Hiroshima, Japan.

Prices

Mazda 323/Protege	Retail Price	Dealer Invoice	Low Price
323 3-door hatchback	$6999	—	—
323 SE 3-door hatchback	8299	—	—
Protege DX 4-door notchback	9999	—	—
Protege LX 4-door notchback	11699	—	—
Destination charge	350	350	350

Dealer invoice and low price not available at time of publication.

Standard equipment:

323: 1.6-liter PFI 4-cylinder engine, 5-speed manual transmission, motorized front shoulder belts, vinyl reclining front bucket seats, one-piece folding rear seat, left remote mirror, coolant temperature gauge, trip odometer, cargo cover, console with storage, rear defogger, 155SR13 tires. **SE** adds: cloth upholstery, 60/40 split rear seat, dual remote mirrors, tinted glass, door pockets, bodyside moldings, wheel covers. **Protege DX:** 1.8-liter SOHC 16-valve 4-cylinder engine, 5-speed manual transmission, motorized front shoulder belts, cloth reclining front bucket seats, 60/40 folding rear seat, remote mirrors, coolant temperature gauge, trip odometer, console with storage, tinted glass, bodyside moldings, door pockets, remote fuel door and decklid releases, right visor mirror, digital clock, rear defogger, 175/70R13 tires. **LX** adds to DX: DOHC 16-valve engine, 4-wheel disc brakes, velour upholstery, power windows and locks, cruise control, AM/FM cassette, power mirrors, intermittent wipers, tachometer, cupholder, left visor mirror, 185/60R14 tires.

Prices are accurate at time of publication; subject to manufacturer's change.

Optional equipment:	Retail Price	Dealer Invoice	Low Price
4-speed automatic transmission	700	630	649
Power steering	250	213	226
Air conditioning	840	NA	NA
Convenience Pkg., 323 SE	125	NA	NA
Rear wiper/washer, remote fuel door and hatch releases, intermittent wipers, digital clock.			
Convenience Pkg., Protege DX	225	NA	NA
Tilt steering column, tachometer, intermittent wipers, cupholder, trunk light, misc. warning lights.			
AM/FM radio, Protege DX	330	NA	NA
AM/FM cassette, 323 SE, Protege DX . . .	450	342	386
Power sunroof, Protege LX	560	NA	NA
Alloy wheels, Protege LX	425	NA	NA
Floormats	65	NA	NA
California emissions pkg.	70	NA	NA

Mazda 626/MX-6

Mazda 626 LX

The slow-selling Touring Sedan 5-door hatchback has been dropped, leaving a 4-door notchback sedan as the only body style for the 626. Otherwise, the 626 and similar MX-6 2-door sports coupe return unchanged for their final season in this form. Redesigned versions of these cars are expected to go on sale in spring 1992 as early 1993 models. Both are built at Mazda's Flat Rock, Michigan, plant, where the

Ford Probe (similar to the MX-6) also is built. The 626 sedan comes in DX and LX guise, both with a 110-horsepower 2.2-liter 4-cylinder engine. The MX-6 also comes in DX and LX trim with the same engine, and in GT trim with a 145-horsepower turbocharged 2.2-liter 4-cylinder. Anti-lock brakes are optional on LX models and the GT. The DX and LX models are known for good fuel economy and above-average reliability, while the performance-oriented MX-6 GT is a little muscle car. The 626 is overshadowed in the market by best-sellers such as the Honda

Specifications

	MX-6 2-door notchback	626 4-door notchback
Wheelbase, in.	99.0	101.4
Overall length, in.	177.0	179.3
Overall width, in.	66.5	66.5
Overall height, in.	53.5	55.5
Curb weight, lbs.	2560	2610
Cargo vol., cu. ft.	15.4	15.9
Fuel capacity, gals.	15.9	15.9
Seating capacity	4	5
Front head room, in.	38.4	39.0
Front leg room, max., in.	43.6	43.7
Rear head room, in.	37.8	37.8
Rear leg room, min., in.	31.8	36.6

Powertrain layout: transverse front engine/front-wheel drive.

Engines

	ohc I-4	Turbo ohc I-4
Size, liters/cu. in.	2.2/133	2.2/133
Fuel delivery	PFI	PFI
Horsepower @ rpm	110 @ 4700	145 @ 4300
Torque (lbs./ft.) @ rpm	130 @ 3000	190 @ 3500
Availability	S	S[1]

EPA city/highway mpg

5-speed OD manual	24/31	21/28
4-speed OD automatic	22/28	19/25

1. MX-6 GT.

Assembly point: Flat Rock, Mich.
Prices are accurate at time of publication; subject to manufacturer's change.

Accord and Toyota Camry, so Mazda dealers should be offering big discounts these days. The slow-selling MX-6 is conservatively styled for a sports coupe, so it lacks the box-office appeal of rivals. That means there should be good deals on the MX-6 as well. Neither car is best in class; both are worth looking at.

Prices

Mazda 626/MX-6	Retail Price	Dealer Invoice	Low Price
626 DX 4-door notchback	$13025	—	—
626 LX 4-door notchback	14595	—	—
MX-6 DX 2-door notchback	13265	—	—
MX-6 LX 2-door notchback	14585	—	—
MX-6 GT 2-door notchback	16905	—	—
Destination charge	350	350	350

Dealer invoice and low price not available at time of publication.

Standard equipment:

DX: 2.2-liter PFI 4-cylinder engine, 5-speed manual transmission, power steering, motorized front shoulder belts, cloth reclining front bucket seats, driver's-seat lumbar and thigh support adjustments, 60/40 folding rear seat, console with storage (626), tachometer, coolant temperature gauge, trip odometer, tilt steering column, dual remote mirrors, intermittent wipers, tinted glass, remote fuel door and decklid release, rear defogger, AM/FM cassette (MX-6), 185/70SR14 tires. **LX** adds: power windows and locks, power mirrors, AM/FM cassette, driver's-seat lateral support adjustments, variable intermittent wipers, folding rear armrest, front door pockets, map lights, cruise control, oscillating center vents, console with storage (MX-6). **GT** adds: turbocharged engine, 4-wheel disc brakes, fog lights and rear spoiler, 195/60VR15 tires on alloy wheels.

Optional equipment:

4-speed automatic transmission	790	NA	NA
Anti-lock brakes, MX-6 GT, 626 LX	1000	850	902
MX-6 LX (includes rear discs)	1150	977	1038
Air conditioning	850	NA	NA
AM/FM cassette, 626 DX	450	342	386
CD player, GT	700	NA	NA
Power moonroof, LX & GT	700	560	615
Cruise control, DX	220	176	193
Rear spoiler, MX-6 DX & LX	375	300	329
Alloy wheels, LX	425	340	373
205/60R15 tires, GT	30	24	26

	Retail Price	Dealer Invoice	Low Price
Anti-theft alarm, LX & GT	200	80	137
Floormats	65	NA	NA
California emissions pkg.	70	NA	NA

Mazda 929

Mazda 929

The name is the same, but Mazda's new premium sedan bears little resemblance to its namesake. The new 929 trades boxy lines for a flowing profile and comes with dual front air bags standard. It's still a rear-drive 4-door, but the wheelbase grows to 112.2 inches from 106.7, overall length decreases half an inch, and the trunk shrinks from 15.1 cubic feet to 12.4. The 1992 version has a twin-cam 24-valve 3.0-liter V-6 with 195 horsepower. A 4-speed automatic with Power and Normal shift modes is the only available transmission. Anti-lock brakes are standard. A moonroof also is standard, but order the optional Premium Package and you get one with a solar ventilation system that ventilates the interior when the car is parked in the sun. The smooth, quiet V-6 delivers more-than-adequate acceleration yet doesn't seem as strong as rivals in the luxury class. Ride and handling are more impressive: Body roll is well controlled in fast corners; the steering feels tight and responsive; and a smooth, controlled ride cushions passengers against impact harshness. The front buckets are firm and supportive, but tall people might find themselves short of leg and head room. In addition, the

Prices are accurate at time of publication; subject to manufacturer's change.

steering wheel position is fixed, so it may not suit everyone. The trunk is deep and fairly wide but too short to hold much luggage. There are several good sedans in the $25,000 to $30,000 range. While the 929 doesn't stand out in that group, it has enough good features to deserve consideration.

Specifications

	4-door notchback
Wheelbase, in.	112.2
Overall length, in.	193.7
Overall width, in.	70.7
Overall height, in.	54.9
Curb weight, lbs.	3596
Cargo vol., cu. ft.	12.4
Fuel capacity, gals.	18.5
Seating capacity	5
Front head room, in.	37.4
Front leg room, max., in.	43.4
Rear head room, in.	37.4
Rear leg room, min., in.	37.0

Powertrain layout: longitudinal front engine/rear-wheel drive.

Engines

	dohc V-6
Size, liters/cu. in.	3.0/180
Fuel delivery	MPI
Horsepower @ rpm	195 @ 5750
Torque (lbs./ft.) @ rpm	200 @ 3500
Availability	S

EPA city/highway mpg

4-speed OD automatic	19/24

Assembly point: Hiroshima, Japan.

Prices

Mazda 929	Retail Price	Dealer Invoice	Low Price
4-door notchback	$27800	—	—
Destination charge	350	350	350

Dealer invoice and low price not available at time of publication.

Standard equipment:

3.0-liter DOHC 24-valve PFI V-6, 4-speed automatic transmission, 4-wheel disc brakes, variable-assist power steering, driver- and passenger-side air bags, automatic climate control, cloth reclining front bucket seats, power driver's seat, console with storage, tachometer, coolant temperature gauge, voltmeter, trip odometer, power mirrors, digital clock, intermittent wipers, cruise control, AM/FM cassette, power antenna, diversity antenna system, power moonroof, tinted glass, remote fuel door and decklid releases, map lights, lighted visor mirrors, rear defogger, 205/65R15 tires on alloy wheels.

Optional equipment:	Retail Price	Dealer Invoice	Low Price
Premium Pkg.	2700	NA	NA
Leather upholstery, multi-disc CD changer, power passenger's seat, solar control glass, cellular phone pre-wiring.			
Leather seats	1000	NA	NA
CD player	700	NA	NA
Requires leather seats.			
Cold Pkg.	300	NA	NA
Heated front seats, all-season tires, upgraded battery.			
Moonroof	600	NA	NA
Requires Premium Pkg.			
Floormats	100	NA	NA
California emissions	70	NA	NA

Mercedes-Benz S-Class

Redesigned for 1992, the S-Class sedans are about the same overall length as before but longer in wheelbase, slightly taller, heavier by some 800 pounds—and much more expensive. All are rear-drive 4-doors that come in two basic sizes: SE models (119.7-inch wheelbase) and SEL (123.6-inch wheelbase). Inline-6-cylinder engines include a 3.2-liter gas unit with 228 horsepower and a 3.5 turbo diesel with 148. V-8s of 4.2 liters (282 horsepower) and 5.0 (322 horsepower) also are offered. The line is topped by the new 600SEL with a 402-horsepower 6.0 V-12. All come with a 4-speed automatic transmission except the 300SE, which has a new 5-speed automatic. Other new shared features include air bags for driver and passenger and double-pane side windows. Traction control is standard on SELs and optional on SEs. Standard on the 600SEL and optional on the others are automatic adjusting suspension, separate

Prices are accurate at time of publication; subject to manufacturer's change.

Mercedes-Benz 500SEL

rear air conditioning, electric rear-window sunshade, compact-disc changer, and cellular telephone. Anti-lock brakes are again standard on all models. These new S-class sedans are mighty impressive, built with an evident cost-no-object attitude that's reflected in fantasyland prices. Our preview drives suggest improved performance across the board compared with last year's models (especially the 300SE). Handling feels better, interiors are usefully roomier, and refinement even higher. But these are heavy, fuelish cars. The Lexus LS 400 and Infiniti Q45 offer almost everything the S-Class does for about half the price.

Specifications	300SD/SE 4-door notchback	400SE 4-door notchback	500SEL 4-door notchback	600SEL 4-door notchback
Wheelbase, in.	119.7	119.7	123.6	123.6
Overall length, in.	201.3	201.3	205.2	205.2
Overall width, in.	74.3	74.3	74.3	74.3
Overall height, in.	58.7	58.9	58.9	58.7
Curb weight, lbs.	4520	4720	4740	4985
Cargo vol., cu. ft.	15.6	15.6	15.6	15.6
Fuel capacity, gals.	29.7	29.7	29.7	29.7
Seating capacity	5	5	5	5
Front head room, in. . . .	38.0	38.0	38.0	38.0
Front leg room, max., in. .	41.3	41.3	41.3	41.3
Rear head room, in.	37.8	37.8	38.5	38.5
Rear leg room, min., in. . .	36.1	36.1	39.6	39.6

Powertrain layout: longitudinal front engine/rear-wheel drive.

Engines

	dohc I-6	Turbodiesel I-6	dohc V-8	dohc V-8	dohc V-12
Size, liters/cu. in. ...	3.2/195	3.5/210	4.2/256	5.0/303	6.0/365
Fuel delivery	PFI	PFI	PFI	PFI	PFI
Horsepower @ rpm .	228 @ 5800	148 @ 4000	282 @ 5700	322 @ 5700	402 @ 5200
Torque (lbs./ft.) @ rpm	229 @ 4100	229 @ 3100	302 @ 3900	354 @ 3900	428 @ 3800
Availability	S[1]	S[2]	S[3]	S[4]	S[5]

EPA city/highway mpg

5-speed OD automatic	15/19				
4-speed automatic		20/23	13/17	13/16	11/15

1. 300SE.   2. 300SD.   3. 400SE.   4. 500SEL.   5. 600SEL.

Assembly point: Stuttgart, Germany.

Prices

Mercedes-Benz S-Class	Retail Price	Dealer Invoice	Low Price
300SD Turbo 4-door notchback	$69400	—	—
350SE 4-door notchback	69400	—	—
400SE 4-door notchback	77900	—	—
500SEL 4-door notchback	93500	—	—
600SEL 4-door notchback	127800	—	—
Destination charge	350	350	350
Gas Guzzler Tax, 300SE	2100	2100	2100
400SE	2600	2600	2600
500SEL	3000	3000	3000
600SEL	4500	4500	4500

Dealer invoice and low price not available at time of publication.

Standard equipment:

300SD: 3.5-liter PFI 6-cylinder turbodiesel engine, 4-speed automatic transmission, power steering, anti-lock 4-wheel disc brakes, Supplemental Restraint System (includes driver-and passenger-side air bags and emergency tensioning seatbelt retractors), anti-theft alarm, power windows and locks, automatic climate control, AM/FM cassette, leather power front seats with 2-position memory, power telescopic steering column, leather-wrapped steering wheel and shift knob, rear defogger, cruise control, headlamp wipers and washers, heated power mirrors, outside temperature indicator, tachometer, coolant temperature and oil pressure gauges, lighted visor mirrors, 225/60VR16 tires on alloy wheels. **300SE** adds: 3.2-liter DOHC PFI 6-cylinder engine, 5-speed automatic transmission. **400SE** adds: 4.2-liter
Prices are accurate at time of publication; subject to manufacturer's change.

DOHC PFI V-8 engine, 4-speed automatic transmission. **500SEL** adds: 5.0-liter DOHC PFI V-8 engine, ASR (Automatic Slip Control), hydropneumatic level control, heated front and rear seats, power rear seat, active charcoal filter. **600SEL** adds: 6.0-liter DOHC PFI V-12 engine, ADS (Adaptive Damping System), rear air conditioner, 10-disc CD changer, cellular telephone, rear window sunshade, orthopedic front backrests.

Optional equipment:

	Retail Price	Dealer Invoice	Low Price
Rear air conditioning (std. 600)	1800	—	—
ASD (Automatic Locking Differential), 300SD	1090	—	—
ASR (Automatic Slip Control), 300SE & 400SE	2565	—	—
ADS (Adaptive Damping System), 300 & 400	2700	—	—
500	2000	—	—
Rear window sunshade (std. 600)	390	—	—
Orthopedic front backrests, each (std. 600) .	345	—	—
Power rear seat, 300 & 400	1020	—	—
Four-place seating, (ex. 600)	5120	—	—
600	3900	—	—
Heated front & rear seats, each, 300 & 400 .	570	—	—
Active charcoal filter, 300 & 400	490	—	—
Rear axle level control, 300 & 400	700	—	—
Power sunroof	380	—	—

Mercedes-Benz 190E

Mercedes-Benz 190E 2.6 Sportline

A Sportline option package is the major change to these rear-drive, compact 4-door sedans. The 190E 2.3 has a 2.3-liter 4-cylinder engine with 130 horsepower and the 190E 2.6 has a 2.6-liter inline-six with 158. Manual transmission is standard on both, automatic is optional. Offered only on the 190E 2.6, the new Sportline package brings a sport-tuned suspension, quicker-ratio power steering, and 205/55VR15 tires instead of the standard 186/65VR15s. A driver-side air bag and anti-lock brakes are standard on all. Traction control is optional on the 190E 2.6 with automatic transmission. The 190E models sacrifice none of Mercedes' usual virtues of rock-solid construction, safety features, and highly developed design and engineering. But while we certainly don't judge cars just on size and passenger capacity, we find it difficult to justify prices this high for a 4-door sedan that has a cramped rear seat and

Specifications

	4-door notchback
Wheelbase, in.	104.9
Overall length, in.	175.1
Overall width, in.	66.5
Overall height, in.	54.1
Curb weight, lbs.	2900
Cargo vol., cu. ft.	11.7
Fuel capacity, gals.	16.1
Seating capacity	5
Front head room, in.	36.9
Front leg room, max., in.	41.9
Rear head room, in.	36.3
Rear leg room, min., in.	31.1

Powertrain layout: longitudinal front engine/rear-wheel drive.

Engines

	ohc I-4	ohc I-6
Size, liters/cu. in.	2.3/140	2.6/158
Fuel delivery	PFI	PFI
Horsepower @ rpm	130 @ 5100	158 @ 5800
Torque (lbs./ft.) @ rpm	146 @ 3500	162 @ 4600
Availability	S[1]	S[2]

EPA city/highway mpg

5-speed OD manual	20/28	19/27
4-speed automatic	20/26	20/25

1. 190E 2.3. 2. 190E 2.6.

Assembly point: Bremen, Germany.
Prices are accurate at time of publication; subject to manufacturer's change.

a rather small trunk. There's little to quibble about when it comes to performance. The 190E 2.3 performs well, though it's slow to gather steam in 30-50-mph passing situations. The 6-cylinder feels more robust and, perhaps because you don't have to be as aggressive with the throttle, returns only slightly less fuel economy. Handling and roadholding are impressive. The taut suspension allows some bumps to be felt through the seats, but in most situations it's absorbent and an ally to high-speed control.

Prices

Mercedes-Benz 190	Retail Price	Dealer Invoice	Low Price
190E 2.3 4-door notchback, 5-speed	$28950	—	—
190E 2.3 4-door notchback, automatic . . .	29850	—	—
190E 2.6 4-door notchback, 5-speed	34000	—	—
190E 2.6 4-door notchback, automatic . . .	34900	—	—
Destination charge	350	350	350

Dealer invoice and low price not available at time of publication.

Standard equipment:

190E 2.3: 2.3-liter PFI 4-cylinder engine, 5-speed manual or 4-speed automatic transmission, power steering, anti-lock 4-wheel disc brakes, Supplemental Restraint System (includes driver-side air bag and emergency tensioning seatbelt retractors), automatic climate control, power windows and locks, cruise control, intermittent wipers, rear defogger, vinyl reclining front bucket seats, heated power mirrors, AM/FM cassette, tachometer, coolant temperature and oil pressure gauges, trip odometer, leather-wrapped steering wheel and shift knob, lighted visor mirrors, wide bodyside moldings, 185/65R15 87H tires on alloy wheels. **190E 2.6** adds: 2.6-liter 6-cylinder engine, power front seats, 185/65R15 87V tires; power sunroof is available at no charge.

Optional equipment:

ASD (Automatic Locking Differential)	1090	NA	—
2.6 w/5-speed	1090	NA	—
ASR (Automatic Slip Control), 2.6			
w/automatic	2565	NA	—
Sportline Pkg., 2.6	2800	NA	—
Leather 4-place sports seats, sport suspension and steering.			
Power front seats, 2.3	1100	NA	—
Rear head restraints	320	NA	—
Headlamp wipers & washers	300	NA	—
Metallic paint	530	NA	—

CONSUMER GUIDE®

	Retail Price	Dealer Invoice	Low Price
Orthopedic front backrests, each	345	NA	—
Not available on 2.6 w/Sportline Pkg.			
Heated front seats	540	NA	—
Reinforced front seat frames, each	30	NA	—
Not available on 2.6 w/Sportline Pkg.			
Memory driver's seat	440	NA	—
Power sunroof, 2.3	995	NA	—
Leather upholstery	1550	NA	—
Anti-theft alarm	565	NA	—
Rear axle level control	665	NA	—

Mercedes-Benz 300/400/500

Mercedes-Benz 300 E

Formerly known as the 300-Class, the Mercedes' lineup of mid-size models has two new members—the 400E and 500E, both powered by V-8 engines. The 400E has a 268-horsepower 4.2-liter V-8 and the 500E a 322-horsepower 5.0-liter V-8. The 500E also has as standard Automatic Slip Control (traction control), 16-inch wheels and tires, and fender flares and a front air dam. The limited-production 500E is assembled for Mercedes by Porsche. A Sportline package with a sport suspension and alloy wheels is a new option for the 300E sedan and 300CE coupe. On the 300E, the package includes the 4-place seating that's standard on the 300CE. Anti-lock brakes and a driver-side air bag are

Prices are accurate at time of publication; subject to manufacturer's change.

standard on all of Mercedes' mid-size cars. A passenger-side air bag is standard on the 400E and 500E and optional on the others. The new V-8 models are clearly in response to Mercedes' Japanese rivals, the Lexus LS 400 and Infiniti Q45, which were offering V-8 power at a lower cost than the 6-cylinder 300E and 300CE. The 400E offers much stronger acceleration than the 300E and performance that's comparable to the Japanese competitors. However, the 400E starts at $55,800, nearly $14,000 more than either the LS 400 or Q45. While Mercedes builds great cars, we'd give serious consideration to the Lexus and Infiniti sedans

Specifications

	2-door notchback	4-door notchback	5-door wagon
Wheelbase, in.	106.9	110.2	110.2
Overall length, in.	183.9	187.2	188.2
Overall width, in.	68.5	68.5	68.5
Overall height, in.	54.9	56.3	59.8
Curb weight, lbs.	3505	3365	3590
Cargo vol., cu. ft.	14.4	14.6	76.8
Fuel capacity, gals.	20.9	20.9	21.4
Seating capacity	4	5	5
Front head room, in.	36.0	36.9	37.4
Front leg room, max., in.	41.9	41.7	41.7
Rear head room, in.	35.5	36.9	36.8
Rear leg room, min., in.	29.6	33.5	33.9

Powertrain layout: longitudinal front engine/rear-wheel drive or automatically engaging 4WD.

Engines	ohc I-6	ohc I-6	dohc I-6	Turbo-diesel ohc I-5	dohc V-8
Size, liters/cu. in. . . .	2.6/158	3.0/181	3.0/181	2.5/152	4.2/256
Fuel delivery	PFI	PFI	PFI	PFI	PFI
Horsepower @ rpm .	158 @ 5800	177 @ 5700	217 @ 6400	121 @ 4600	268 @ 5700
Torque (lbs./ft.) @ rpm	162 @ 4600	188 @ 4400	195 @ 4600	165 @ 2400	295 @ 3900
Availability	S[1]	S[2]	S[3]	S[4]	S[5]

EPA city/highway mpg

4-speed automatic . .	20/25	18/23	17/23	26/31	15/20

1. 300E 2.6.   2. 300E, 300TE.   3. 300CE.   4. 300D 2.5 Turbo.   5. 400E

Assembly points: Bremen, Germany; Stuttgart, Germany.

before spending more money on one of Mercedes' mid-size models. Intense competition means Mercedes dealers should be willing to bargain.

Prices

Mercedes-Benz 300/400/500	Retail Price	Dealer Invoice	Low Price
300D 2.5 Turbo 4-door notchback	$42950	—	—
300E 2.6 4-door notchback	42950	—	—
300E 4-door notchback	49500	—	—
300E 4Matic 4-door notchback	57100	—	—
300CE 2-door notchback	60400	—	—
300TE 5-door wagon	53900	—	—
300TE 4Matic 5-door wagon	61100	—	—
400E 4-door notchback	55800	—	—
500E 4-door notchback	79200	—	—
Destination charge	350	350	350
Gas Guzzler Tax, 300E 4Matic, 300TE ...	1000	1000	1000
300TE 4Matic	1300	1300	1300
400E	NA	NA	NA
500E	2600	2600	2600

Dealer invoice and low price not available at time of publication.

Standard equipment:

300D 2.5 Turbo/300E 2.6: 2.5-liter turbocharged 5-cylinder diesel engine/ 2.6-liter PFI 6-cylinder gasoline engine, 4-speed automatic transmission, power steering, anti-lock 4-wheel disc brakes, Supplemental Restraint System (includes driver-side air bag and emergency tensioning seatbelt retractors), cruise control, rear headrests, heated power mirrors, automatic climate control, power windows and locks, rear defogger, tachometer, coolant temperature and oil pressure gauges, trip odometer, intermittent wipers, heated windshield washer fluid reservoir and nozzles, leather-wrapped steering wheel and shift knob, 195/65R15 91H tires (300D 2.5), 195/65R15 91V tires (300E 2.6); power sunroof is available at no charge. **300E** adds: 3.0-liter engine, headlamp wipers and washers, anti-theft alarm system, power telescopic steering column, power front seat, leather upholstery, outside temperature indicator, high-performance sound system. **300CE** adds: DOHC 24-valve engine. **300TE wagon** adds to 300E: automatic level control, roof rack, rear wiper/washer; deletes leather upholstery. **4Matic** models have automatic 4WD. **400E** adds to 300E: 4.2-liter V-8 engine, passenger-side air bag. **500E** adds: 5.0-liter V-8 engine, ASR (Automatic Slip Control), heated front seats, rear reading lamps and sunshade, hydropneumatic level control, rear console storage box, fog lamps, 225/55R16 tires.

Prices are accurate at time of publication; subject to manufacturer's change.

Optional equipment:

	Retail Price	Dealer Invoice	Low Price
Passenger-side airbag	730	NA	—
Anti-theft alarm, 300D & 2.6	630	NA	—
ASD (Automatic Locking Differential), 300D .	1090	NA	—
ASR (Automatic Slip Control)	2565	NA	—
Not available on 300D and 4-matic.			
Rear axle level control (NA 300D)	665	NA	—
Headlamp wipers & washers, 300D & 2.6 .	300	NA	—
High-performance sound system, 300D & 2.6	475	NA	—
Metallic paint, 300D & 2.6	600	NA	—
Sportline Pkg., 300E	2000	NA	—
300CE	1300	NA	—
Sport suspension and steering, 8-hole alloy wheels. 300E adds 4-place sport seats.			
Partition net & luggage cover, wagons . . .	460	NA	—
Rear reading lamps, 4-doors	85	NA	—
Rear window sunshade (NA wagons)	390	NA	—
Orthopedic front backrests, each	345	NA	—
Heated front seats	540	NA	—
Reinforced front seat frames, each	30	NA	—
Memory driver's seat, 300D & 2.6	440	NA	—
Telescopic steering column, 300D & 2.6 .	345	NA	—
Third rear-facing seat, wagons	1160	NA	—
Leather upholstery, 300D, 2.6, wagons . .	1550	NA	—

Mercedes-Benz 300/500SL

The 2-seat, rear-drive SL roadster returns for its third season unchanged. The 300SL has a 228-horsepower 3.0-liter inline 6-cylinder engine that teams with a 5-speed manual or 5-speed automatic transmission. The 500SL has a 322-horsepower 5.0-liter V-8 and a 4-speed automatic transmission. Standard equipment on both includes dual front air bags, anti-lock brakes, a power convertible top, and a removable aluminum top with a glass rear window and electric defogger. The SL's most innovative safety feature is a rollover bar designed to flip into place behind the front seats just before it's needed. It's designed to deploy in 0.3 seconds if various roll-angle, deceleration, and suspension-extension sensors indicate an impending flip. The roll bar works with either top in place and can be raised and lowered by a dashboard button. Mercedes' automatically adjusting suspension (ADS, for Adaptive Damping System) is op-

Mercedes-Benz 500SL

Specifications

	2-door conv.
Wheelbase, in.	99.0
Overall length, in.	176.0
Overall width, in.	71.3
Overall height, in.	50.7
Curb weight, lbs.	4010
Cargo vol., cu. ft.	7.9
Fuel capacity, gals.	23.7
Seating capacity	2
Front head room, in.	37.1
Front leg room, max., in.	42.4
Rear head room, in.	—
Rear leg room, min., in.	—

Powertrain layout: longitudinal front engine/rear-wheel drive.

Engines

	dohc I-6	dohc V-8
Size, liters/cu. in.	3.0/181	5.0/303
Fuel delivery	PFI	PFI
Horsepower @ rpm	228 @ 6300	322 @ 5500
Torque (lbs./ft.) @ rpm	201 @ 4600	332 @ 4000
Availability	S[1]	S[2]

EPA city/highway mpg

5-speed manual	16/23	
5-speed OD automatic	16/23	
4-speed automatic		14/18

1. 300SL.   2. 500SL.

Assembly point: Bremen, Germany.
Prices are accurate at time of publication; subject to manufacturer's change.

tional on both models. Acceleration is swift and effortless on the 500SL and the V-8 engine has a muted, refined purr. The 300SL is just as refined but the 6-cylinder engine has little low-speed torque, so you have to floor the throttle and wait for engine speed to climb before there's much action. The SL is a great-looking car with outstanding performance and intriguing features.

Prices

Mercedes-Benz 300/500SL	Retail Price	Dealer Invoice	Low Price
300SL 2-door convertible, 5-speed	$82500	—	—
300SL 2-door convertible, automatic	83500	—	—
500SL 2-door convertible, automatic	97500	—	—
Destination charge	350	350	350

Dealer invoice and low price not available at time of publication.

Gas Guzzler tax, 300SL automatic	1000	1000	1000
300SL 5-speed	1300	1300	1300
500SL	2100	2100	2100

Standard equipment:

300SL: 3.0-liter DOHC 24-valve 6-cylinder engine, 5-speed manual or 5-speed automatic transmission, power steering, anti-lock 4-wheel disc brakes, driver- and passenger-side air bags, automatic soft top, removable hard top, power seats with 3-position memory, heated power mirrors, electrically adjustable steering column, outside temperature readout, cruise control, AM/FM cassette with power antenna, power windows and locks, infrared keyless entry, anti-theft alarm, automatic climate control, fog lamps, headlamp wipers and washers, rear defogger (for hard top), tachometer, coolant temperature and oil pressure gauges, trip odometer, 225/55VR16 tires on alloy wheels. **500SL** adds: 5.0-liter DOHC 32-valve V-8, 4-speed automatic transmission, ASR (Automatic Slip Control).

Optional equipment:

ADS (Adaptive Damping System)	3935	NA	NA
ASD (Automatic Locking Differential), 300 w/manual	1090	NA	NA
ASR (Automatic Slip Control), 300 w/automatic	2565	NA	NA
Heated front seats, each	540	NA	NA
Othopedic front seats, each	345	NA	NA
Cellular telephone	1295	NA	NA
10-disc CD changer	1200	NA	NA

Mercury Capri

Mercury Capri

New wheels, tires, and interior trim for the top-line model head the changes to this 4-seat, front-drive convertible. Capri is built by Ford of Australia with major components borrowed from Mazda's previous-generation 323 subcompact. The base model has a 1.6-liter 4-cylinder engine with 100 horsepower; the sportier XR2 uses a turbocharged version with 132. Manual transmission is standard, automatic is optional on the base model and this year gains an interlock that prevents shifting from park unless the brake pedal is applied. The XR2 gains 195/50R15 tires on new three-spoke alloy wheels. These replace 185/60R14 tires, which remain standard on the base Capri. Cruise control is a new option on the base model and power door locks are dropped from both. Both models have a driver-side air bag. The standard cloth top folds manually and is stored beneath a hinged hard cover behind the back seat. A removable steel hard top with an electric rear-window defroster is optional. Capri isn't a sports car as much as a pleasant small convertible with some conveniences absent in real sports cars—namely a rear seat that holds a couple of children or an adult riding sidesaddle. The base Capri accelerates like an economy sedan. The zestier XR2 is quicker but the front end pulls to one side in hard acceleration. Noise levels are high and thick rear roof pillars create big blind spots. The front-drive Capri is nimble on the road and has better wet-weather traction than rear-drive sports cars.

Prices are accurate at time of publication; subject to manufacturer's change.

Specifications

	2-door conv.
Wheelbase, in.	94.7
Overall length, in.	166.1
Overall width, in.	64.6
Overall height, in.	50.2
Curb weight, lbs.	2404
Cargo vol., cu. ft.	8.6
Fuel capacity, gals.	11.1
Seating capacity	4
Front head room, in.	37.8
Front leg room, max., in.	41.2
Rear head room, in.	34.4
Rear leg room, min., in.	25.8

Powertrain layout: transverse front engine/front-wheel drive.

Engines	dohc I-4	Turbo dohc I-4
Size, liters/cu. in.	1.6/97	1.6/97
Fuel delivery	PFI	PFI
Horsepower @ rpm	100 @ 5750	132 @ 6000
Torque (lbs./ft.) @ rpm	95 @ 5500	136 @ 3000
Availability	S	S[1]

EPA city/highway mpg

5-speed OD manual	25/31	23/28
4-speed OD automatic	23/27	

1. XR2.

Assembly point: Broadmeadows, Australia.

Prices

Mercury Capri	Retail Price	Dealer Invoice	Low Price
2-door convertible	$14452	$13038	—
XR2 2-door convertible	17250	15528	—
Destination charge	375	375	375

Low price not available at time of publicaton.

Standard equipment:

1.6-liter DOHC 16-valve PFI 4-cylinder engine, 5-speed manual transmission, power steering, 4-wheel disc brakes, driver-side air bag, cloth reclining front bucket seats, driver-seat tilt, height, and lumbar support adjustments, folding rear seatback, tinted glass, power windows and mirrors, leather-wrapped steering wheel, AM/FM radio, intermittent wipers, 185/60R14 tires.
XR2 adds: turbocharged, intercooled engine, air conditioning, cruise control, AM/FM cassette, fog lights, rear spoiler, alloy wheels.

Optional equipment:	Retail Price	Dealer Invoice	Low Price
4-speed automatic transmission, base . . .	732	622	—
Air conditioning, base	817	695	—
Removable hardtop	1383	1175	—
Includes dome light, map lights, and rear defogger.			
Preferred Pkg. 651A, base	1047	892	—
Air conditioning, AM/FM cassette, alloy wheels, cruise control.			
Alloy wheels, base	351	299	—
AM/FM cassette, base	155	132	—
Premium AM/FM cassette, base	435	370	—
XR2	280	238	—
AM/FM radio delete, base (credit)	(245)	(208)	(208)
AM/FM cassette delete, XR2 (credit)	(400)	(340)	(340)
Tonneau cover	195	166	—
California emissions pkg.	100	85	—

Mercury Cougar/ Ford Thunderbird

Mercury marks the 25th anniversary of the Cougar with a special model later in the year, while the similar Ford Thunderbird adds a new Sport model with a standard V-8. The base Cougar LS model has a 140-horsepower 3.8-liter V-6. Optional on the LS and standard on the sportier Cougar XR7 is a 200-horsepower 5.0-liter V-8. Due later is an anniversary LS model with the V-8, a monochromatic color scheme, BBS wheels, and special trim. The XR7 has new alloy wheels. The Thunderbird lineup includes base and LX models with the 140-horsepower V-6; the new Sport with the V-8; and the Super Coupe with a 210-horsepower supercharged 3.8-liter V-6. The V-8 is optional on the base and LX T-Birds. The LX and Sport models have the same front-end appearance as the SC this year and all Thunder-

Prices are accurate at time of publication; subject to manufacturer's change.

Mercury Cougar

birds have new full-width taillamps. The Cougar and Thunderbird are kissing cousins except for the Super Coupe's supercharged engine. The Super Coupe has impressive acceleration, but the V-8 is the best engine for these luxury coupes. It's smoother and quieter than the supercharged engine, and nearly as powerful. The Cougar XR7 and Thunderbird Sport models ride too stiffly for our tastes, so we would look for one of the less-expensive models with the optional V-8 engine to get a more comfortable ride. Both these coupes are small inside for their exterior size, and their wide, heavy doors are a chore to deal with in crowded parking spots.

Specifications

	2-door notchback
Wheelbase, in.	113.0
Overall length, in.	198.7
Overall width, in.	72.7
Overall height, in.	52.7
Curb weight, lbs.	3550
Cargo vol., cu. ft.	15.2
Fuel capacity, gals.	18.0
Seating capacity	5
Front head room, in.	38.1
Front leg room, max., in.	42.5
Rear head room, in.	37.5
Rear leg room, min., in.	35.8

Powertrain layout: longitudinal front engine/rear-wheel drive.

Engines

	ohv V-6	ohv V-8	Supercharged ohv V-6
Size, liters/cu. in.	3.8/232	5.0/302	3.8/232
Fuel delivery	PFI	PFI	PFI
Horsepower @ rpm	140 @	200 @	210 @
	3800	4000	4000
Torque (lbs./ft.) @ rpm	215 @	275 @	315 @
	2400	3000	2600
Availability	S[1]	S[2]	S[3]
EPA city/highway mpg			
5-speed OD manual			17/24
4-speed OD automatic	20/27	17/24	17/23

1. Cougar LS, base Thunderbird and LX.   2. Cougar XR7, Thunderbird Sport.
3. Thunderbird SC.

Assembly point: Lorain, Ohio.

Prices

Mercury Cougar	Retail Price	Dealer Invoice	Low Price
LS 2-door notchback	$16460	$14186	$14536
XR7 2-door notchback	22054	18941	19291
Destination charge	495	495	495

Standard equipment:

LS: 3.8-liter PFI V-6, 4-speed automatic transmission, power steering, motorized front shoulder belts, air conditioning, cloth reclining front bucket seats, intermittent wipers, tinted glass, power windows, AM/FM radio, coolant temperature gauge, center console, power mirrors, rear armrest, visor mirrors, 205/70R15 tires. **XR7** adds: 5.0-liter PFI V-8, anti-lock 4-wheel disc brakes, Traction-Lok axle, adjustable handling suspension, fog lights, tachometer, oil pressure gauge, voltmeter, sport seats with power lumbar, seatback pockets, 225/60R16 tires on alloy wheels.

Optional equipment:

5.0-liter V-8, LS w/Pkg. 262A or 263A . .	1184	1007	1036
LS w/Pkg. 260A	1080	918	945
Includes variable-assist power steering, except with Pkg. 260A.			
Anti-lock brakes, LS	695	591	608
Includes Traction-Lok axle.			
Traction-Lok axle, LS	100	85	88
Preferred Pkg. 260B, LS	1345	1143	1177
Tilt steering column, cruise control, rear defogger, sport wheel covers.			

Prices are accurate at time of publication; subject to manufacturer's change.

	Retail Price	Dealer Invoice	Low Price
Preferred Pkg. 262A, LS	1947	1654	1704

Pkg. 261A plus power driver's seat, Luxury Trim Option (sport instrument cluster with tachometer, cloth and leather upholstery, upgraded carpet, woodtone dashboard applique), illuminated entry, leather-wrapped steering wheel, cassette player, lighted visor mirrors, power locks, remote fuel door and decklid releases, Light Group, floormats, 215/70R15 tires on alloy wheels.

Preferred Pkg. 263A, LS	2953	2510	2584

Pkg. 262A plus keyless entry, diagnostic maintenance monitor, power passenger seat, High Level Audio Sytem, power antenna, Luxury Lamp Group.

Preferred Pkg. 265A, XR7	NC	NC	NC

Power driver's seat, tilt steering column, cruise control, rear defogger, cassette player, power locks, remote fuel door and decklid releases.

Preferred Pkg. 266A, XR7	1237	1052	1082

Pkg. 265A plus keyless illuminated entry, diagnostic maintenance monitor, High Level Audio System, power antenna, Luxury Lamp Group, Light Group, lighted visor mirrors, floormats.

Luxury Trim Option, LS	674	573	590

Sport instrument cluster with tachometer, cloth and leather upholstery, upgraded carpet, woodtone dashboard applique.

Anti-theft alarm system	245	208	214

Requires Power Lock Group.

Automatic temperature control	162	138	142
Rear defogger	170	144	149
Diagnostic Maintenance Monitor	89	76	78

LS requires Luxury Trim Option.

Illuminated entry	82	69	72
Keyless illuminated entry	228	194	200
LS w/Pkg. 262A	146	124	128

Requires Power Lock Group.

Luxury Lamp Group	261	222	228

Headlamp Convenience Group, cornering lamps.

Light Group	146	124	128
Power Lock Group	311	264	272

Power locks, remote fuel door and decklid releases.

Power moonroof	776	659	679

Requires lighted visor mirrors.

AM/FM cassette	155	132	136
High Level Audio System, w/LS (263A) or			
XR7 (266A)	460	391	403
w/LS (263A) or XR7 (265A)	305	259	267

Base requires Luxury Trim Option.

Ford JBL audio system	526	447	460

LS requires Luxury Trim Option; LS and XR7 require High Level Audio System.

CONSUMER GUIDE®

	Retail Price	Dealer Invoice	Low Price
CD player	491	418	430
Requires Ford JBL audio system.			
Power antenna	85	73	74
Power front seats, each	305	259	267
Split folding rear seat	133	113	116
Leather seat trim	515	437	451
Cruise control	224	191	196
Requires tilt steering column.			
Leather-wrapped steering wheel	96	82	84
Requires cruise control and tilt steering column.			
Tilt steering column	145	123	127
Requires cruise control.			
Cold Weather Group, LS	215	182	188
LS w/any Preferred Pkg.	45	38	39
XR7	188	160	165
XR7 w/any Preferred Pkg.	18	16	16
Sport wheel covers, LS	85	73	74
Alloy wheels & 215/70R15 tires, LS	306	260	268
Requires Luxury Trim Option.			
205/70R15 whitewall tires, LS	73	62	64
225/60ZRR16 BSW performance tires, XR7 .	NC	NC	NC
Front floormats	33	28	29
California emissions pkg.	100	85	88

Ford Thunderbird

2-door notchback	$16345	$14098	$14498
Sport 2-door notchback	18611	16024	16424
LX 2-door notchback	18783	16170	16570
Super Coupe 2-door notchback	22046	18944	19344
Destination charge	495	495	495

Standard equipment:

3.8-liter PFI V-6, 4-speed automatic transmission, power steering, air conditioning, motorized front shoulder belts, cloth reclining front bucket seats, center console, left remote mirror, visor mirrors, tinted glass, coolant temperature gauge, trip odometer, AM/FM radio, power windows, intermittent wipers, 205/70R15 tires. **Sport** adds: 5.0-liter V-8, cruise control, tilt steering column, variable-assist power steering, leather-wrapped steering wheel, fog lights, tachometer, Handling Package, 215/65R15 handling tires on alloy wheels. **LX** adds: 3.8-liter V-6 engine, cloth/leather/vinyl seat trim, power driver's seat, Power Lock Group, cassette player, illuminated entry, misc. lights, lighted visor mirrors, rear armrest, 205/70R15 tires on styled wheels; Handling Package is deleted. **Super Coupe** adds to base: 3.8-liter supercharged V-6, 5-speed manual transmission, anti-lock 4-wheel disc brakes,
Prices are accurate at time of publication; subject to manufacturer's change.

adjustable sport suspension, Traction-Lok axle, articulated sport seats with power lumbar and side bolsters, seatback pockets, tachometer, boost gauge, speed-sensitive power steering, lower bodyside cladding, fog lights, power mirrors, rear armrest, misc. lights, 225/60ZR16 tires on alloy wheels.

Optional equipment:

	Retail Price	Dealer Invoice	Low Price
5.0-liter V-8, base & LX	1080	918	945
4-speed automatic transmission, SC	595	506	521
Anti-lock brakes, base, Sport & LX	695	591	608
Includes Traction-Lok axle.			
Preferred Pkg. 151A, base	762	646	667
Power driver's seat, cassette player, rear defogger, cruise control, tilt steering column, power mirrors, alloy wheels.			
Preferred Pkg. 152A, Sport	NC	NC	NC
Power driver's seat, cassette player, rear defogger.			
Preferred Pkg. 155A, LX	1038	882	908
Rear defogger, automatic climate control, premium cassette player with premium sound, power antenna, Autolamp system, cornering lamps, keyless entry, power passenger seat, front floormats, alloy wheels.			
Preferred Pkg. 157A, SC	858	729	751
Power driver's seat, automatic climate control, cassette player, power antenna, rear defogger, cruise control, tilt steering column, power locks.			
Leather seat trim, LX	515	437	451
SC	648	550	567
Anti-theft system	245	208	214
Autolamp Group	193	164	169
Autolamp system, automatic day/night mirror.			
Traction-Lok axle, base, Sport & LX	100	85	88
Cornering lamps	68	58	60
Rear defogger	170	144	149
Automatic climate control, LX & SC	162	138	142
Electronic instruments, LX	270	229	236
Cassette player	155	132	136
Premium cassette w/o Preferred Pkg. . . .	460	391	403
w/Preferred Pkg.	305	259	267
Ford JBL audio system	526	447	460
CD player	491	418	430
Power antenna	85	73	74
Illuminated entry	82	69	72
Keyless entry, base & SC w/o illuminated entry	228	194	200
Base, LX & SC w/illuminated entry . . .	146	124	128
Light Convenience Group, base	146	124	128
SC	100	85	88
Misc. lights, lighted visor mirrors.			
Power Lock Group	311	264	272
Power locks, remote fuel door and decklid releases.			

CONSUMER GUIDE®

	Retail Price	Dealer Invoice	Low Price
Luxury Group, base w/Pkg. 151A	561	477	491
SC w/Pkg. 157A	370	314	324
Sport w/Pkg. 152A	106	90	93
Cruise control, tilt steering column, power mirrors.			
Cruise control & tilt steering wheel, base .	370	314	324
Power moonroof, base & SC	876	744	767
Base, LX, or SC w/Light Convenience Group	776	659	679
Power seats (each)	305	259	267
Vehicle maintenance monitor	89	76	78
Alloy wheels, base	306	260	268
Base w/Pkg. 151A & LX w/155A	221	188	193
Includes 215/70R15 tires.			
Cold Weather Group	205	174	179
SC w/automatic	178	151	156
W/Pkg. 151A, 155A, SC w/5-speed & 157A	45	38	39
SC w/automatic & Pkg. 157A	18	16	17
All-season tires, SC	73	62	64
Conventional spare tire, base & LX	73	62	64
Front floormats	33	28	29
California emissions pkg.	100	85	88

Mercury Grand Marquis/ Ford Crown Victoria

Mercury Grand Marquis

A front passenger-side air bag is supposed to become available later in the model year as a new option for the Grand Marquis and nearly identical Crown Victoria, the full-size, rear-drive cars from Ford Motor Company. A driver-side

Prices are accurate at time of publication; subject to manufacturer's change.

air bag is standard on both. These 6-passenger, 4-door sedans arrived as early 1992 models with new styling, redesigned interiors, and a new overhead-camshaft 4.6-liter V-8 engine. This engine makes 190 horsepower in standard form and 210 with the optional dual exhausts. The 4-speed automatic transmission is supposed to gain electronic controls during the 1992 model run. A sporty Touring Sedan model joined the Crown Vic line in fall 1991. Anti-lock brakes and traction control are teamed as a single option for both models. The Grand Marquis and Crown Vic have the same traditional big car feel and spacious cabin as before. They now look much more modern and offer contemporary safety features. The smooth-as-glass 4.6-liter V-8

Specifications

	4-door notchback
Wheelbase, in.	114.4
Overall length, in.	212.4
Overall width, in.	77.8
Overall height, in.	56.9
Curb weight, lbs.	3768
Cargo vol., cu. ft.	20.6
Fuel capacity, gals.	20.0
Seating capacity	6
Front head room, in.	39.4
Front leg room, max., in.	42.5
Rear head room, in.	38.1
Rear leg room, min., in.	39.7

Powertrain layout: longitudinal front engine/rear-wheel drive.

Engines

	ohc V-8
Size, liters/cu. in.	4.6/281
Fuel delivery	PFI
Horsepower @ rpm	190 @ 4200[1]
Torque (lbs./ft.) @ rpm	260 @ 3200[2]
Availability	S

EPA city/highway mpg

4-speed OD automatic	18/25

1. 210 @ 4600 with dual exhaust.   2. 270 @ 3400 with dual exhaust.

Assembly point: St. Thomas, Ontario, Canada.

gets these heavy cars away from stops smartly, but it's slow to respond in the 30-50-mph range. Front-drive rivals like the Buick LeSabre and Oldsmobile Eighty-Eight are more nimble than the Grand Marquis and Crown Vic and deliver similar acceleration with their V-6 engines. However, they can't tow as much as the Ford cars, which can haul trailers up to 5000 pounds. Against the rear-drive Chevrolet Caprice, it's no contest. The Mercury and Ford sedans are clearly superior. General Motors' only advantage is that it still offers full-size, rear-drive wagons.

Prices

Mercury Grand Marquis	Retail Price	Dealer Invoice	Low Price
GS 4-door notchback	$20216	$17423	—
LS 4-door notchback	20644	17787	—
Destination charge	535	535	535

Low price not available at time of publication.

Standard equipment:

GS: 4.6-liter PFI V-8, 4-speed automatic transmission, 4-wheel disc brakes, power steering, driver-side air bag, cloth split bench seat with recliners and dual armrests, air conditioning, power windows and mirrors, tinted glass, AM/FM radio, right visor mirror, intermittent wipers, tilt steering column, trip odometer, Autolamp system, remote fuel door release, automatic parking brake release, 215/70R15 tires. **LS** adds: upgraded upholstery, rear head restraints. Major options will include: anti-lock brakes, Traction Assist, passenger airbag, Performance and Handling Pkg. (anti-lock brakes, uprated suspension, rear air suspension, dual exhaust, 3.27 axle ratio, 225/70R15 tires on alloy wheels), Trailer Towing Pkg. (5000-lb capacity; includes dual exhaust, 3.55 axle ratio, rear air suspension, heavy-duty chassis components), Electronic Group (electronic instruments, trip computer, automatic temperature control).

Optional equipment:

Anti-lock brakes w/Traction Assist	695	591	626
Passenger-side airbag	488	415	439
Preferred Pkg. 156A, GS	1159	983	1043
Power driver's seat, illuminated entry, cruise control, rear defogger, Power Lock Group, Luxury Light Group, bodyside paint stripe, floor mats, WSW tires.			
Preferred Pkg. 157A, GS	1425	1209	1283
Pkg. 156A plus cassette player, locking radial-spoked wheel covers.			

Prices are accurate at time of publication; subject to manufacturer's change.

	Retail Price	Dealer Invoice	Low Price
Preferred Pkg. 172A, LS	1662	1411	1496

Pkg. 157A plus front cornering lamps, leather-wrapped steering wheel, cassette player, aluminum wheels, power antenna.

Rear defogger	170	144	153
Insta-Clear windshield	305	259	275
Power Lock Group	310	263	279

Includes remote deck lid release.

Illuminated entry system	82	69	74
Keyless entry system	146	124	131
Handling and Performace Pkg.	1612	1370	1451
w/Pkg. 172A	1090	927	981
w/Pkgs. 156A or 157A	1530	1301	1377

Includes performance springs, shocks and stabilizer bars, alloy wheels, anti-lock brakes w/electronic traction control, dual exhaust w/ 210 bhp engine rating, 3.27 axle ratio, 225/70R15 tires. Not available with Trailer Towing Pkg., Electronic Group, other wheel, wheel cover, tire options, or conventional spare tire w/JBL audio system.

Rear air-spring suspension	285	242	257
Trailer Towing Pkg.	490	417	441
Power driver's seat	305	259	275
Power front seats w/power lumbar	809	687	728
With Pkg. 156A, 157A, or 172A	504	428	454
Leather seat trim, LS	555	472	500

Requires power front seats.

Cruise control	224	191	202
AM/FM cassette	155	132	140
Radio delete option (credit)	(206)	(175)	(175)
High-level audio system	490	417	441
With Pkg. 157A or 172A	335	285	302
Ford JBL audio system	526	447	473
Power antenna	85	73	77
Electronic Group	516	439	464

Automatic climate control, digital instrumentation, trip computer. Requires rear window defogger.

215/70R15 WSW all-season tires	82	70	74
Conventional spare tire	85	72	77
Cast aluminum wheels	440	374	396
With Pkg. 157A	129	110	116
Locking radial-spoked wheel covers	311	264	280
Front cornering lamps	68	58	61
Luxury Light Group	179	152	161
Leather-wrapped steering wheel	96	82	86

Requires cruise control.

Heavy duty battery	27	23	24
Front floormats	26	22	23
Rear floormats	20	17	18

	Retail Price	Dealer Invoice	Low Price
Engine block heater	26	22	23
Bodyside paint stripe	61	52	55
Rear license plate frame	9	8	8

Ford Crown Victoria

4-door notchback	$19563	$16864	$17214
LX 4-door notchback	20887	17989	18339
Touring Sedan 4-door notchback	23832	20492	20842
Destination charge	545	545	545

Standard equipment:

4.6-liter PFI V-8, 4-speed automatic transmission 4-wheel disc brakes, power steering, driver-side air bag, air conditioning, cloth reclining split bech seat, map pockets, digital clock, power windows, coolant temperature gauge, trip odometer, tilt steering column, tinted glass, automatic parking brake release, intermittent wipers, AM/FM radio, 215/70R15 all-season tires. **LX** adds: trunk cargo net, upgraded interior trim, Light/Decor Group, remote fuel door release, carpeted spare tire cover. **Touring Sedan** adds: leather-wrapped steering wheel, cruise control, power front seats with armrest and cup holders, floormats, Handling and Performance Package.

Optional equipment:

Passenger-side air bag	488	415	439
Anti-lock brakes w/electronic traction assist	695	591	932
Preferred Pkg. 110B, base	943	802	849

Rear defogger, floormats, illuminated entry system, Light/Decor Group, Power Lock Group, cassette player, remote fuel door release, power driver's seat, leather-wrapped steering wheel, cruise control, spare tire cover, trunk cargo net, wheel covers.

Preferred Pkg. 113B, LX	827	702	744

Rear defogger, floormats, illuminated entry system, Power Lock Group, cassette player, power driver's seat, leather-wrapped steering, cruise control, cornering lamps, power antenna, alloy wheels.

Pkg. 114A, LX	3158	2684	2842

Preferred Pkg. 113A plus anti-lock brakes, electronic traction control, high-level audio system, electronic climate control, trip computer, electronic instrumentation, keyless entry system, rear air suspension, power front seats.

Pkg. 115A, Touring Sedan	961	816	865

Rear defogger, illuminated entry, Power Lock Group, cornering lamps, power antenna, high-level audio system, keyless entry system.

Leather seating surfaces, LX	555	472	500
Touring Sedan	339	288	305

Prices are accurate at time of publication; subject to manufacturer's change.

	Retail Price	Dealer Invoice	Low Price
Heavy-duty battery	27	23	24
Front cornering lamps	68	58	61
Rear window defroster	170	144	153
Floormats, front	26	22	23
Floormats, rear	20	17	18
Engine block heater	26	22	23
Illuminated entry system	82	69	74
Keyless entry, (NA base)	146	124	131
Rear air suspension	285	243	257
Remote fuel door release (std. LX)	41	35	37
Power driver's seat	305	259	275
Power driver/passenger seats, LX	504	428	454
Spare tire cover	18	16	16
Cruise control	321	273	289
Includes leather-wrapped steering wheel.			
Trailer Towing Pkg.	490	417	441
w/Pkg. 114A	205	174	185
Includes rear air spring suspension, heavy-duty battery, flasher system and U-joint, extra cooling, dual exhaust, wiring harness, power steering and transmission oil coolers, full-size spare tire, Traction-Lok axle (except w/anti-lock brakes). Not available with Handling and Performance Package.			
Alloy wheels	440	374	396
Not available with Handling and Performance Package.			
Spoke wheel covers	311	264	280
Insta-Clear windshield, (NA base)	305	259	275
Light/Decor Group	222	189	200
Includes illuminated visor mirrors, misc. lights, striping.			
Power Lock Group	310	263	279
Includes power door locks, remote decklid release.			
Electronic Group	516	438	464
Automatic climate control, electronic instrumentation, trip computer. Requires rear defogger. Not available with Handling and Performance Pkg.			
Handling and Performance Pkg.	1612	1370	1451
w/Pkg. 113B	1172	996	1055
w/Pkg. 114A	191	163	172
Includes performance springs, shocks and stabilizer bars, alloy wheels, anti-lock brakes w/electronic traction control, dual exhaust w/210 bhp engine rating, 3.27 axle ratio, 225/70R15 tires. Not available with Trailer Towing Pkg., Electronic Group, other wheel, wheel cover, and tire options, or with conventional spare tire w/JBL audio system.			
Cassette player	155	132	140
High Level audio system	490	417	441
w/Pkg. 110B or 113B	335	285	302
60-watt AM/FM stereo cassette w/electronic volume control, scan and search feature, upgraded amplifier and speakers.			
JBL audio system	526	447	440
Power antenna	85	73	77

Mercury Topaz/Ford Tempo

Mercury Topaz LTS 4-door

The front-drive Topaz and Tempo gain available V-6 power but lose their 4-wheel-drive option. The 3.0-liter V-6 is standard on the Topaz XR5 2-door and LTS 4-door, and the Tempo GLS, which comes in both body styles. The V-6 is optional on other Topaz and Tempo models. A 96-horsepower 2.3-liter 4-cylinder is standard on Topaz GS and LS models, and Tempo GL and LX models. A 5-speed manual transmission is standard and a 3-speed automatic is optional with both engines. The Topaz has new bumpers and a simulated light-bar grille this year, while 4-door Tempos get a new monotone exterior appearance and new taillamps. Topaz and Tempo are strong sellers because fully equipped they're less expensive than most Japanese compacts, even basically equipped versions. Passenger room and trunk space are just average for the compact field. Neither the Topaz nor the Tempo are as refined as Japanese rivals. But the new V-6 gives them more driving appeal, as it pulls strongly at all speeds and works well with the 3-speed automatic. It's a big improvement over the tepid, coarse 4-cylinder engine. The Topaz and Tempo were among the first domestic family cars to offer an optional driver-side air bag. However, we'd like to see the air bag made standard, or at least optional on 2-door models. And note also that rivals such as the Chevrolet Corsica now have standard anti-lock brakes, while Ford Motor Company doesn't offer them on its compacts. The Topaz and Tempo are hardly the most modern compacts, but they offer good value for the money.

Specifications

	2-door notchback	4-door notchback
Wheelbase, in.	99.9	99.9
Overall length, in.	176.7	177.0
Overall width, in.	68.3	68.3
Overall height, in.	52.8	52.9
Curb weight, lbs.	2546	2602
Cargo vol., cu. ft.	13.2	12.9
Fuel capacity, gals.	15.9	15.9
Seating capacity	5	5
Front head room, in.	37.5	37.5
Front leg room, max., in.	41.5	41.5
Rear head room, in.	36.8	37.0
Rear leg room, min., in.	36.0	36.0

Powertrain layout: transverse front engine/front-wheel drive.

Engines

	ohv I-4	ohv V-6
Size, liters/cu. in.	2.3/141	3.0/182
Fuel delivery	PFI	PFI
Horsepower @ rpm	96 @ 4400	135 @ 5500
Torque (lbs./ft.) @ rpm	128 @ 2600	150 @ 3250
Availability	S[1]	S[2]

EPA city/highway mpg

5-speed OD manual	23/33	21/28
3-speed automatic	21/26	20/24

1. Topaz GS, LS; Tempo GL, LX. 2. Topaz XR5, LTS; Tempo GLS.

Assembly points: Kansas City, Mo.; Oakville, Ontario, Canada.

Prices

Mercury Topaz	Retail Price	Dealer Invoice	Low Price
GS 2-door notchback	$10512	$9490	$9865
XR5 2-door notchback	13452	12108	12483
GS 4-door notchback	10678	9638	10013

	Retail Price	Dealer Invoice	Low Price
LS 4-door notchback	12057	10866	11241
LTS 4-door notchback	14244	12812	13187
Destination charge	465	465	465

Standard equipment:

GS: 2.3-liter PFI 4-cylinder engine, 5-speed manual transmission, power steering, motorized front shoulder belts, cloth reclining front bucket seats, tinted glass, intermittent wipers, power mirrors, tachometer, coolant temperature gauge, trip odometer, AM/FM radio, center console, 185/70R14 tires. **LS adds:** sport suspension, performance tires, power windows and locks, remote fule door and decklid releases, rear defogger, illuminated entry, Light Group, decklid luggage rack, cassette player, tilt steering column, cruise control, cassette storage in console, lighted visor mirrors, cargo net. **XR5 adds to GS:** 3.0-liter PFI V-6 engine, performance axle ratio, sport suspension, remote fuel door and decklid releases, rear defogger, Light Group, leather-wrapped steering wheel, cassette player, tilt steering column, sport seats with power lumbar, center armrest, cargo net, 185/60HR15 tires on alloy wheels. **LTS adds to LS:** 3.0-liter PFI V-6 engine, performance axle ratio, air conditioning, power driver's seat, alloy wheels, leather-wrapped steering wheel, premium sound, sport seats with power lumbar.

Optional equipment:

3.0-liter V-6 engine	685	583	603
Requires air conditioning.			
3-speed automatic transmission	563	479	495
Driver-side air bag, GS	369	314	325
LS	NC	NC	NC
Available only on 4-door models. Deletes tilt steering column and cruise control (where applicable); requires automatic transmission.			
Air conditioning	817	695	719
Preferred Pkg. 352A, GS 2-door	875	744	770
4-door	915	779	805
Automatic transmission, Comfort/Convenience Group, rear defogger, air conditioning, Power Lock Group.			
Preferred Pkg. 353A, GS 4-door	1302	1108	1146
Pkg. 352A plus power windows, tilt steering column, cruise control, cassette player.			
Preferred Pkg. 365A, LS	NC	NC	NC
3-speed automatic transmission.			
Preferred Pkg. 371A, XR5	272	231	239
Cruise control, Power Lock Group, premium sound system.			
Preferred Pkg. 375A, LTS	NC	NC	NC
Automatic transmission.			
Rear defogger	170	144	150
Comfort/Convenience Group	198	168	174

Prices are accurate at time of publication; subject to manufacturer's change.

	Retail Price	Dealer Invoice	Low Price
Power Lock Group, GS 2-door	311	264	274
GS 2-door w/Comfort/Convenience Group & XR5	210	178	185
GS 4-door	351	299	309
GS 4-door w/Comfort/Convenience Group	250	213	220
Includes remote fuel door and decklid releases.			
Power windows, 4-doors	330	281	290
Power driver's seat	305	259	268
Tilt steering column	145	123	128
Cruise control	224	191	197
Cassette player, GS	155	132	136
Premium sound system (std. LTS)	138	117	121
Clearcoat paint	91	78	80
Two-tone paint	159	135	140
Decklid luggage rack (NA XR5)	115	97	101
GS w/o clearcoat paint	NC	NC	NC
Polycast wheels	193	164	170
Alloy wheels, GS	278	236	245
185/70R14 WSW tires, GS w/2.3L	82	69	72
Engine block heater	20	17	18
California emissions	100	85	88

Ford Tempo

	Retail Price	Dealer Invoice	Low Price
GL 2-door notchback	$9987	$9014	$9214
GLS 2-door notchback	12652	11386	11564
GL 4-door notchback	10137	9147	9347
LX 4-door notchback	11115	10017	10217
GLS 4-door notchback	12800	11517	11717
Destination charge	465	465	465

Standard equipment:

GL: 2.3-liter PFI 4-cylinder engine, 5-speed manual transmission, power steering, motorized front shoulder belts, cloth reclining front bucket seats, tinted glass, intermittent wipers, coolant temperature gauge, AM/FM radio, 185/70R14 tires. **GLS** adds: 3.0-liter V-6 engine, air conditioning, sport suspension, performance front seats with power lumbar, rear spoiler, Light Group, leather-wrapped steering wheel, tachometer and trip odometer, cassette player, fog lamps performance tires on alloy wheels. **LX** adds to GL: touring suspension, illuminated entry, power locks, remote fuel door and decklid releases, tilt steering column, power mirrors, front armrest, cargo tiedown net, seatback pockets, Light Group, tachometer and trip odometer, floormats, performance tires.

Optional equipment:

	Retail Price	Dealer Invoice	Low Price
3.0-liter V-6 engine	685	583	589
Requires air conditioning.			
3-speed automatic transmission	563	479	484
Air conditioning	817	695	703
Driver-side air bag, GL	369	314	317
LX (deletes tilt steering column)	224	191	193
Preferred Pkg. 225A, GL	304	258	261
Air conditioning, Light Group, power mirrors, tilt steering column.			
Preferred Pkg. 226A, GL 2-door	1305	1109	1122
GL 4-door	1345	1144	1157
Pkg. 225B plus 3-speed automatic transmission, front armrest, rear defogger, power locks, remote fuel door and decklid releases, cassette player, alloy wheels.			
SRS Pkg. 227A, GL 2-door	1081	919	930
GL 4-door	1121	954	964
Driver-side air bag, 3-speed automatic transmission, air conditioning, Light Group, power mirrors, front armrest, rear defogger, power locks, remote fuel door and decklid releases, floormats.			
Preferred Pkg. 229A, GLS 2-door	642	545	552
GLS 4-door	682	580	587
Air conditioning, tilt steering column, power locks, remote fuel door and decklid releases, cruise control, power driver's seat, premium sound.			
Preferred Pkg. 233A, LX	1755	1492	1509
3-speed automatic transmission, air conditioning, rear defogger, cassette player, decklid luggage rack.			
Front armrest	59	50	51
Rear defogger	170	145	146
Sport Instrument Cluster	87	74	75
Tachometer and trip odometer.			
Light Group	38	32	33
Power Lock Group, 2-doors	311	264	267
4-doors	351	299	302
Power locks, remote fuel door and decklid releases.			
Decklid luggage rack (NA GLS 2-door) . . .	115	97	99
Power mirrors	121	103	104
Cassette player	155	132	133
Premium sound	138	117	119
Power driver's seat	305	259	262
Cruise control (NA w/airbag)	224	191	193
Tilt steering column (NA w/airbag)	145	123	125
Polycast wheels, GL	193	164	166
Power windows, 4-doors	330	281	284
Whitewall performance tires, GL & LX . . .	82	69	71
Front floormats	24	20	21
Rear floormats	9	8	8
Clearcoat paint	91	78	78

Prices are accurate at time of publication; subject to manufacturer's change.

Mitsubishi Diamante

Mitsubishi Diamante

Diamante replaces the Sigma as Mitsubishi's flagship sedan for 1992. It's a front-drive 4-door notchback that comes in two price levels. The base Diamante has a 175-horsepower 3.0-liter V-6 engine and the LS has a dual-cam 202-horsepower version of that engine. Automatic is the sole transmission. A driver-side air bag is standard on both. Anti-lock brakes are standard on the LS, optional on the base car. Optional on the LS is the Euro Handling Package with two key components: Active Electronically Controlled Suspension, and a traction-control system that has what Mitsubishi calls "trace control," which reduces power when cornering speeds threaten to exceed vehicle cornering ability. We've driven both Diamantes and neither has strong enough acceleration to stand out in the competitive $20,000-$30,000 sedan market. The base model feels as responsive to the throttle as the LS in most driving. The LS's advantage is in highway passing, when it s dual-cam engine gives it quicker, stronger response. The Diamante has capable handling and feels stable at highway speeds. Driver comfort is top-notch, though the stereo and electronic climate controls are hard to decipher and hard to see in sunlight. Room in front is good, though the optional power sunroof crowds head space for those over 6-feet. Rear seat room and cargo space are adequate.

Specifications

	4-door notchback
Wheelbase, in.	107.1
Overall length, in.	190.2
Overall width, in.	69.9
Overall height, in.	55.5
Curb weight, lbs.	3428
Cargo vol., cu. ft.	13.6
Fuel capacity, gals.	19.0
Seating capacity	5
Front head room, in.	38.6
Front leg room, max., in.	43.9
Rear head room, in.	36.9
Rear leg room, min., in.	34.2

Powertrain layout: transverse front engine/front-wheel drive.

Engines

	ohc V-6	dohc V-6
Size, liters/cu. in.	3.0/182	3.0/182
Fuel delivery	PFI	PFI
Horsepower @ rpm	175 @ 5500	202 @ 6000 @
Torque (lbs./ft.) @ rpm	185 @ 3000	199 @ 3000
Availability	S	S[1]

EPA city/highway mpg

4-speed OD automatic	18/25	18/24

1. LS.

Assembly point: Oye, Japan.

Prices

Mitsubishi Diamante	Retail Price	Dealer Invoice	Low Price
4-door notchback	$19939	$16749	—
LS 4-door notchback	25135	20611	—
Destination charge	343	343	343

Low price not available at time of publication.

Standard equipment:

3.0-liter PFI V-6, 4-speed automatic transmission, 4-wheel disc brakes, power steering, driver-side air bag, cloth reclining front bucket seats, au-

Prices are accurate at time of publication; subject to manufacturer's change.

tomatic climate control, power windows, speed-sensitive power locks, power mirrors, cruise control, rear defogger, console with armrest, folding rear armrest, dual cupholders, tinted glass, front and rear map lights, remote fuel door and decklid releases, woodgrain interior accents, tachometer, coolant temperature gauge, trip odometer, intermittent wipers, headlamp auto-off system, AM/FM cassette with diversity antenna, 205/65R15 V-rated tires with full-size spare. **LS** adds: DOHC 24-valve engine, anti-lock brakes, cruise control, power driver's seat with 2-position memory, AM/FM cassette and CD player with EQ and steering-wheel-mounted controls, alloy wheels.

Optional equipment:	Retail Price	Dealer Invoice	Low Price
Anti-lock brakes, base	1100	880	—
AM/FM cassette w/equalizer, base	357	250	—
AM/FM cassette w/compact disc, base . . .	860	602	—
LS	259	181	—
Cruise control, base	188	150	—
Power sunroof	863	690	—
Alloy wheels, base	388	310	—
Luxury Package, LS	2100	1723	—
Includes leather seats, power passenger seat.			
Euro Handling Package, LS	1670	1336	—
Includes active ECS suspension, traction control.			
Floormats	90	58	—

Mitsubishi Eclipse/ Eagle Talon/ Plymouth Laser

This trio of sports coupes gets new front styling with exposed aerodynamic headlamps, a new hood that dips lower into the nose, and new front fascia. The Plymouth Laser joins its siblings in offering all-wheel drive this year; previously, the Laser came only with front-wheel drive. The Laser RS Turbo AWD, however, comes only with a 5-speed manual transmission; the AWD models in the Mitsubishi and Eagle lines are available with the manual or a 4-speed automatic. All these cars are built in Illinois and use Mitsubishi designed powertrains and other mechanical components. Anti-lock brakes are optional in all three model lines. Base models in the Eclipse and Laser lines have a mild-mannered 1.8-liter 4-cylinder engine. Models with

Mitsubishi Eclipse GSX

the dual-cam 2.0-liter engine have much livelier acceleration, though this engine performs better with the 5-speed
manual than with the automatic because it doesn't produce
much power at low speeds. The turbocharged AWD models
have stellar acceleration and exemplary all-weather traction. As with most sports coupes, the rear seat is minuscule,
cargo space is short even for this category, and shorter
drivers feel as if they're sitting in a bathtub. The ride is
stiff on most models and noise from engine and road are
prominent, but the Eclipse and its cousins are top conten-
ders in the competitive sports coupe class. While the AWD
models are our favorites, a front-drive version with the
dual-cam 2.0-liter engine will be the best all-around value.

Specifications

	3-door hatchback
Wheelbase, in.	97.2
Overall length, in.	170.5
Overall width, in.	66.5
Overall height, in.	51.4
Curb weight, lbs.	2524
Cargo vol., cu. ft.	10.2
Fuel capacity, gals.	15.9
Seating capacity	4
Front head room, in.	37.9
Front leg room, max., in.	43.9
Rear head room, in.	34.1
Rear leg room, min., in.	28.5

Powertrain layout: transverse front engine/front-wheel drive or permanent 4WD.

Prices are accurate at time of publication; subject to manufacturer's change.

Engines

Engines	ohc I-4	dohc I-4	Turbo dohc I-4
Size, liters/cu. in.	1.8/107	2.0/122	2.0/122
Fuel delivery	PFI	PFI	PFI
Horsepower @ rpm	92 @ 5000	135 @ 6000	190 @ 6000[1]
Torque (lbs./ft.) @ rpm	105 @ 3500	125 @ 3000	203 @ 3000
Availability	S[2]	S[3]	S[4]

EPA city/highway mpg

	ohc I-4	dohc I-4	Turbo dohc I-4
5-speed OD manual	23/32	22/29	21/28
4-speed OD automatic	23/30	22/27	19/23

1. 195 horsepower w/AWD; 180 horsepower with automatic. 2. Base Eclipse, GS; base Laser. 3. Eclipse GS DOHC; base Talon; Laser RS. 4. Eclipse GS Turbo, GSX; Talon TSi; Laser RS Turbo.

Assembly point: Normal, Ill.

Prices

Mitsubishi Eclipse	Retail Price	Dealer Invoice	Low Price
3-door hatchback, 5-speed	$11259	$9852	$10556
3-door hatchback, automatic	11919	10427	11173
GS 1.8 3-door hatchback, 5-speed	12529	10900	11715
GS 1.8 3-door hatchback, automatic	13189	11475	12332
GS DOHC 3-door hatchback, 5-speed . . .	13469	11719	12594
GS DOHC 3-door hatchback, automatic . .	14129	12294	13212
GS Turbo 3-door hatchback, 5-speed . . .	17109	14886	15998
GS Turbo 3-door hatchback, automatic . .	17899	15575	16737
GSX 3-door hatchback, 5-speed	18849	16402	17626
GSX 3-door hatchback, automatic	19649	17091	18370
Destination charge	368	368	368

Standard equipment:

1.8-liter PFI 4-cylinder engine, 5-speed manual or 4-speed automatic transmission, 4-wheel disc brakes, motorized front shoulder belts, cloth reclining front bucket seats, split folding rear seat, tilt steering column, map lights, remote fuel door and hatch releases, visor mirrors, tachometer, coolant temperature gauge, dual trip odometers, intermittent wipers, automatic-off headlamp feature, AM/FM radio, tinted glass, remote mirrors, 185/70R14 tires. **GS** adds: power steering, 3-way driver's seat, upgraded door panels, power mirrors, rear defogger, cargo cover, center console with coin and cup holders, AM/FM cassette, full wheel covers. **GS DOHC** adds: 2.0-liter DOHC 16-valve engine, sport suspension, power antenna, 205/55HR16 tires.

CONSUMER GUIDE®

GS DOHC Turbo adds: turbocharged engine, air conditioning, rear wiper/washer, air dam and rear spoiler, sill extensions, 6-way front sport seats, cruise control, power windows and door locks, leather-wrapped steering wheel, V-rated tires on alloy wheels. **GSX** adds: permanent 4-wheel drive, limited-slip differential, dual exhausts.

Optional equipment:	Retail Price	Dealer Invoice	Low Price
Anti-lock brakes, GS Turbo, GSX	943	773	858
Power steering, base	267	219	243
Air conditioning	827	678	753
AM/FM cassette, base	173	142	158
AM/FM cassette w/EQ, GS DOHC & GSX .	212	174	193
AM/FM cassette w/CD player, Turbo & GSX .	718	589	654
Power Pkg., exc. base	459	376	418
Power windows and locks.			
Alloy wheels, GS DOHC	321	263	292
Rear wiper/washer (std. Turbo)	132	108	120
Cruise control (std. Turbo)	213	175	194
Sunroof (NA base)	373	306	340
Rear defogger, base	121	103	112
Wheel covers, base	102	84	93
Rear spoiler, GS DOHC	339	278	309
Wheel locks, Turbo & GSX	29	19	24
Floormats	56	37	47

Eagle Talon

	Retail Price	Dealer Invoice	Low Price
3-door hatchback (5-speed)	$13631	$12498	$12903
w/Pkg. 23B (5-speed)	14458	13201	13659
w/Pkg. 24B (automatic)	15159	13797	14299
B Pkgs. add: air conditioning.			
w/Pkg. 23C (5-speed)	15255	13878	14387
w/Pkg. 24C (automatic)	15956	14474	15027
C Pkgs. add to B: cruise control, rear wiper/washer, power windows and locks.			
w/Pkg. 23D (5-speed)	15751	14300	14840
w/Pkg. 24D (automatic)	16452	14896	15480
D Pkgs. add to C: premium audio system with EQ, alloy wheels.			
TSi 3-door hatchback (5-speed)	14963	13697	14153
TSi 3-door hatchback (automatic)	15803	14411	14920
w/Pkg. 25F (5-speed)	16587	15077	15637
w/Pkg. 26F (automatic)	17427	15791	16404
F Pkgs. add: air conditioning, cruise control, rear wiper/washer, power windows and locks.			
w/Pkg. 25G (5-speed)	17083	15499	16090
w/Pkg. 26G (automatic)	17923	16213	16857
G Pkgs. add to F: premium audio system with EQ, alloy wheels.			

Prices are accurate at time of publication; subject to manufacturer's change.

	Retail Price	Dealer Invoice	Low Price
TSi AWD 3-door hatchback (5-speed) ...	16905	15445	15975
TSi AWD 3-door hatchback (automatic) ..	17745	16159	16743
w/Pkg. 25J (5-speed)	18529	16825	17459
w/Pkg. 26J (automatic)	19369	17539	18226

J Pkgs. add: air conditioning, cruise control, rear wiper/washer, power windows and locks.

Destination charge	343	343	343

Standard equipment:

2.0-liter DOHC 16-valve PFI 4-cylinder engine, 5-speed manual or 4-speed automatic transmission, 4-wheel disc brakes, power steering, motorized front shoulder belts, cloth reclining front bucket seats, driver-seat lumbar support adjustment, folding rear seat, console (with armrest, storage, and cup holders), rear defogger, tinted glass, tachometer, coolant temperature and oil pressure gauges, trip odometer, map lights, power mirrors, visor mirrors, AM/FM cassette, remote fuel door and hatch releases, tilt steering column, tonneau cover, intermittent wipers, floormats, 205/55HR16 tires. **TSi** adds: turbocharged engine, sill extensions and specific fascias, driving lamps, performance seats, turbo boost gauge, leather-wrapped steering wheel and shift handle, 205/55VR16 tires. **TSi AWD** adds: permanent 4-wheel drive, limited-slip differential, uprated suspension, alloy wheels.

Optional equipment:

Anti-lock brakes (base and TSi)	943	802	830
w/TSi AWD	681	579	599

Requires security alarm on TSi & AWD; deletes limited-slip differential from AWD.

Security alarm, TSi & AWD	163	139	143

Requires anti-lock brakes.

Premium audio system, AWD	212	180	187
AM/FM cassette w/CD player (TSi)	506	430	436
w/TSi AWD	718	610	620
Pop-up sunroof	373	317	328
Leather upholstery, TSi & AWD	435	370	383
Alloy wheels, base & TSi	234	241	206

Plymouth Laser

	Retail Price	Dealer Invoice	Low Price
3-door hatchback (5-speed)	$11206	$10331	$10731
w/Pkg. 21B (5-speed)	11814	10848	11248
w/Pkg. 22B (automatic)	12515	11444	11844

B Pkgs. add: power steering, rear defogger, tonneau cover, console cupholder, wheel covers, floormats.

w/Pkg. 21C (5-speed)	12641	11551	11951

	Retail Price	Dealer Invoice	Low Price
w/Pkg. 22C (automatic)	13342	12147	12547
C Pkgs. add to B: air conditioning.			
w/Pkg. 21D (5-speed)	13052	11901	12301
w/Pkg. 22D (automatic)	13753	12496	12896
D Pkgs. add to C: cassette player, cruise control.			
RS 3-door hatchback (5-speed)	13101	11981	12381
w/Pkg. 23F (5-speed)	13928	12683	13083
w/Pkg. 24F (automatic)	14629	13280	13680
F Pkgs. add: air conditioning.			
w/Pkg. 23G (5-speed)	14311	13009	13409
w/Pkg. 24G (automatic)	15012	13605	14005
G Pkgs. add to F: cassette player w/EQ, console cupholder, rear wiper/washer, floormats.			
w/Pkg. 23H (5-speed)	15032	13622	14022
w/Pkg. 24H (automatic)	15733	14218	14618
H Pkgs. add to G: power windows and locks, cruise control, fog lights.			
RS Turbo 3-door hatchback (5-speed) . . .	14392	13143	13543
w/Pkg. 25G (5-speed)	15602	14171	14571
w/Pkg. 26G (automatic)	16442	14885	15285
G Pkgs. add to F: air conditioning, cassette player with EQ, console cupholder, rear wiper/washer, floormats.			
w/Pkg. 25H (5-speed)	16323	14784	15184
w/Pkg. 26H (automatic)	17163	15498	15898
K Pkgs. add to G: power windows and locks, cruise control, fog lights.			
RS Turbo 4WD 3-door hatchback (5-speed) .	16368	14921	15321
w/Pkg. 25N (5-speed)	17195	15624	16024
N Pkg. adds: air conditioning.			
w/Pkg. 25P (5-speed)	17578	15950	16350
P Pkg. adds to N: console with cupholder, floormats, cassette player with EQ, rear wiper/washer.			
w/Pkg. 25Q (5-speed)	18299	16563	16963
Q Pkg. adds to P: power windows and locks, cruise control, fog lights.			
Destination charge	368	368	368

Standard equipment:

1.8-liter PFI 4-cylinder engine, 5-speed manual or 4-speed automatic transmission, motorized front shoulder belts, cloth reclining front bucket seats, split folding rear seatback, center console, tachometer, coolant temperature and oil pressure gauges, trip odometer, tinted glass, remote fuel door and hatch releases, dual remote mirrors, visor mirrors, AM/FM radio, tilt steering column, intermittent wipers, 185/70R14 tires. **RS** adds: 2.0-liter DOHC PFI 4-cylinder engine, power steering, driver-seat lumbar support adjustment, rear defogger, center armrest, power mirrors, cassette player, tonneau cover, 205/55HR16 tires. **RS Turbo** adds: turbocharged, intercooled engine, 205/55VR16 tires. **RS Turbo 4WD** adds: sport suspension, alloy wheels.

Prices are accurate at time of publication; subject to manufacturer's change.

Optional equipment:

	Retail Price	Dealer Invoice	Low Price
4-speed automatic transmission, Base & RS	701	596	631
RS Turbo 2WD	840	714	756
Anti-lock brakes, RS & RS Turbo	943	802	849
RS requires Pkg. H; RS Turbo 2WD requires Pkg. H; RS Turbo 4WD requires Pkg. Q.			
Cassette player, base w/Pkg. B or C	198	168	178
CD player, RS & RS Turbo 2WD w/Pkg. H; RS Turbo 4WD w/Pkg. Q	506	430	455
Rear defogger, base	127	108	114
Sunroof	373	317	336
Alloy wheels, RS & RS Turbo 2WD	321	273	289
RS requires Pkg. G or H.			

Mitsubishi Expo/ Eagle Summit Wagon/ Plymouth Colt Vista

Mitsubishi Expo LRV Sport

The new Expo and its slightly smaller sibling, the Expo LRV (Light Recreation Vehicle) are sized between subcompact station wagons and minivans. Expo is a 7-passenger wagon with four side doors and a one-piece rear liftgate. It has a 116-horsepower 2.4-liter 4-cylinder engine. The Expo LRV seats five and is nine inches shorter than the Expo. It has two front doors, a liftgate, and a sliding right-rear door, like most vans. The LRV's engine is a 113-horse-power 1.8-liter four. With either, manual transmission is standard, automatic is optional. Nearly identical versions of the LRV are sold as the Eagle Summit Wagon and Plymouth Colt Vista. One difference: The 1.8-liter engine is standard on the Summit and Colt Vista and the 2.4-liter engine is optional. All versions of these vehicles are available with front-wheel drive or permanently engaged 4-wheel drive. Anti-lock brakes are optional on most models. Pleasant and easy to drive, the Expos and their siblings at Eagle and Plymouth deliver similar performance despite

Specifications

	4-door wagon	5-door wagon
Wheelbase, in.	99.2	107.1
Overall length, in.	168.6	177.4
Overall width, in.	66.7	66.7
Overall height, in.	64.4	62.6
Curb weight, lbs.	2701	2942
Cargo vol., cu. ft.	79.0	75.0
Fuel capacity, gals.	14.5	15.8
Seating capacity	5	7
Front head room, in.	40.0	39.3
Front leg room, max., in.	40.8	40.5
Rear head room, in.	38.6	39.3
Rear leg room, min., in.	36.1	37.7

Powertrain layout: transverse front engine/front-wheel drive or permanent 4WD.

Engines

	ohc I-4	ohc I-4
Size, liters/cu. in.	1.8/112	2.4/144
Fuel delivery	PFI	PFI
Horsepower @ rpm	113 @ 6000	116 @ 5000
Torque (lbs./ft.) @ rpm	116 @ 4500	136 @ 3500
Availability	S[1]	S[2]

EPA city/highway mpg

5-speed OD manual	23/29	21/27
4-speed OD automatic	23/28	20/25

1. Expo LRV; Summit; Colt Vista. 2. Expo; opt. Summit, Colt Vista.

Assembly point: Okazaki, Japan.
Prices are accurate at time of publication; subject to manufacturer's change.

their differences in size, weight, and horsepower. Each has adequate acceleration, though they feel taxed under a full load. Tight cornering produces marked body roll, tire squealing, and lots of understeer (resistance to turning). All have a comfortably compliant ride. Various combinations of folding seats and, on all except the Expo, a removable rear seat, give them versatile passenger and cargo arrangements. These Mitsubishi-built vehicles are good choices for those who need more than a small wagon but less than a minivan.

Prices

Mitsubishi Expo	Retail Price	Dealer Invoice	Low Price
LRV base 4-door wagon, 5-speed	$11169	$10055	—
LRV base 4-door wagon, automatic	11839	10655	—
LRV Sport 4-door wagon, 5-speed	11989	10434	—
LRV Sport 4-door wagon, automatic	12679	11034	—
LRV Sport 4WD 4-door wagon, 5-speed . .	13889	12081	—
LRV Sport 4WD 4-door wagon, automatic .	14579	12681	—
Base 5-door wagon, 5-speed	13549	11926	—
Base 5-door wagon, automatic	14229	12526	—
SP 5-door wagon, 5-speed	14509	12476	—
SP 5-door wagon, automatic	15209	13076	—
SP 4WD 5-door wagon, 5-speed	15839	13626	—
SP 4WD 5-door wagon, automatic	16539	14226	—
Destination charge	368	368	368

Low price not available at time of publication.

Standard equipment:

LRV base: 1.8-liter PFI 4-cylinder engine, 5-speed manual or 4-speed automatic transmission, passive front shoulder belts, power steering, tilt steering column, reclining front bucket seats, folding and removable rear seat, coolant temperature gauge, trip odometer, remote fuel door and tailgate releases, dual outside mirrors, intermittent wipers, 185/75R14 tires. **LRV Sport** adds: rear defogger, power mirrors, digital clock, front armrest, split folding rear seat, wheel covers, 205/70R14 tires. **LRV Sport 4WD** adds: full-time 4-wheel drive, two-tone paint, rear stabilizer bar, mud guards. **Base 5-door** adds to LRV base: 2.4-liter PFI 4-cylinder engine, 7-passenger seating with split folding middle and back seats, rear defogger, rear wiper/washer, map pockets, dual visor mirrors, wheel covers, 205/70R14 tires. **SP** adds: power mirrors, digital clock, front armrest, tachometer, AM/FM cassette. **SP 4WD** adds: full-time 4-wheel drive.

Optional equipment:	Retail Price	Dealer Invoice	Low Price
Anti-lock brakes, ex. base	924	758	—
Air conditioning	775	620	—
Power Pkg., SP	459	367	—
LRV Sport	528	422	—
Power windows and locks. LRV adds: power mirrors, power tailgate lock, right door map pocket.			
Preferred Equipment Pkg., LRV Sport . . .	445	356	—
Rear wiper/washer and deflector, tachometer, low-fuel warning light, rear storage area, cloth-trimmed door panels, dual horns.			
Cruise control, ex. base	194	155	—
Rear defogger, LRV base	69	55	—
Roof rack, ex. base	260	180	—
Two-tone paint, ex. base	205	164	—
Power sunroof, ex. base	685	548	—
Power tailgate lock, LRV Sport	53	42	—
Tonneau cover, LRV Sport	53	42	—
SP	50	40	—
Cargo Kit, LRV Sport	98	69	—
Cargo tray and net.			
Radio Accommodation Pkg., LRV base . . .	136	95	—
AM/FM stereo, LRV base	327	229	—
AM/FM cassette, LRV	526	368	—
AM/FM cassette w/EQ, LRV	870	609	—
SP	344	241	—
Tire & Wheel Pkg., LRV Sport 2WD	348	278	—
Rear stabilizer bar, 205/70R14 tires on alloy wheels.			
Trim rings, LRV base	72	46	—
Alloy wheels, 4WD	291	233	—
Floormats, LRV Sport	71	47	—
SP	85	55	—
Rear mud guards, LRV 4WD, SP	49	34	—
Mud guards (front & rear), LRV Sport 2WD .	94	66	—

Eagle Summit Wagon

	Retail Price	Dealer Invoice	Low Price
DL 4-door wagon w/Pkg. 21A (5-speed) . .	$11397	$10447	—
w/Pkg. 22A (automatic)	12120	11069	—
DL standard equipment.			
w/Pkg. 21B (5-speed)	11463	10504	—
w/Pkg. 22B (automatic)	12186	11126	—
Pkg. 21/22A plus rear defogger.			
w/Pkg. 21C (5-speed)	12058	11016	—
w/Pkg. 22C (automatic)	12781	11638	—
Pkg. 21/22B plus tinted glass, power mirrors, rear stabilizer bar, rear wiper/washer, AM/FM stereo, air conditioning.			
w/Pkg. 21D (1.8-liter/5-speed)	12683	11553	—

Prices are accurate at time of publication; subject to manufacturer's change.

	Retail Price	Dealer Invoice	Low Price
w/Pkg. 22D (1.8-liter/automatic)	13406	12175	—
w/Pkg. 23D (2.4-liter/5-speed)	12864	11709	—
w/Pkg. 24D (2.4-liter/automatic)	13587	12331	—

Pkg. 21/22C plus cassette player, floormats, remote tailgate release, roof rack, cruise control.

LX 4-door wagon w/Pkg. 21H (1.8-liter/

	Retail Price	Dealer Invoice	Low Price
5-speed)	12894	11767	—
w/Pkg. 22H (1.8-liter/automatic)	13617	12385	—
w/Pkg. 23H (2.4-liter/5-speed)	13075	11919	—
w/Pkg. 24H (2.4-liter/automatic)	13798	12540	—

LX standard equipment plus rear defogger, floormats, cargo security cover, cassette player, air conditioning, roofrack.

	Retail Price	Dealer Invoice	Low Price
w/Pkg. 21K (1.8-liter/5-speed)	13473	12261	—
w/Pkg. 22K (1.8-liter/automatic)	14195	12883	—
w/Pkg. 23K (2.4-liter/5-speed)	13654	12417	—
w/Pkg. 24K (2.4-liter/automatic)	14377	13038	—

Pkg. 21-24H plus cruise control, power windows and locks.

AWD 4-door wagon w/Pkg. 21P (1.8-liter/

	Retail Price	Dealer Invoice	Low Price
5-speed)	13469	12312	—

AWD standard equipment.

	Retail Price	Dealer Invoice	Low Price
w/Pkg. 21R (1.8-liter/5-speed)	13535	12369	—

Pkg. 21P plus rear defogger.

	Retail Price	Dealer Invoice	Low Price
w/Pkg. 21S (1.8-liter/5-speed)	14013	12780	—
w/Pkg. 22S (1.8-liter/automatic)	14736	13402	—
w/Pkg. 23S (2.4-liter/5-speed)	14194	12936	—
w/Pkg. 24S (2.4-liter/automatic)	14917	13557	—

Pkg. 21R plus cargo security cover, Gauge Group, tinted glass, AM/FM stereo.

	Retail Price	Dealer Invoice	Low Price
w/Pkg. 23T (2.4-liter/5-speed)	15029	13654	—
w/Pkg. 24T (2.4-liter/automatic)	15752	14275	—

Pkg. 21-24S plus cassette player, air conditioning, Custom Group, floormats, roof rack, cruise control.

	Retail Price	Dealer Invoice	Low Price
w/Pkg. 23W (2.4-liter/5-speed)	15421	13991	—
w/pkg. 24W (2.4-liter/automatic)	16144	14613	—

Pkg. 23/24T plus power windows and locks.

Destination charge	—	—	—

Low price not available at time of publication.

Standard equipment:

DL: 1.8-liter PFI 4-cylinder engine, 5-speed manual or 4-speed automatic transmission, passive front shoulder belts, power steering, reclining front bucket seats, folding and removable rear seat, coolant temperature gauge, trip odometer, remote fuel door release, dual outside mirrors, intermittent wipers, 185/75R14 tires. **LX** adds: tinted glass, bodyside moldings, color-keyed bumpers, wheel covers, 205/70R14 tires. **AWD** adds: full-time 4-wheel drive, front and rear mudguards; deletes tinted glass.

Optional equipment:	Retail Price	Dealer Invoice	Low Price
Anti-lock brakes	913	785	—
Available on DL w/C or D Pkg., LX, and AWD w/S, T or W Pkg.			
Air conditioning	753	648	—
Roof rack, DL w/Pkg. C & AWD w/Pkg. S .	151	130	—
AM/FM stereo	288	248	—
AM/FM cassette, DL w/Pkg. C & AWD w/Pkg. S	181	156	—
Requires AM/FM stereo.			
Two-tone paint, LX & AWD	193	166	—
Floormats, DL w/Pkg. C & AWD w/Pkg. S .	55	47	—

Plymouth Colt Vista

	Retail Price	Dealer Invoice	Low Price
Base 4-door wagon w/Pkg. 21A (5-speed) .	$11397	$10447	—
w/Pkg. 22A (automatic)	12120	11069	—
Standard equipment.			
w/Pkg. 21B (5-speed)	11463	10504	—
w/Pkg. 22B (automatic)	12186	11126	—
Pkg. 21/22A plus rear defogger.			
w/Pkg. 21C (5-speed)	12058	11016	—
w/Pkg. 22C (automatic)	12781	11638	—
Pkg. 21/22B plus tinted glass, power mirrors, rear stabilizer bar, rear wiper/washer, AM/FM stereo, air conditioning.			
w/Pkg. 21D (1.8-liter/5-speed)	12683	11553	—
w/Pkg. 22D (1.8-liter/automatic)	13406	12175	—
w/Pkg. 23D (2.4-liter/5-speed)	12864	11709	—
w/Pkg. 24D (2.4-liter/automatic)	13587	12331	—
Pkg. 21/22C plus cassette player, floormats, remote tailgate release, roof rack, cruise control.			
SE 4-door wagon w/Pkg. 21H (1.8-liter/ 5-speed)	12894	11767	—
w/Pkg. 22H (1.8-liter/automatic)	13617	12385	—
w/Pkg. 23H (2.4-liter/5-speed)	13075	11919	—
w/Pkg. 24H (2.4-liter/automatic)	13798	12540	—
SE standard equipment plus rear defogger, floormats, cargo security cover, cassette player, air conditioning, roofrack.			
w/Pkg. 21K (1.8-liter/5-speed)	13473	12261	—
w/Pkg. 22K (1.8-liter/automatic)	14195	12883	—
w/Pkg. 23K (2.4-liter/5-speed)	13654	12417	—
w/Pkg. 24K (2.4-liter/automatic)	14377	13038	—
Pkg. 21-24H plus cruise control, power windows and locks.			

Prices are accurate at time of publication; subject to manufacturer's change.

	Retail Price	Dealer Invoice	Low Price
AWD 4-door wagon w/Pkg. 21P (1.8-liter/ 5-speed)	13469	12312	—
AWD standard equipment.			
w/Pkg. 21R (1.8-liter/5-speed)	13535	12369	—
Pkg. 21P plus rear defogger.			
w/Pkg. 21S (1.8-liter/5-speed)	14013	12780	—
w/Pkg. 22S (1.8-liter/automatic)	14736	13402	—
w/Pkg. 23S (2.4-liter/5-speed)	14194	12936	—
w/Pkg. 24S (2.4-liter/automatic)	14917	13557	—
Pkg. 21R plus cargo security cover, Gauge Group, tinted glass, AM/FM stereo.			
w/Pkg. 23T (2.4-liter/5-speed)	15029	13654	—
w/Pkg. 24T (2.4-liter/automatic)	15752	14275	—
Pkg. 21-24S plus cassette player, air conditioning, Custom Group, floormats, roof rack, cruise control.			
w/Pkg. 23W (2.4-liter/5-speed)	15421	13991	—
w/Pkg. 24W (2.4-liter/automatic)	16144	14613	—
Pkg. 23/24T plus power windows and locks.			
Destination charge	—	—	—

Low price not available at time of publication.

Standard equipment:

Base: 1.8-liter PFI 4-cylinder engine, 5-speed manual or 4-speed automatic transmission, passive front shoulder belts, power steering, reclining front bucket seats, folding and removable rear seat, coolant temperature gauge, trip odometer, remote fuel door release, dual outside mirrors, intermittent wipers, 185/75R14 tires. **SE** adds: tinted glass, bodyside moldings, color-keyed bumpers, wheel covers, 205/70R14 tires. **AWD** adds: full-time 4-wheel drive, front and rear mudguards; deletes tinted glass.

Optional equipment:

Anti-lock brakes	913	785	—
Available on base w/C or D Pkg., SE, and AWD w/S, T or W Pkg.			
Air conditioning	753	648	—
Roof rack, base w/Pkg. C & AWD w/Pkg. S .	151	130	—
AM/FM stereo	288	248	—
AM/FM cassette, base w/Pkg. C & AWD			
w/Pkg. S	181	156	—
Requires AM/FM stereo.			
Two-tone paint, SE & AWD	193	166	—
Floormats, base w/Pkg. C & AWD w/Pkg. S .	55	47	—

CONSUMER GUIDE®

Mitsubishi Galant

Mitsubishi Galant GSR

Mitsubishi's compact 4-door sedan gets a mild facelift. A color-keyed grille and bumper are new in front, plus there are new taillamps and the LS has new wheels. The lineup again starts with base and LS models powered by a 102-horsepower 2.0-liter 4-cylinder engine. GS and GSR models get a twin-cam version of the 2.0 with 144 horsepower, up from 135 a year ago. All these models have front-wheel drive. Discontinued is the GSX, which had permanently engaged all-wheel drive. It's been rendered redundant by the VR-4, which arrived for 1991. The VR-4 has AWD, a 195-horsepower turbocharged 2.0, 4-wheel steering, leather interior trim, and a bolder exterior look. The VR-4 and GSR models come only with a 5-speed manual transmission; the LS only with a 4-speed overdrive automatic. Base and GS models come with either transmission. Anti-lock brakes are standard on the VR-4, optional on the GS and GSR. Mitsubishi's Electronically Controlled Suspension (ECS) is standard on the VR-4 and GSR. The VR-4 — an engineering marvel — offers turbocharged performance and all-wheel drive in a roomy family sedan. A Galant LS has much milder performance, but offers power windows, locks, and mirrors, good mileage, and a supple, well-damped suspension. The GS has those same features, plus better acceleration, and is available with anti-lock brakes, which we recommend. The Galant is price competitive with Japanese

Prices are accurate at time of publication; subject to manufacturer's change.

rivals but upstream of comparable domestics and the Hyundai Sonata. However, its range of models and variety of features is hard to equal.

Specifications

	4-door notchback
Wheelbase, in.	102.4
Overall length, in.	183.9
Overall width, in.	66.7
Overall height, in.	53.5
Curb weight, lbs.	2601[1]
Cargo vol., cu. ft.	12.3
Fuel capacity, gals.	15.9
Seating capacity	5
Front head room, in.	38.6
Front leg room, max., in.	41.9
Rear head room, in.	37.4
Rear leg room, min., in.	36.0

1. Base model; 3251 lbs., VR-4.

Powertrain layout: transverse front engine/front-wheel drive or permanent 4WD.

Engines	ohc I-4	dohc I-4	Turbo dohc I-4
Size, liters/cu. in.	2.0/122	2.0/122	2.0/122
Fuel delivery	PFI	PFI	PFI
Horsepower @ rpm	102 @ 5000	144 @ 6000	195 @ 6000
Torque (lbs./ft.) @ rpm	116 @ 2500	134 @ 4500	203 @ 3000
Availability	S[1]	S[2]	S[3]
EPA city/highway mpg			
5-speed OD manual	23/30	20/26	19/25
4-speed OD automatic	21/27	19/25	

1. Base, LS.   2. GS, GSR.   3. VR-4.

Assembly point: Okazaki, Japan.

Prices

Mitsubishi Galant	Retail Price	Dealer Invoice	Low Price
4-door notchback, 5-speed	$11699	—	—
4-door notchback, automatic	13159	—	—

	Retail Price	Dealer Invoice	Low Price
LS 4-door notchback, automatic	14809	—	—
GS 4-door notchback, 5-speed	15179	—	—
GS 4-door notchback, automatic	15939	—	—
GSR 4-door notchback, 5-speed	16689	—	—
VR-4 4-door notchback, 5-speed	22500	—	—
Destination charge	368	368	368

Dealer invoice and low price not available at time of publication.

Standard equipment:

2.0-liter PFI 4-cylinder engine, 5-speed manual or 4-speed automatic transmission, power steering, motorized front shoulder belts, reclining front bucket seats, 4-way driver's seat, tinted glass, remote mirrors, intermittent wipers, tachometer, tilt steering column, center console, rear defogger, remote fuel door and decklid releases, 185/70SR14 tires. **LS** adds: power windows and locks, power mirrors, AM/FM cassette with power antenna, 6-way driver's seat, split folding rear seatback, velour upholstery, cruise control, wheel covers. **GS** adds: DOHC 16-valve engine, 4-wheel disc brakes, 5-way driver's seat, sport tweed upholstery, theft-deterrent system, 195/65HR14 tires. **GSR** adds: anti-lock brakes, electronically controlled suspension, rear spoiler, floormats, 195/60HR15 tires on alloy wheels. **VR-4** adds: turbocharged engine, anti-lock brakes, 4-wheel steering, air conditioning, leather upholstery, anti-theft system, rear spoiler, 6-way driver's seat.

Optional equipment:

Anti-lock brakes, GS	924	758	831
Air conditioning (std. VR-4)	802	658	721
AM/FM cassette, base	554	388	465
AM/FM cassette w/EQ (NA base)	316	221	265
AM/FM cassette w/CD player (NA base) ..	799	577	680
Power glass sunroof (NA base)	685	548	609
Wind deflector for sunroof	45	30	37
Power Pkg., base	463	370	411
Power windows and locks.			
Rear spoiler, GS	175	140	156
Alloy wheels, LS & GS	294	235	261
Wheel covers, base	78	62	69
Floormats, base, LS, & GS	69	46	57
Fog lights (NA VR-4)	235	165	198
Accessory kit, base & GS	166	116	139
Floormats and mud guards.			
Mud guards, base & GS	112	78	94

Prices are accurate at time of publication; subject to manufacturer's change.

Mitsubishi Mirage

Mitsubishi Mirage GS 4-door

Base versions of this front-drive subcompact get new full-cloth seat inserts in place of a combination vinyl and cloth, and LS versions have new wheels and rear trim. All models except the GS use a 1.5-liter 4-cylinder engine with three valves per cylinder and 92 horsepower. The GS has a twin-cam, 16-valve 1.6-liter four with 123 horsepower. Mirage's line begins with the VL 3-door hatchback with either a 4-speed manual transmission or a 3-speed automatic. Base hatchbacks have a 5-speed manual standard and a 3-speed automatic optional. Other models have the 5-speed standard and a 4-speed automatic optional. Standard features exclusive to the GS include 4-wheel disc brakes, a tachometer, and sport bucket seats. Dodge and Plymouth dealers sell similar hatchbacks as the Colt; Eagle dealers sell both body styles as the Summit. Among the Mirage models, we especially like the GS for its sporting flair, above-average handling, and brisk acceleration. Fuel economy is the biggest plus for the other Mirages; we averaged a pleasing 37 mpg with a 4-door/5-speed. Work the 1.5-liter engine hard, however, and it growls back. A sensible dashboard design, a surprisingly comfortable ride, and a fairly solid feel are other credits. The hatchback loses a lot of cargo room and rear-seat space compared to the 4-door. However, the hatchback is the way to go if you're on a tight budget.

Specifications

	3-door hatchback	4-door notchback
Wheelbase, in.	93.9	96.7
Overall length, in.	158.7	170.1
Overall width, in.	65.7	65.7
Overall height, in.	52.0	52.8
Curb weight, lbs.	2238	2271
Cargo vol., cu. ft.	34.7	10.3
Fuel capacity, gals.	13.2	13.2
Seating capacity	5	5
Front head room, in.	38.3	39.1
Front leg room, max., in.	41.9	41.9
Rear head room, in.	36.9	37.5
Rear leg room, min., in.	32.5	34.4

Powertrain layout: transverse front engine/front-wheel drive.

Engines

	ohc l-4	dohc l-4
Size, liters/cu. in.	1.5/90	1.6/97
Fuel delivery	PFI	PFI
Horsepower @ rpm	92 @ 6000	123 @ 6500
Torque (lbs./ft.) @ rpm	93 @ 3000	101 @ 5000
Availability	S[1]	S[2]

EPA city/highway mpg

4-speed OD manual	31/36	
5-speed OD manual	29/35	23/28
3-speed automatic	28/31	
4-speed OD automatic	26/32	22/28

1. All except GS.   2. GS.

Assembly point: Mizushima, Japan.

Prices

Mitsubishi Mirage	Retail Price	Dealer Invoice	Low Price
VL 3-door hatchback, 4-speed	$7319	$6614	$6967
VL 3-door hatchback, automatic	7889	7123	7506
3-door hatchback, 5-speed	7919	7135	7527
3-door hatchback, automatic	8389	7557	7973
4-door notchback, 5-speed	8939	—	—
4-door notchback, automatic	9579	—	—

Prices are accurate at time of publication; subject to manufacturer's change.

	Retail Price	Dealer Invoice	Low Price
LS 4-door notchback, 5-speed	9489	—	—
LS 4-door notchback, automatic	10129	—	—
GS DOHC 4-door notchback, 5-speed . . .	10899	—	—
GS DOHC 4-door notchback, automatic . .	11559	—	—
Destination charge	368	368	368

Sedan dealer invoice and low price not available at time of publication.

Standard equipment:

VL: 1.5-liter PFI 4-cylinder engine, 4-speed manual transmission, motorized front shoulder belts, reclining front bucket seats, split folding rear seat, center console with storage, coolant temperature gauge, trip odometer, locking fuel door. **Sedan** has tinted glass, carpeting, dual mirrors; deletes split folding rear seat. **Base** adds: 5-speed manual or 3-speed automatic transmission (3-door; automatic on 4-door is 4-speed), dual mirrors, cigarette lighter, rear defogger (3-door). **LS** adds: digital clock, remote fuel door and decklid releases, rear defogger, map pockets, split folding rear seat, wheel covers 175/70R13 tires. **GS DOHC** adds: 1.6-liter DOHC 16-valve engine, 4-wheel disc brakes, power steering, tilt/telescopic steering wheel, tachometer, sport seats, 195/60R14 tires.

Optional equipment:

Air conditioning	756	620	688
Power steering (NA VL; std. GS)	262	215	239
AM/FM radio, base 4-door	280	196	238
VL	380	271	326
Base 3-door	333	238	286
3-door includes cargo cover.			
AM/FM cassette w/4 speakers, base 4-door .	479	335	407
AM/FM cassette w/4 speakers, base 3-door .	539	377	458
Includes cargo cover.			
AM/FM cassette w/6 speakers, LS & GS . .	507	355	431
AM/FM cassette w/EQ, GS	823	576	700
Dual rear speakers, base 4-door	29	20	25
Radio Accommodation Pkg., VL	47	33	40
Base 3-door	89	62	76
Base includes cargo cover.			
Accessory kit, 3-door	191	136	164
Digital clock, floormats, mud guards.			
Rear defogger, VL, base sedan	62	53	58
Convenience Pkg., GS	501	401	451
Power windows and locks, power mirrors.			
Cruise control, GS	216	173	195
Includes variable intermittent wipers.			
Alloy wheels, GS	285	228	257
Dual mirrors, base 3-door	32	26	29

Mitsubishi Precis

The Korean-built Precis, Mitsubishi's price leader, is a front-drive subcompact that's nearly identical to the Hyundai Excel, though Precis comes only as a 3-door hatchback, while the Excel also comes as a 4-door sedan. The only engine is an 81-horsepower 1.5-liter 4-cylinder. Base models come with a 4-speed manual or a 4-seed automatic transmission. RS models add such items as wider wheels, a tachometer, cloth upholstery, and a split, folding rear seatback. A 5-speed manual is standard on the RS. See the Hyundai Excel for more information on this car.

Specifications

	3-door hatchback
Wheelbase, in.	93.9
Overall length, in.	161.4
Overall width, in.	63.3
Overall height, in.	51.6
Curb weight, lbs.	2040
Cargo vol., cu. ft.	37.9
Fuel capacity, gals.	11.9
Seating capacity	5
Front head room, in.	37.8
Front leg room, max., in.	41.9
Rear head room, in.	37.5
Rear leg room, min., in.	32.9

Powertrain layout: transverse front engine/front-wheel drive.

Engines

	ohc I-4
Size, liters/cu. in.	1.5/90
Fuel delivery	PFI
Horsepower @ rpm	81 @ 5500
Torque (lbs./ft.) @ rpm	91 @ 3000
Availability	S

EPA city/highway mpg

4-speed OD manual	29/33
4-speed OD automatic	28/32

Assembly point: Ulfan, South Korea.

Prices are accurate at time of publication; subject to manufacturer's change.

Prices

Mitsubishi Precis (1991 Prices)	Retail Price	Dealer Invoice	Low Price
3-door hatchback, 4-speed	$6469	$5896	$6189
3-door hatchback, automatic	7119	6498	6809
RS 3-door hatchback, 5-speed	6929	6267	6598
RS 3-door hatchback, automatic	7479	6767	7123
Destination charge	343	343	343

Standard equipment:

1.5-liter PFI 4-cylinder engine, 4-speed manual or 4-speed automatic transmission, door-mounted front shoulder belts, cloth and vinyl reclining front bucket seats, detachable cargo cover, variable intermittent wipers, rear defogger, coolant temperature gauge, trip odometer, locking fuel door, 155/80R13 tires. **RS** adds: 5-speed manual or 4-speed automatic transmission, tachometer, cloth upholstery, 60/40 split folding rear seat, upgraded interior trim, rear wiper/washer, wheel covers, 175/70R13 tires.

Optional equipment:

Power steering	260	221	235
Air conditioning	758	606	665
AM/FM cassette	295	221	252
High Power AM/FM cassette, RS	471	330	391
Floormats	55	35	44
Wheel trim rings	67	42	55

Mitsubishi 3000GT/ Dodge Stealth

A removable glass sunroof is supposed to become available later in the year on the Stealth as the major change for these Mitsubishi-built twins. The 3000GT and Stealth differ slightly in appearance trim, features, and pricing. The 3000GT line consists of base and SL models with front-wheel drive and a twin-cam 3.0-liter V-6 rated at 222 horsepower. The flagship VR-4 has permanently engaged 4-wheel drive, 4-wheel steering, and a 300-horsepower twin-turbo version of the V-6. The Stealth lineup includes a base model with a 164-horsepower single cam V-6 that's not available on the 3000GT. The Stealth ES and R/T models

CONSUMER GUIDE®

Mitsubishi 3000GT

have the 222-horsepower engine and the R/T Turbo gets the 300-horsepower engine, plus 4WD and 4WS. All models have a driver-side air bag. Anti-lock brakes are optional on the base 3000GT, standard on the other Mitsubishi models. At Dodge, anti-lock brakes are standard on the R/T models, optional on the others. While Dodge emphasizes the lower-rung versions of this car, Mitsubishi spotlights the VR-4. It's virtually a twin of the Stealth R/T Turbo, with the same Apollo-launch acceleration, tenacious AWD roadholding, teeth-jarring ride, and poor gas mileage. Other models aren't as fast, but quick enough, and they have most of the VR-4's admirable qualities. As with most sports cars, the cockpit is snug and low-slung, with a back seat strictly for show. Probably the best values are the base 3000GT and the base and ES Stealths.

Specifications

	3-door hatchback
Wheelbase, in.	97.2
Overall length, in.	180.5
Overall width, in.	72.4
Overall height, in.	49.1
Curb weight, lbs.	3086
Cargo vol., cu. ft.	11.1
Fuel capacity, gals.	19.8
Seating capacity	4

Prices are accurate at time of publication; subject to manufacturer's change.

	3-door hatchback
Front head room, in.	37.1
Front leg room, max., in.	44.2
Rear head room, in.	34.1
Rear leg room, min., in.	28.5

Powertrain layout: transverse front engine/front-wheel drive or permanent 4WD.

Engines	ohc V-6	dohc V-6	Turbo dohc V-6
Size, liters/cu. in.	3.0/181	3.0/181	3.0/181
Fuel delivery	PFI	PFI	PFI
Horsepower @ rpm	164 @ 5500	222 @ 6000	300 @ 6000
Torque (lbs./ft.) @ rpm	185 @ 4000	201 @ 4500	307 @ 2500
Availability	S[1]	S[2]	S[3]

EPA city/highway mpg

	ohc V-6	dohc V-6	Turbo dohc V-6
5-speed OD manual	18/24	19/24	18/24
4-speed OD automatic	18/23	18/24	

1. Base Stealth.　2. Base 3000GT, SL; Stealth ES, R/T.　3. 3000GT VR-4; Stealth R/T Turbo.

Assembly point: Nagoya, Japan.

Prices

Mitsubishi 3000GT	Retail Price	Dealer Invoice	Low Price
3-door hatchback, 5-speed	$20049	$17049	—
3-door hatchback, automatic	20869	17744	—
SL 3-door hatchback, 5-speed	26209	21499	—
SL 3-door hatchback, automatic	27059	22194	—
VR-4 3-door hatchback, 5-speed	32800	26848	—
Destination charge	368	368	368

Low price not available at time of publication.

Standard equipment:

3.0-liter DOHC 24-valve PFI V-6, 5-speed manual or 4-speed automatic transmission, 4-wheel disc brakes, power steering, driver's-side airbag, cloth reclining front bucket seats, split folding rear seat, tachometer, coolant temperature and oil pressure gauges, voltmeter, trip odometer, power mirrors, remote fuel door and hatch releases, AM/FM cassette with four speakers, power antenna, tilt steering column, leather-wrapped steering wheel, fog lamps, coin and cup holders, visor mirrors, rear defogger, digital clock, tinted glass, 225/55VR16 tires on alloy wheels. **SL** adds: anti-lock brakes, electronically controlled suspension, automatic climate control, power windows and locks, cruise control, rear wiper/washer, upgraded audio system (with six speakers, EQ, and steering-wheel-mounted controls), anti-theft system, heated mirrors. **VR-4** adds: turbocharged engine, permanent 4-wheel drive, 4-wheel steering, limited-slip rear differential, Active Aero front air dam and rear spoiler, Active Exhaust, 245/45ZR17 tires.

Optional equipment:

	Retail Price	Dealer Invoice	Low Price
Anti-lock brakes, base	1130	904	—
Air conditioning, base	840	688	—
Upgraded cassette audio system, base . . .	386	270	—
Includes six speakers and EQ.			
CD player, base	889	622	—
SL	503	352	—
VR-4	274	192	—
Premium Sound System, SL	229	160	—
Sunroof	375	300	—
Anti-theft system, base	168	134	—
Rear wiper/washer, base	138	110	—
Rear spoiler, SL	200	160	—
Power Pkg., base	569	455	—
Power windows and locks, cruise control.			
Leather seat trim, SL & VR-4	1120	896	—
Mud guards	134	94	—

Dodge Stealth
(Preliminary prices)

3-door hatchback	$17155	—	—
ES 3-door hatchback	19028	—	—
R/T 3-door hatchback	25500	—	—
R/T Turbo 3-door hatchback	30855	—	—
Destination charge	343	343	343

Dealer invoice and low price not available at time of publication.

Standard equipment:

3.0-liter PFI V-6, 5-speed manual transmission, 4-wheel disc brakes, power steering, driver-side air bag, cloth reclining front bucket seats, tachometer, coolant temperature and oil pressure gauges, remote fuel door and hatch releases, remote mirrors, AM/FM radio, tilt steering column, leather-wrapped steering wheel, tinted glass, intermittent wipers, 205/65HR15 tires. **ES** adds: DOHC 24-valve engine, fog/driving lights, 225/55VR16 unidirectional tires on alloy wheels. **R/T** adds: anti-lock brakes, Variable Damped Electronic Suspension, automatic climate control, heated mirrors, power windows and locks, power driver-seat lumbar and side bolsters, AM/FM cassette, power

Prices are accurate at time of publication; subject to manufacturer's change.

antenna, cruise control, security alarm, rear spoiler, rear wiper/washer. **R/T Turbo** adds: turbocharged engine, permanent 4-wheel drive, 4-wheel steering, 245/45ZR17 unidirectional tires.

Optional equipment:	Retail Price	Dealer Invoice	Low Price
4-speed automatic transmission (NA 4WD) .	813	699	—
Air conditioning, base & ES	846	728	—
Leather trim	843	725	—
Option Pkg. IFA, base	259	223	—
Alloy wheels.			
Option Pkg. IFB, base	836	719	—
Pkg. IFA plus power windows and locks, cruise control, floormats.			
Option Pkg. IFC, base	969	833	—
Pkg. IFB plus rear wiper/washer.			
Option Pkg. IFD, base	1445	1243	—
Pkg. IFC plus Ultimate Sound audio system.			
Option Pkg. IFE, base	2219	1908	—
Anti lock brakes, security alarm, alloy wheels, power windows and locks, cruise control, rear wiper/washer, floormats.			
Option Pkg. IFF, base	3119	2682	—
Pkg. IFE plus Ultimate Sound audio system with CD player.			
Option Pkg. IFB, ES	891	766	—
Power windows and locks, cruise control, rear wiper/washer, cassette player, floormats.			
Option Pkg. IFC, ES	1186	1020	—
Pkg. IFB plus Ultimate Sound audio system.			
Option Pkg. IFD, ES	2436	2095	—
Pkg. IFC plus anti-lock brakes, security alarm.			
Option Pkg. IFE, ES	2860	2460	—
Pkg. IFD plus CD player.			
Option Pkg. IFF, ES	3221	2770	—
Pkg. IFE plus Electronic Variable Damped Suspension.			
Option Pkg. IFB, R/T, R/T Turbo	424	365	—
Ultimate Sound audio system with CD player.			
Cassette player, base	181	156	—
Floormats, base	28	24	—

Nissan Maxima

An optional driver-side air bag and a more powerful engine for the sporty SE model are new for this front-drive 4-door. Maxima returns in posh GXE and sporty SE guise. Now standard on the SE is a new twin-cam 190-horsepower 3.0-liter V-6. A single-cam 160-horsepower 3.0 V-6 remains standard on the GXE. A 5-speed manual transmission is

Nissan Maxima SE

Specifications

	4-door notchback
Wheelbase, in.	104.3
Overall length, in.	187.6
Overall width, in.	69.3
Overall height, in.	55.1
Curb weight, lbs.	3129
Cargo vol., cu. ft.	14.5
Fuel capacity, gals.	18.5
Seating capacity	5
Front head room, in.	39.5
Front leg room, max., in.	43.7
Rear head room, in.	36.9
Rear leg room, min., in.	33.2

Powertrain layout: transverse front engine/front-wheel drive.

Engines

	ohc V-6	dohc V-6
Size, liters/cu. in.	3.0/181	3.0/181
Fuel delivery	PFI	PFI
Horsepower @ rpm	160 @ 5200	190 @ 5600
Torque (lbs./ft.) @ rpm	182 @ 2800	190 @ 4000
Availability	S[1]	S[2]

EPA city/highway mpg

5-speed OD manual		21/26
4-speed OD automatic	19/26	19/26

1. GXE.   2. SE.

Assembly point: Yokosuka, Japan.

Prices are accurate at time of publication; subject to manufacturer's change.

standard on the SE and a 4-speed automatic is optional. The GXE comes only with the automatic. A driver-side air bag is optional for the first time on both models. Anti-lock brakes, previously optional only on the SE, are also optional on the GXE this year. Both versions also wear a new grille and taillamps. Also for 1992, the SE's power glass sunroof jumps from the standard-equipment list to the options roster, but the SE gains a new viscous limited-slip differential and, on models with the manual transmission, high-performance all-season tires. The current Maxima bowed for 1989, so it's a little old compared to recent arrivals such as the Lexus ES 300 and Mitsubishi Diamante. It's still a sterling blend of roominess, quality, performance, and value. We're disappointed that the air bag and anti-lock brakes aren't standard across the Maxima line, but the SE's new engine is smoother, quieter, and more responsive than the base V-6. The SE takes to winding roads with aplomb while the GXE clearly favors luxury, a strategy evident in its higher degree of body lean in turns, cushier ride, and lower horsepower and more subdued powertrain. However, both versions belong at the top of your shopping list for luxury sedans under $30,000.

Prices

Nissan Maxima	Retail Price	Dealer Invoice	Low Price
GXE 4-door notchback, automatic	$19695	$17076	$17937
SE 4-door notchback, 5-speed	20815	18047	18957
SE 4-door notchback, automatic	21750	18858	19809
Destination charge	300	300	300

Standard equipment:

3.0-liter PFI V-6, 4-speed automatic transmission, power steering, motorized front shoulder belts, air conditioning, power windows and locks with keyless entry, velour reclining front bucket seats, driver's seat height and lumbar adjustments, power mirrors, cruise control, tinted glass, AM/FM cassette with diversity antenna, motorized front shoulder belts with manual lap belts, theft deterrent system, tilt steering column, variable-intermittent wipers, rear defogger, remote fuel door and decklid releases, illuminated entry, tachometer, trip odometer, coolant temperature gauge, digital clock, 205/65R15 tires on alloy wheels. **SE** deletes keyless entry and adds: 3.0-liter DOHC PFI V-6 engine, 5-speed manual or 4-speed automatic transmission, 4-wheel disc brakes, limited slip differential, Nissan-Bose audio system, rear spoiler, leather-wrapped steering wheel and shifter.

Optional equipment:

	Retail Price	Dealer Invoice	Low Price
Anti-lock brakes	995	843	897
Driver-side air bag	500	423	450
Luxury Pkg., GXE	2225	1884	2004
Power sunroof, 4-way power front seats, Nissan-Bose audio system, automatic climate control, leather-wrapped steering wheel and shifter.			
Leather Trim Pkg., GXE	1000	847	901
SE	1400	1185	1261
SE includes 4-way power front seats; requires Luxury Pkg. on GXE.			
Pearlglow paint	350	297	316
Power sunroof	825	699	743
California emissions	70	59	63

Nissan NX 1600/2000

Nissan NX 2000

New convenience items are available for the front-drive NX 2000 and similar NX 1600. Introduced during 1991 to replace the Pulsar NX, they're based on Nissan's Sentra subcompact, but have their own 3-door hatchback styling. The NX 2000 uses a 2.0-liter 4-cylinder engine with 140 horsepower. The NX 1600 has a 1.6-liter four with 110. A 5-speed manual transmission is standard and a 4-speed automatic is optional on both. The NX 2000 adds firmer suspension, larger tires, rear disc brakes, and a limited-slip differential. Its standard rear spoiler and fog lights are optional on the NX 1600. New for 1992 on the 2000 is a

Prices are accurate at time of publication; subject to manufacturer's change.

Power Package option with electric windows, door locks, and cruise control. The T-bar roof option expands from the NX 2000 to the NX 1600. A driver-side air bag is standard on both. Anti-lock brakes are optional on the NX 2000 with the 5-speed manual. With the NX 1600 you get sporty looks, high fuel economy, and acceleration on a par with the lower-rung models of rivals such as the Ford Probe and Toyota Celica. The quicker NX 2000 will please enthusiast drivers. Neither engine has much power below 3500 rpm, so we recommend the easy-shifting manual transmission for best performance. These cars score with their standard air bag, solid feel, supportive front buckets, and good fuel economy.

Specifications

	3-door hatchback
Wheelbase, in.	95.7
Overall length, in.	162.4
Overall width, in.	66.1
Overall height, in.	51.4
Curb weight, lbs.	2350
Cargo vol., cu. ft.	16.9
Fuel capacity, gals.	13.2
Seating capacity	4
Front head room, in.	37.3
Front leg room, max., in.	41.6
Rear head room, in.	35.2
Rear leg room, min., in.	25.7

Powertrain layout: transverse front engine/front-wheel drive.

Engines	dohc I-4	dohc I-4
Size, liters/cu. in.	1.6/97	2.0/122
Fuel delivery	PFI	PFI
Horsepower @ rpm	110 @ 6000	140 @ 6400
Torque (lbs./ft.) @ rpm	108 @ 4000	130 @ 4800
Availability	S[1]	S[2]

EPA city/highway mpg

5-speed OD manual	28/38	23/30
4-speed OD automatic	27/36	23/29

1. NX 1600.   2. NX 2000.

Assembly point: Zama, Japan.

Prices

Nissan NX 1600/2000	Retail Price	Dealer Invoice	Low Price
1600 3-door hatchback, 5-speed	$11300	$10143	—
1600 3-door hatchback, automatic	12125	10883	—
2000 3-door hatchback, 5-speed	13480	11963	—
2000 3-door hatchback, automatic	14315	12703	—
Destination charge	300	300	300

Low price not available at time of publication.

Standard equipment:

1600: 1.6-liter DOHC 16-valve PFI 4-cylinder engine, 5-speed manual or 4-speed automatic transmission, power steering, driver-side air bag, cloth reclining front bucket seats, folding rear seat, tachometer, trip odometer, coolant temperature gauge, power mirrors, tilt steering column, tinted glass, intermittent wipers, rear defogger, remote fuel door and hatch releases, center console, right visor mirror, cupholder, 175/70R13 tires. **2000** adds: 2.0-liter engine, 4-wheel disc brakes, limited-slip differential, front air dam, rear spoiler, upgraded carpet, leather-wrapped steering wheel and shift knob, fog lights, AM/FM cassette, 195/55R14 tires on alloy wheels.

Optional equipment:

Anti-lock brakes, 2000 w/5-speed	700	593	—
Air conditioning	850	720	—
Power Pkg., 2000	730	618	—
AM/FM cassette, 1600	450	381	—
T-bar roof, 2000	900	762	—
Pearlglow paint, 1600	350	297	—
California emissions pkg.	70	59	—

Nissan Pathfinder

Nissan's compact sport-utility vehicle is unchanged this year, though there may be a facelift in spring 1992. Pathfinder comes only as a 5-door wagon in XE and SE trim levels. XE versions are available with either rear- or 4-wheel drive; the SE comes only with 4-wheel drive. The 4WD system has automatic locking front hubs and limited shift-on-the-fly capability. Pathfinder uses a 153-horsepower 3.0-liter V-6 engine teamed with either a 5-speed manual or 4-speed automatic transmission. Standing-start accelera-

Prices are accurate at time of publication; subject to manufacturer's change.

Nissan Pathfinder SE 5-door

Specifications

	5-door wagon
Wheelbase, in.	104.3
Overall length, in.	171.9
Overall width, in.	66.5
Overall height, in.	65.7
Curb weight, lbs.	3795
Cargo vol., cu. ft.	31.4
Fuel capacity, gals.	21.1
Seating capacity	5
Front head room, in.	39.3
Front leg room, max., in.	42.6
Rear head room, in.	36.8
Rear leg room, min., in.	33.1

Powertrain layout: longitudinal front engine/rear-wheel drive or on-demand 4WD.

Engines

	ohc V-6
Size, liters/cu. in.	3.0/181
Fuel delivery	PFI
Horsepower @ rpm	153 @ 4800
Torque (lbs./ft.) @ rpm	180 @ 4000
Availability	S
EPA city/highway mpg	
5-speed OD manual	15/18
4-speed OD automatic	15/18

Assembly point: Kyoto, Japan.

CONSUMER GUIDE®

tion is brisk for this class, but Pathfinder's V-6 doesn't have enough torque to stay with such domestic rivals as the Ford Explorer and Jeep Cherokee when climbing hills or hauling heavy loads. Gas mileage was dismal in our test: 14.7 mpg with automatic transmission. The 4WD system lacks full shift-on-the-fly, so it isn't as convenient as those on the Chevrolet S10 Blazer, Ford Explorer, Cherokee, and other rivals. There's a fairly high step up into the Pathfinder's interior and the rear doors are narrow, two big minuses for a family vehicle. The cargo area is long and wide. The rear seat splits 60/40 and folds flat if you tilt the cushions forward and remove the headrests. Pathfinder has good points, but it needs a more convenient 4WD system with full shift-on-the-fly capability to move to the front of the pack of compact 4×4s.

Prices

Nissan Pathfinder	Retail Price	Dealer Invoice	Low Price
XE 2WD 5-door wagon, 5-speed	$17265	$15233	$15853
XE 2WD 5-door wagon, automatic	18480	16305	16968
XE 4WD 5-door wagon, 5-speed	18910	16684	17363
XE 4WD 5-door wagon, automatic	20125	17756	18479
SE 4WD 5-door wagon, 5-speed	21980	19393	20182
SE 4WD 5-door wagon, automatic	22925	20227	21050
Destination charge	300	300	300

Standard equipment:

XE: 3.0-liter PFI V-6, 5-speed manual or 4-speed automatic transmission, anti-lock rear brakes, power steering, automatic locking front hubs (4WD), cloth reclining front bucket seats, split folding and reclining rear seat, tachometer, coolant temperature gauge, trip odometer, digital clock, rear wiper/washer, tinted glass, dual outside mirrors, skid plates, front tow hooks, AM/FM cassette with diversity antenna, tilt steering column, rear defogger, left front door pocket, remote fuel door release, cargo tiedown hooks, 235/75R15 tires. **SE** adds: semi-automatic air conditioning, power windows and locks, cruise control, intermittent wipers, power mirrors, misc. lights, remote rear window release, two trip odometers, voltmeter, rear quarter privacy glass, upgraded upholstery and carpet, driver-seat height and lumbar support adjustments, right front door pocket, outboard folding rear armrests.

Prices are accurate at time of publication; subject to manufacturer's change.

Optional equipment:

	Retail Price	Dealer Invoice	Low Price
Air conditioning, XE	850	720	766
Sport/Power Pkg., XE 2WD	1050	889	946
XE 4WD	1250	1059	1126
SE	2000	1693	1801

XE: outside spare tire carrier, spare tire cover, fender flares, fog lights, power windows and locks, power mirrors, remote hatch release, limited-slip differential (4WD). SE adds: adjustable shock absorbers, 4-wheel disc brakes, removable glass sunroof, step rail, 31 × 10.5R15 tires on alloy wheels.

	Retail Price	Dealer Invoice	Low Price
Leather Trim Pkg., SE	1000	847	901
Requires Sport/Power Pkg.			
CD player	375	317	338
Two-tone paint, SE	300	254	270
Luggage rack/air deflector	175	148	158
California emissions	70	59	63

Nissan Sentra

1991 Nissan Sentra GXE 4-door

Nissan's front-drive subcompact gets only minor changes. Newly standard on 2-door models are a passenger-side vanity mirror and black body side moldings. And the Value Option Package, previously limited to XE models, is extended to the SE and SE-R versions. It consists of air conditioning, cruise control, and a 4-speaker AM/FM stereo. Model offerings are unchanged: The budget E and the XE come as 2- and 4-door notchbacks; the sporty SE and SE-R are available only in 2-door styling; and the luxury GXE comes only as a 4-door. All but the SE-R have a 1.6-liter 4-cylinder engine with 110 horsepower. The SE-R has a 140-horsepower 2.0-liter four. E models come with a 4-speed manual transmission standard and a 3-speed automatic optional. A 5-speed manual is standard on the others—and mandatory on the SE-R—and a 4-speed automatic is optional. Anti-lock brakes are optional only on the SE-R and GXE. Automatic transmission saps most of the base engine's verve, and brisk acceleration means flooring the throttle and enduring jolting shifts. Fuel economy is great, however: Our test GXE with automatic averaged 26 mpg in urban driving. The SE-R is a "pocket rocket" with zesty get-up-and-go from its smooth 2.0-liter engine. Sentra corners with modest body roll, but good grip from the tires. Availability of anti-lock brakes is still unusual for the sub-compact class. Too bad they aren't available on the less-expensive Sentras. Sentra is an efficient, comfortable, reasonably priced small car that ranks at the top of its class.

Specifications

	2-door notchback	4-door notchback
Wheelbase, in.	95.7	95.7
Overall length, in.	170.3	170.3
Overall width, in.	65.6	65.6
Overall height, in.	53.9	53.9
Curb weight, lbs.	2266	2288
Cargo vol., cu. ft.	11.7	11.7
Fuel capacity, gals.	13.2	13.2
Seating capacity	5	5
Front head room, in.	38.5	38.5
Front leg room, max., in.	41.9	41.9
Rear head room, in.	36.6	36.6
Rear leg room, min., in.	30.9	30.9

Powertrain layout: transverse front engine/front-wheel drive.

Engines

	dohc I-4	dohc I-4
Size, liters/cu. in.	1.6/97	2.0/122
Fuel delivery	PFI	PFI
Horsepower @ rpm	110 @ 6000	140 @ 6400
Torque (lbs./ft.) @ rpm	108 @ 4000	132 @ 4800
Availability	S	S[1]

Prices are accurate at time of publication; subject to manufacturer's change.

	dohc I-4	dohc I-4
EPA city/highway mpg		
4-speed manual	29/37	
5-speed OD manual	29/39	24/32
3-speed automatic	28/33	
4-speed OD automatic	27/36	24/31

1. SE-R.

Assembly points: Kyoto, Japan; Smyrna, Tenn.

Prices

Nissan Sentra	Retail Price	Dealer Invoice	Low Price
E 2-door notchback, 4-speed	$8495	$7971	$8233
E 2-door notchback, automatic	9565	8976	9271
XE 2-door notchback, 5-speed	9880	8768	9324
XE 2-door notchback, automatic	10605	9411	10008
SE 2-door notchback, 5-speed	10560	9317	9939
SE 2-door notchback, automatic	11285	9957	10621
SE-R 2-door notchback	11850	10455	11153
E 4-door notchback, 5-speed	9550	8475	9013
E 4-door notchback, automatic	10525	9340	9933
XE 4-door notchback, 5-speed	10565	9376	9971
XE 4-door notchback, automatic	11290	10018	10654
GXE 4-door notchback, 5-speed	12950	11426	12188
GXE 4-door notchback, automatic	13675	12066	12871
Destination charge	300	300	300

Standard equipment:

E 2-door: 1.6-liter DOHC 16-valve PFI 4-cylinder engine, 4-speed manual or 3-speed automatic transmission, door-mounted automatic front shoulder belts, cloth reclining front bucket seats, rear defogger, coolant temperature gauge, trip odometer, 155/80R13 tires (models with automatic transmission have 175/70R13 tires, power steering, and tilt steering column); 4-door has motorized front shoulder belts, 5-speed manual or 3-speed automatic transmission, right visor mirror. **XE** adds: 5-speed manual or 4-speed automatic transmission, power steering, tilt steering column, power mirrors, bodyside molding, intermittent wipers, right visor mirror, digital clock, 175/70R13 tires. **GXE** adds: air conditioning, power windows and locks, AM/FM cassette with diversity antenna, cruise control, velour upholstery, tachometer, storage bin under passenger seat, alloy wheels. **SE** adds to XE: multi-adjustable seats with upgraded upholstery, rear spoiler; deletes bodyside molding. **SE-R** adds: 2.0-liter engine, 4-wheel disc brakes, limited-slip differential, sport suspension, bodyside molding, fog lights, 185/60R14 tires on alloy wheels.

CONSUMER GUIDE®

Optional equipment:	Retail Price	Dealer Invoice	Low Price
Anti-lock brakes, GXE & SE-R	700	593	647
Air conditioning (std. GXE)	850	720	785
Power sunroof, GXE & SE-R	825	699	762
Not available with anti-lock brakes on GXE.			
Value Option Pkg., E & XE	995	843	919
SE & SE-R	1295	1097	1196
Air conditioning, AM/FM cassette, cruise control.			
Cruise control, XE, SE & SE-R	220	187	204
AM/FM cassette (NA E)	450	381	416
Metallic paint, E	100	85	93
California emissions	70	59	NA

Nissan Stanza

Nissan Stanza SE

A new sporty SE model joins the Stanza lineup of front-drive 4-doors. The SE has most of the same standard features as the luxury-oriented GXE model, but adds a blackout grille, rear spoiler, fog lights, and leather-wrapped steering wheel and shift knob. Like all Stanzas, it uses a 138-horsepower 2.4-liter 4-cylinder engine. A 5-speed manual transmission is standard on the base XE and the SE and a 4-speed automatic is optional. The GXE comes only with the automatic. Anti-lock brakes are optional on the GXE and SE. Stanza's road manners are sportier than those of most compact sedans. It has responsive steering, nimble handling, and good cornering grip. Standing-start acceleration is middle-of-the pack, but there's ample low-speed

Prices are accurate at time of publication; subject to manufacturer's change.

power for brisk takeoffs and the engine mates well to the smooth-shifting automatic transmission. The engine gets quite raucous under hard throttle, however. Combined with constant road noise and suspension thumping, it marks Stanza as an annoyingly loud car. Some of our drivers find it a stiff-riding compact, as well. The front seats are comfortable and roomy, but there's not enough rear leg room for tall people to relax. Stanza's not as big inside as some competitors, such as the new Toyota Camry, Hyundai Sonata, and Dodge Spirit/Plymouth Acclaim, and it doesn't offer a V-6. However, it's a competent, well-built compact and has more of a sporting flair than most rivals.

Specifications

	4-door notchback
Wheelbase, in.	100.4
Overall length, in.	179.9
Overall width, in.	66.9
Overall height, in.	54.1
Curb weight, lbs.	2788
Cargo vol., cu. ft.	14.0
Fuel capacity, gals.	16.4
Seating capacity	5
Front head room, in.	38.6
Front leg room, max., in.	42.6
Rear head room, in.	36.8
Rear leg room, min., in.	33.6

Powertrain layout: transverse front engine/front-wheel drive.

Engines

	ohc I-4
Size, liters/cu. in.	2.4/146
Fuel delivery	PFI
Horsepower @ rpm	138 @ 5600
Torque (lbs./ft.) @ rpm	148 @ 4400
Availability	S

EPA city/highway mpg

5-speed OD manual	22/29
4-speed OD automatic	21/27

Assembly point: Yokosuka, Japan.

Prices

Nissan Stanza

	Retail Price	Dealer Invoice	Low Price
XE 4-door notchback, 5-speed	$12750	$11029	$11600
XE 4-door notchback, automatic	13700	11851	12464
GXE 4-door notchback, automatic	17070	14595	15446
SE 4-door notchback, 5-speed	16690	14270	—
SE 4-door notchback, automatic	17525	14984	—
Destination charge	300	300	300

SE low price not available at time of publication.

Standard equipment:

XE: 2.4-liter PFI 4-cylinder engine, 5-speed manual or 4-speed automatic transmission, cruise control (with automatic), power steering, motorized front shoulder belts, cloth reclining front bucket seats, power mirrors, intermittent wipers, tilt steering column, coolant temperature gauge, trip odometer, remote fuel door and decklid releases, front door pockets, tinted glass, digital clock, console with storage and cupholders, 195/65R14 tires. **GXE** adds: air conditioning, limited-slip differential, power windows and locks, AM/FM cassette with power antenna and diversity antenna system, tachometer, cruise control, velour upholstery, driver-seat height and lumbar support adjustments, map lights, alloy wheels. SE adds: rear spoiler, fog lamps, leather-wrapped steering wheel and shifter; automatic deletes cruise control, height and lumbar adjustable driver-seat, rear armrest.

Optional equipment:

Anti-lock brakes, GXE & SE	995	826	888
Value Option Pkg., XE	1690	1403	1509

Air conditioning, power windows and locks, AM/FM cassette, velour upholstery, driver's-seat height and lumbar adjustments, rear armrest, tachometer.

Cruise control, XE 5-speed	220	183	197
Power sunroof, GXE & SE	825	685	737
Pearlglow paint	350	291	313

XE requires Value Option Pkg.

Nissan 240SX

The big news is the addition of a convertible model scheduled to go on sale in spring 1992. Nissan is mum on details, but the convertible 240SX is expected to have a power top. Anti-lock brakes are no longer available on the LE version

Prices are accurate at time of publication; subject to manufacturer's change.

Nissan 240SX SE 3-door

as the only change this fall on the returning models, which comprise 2-door notchback and 3-door fastback coupes in base and SE trim, plus the luxury LE fastback. All have a 155-horsepower 2.4-liter 4-cylinder engine driving the rear wheels. Optional on the SE fastback is a Handling Package that includes Nissan's Super-HICAS 4-wheel steering system, a limited-slip differential, sport suspension, and wider tires. Anti-lock brakes are now optional only on the SE fastback with air conditioning, the Handling Package, and a sunroof. Standard on the SE 2-door is a head-up display, which projects a digital speedometer reading onto the windshield. With a large-displacement 4-cylinder, the 240SX has enough torque to move out fairly quickly with automatic transmission. But the car is best enjoyed with the slick-shifting manual. The engine is too coarse and loud, however, and there's too much road noise at highway speeds. Sports-car handling is the best quality, though the rear-drive layout makes for poor traction on slick pavement. The ride is firm but not harsh. We're sorry to see the added security of anti-lock brakes limited to the SE model, and then made available only with a host of expensive options.

Specifications

	2-door notchback	3-door hatchback
Wheelbase, in.	97.4	97.4
Overall length, in.	178.0	178.0
Overall width, in.	66.5	66.5
Overall height, in.	50.8	50.8

	2-door notchback	3-door hatchback
Curb weight, lbs.	2699	2730
Cargo vol., cu. ft.	8.6	14.2
Fuel capacity, gals.	15.9	15.9
Seating capacity	4	4
Front head room, in.	37.8	37.8
Front leg room, max., in.	42.0	42.0
Rear head room, in.	34.5	33.3
Rear leg room, min., in.	23.8	23.8

Powertrain layout: longitudinal front engine/rear-wheel drive.

Engines

	dohc I-4
Size, liters/cu. in.	2.4/146
Fuel delivery	PFI
Horsepower @ rpm	155 @ 5600
Torque (lbs./ft.) @ rpm	160 @ 4400
Availability	S

EPA city/highway mpg

5-speed OD manual	22/27
4-speed OD automatic	21/26

Assembly point: Kyoto, Japan.

Prices

Nissan 240SX	Retail Price	Dealer Invoice	Low Price
2-door notchback, 5-speed	$14515	$12881	$13364
2-door notchback, automatic	15345	13617	14128
SE 2-door notchback, 5-speed	16690	14810	15366
SE 2-door notchback, automatic	17515	15543	16126
3-door hatchback, 5-speed	14785	13120	13612
3-door hatchback, automatic	15615	13857	14377
SE 3-door hatchback, 5-speed	16885	14984	15546
SE 3-door hatchback, automatic	17715	15720	16310
LE 3-door hatchback, 5-speed	18725	16617	17240
LE 3-door hatchback, automatic	19550	17349	18000
Destination charge	300	300	300

Standard equipment:

2.4-liter DOHC 16-valve PFI 4-cylinder engine, 5-speed manual or 4-speed automatic transmission, 4-wheel disc brakes, power steering, motorized

Prices are accurate at time of publication; subject to manufacturer's change.

front shoulder belts, cloth reclining front bucket seats, folding rear seat, AM/FM cassette with power antenna and diversity antenna system, tachometer, coolant temperature gauge, trip odometer, digital clock, tilt steering column, intermittent wipers, rear defogger, remote fuel door and decklid/hatch releases, console with storage, door pockets, visor mirrors, cargo area cover (3-door), tinted glass, remote mirrors, 195/60R15 tires. **SE** adds: power windows and locks, cruise control, leather-wrapped steering wheel and shift knob, map lights, premium speakers, digital speedometer with head-up display (2-door), front air dam, rear wiper/washer (3-door), alloy wheels. **LE** adds: leather upholstery, air conditioning.

Optional equipment:	Retail Price	Dealer Invoice	Low Price
Anti-lock brakes, SE 3-door	995	843	897
SE requires air conditioning.			
Air conditioning, base & SE	850	720	766
Power sunroof, SE 2-door	825	699	743
Flip-up sunroof, SE 3-door, LE	450	381	405
Handling Pkg., SE 3-door	500	423	450
Sport suspension, 4-wheel steering, limited-slip differential, 205/60R15 tires.			
California emissions	70	59	NA

Nissan 300ZX

Nissan 300ZX Turbo

A driver-side air bag, optional last year, is standard this year as the major change for this rear-drive sports car. The 300ZX returns in 2-seat and 2+2 configurations, and a 2-seat convertible model is due for a spring introduction.

Meanwhile, the 2-seat base model remains available only with a 5-speed manual transmission. A higher-priced 2-seater comes with a T-bar roof and is offered with either the manual or a 4-speed automatic. The 2 + 2 also is available with either transmission but has a fixed roof. The top-of-the-line 300ZX Turbo is a 2-seater with a T-bar roof and a choice of manual or automatic. The Turbo model has a 300-horsepower 3.0-liter V-6 and the others a 222-horsepower 3.0-liter. The Turbo adds Nissan's Super-HICAS 4-

Specifications

	3-door hatchback	2+2 3-door hatchback
Wheelbase, in.	96.5	101.2
Overall length, in.	169.5	178.0
Overall width, in.	70.5	70.9
Overall height, in.	49.2	49.4
Curb weight, lbs.	3186[1]	3313
Cargo vol., cu. ft.	23.7	21.8
Fuel capacity, gals.	19.0	19.0
Seating capacity	2	4
Front head room, in.	36.8	37.1
Front leg room, max., in.	43.0	43.0
Rear head room, in.	—	34.4
Rear leg room, min., in.	—	22.7

1. 3474 lbs., Turbo.

Powertrain layout: longitudinal front engine/rear-wheel drive.

Engines

	dohc V-6	Turbo dohc V-6
Size, liters/cu. in.	3.0/181	3.0/181
Fuel delivery	PFI	PFI
Horsepower @ rpm	222 @ 6400	300 @ [1] 6400
Torque (lbs./ft.) @ rpm	198 @ 4800	283 @ 3600
Availability	S	S[2]

EPA city/highway mpg

5-speed OD manual	18/24	18/24
4-speed OD automatic	18/24	18/23

1. 280 horsepower with automatic transmission.   2. Turbo.

Assembly point: Hiratscka, Japan.

Prices are accurate at time of publication; subject to manufacturer's change.

wheel steering. Anti-lock brakes are standard across the board. Naturally aspirated 300ZXs have strong acceleration but the Turbo is seriously fast. Rain and snow demand caution lest the rear end break loose. Handling is outstanding on dry roads, but the ride is stiff—harsh even. The dashboard is accommodating, but the annoying automatic temperature control must be reset with virtually each start. The 300ZX Turbo is a stellar performer, though the less-expensive, naturally aspirated models should have more than enough performance for most drivers. For comparison, look at the new Mitsubishi 3000GT and similar Dodge Stealth.

Prices

Nissan 300ZX	Retail Price	Dealer Invoice	Low Price
3-door hatchback w/o T-roof, 5-speed . . .	$29120	$24950	$28120
3-door hatchback, 5-speed	31190	26724	30190
3-door hatchback, automatic	32135	27533	31135
Turbo 3-door hatchback, 5-speed	35890	30751	34890
Turbo 3-door hatchback, automatic	36840	31565	35840
2+2 3-door hatchback, 5-speed	32440	27795	31440
2+2 3-door hatchback, automatic	33390	28609	32390
Destination charge	300	300	300

Standard equipment:

3.0-liter DOHC 24-valve PFI V-6, 5-speed manual or 4-speed automatic transmission, anti-lock 4-wheel disc brakes, driver-side air bag, limited-slip differential, power steering, door-mounted automatic front shoulder belts, power cloth reclining front bucket seats, driver-seat lumbar support and bolster adjustments, folding rear seat (2+2), air conditioning, power windows and locks, cruise control, heated power mirrors, theft-deterrent system, Nissan Bose AM/FM cassette with power antenna and diversity antenna system (models with T-roof), tachometer, coolant temperature and oil pressure gauges, trip odometer, digital clock, intermittent wipers, rear defogger and wiper/washer, remote fuel door and hatch releases, illuminated entry, cargo area cover, seatback pockets, tinted glass, fog lights, 225/50VR16 tires on alloy wheels. **Turbo** adds: turbocharged engine, 4-wheel steering, adjustable shock absorbers, rear spoiler.

Optional equipment:

Leather Pkg., 2-seater w/T-roof	1075	910	1018
2+2	1275	1079	1207
Bose audio system (std. w/T-roof)	700	593	663
Pearlglow paint, w/T-roof	350	297	332

Oldsmobile Cutlass Ciera/ Buick Century

Oldsmobile Cutlass Ciera SL 4-door

For 1992, Buick's mid-size front-drive Century receives only detail changes, while Oldsmobile drops the 2-door body style and the base 4-door sedan of the similar Cutlass Ciera. First introduced in 1982 along with the Chevy Celebrity and Pontiac 6000, the Century and Ciera are the only survivors. Century comes in 2- and 4-door notchback and 5-door wagon body styles, in Special, Custom, and Limited trim. Ciera comes only as a 4-door notchback or 5-door wagon in S or up-level SL trim. All Centurys get a 105-horsepower 2.5-liter 4-cylinder as standard equipment, with a 160-horsepower 3.3-liter V-6 optional. The 4-cylinder comes only with a 3-speed automatic; the V-6 can have either a 3-speed or 4-speed automatic. Mid-level Custom models gain a 55/45 split front seat with center armrest/storage compartment as standard, and a gauge cluster with trip odometer as an option. Both Custom and Limited models get standard power seatback recliners. Besides the loss of body style choices, the Cutlass Ciera and Cutlass Cruiser wagon continue with few changes. S models get the 2.5-liter four with 3-speed automatic standard; SL comes with the 3.3-liter V-6 and 3-speed automatic, though the 4-speed automatic is optional. The V-6 and 4-speed automatic are optional on the S. Cutlass Cruiser S gets woodgrain exterior paneling as a new option, and Ciera S is offered with the remote lock package previously available only on up-

Prices are accurate at time of publication; subject to manufacturer's change.

level Cieras. All Centurys and Cieras now come with automatic door locks. Neither offers an air bag or anti-lock brakes. We strongly recommend the smooth V-6 over the rough, weak 4-cylinder engine. Compared to others in this class, Ciera and Century ride on a softer suspension, which some people might prefer, but don't handle as well as most newer designs. Interior space is competitive: Four adults will fit in the sedan comfortably (six in a pinch), and wagons can hold up to eight passengers. Cargo space is also about par for this class. Though the Ciera and Century have long since begun showing their age, they are priced lower than many similarly sized competitors.

Specifications	2-door notchback	4-door notchback	5-door wagon
Wheelbase, in.	104.9	104.9	104.9
Overall length, in.	190.3	190.3	194.4
Overall width, in.	69.5	69.5	69.5
Overall height, in.	54.1	54.1	54.5
Curb weight, lbs.	2771	2813	2975
Cargo vol., cu. ft.	15.8	15.8	74.4
Fuel capacity, gals.	15.7	15.7	15.7
Seating capacity	6	6	8
Front head room, in.	38.6	38.6	38.6
Front leg room, max., in.	42.1	42.1	42.1
Rear head room, in.	37.6	38.0	38.9
Rear leg room, min., in.	35.8	35.8	34.7

Powertrain layout: transverse front engine/front-wheel drive.

Engines	ohv I-4	ohv V-6
Size, liters/cu. in.	2.5/151	3.3/204
Fuel delivery	TBI	PFI
Horsepower @ rpm	110 @ 5200	160 @ 5200
Torque (lbs./ft.) @ rpm	135 @ 3200	185 @ 2000
Availability	S	O[1]

EPA city/highway mpg		
3-speed automatic	22/31	19/26
4-speed OD automatic		19/30

1. Std., Cutlass Ciera SL.

Assembly point: Oklahoma City, Okla.

Prices

Oldsmobile Cutlass Ciera	Retail Price	Dealer Invoice	Low Price
S 4-door notchback	$12755	$11837	$12187
SL 4-door notchback	16895	14665	15015
Cruiser S 5-door 2-seat wagon	13860	12862	13212
Cruiser SL 5-door 3-seat wagon	17395	15099	15449
Destination charge	500	500	500

Standard equipment:

2.5-liter TBI 4-cylinder engine, 3-speed automatic transmission, power steering, door-mounted automatic front seatbelts, custom bench seat with armrest, AM/FM radio, power locks, front door pockets, tinted glass, left remote and right manual mirrors, split folding rear seat (wagon), 185/75R14 whitewall tires. **SL** adds: 3.3-liter PFI V-6, air conditioning, cassette player, 55/45 front seat with power seatback recliners, misc. lights, visor mirrors, remote decklid release.

Optional equipment:

3.3-liter V-6, S	710	604	618
4-speed automatic transmission, S & SL	200	170	174
Available only with V-6.			
Option Pkg. 1SB, S	830	706	722
Air conditioning.			
Option Pkg. 1SC, S	1040	884	905
Pkg. 1SB plus tilt steering column, intermittent wipers.			
Option Pkg. 1SD, S	1380	1173	1201
Pkg. 1SC plus power windows.			
Option Pkg. 1SE, S	2007	1706	1746
Pkg. 1SD plus cruise control, 55/45 front seat with storage armrest and power recliners.			
Option Pkg. 1SF, S	1085	922	944
Pkg. 1SE plus remote decklid release, remote mirrors, door edge guards, rocker panel, wheel opening, and bodyside moldings.			
Option Pkg. 1SB, S wagon	1125	956	979
Air conditioning, tilt steering column, intermittent wipers, rear window air deflector, floormats.			
Option Pkg. 1SC, S wagon w/o YP9	1971	1675	1715
w/YP0	1493	1269	1299
Pkg. 1SB plus 55/45 front seat with storage armrest and power seatback recliners, cruise control, Lamp & Mirror Group, rocker panel and wheel opening moldings, roof luggage rack, remote mirrors, door edge guards, striping.			

Prices are accurate at time of publication; subject to manufacturer's change.

	Retail Price	Dealer Invoice	Low Price
Option Pkg. 1SD, S wagon w/o YP9	2725	2316	2371
w/YP9	2247	1910	1955

Pkg. 1SC plus power windows, power antenna, lower bodyside moldings, rear-facing third seat.

Option Pkg. 1SB, SL 4-door	1006	855	875
SL wagon	981	834	853

Power windows, cruise control, tilt steering column, intermittent wipers, lighted visor mirrors, remote mirrors, door edge guards (4-door), floormats, striping.

Option Pkg. 1SC, SL 4-door	1521	1293	1323
SL wagon	1496	1272	1302

Pkg. 1SB plus Remote Lock Control Pkg., power driver's seat, power antenna.

55/45 front seat w/storage armrest, S ...	293	249	255

Includes power driver's seat recliner.

45/45 front seat w/console, SL 4-door ...	125	106	109

Includes power driver's seat recliner, leather-wrapped steering wheel; requires tilt steering column, intermittent wipers.

Leather seats, SL w/o 45/45 front seat ...	515	438	448
w/45/45 front seats	425	361	370

includes leather-wrapped steering wheel.

Power driver's seat	305	259	265
Power front seat recliners, each	55	47	48
Rear defogger	170	145	148
Remote mirrors	30	26	26
Load Carrying Pkg	106	90	92

Manually adjustable rear shocks, 195/75R14 whitewall tires.

Cruise control	230	196	200

Requires intermittent wipers, tilt steering column.

Tilt steering column	145	123	126
Intermittent wipers	65	55	57
Power windows	340	289	296
Remote decklid release, S 4-door	60	51	52
Wire wheel covers	240	204	209
185/75R14 blackwall tires (credit), S	(48)	(41)	(41)
195/70R14 tires on alloy wheels	295	251	257
Rallye instruments, S & SL	104	88	90

Includes tachometer, trip odometer, voltmeter, temperature and oil pressure gauges.

Convenience Group, S 4-door	64	54	56
S wagon	57	48	50

Lighted visor mirrors, reading lights, underhood light, day/night rearview mirror.

Cassette player, S	165	140	144
UX1 cassette system w/EQ, SL	235	200	204

Requires power windows.

CONSUMER GUIDE®

	Retail Price	Dealer Invoice	Low Price
6-speaker enhanced audio system, SL . . .	85	72	74
Requires power windows.			
Power antenna	85	72	74
High-capacity cooling	40	34	35
Decklid luggage rack, 4-doors	115	98	100
Roof rack, wagons	115	98	100
Rear air deflector, wagons	40	34	35
YP9 Sport Appearance Pkg., S wagon . . .	851	723	740
Unique exterior treatment, 195/70R14 tires on alloy wheels, floor console and shifter, leather-wrapped steering wheel, rallye instruments, roof rack.			
Woodgrain paneling, wagons	265	225	231
w/Pkg. 1SC or 1SD	220	187	191
Engine block heater	18	15	16
Front floormats	25	21	22
Rear floormats	20	17	17
Door edge guards (ex. SL wagon)	25	21	22
Rocker panel moldings, S	26	22	23
Wheel opening moldings, S	30	26	26
Bodyside moldings, S	70	60	61
Striping	45	38	39
Warranty enhancements for New York . . .	25	21	22
California emissions pkg	100	85	87

Buick Century

	Retail Price	Dealer Invoice	Low Price
Special 4-door notchback	$13795	$12250	$12550
Custom 2-door notchback	14550	12629	12929
Custom 4-door notchback	14755	12807	13107
Custom 5-door wagon	15660	13593	13893
Limited 4-door notchback	15695	13623	13923
Limited 5-door wagon	16395	14231	14531
Destination charge	500	500	500

Standard equipment:

Special: 2.5-liter TBI 4-cylinder engine, 3-speed automatic transmission, power steering, air conditioning, door-mounted automatic front seatbelts, power locks, left remote and right manual mirrors, tinted glass, map lights, instrument panel courtesy lights, cloth bench seat w/armrest, AM/FM radio, 185/75R14 tires. **Custom** adds: 55/45 cloth front seat, power front seat back recliners, front seat armrest w/cupholders, whitewall tires, split folding rear seatback; **wagon** has: two-way tailgate, cargo area lights, and storage compartments. **Limited** adds: 55/45 front seat with storage armrest & cupholders, voltmeter, coolant temperature gauge, trip odometer, courtesy lights; **wagon** has load floor carpeting.

Prices are accurate at time of publication; subject to manufacturer's change.

Optional equipment:

	Retail Price	Dealer Invoice	Low Price
3.3-liter V-6	710	604	639
4-speed automatic transmission (V-6 req.) .	200	170	180
Premium Pkg. SC, Special	668	568	601

Tilt steering column, 55/45 front seat, intermittent wipers, cruise control, floormats, power passenger seat recliner.

Luxury Pkg. SD, Special	978	831	880

Pkg. SC plus cassette player, rear defogger.

Prestige Pkg. SE, Special	1332	1132	1199

Pkg. SD plus power windows, visor mirrors.

Popular Pkg. SB, Custom notchbacks . . .	425	361	383
Custom wagon	480	408	432

Notchbacks: tilt steering column, rear defogger, intermittent wipers, floormats. Wagon: tilt steering column, cruise control, floormats, intermittent wipers.

Premium Pkg. SC, Custom 2-door	1030	876	927
Custom 4-door	1030	876	927
Custom wagon	790	672	711

Notchbacks: Pkg. SB plus cruise control, cassette player, wire wheels. Wagon Pkg. SB plus: rear defogger, cassette player.

Luxury Pkg. SD, Custom 2-door	1577	1340	1419
Custom 4-door	1642	1396	1478
Custom wagon	1213	1031	1092

Pkg. SC plus power windows, power antenna, lighted visor mirrors, accent stripes, power trunk release. Wagon Pkg. SC plus: power windows, misc. gauges, trip odometer, accent stripes.

Prestige Pkg. SE, Custom 2-door	2237	1901	2013
Custom 4-door	2302	1957	2072
Custom wagon	1648	1401	1483

Pkg. SD plus: power driver's seat, remote keyless entry, power mirrors, premium speakers, misc. gauges, trip odometer, front reading lights. Wagon Pkg. SD plus: third seat, rear vent windows, roof rack, remote tailgate release, rear air deflector.

Premium Pkg. SC, Ltd. 4-door	1030	876	927
Ltd. wagon	1250	1063	1125

Tilt steering column, rear defogger, intermittent wipers, power locks, cruise control, floormats, cassette player, wire wheel covers. Wagon adds: luggage rack, remote tailgate release, rear air deflector.

Luxury Pkg. SD, Ltd. 4-door	1699	1444	1529
Ltd. wagon	2074	1763	1867

4-door: Pkg. SC plus power antenna, power windows, lighted visor mirrors, front reading lights, power mirrors, remote trunk release. Wagon adds: third seat.

Prestige Pkg. SE, Ltd. 4-door	2364	2009	2128
Ltd. wagon	2704	2298	2434

Pkg. SD plus power driver's seat, cassete player with search/repeat, premium speakers, steering-wheel-mounted radio controls, remote keyless entry.

	Retail Price	Dealer Invoice	Low Price
Rear defogger, Special & Custom wagon .	170	145	153
Remote keyless entry (NA Special)	135	115	122
Decklid luggage rack, notchbacks	115	98	104
Cassette player, Cust/Spcl w/Pkg. SB, Ltd w/SC	140	119	126
Cassette player w/seach/repeat			
Custom & Pkg. SB	170	145	153
Custom w/SC/SD/SE, Ltd w/SC/SD . . .	30	26	27
CD player, Custom w/SC/SD/SE, Ltd w/SC/SD	274	233	247
Ltd w/SE	244	207	220
Premium speakers, notchbacks	70	60	63
Wagons	35	30	32
Steering-wheel-mounted radio controls, Custom	125	106	113
Requires CD player or cassette player with search/repeat.			
Power antenna, Special & Custom wagon .	85	72	77
55/45 seat with armest, Special	133	113	120
Empress cloth 55/45 seat w/storage armrest, Custom	368	204	216
Custom w/SC/SD/SE	240	204	216
Leather/vinyl seat, Ltd. 4-door	500	425	450
Remote decklid release, notchbacks	60	51	54
Wire wheel covers, Custom	240	204	216
Styled steel wheels, Special & Custom . . .	115	98	104
Alloy wheels	295	251	266
w/Pkg. containing wire wheel covers . .	85	72	77
185/75R14 Whitewall tires, Special	68	58	61
Rear wiper, wagons	125	106	113
w/any option pkg.	85	72	77
Deletes air deflector from option packages.			
Woodgrain applique, Custom wagon w/SB/SC	350	298	315
Custom wagon w/SD/SE, Ltd wagon . .	305	259	275

Oldsmobile Toronado/ Buick Riviera

Neither of these front-drive luxury coupes changes much for 1992. Oldsmobile offers a base Toronado and sportier Trofeo version, the latter of which gets a firmer suspension and larger performance tires. Front bucket seats are standard, but a 3-place bench can be substituted on the base model. Toronados with the bench seat gain an interlock

Prices are accurate at time of publication; subject to manufacturer's change.

1991 Oldsmobile Toronado Trofeo

that prevents shifting out of park unless the brake pedal is applied. Bucket-seat models are due to get this safety feature later in the model year. Unlike the Toronado, Riviera comes in a single trim level, though option packages allow some individuality in appearance and personality. Anti-lock brakes and a driver-side air bag are standard on all, as is a 170-horsepower 3.8-liter V-6 engine and 4-speed electronically controlled automatic transmission. This powertrain combination provides brisk acceleration whether around town or on the highway, and smooth power delivery. The base suspension allows too much wallowing over freeway dips and reduces anything but gentle cornering to a display of tire squealing and body lean. The Trofeo has wider tires and a stiffer suspension that give it a more controlled feel, but also provokes a rather choppy ride on anything but smooth pavement. A Riviera equipped with the optional Gran Sport package provides a similar ride/handling combination. The Riviera's dashboard has electronic readouts that mimic analog gauges; Toronado has regular analog gauges. In both cars, over-the-shoulder visibility is obscured by the wide rear pillars, and the large, heavy doors require a lot of room to open fully. Even then, passengers will have a hard time climbing into the back seat. Leg room in back is acceptable, but rear head room is skimpy, and the seat's low cushion and hard backrest make long trips rather uncomfortable. The trunk is wide enough, but it's not very deep. Yet as long as you don't need room for four or a lot of luggage, either car makes for a competent touring machine.

Specifications

	2-door notchback
Wheelbase, in.	108.0
Overall length, in.	200.3
Overall width, in.	72.8
Overall height, in.	53.0
Curb weight, lbs.	3462
Cargo vol., cu. ft.	15.8
Fuel capacity, gals.	18.8
Seating capacity	6
Front head room, in.	37.8
Front leg room, max., in.	43.0
Rear head room, in.	37.8
Rear leg room, min., in.	35.7

Powertrain layout: transverse front engine/front-wheel drive.

Engines

	ohv V-6
Size, liters/cu. in.	3.8/231
Fuel delivery	PFI
Horsepower @ rpm	170 @ 4800
Torque (lbs./ft.) @ rpm	220 @ 3200
Availability	S

EPA city/highway mpg

4-speed OD automatic	18/27

Assembly point: Hamtramck, Mich.

Prices

Oldsmobile Toronado/Trofeo	Retail Price	Dealer Invoice	Low Price
Toronado 2-door notchback	$24695	$21435	$21785
Trofeo 2-door notchback	27295	23692	24042
Destination charge	600	600	600

Standard equipment:

Toronado: 3.8-liter PFI V-6, 4-speed automatic transmission, anti-lock 4-wheel disc brakes, power steering, driver-side air bag, automatic climate control, cloth reclining front bucket seats, power driver's seat, center console, power windows and locks, cruise contol, AM/FM cassette, power

Prices are accurate at time of publication; subject to manufacturer's change.

antenna, power mirrors with heated left, remote fuel door and decklid releases, tachometer and gauges, leather-wrapped steering wheel, tilt steering column, visor mirror, intermittent wipers, automatic leveling, cargo net, Twilight Sentinel, PASS-Key theft-deterrent system, rear defogger, floormats, 215/65R15 tires on alloy wheels. **Trofeo** adds: FE3 Touring Car suspension, power sport seats with power lumbar and side bolsters, air dam with fog lamps, compass, steering wheel touch controls, Remote Lock Control Pkg., automatic day/night mirror, lighted visor mirrors, 215/60R16 tires.

Optional equipment:

	Retail Price	Dealer Invoice	Low Price
Option Pkg. 1SB, base	819	696	721
Power passenger seat, Illumination Pkg., lighted visor mirrors, automatic day/night mirror, Remote Lock Control Pkg., steering wheel touch controls.			
55/45 seat & electronic instruments, base .	NC	NC	NC
Astroroof	1350	1148	1188
Heated windshield	250	213	220
Upgraded audio system w/EQ	120	102	106
CD player w/EQ	394	335	347
Cassette & CD players w/EQ	516	439	454
FE3 Touring Car suspension, base	60	51	53
Mobile cellular telephone	995	846	876
Visual Information Center	1295	1101	1140
Requires audio system with EQ.			
Custom leather trim, base	425	361	374
Glamour paint (base) or special paint (Trofeo)	210	179	185
Two-tone paint, base	101	86	89
Wire wheel covers, base	NC	NC	NC
205/70R15 whitewall tires	NC	NC	NC
Engine block heater	18	15	16
Warranty enhancements for New York state .	25	21	22
California emissions pkg.	100	85	88

Buick Riviera

2-door notchback	$25415	$21806	$22156
Destination charge	600	600	600

Standard equipment:

3.8-liter PFI V-6, 4-speed automatic transmission, anti-lock 4-wheel disc brakes, power steering, driver-side air bag, automatic climate control, cloth reclining front bucket seats, power driver's seat, automatic level control, cruise control, solar control glass, power windows and locks, power mirrors, illuminated entry, tachometer, coolant temperature and oil pressure gauges, voltmeter, trip odometer, remote fuel door and decklid releases, rear defogger, console with armrest, cornerning lamps, lighted visor mirror, AM/FM cassette with tape search/repeat, tinted glass, tilt steering column, intermittent wipers, leather-wrapped steering wheel, floormats, door edge guards, 205/70R15 whitewall tires, wire wheel covers.

Optional equipment:

	Retail Price	Dealer Invoice	Low Price
Luxury Pkg. SD	520	442	452
Power passenger seat with power recliner, automatic day/night mirror, Twilight Sentinel.			
Prestige Pkg. SE	1069	909	930
Pkg. SD plus power decklid pulldown, heated left mirror, remote keyless entry, automatic power locks, theft-deterrent system.			
Gran Touring Pkg.	134	114	117
Gran Touring suspension, 215/65R15 Eagle GT + 4 tires on alloy wheels, leather-wrapped sport steering wheel and shift handle, fast-ratio steering.			
Riviera Appearance Pkg.	235	200	204
Light Driftwood lower accent paint, bodyside stripe, painted alloy wheels.			
Delco/Bose music system w/CD player . . .	1399	1189	1217
CD player w/EQ	516	439	449
Astroroof	1350	1148	1175
Heavily padded vinyl top	695	591	605
Leather & vinyl upholstery	600	510	522
14-way driver's seat w/leather & vinyl . . .	945	803	822
Alloy wheels	85	72	74
Painted alloy wheels	185	157	161
Firemist paint	250	213	218
Pearlescent white diamond paint	250	213	218
Lower accent paint	190	162	165
Warranty enhancements for New York . . .	25	21	22
California emissions pkg.	100	85	87

Plymouth Acclaim/Dodge Spirit

The compact, front-drive Acclaim and Spirit are virtual twins, though the Spirit is marketed as the sportier car, while Acclaim is promoted as a value leader. Spirit is offered in base, LE, ES, and R/T versions; Acclaim this year is trimmed back to only one model. The main reason is that 85 percent of Acclaim sales were base versions. Standard on Acclaim is a 2.5-liter 4-cylinder engine with 100 horsepower; optional is a 3.0-liter V-6 with 141. The V-6 this year is available with a lower-cost 3-speed automatic as well as a 4-speed automatic. Spirit's base and LE models come with the 2.5-liter four, while the ES gets a 152-horse-

Prices are accurate at time of publication; subject to manufacturer's change.

Plymouth Acclaim

power turbo version of the 2.5. The 3.0-liter V-6 is optional on all three. The limited-edition high-performance Spirit R/T comes only with a 224-horsepower turbocharged 2.2-liter 4-cylinder with double-overhead camshafts and four valves per cylinder. A 5-speed manual transmission is standard with the 4-cylinder engines and is mandatory on the R/T. A 3-speed automatic is optional with the 2.5 fours, and for the first time is offered with the V-6. Previously, the six had been available only with a 4-speed overdrive automatic. Spirit also gets a new design for its standard 14-inch wheel covers and for the 15-inch alloys standard on ES and R/T and optional on the others. Driver-side air bags are standard on every Acclaim and Spirit, and anti-lock brakes are optional across the board. If you're after fuel economy instead of brisk acceleration, the base 2.5-liter four isn't a bad choice. Sportier types will enjoy the 2.5 turbo, which has better-than-average low-speed response for a turbocharged engine, though it suffers a noisy, somewhat coarse disposition. However, the V-6 delivers the best blend of acceleration and good manners, and we're happy to see it's now available with a 3-speed automatic. Spirit has firmer shock absorbers than the Acclaim for a tauter ride and sharper steering and handling. Both have readable gauges and a simple dashboard layout, as well as fine outward visibility. Front-seat comfort is good, but the trade-off for adequate rear head and knee room is a back-seat cushion that's low and short. The roomy trunk has a flat floor and low liftover. Neither car is exceptional, but they're solid and competent domestic sedans.

Specifications

	4-door notchback
Wheelbase, in.	103.5
Overall length, in.	181.2
Overall width, in.	68.1
Overall height, in.	53.5
Curb weight, lbs.	2788
Cargo vol., cu. ft.	14.4
Fuel capacity, gals.	16.0
Seating capacity	6
Front head room, in.	38.4
Front leg room, max., in.	41.9
Rear head room, in.	37.9
Rear leg room, min., in.	38.3

Powertrain layout: transverse front engine/front-wheel drive.

Engines	ohc I-4	Turbo ohc I-4	ohc V-6	Turbo dohc I-4
Size, liters/cu. in.	2.5/153	2.5/153	3.0/181.4	2.2/135
Fuel delivery	TBI	PFI	PFI	PFI
Horsepower @ rpm	100 @ 4800	152 @ 4800	141 @ 5000	224 @ 2800
Torque (lbs./ft.) @ rpm	135 @ 2800	210 @ 2400	171 @ 2800	217 @ 6000
Availability	S[1]	S[2]	O	S[3]
EPA city/highway mpg				
5-speed OD manual	23/31	21/27		19/26
3-speed automatic	23/27	19/24	21/25	
4-speed OD automatic			20/27	

1. Base Spirit, LE; Acclaim. 2. Spirit ES. 3. Spirit R/T.

Assembly point: Newark, Del.

Prices

Plymouth Acclaim	Retail Price	Dealer Invoice	Low Price
4-door notchback w/Pkg. 21A (2.5-liter/ 5-speed)	$11470	$10264	$10549
w/Pkg. 22A (2.5-liter/automatic 3)	12027	10737	11022
Standard equipment.			
w/Pkg. 21C (2.5-liter/5-speed)	11900	10629	10914
w/Pkg. 22D (2.5-liter/automatic 3)	12457	11103	11388

Prices are accurate at time of publication; subject to manufacturer's change.

	Retail Price	Dealer Invoice	Low Price
w/Pkg. 26D (3.0-liter/automatic 3)	13182	11719	12004

Pkg. 21A plus air conditioning, rear defogger, tilt steering column, cruise control, 4 speakers, tinted glass, floormats.

	Retail Price	Dealer Invoice	Low Price
w/Pkg. 22E (2.5-liter/automatic 3)	13194	11729	12014
w/Pkg. 26E (3.0-liter/automatic 3)	13919	12345	12630
w/Pkg. 28E (3.0-liter/automatic 4)	14002	12416	12701

Pkg. 21C/22D/26D plus power windows and locks, power mirrors, remote decklid release.

	Retail Price	Dealer Invoice	Low Price
Destination charge	485	485	485

Standard equipment:

2.5-liter TBI 4-cylinder engine, 5-speed manual transmission, power steering, driver-side air bag, cloth reclining front bucket seats, coolant temperature gauge, voltmeter, trip odometer, dual remote mirrors, AM/FM radio with two speakers, remote decklid release, intermittent wipers, misc. lights, visor mirrors, bodyside moldings, 185/70R14 tires.

Engines and transmissions: 2.5-liter TBI 4-cylinder with 5-speed manual or 3-speed automatic transmission, 3.0-liter PFI V-6 with 3- or 4-speed automatic transmission.

Optional equipment:

	Retail Price	Dealer Invoice	Low Price
Anti-lock brakes	899	764	791
Console & Armrest Group, w/21C	81	69	71
Front armrest; requires bucket seats.			
w/Pkg. D or E	155	132	136
Full floor console with armrest; requires bucket seats.			
Interior Illumination Group	293	249	258
Illuminated entry system, lighted visor mirrors, message center, map and underhood lights, cigarette lighter; requires Pkg. E.			
Rear defogger	173	147	152
50/50 split front seat	102	87	90
Requires automatic transmission.			
w/split folding rear seat	250	213	220
Requires Pkg. D or E.			
Front bucket seats	148	126	130
Includes split folding rear seat.			
Cassette player w/4 speakers	155	132	136
Cassette player w/Infinity speakers	430	366	378
Power driver's seat	296	252	260
195/70R14 whitewall tires, w/22D & 22E .	104	88	92
w/26 or 28E	73	62	64
Conventional spare tire	95	81	84
w/195/70R14	95	81	84
Extra-cost paint	77	65	68
California emissions pkg.	102	87	90

Dodge Spirit

	Retail Price	Dealer Invoice	Low Price
4-door notchback w/Pkg. 21A	$11470	$10264	$10549
w/Pkg. 22A (2.5-liter/automatic 3)	12027	10737	11022
w/Pkg. 21C (2.5-liter/5-speed)	11900	10629	10914
w/Pkg. 22D (2.5-liter/automatic 3)	12457	11103	11388
w/Pkg. 26D (3.0-liter/automatic 3)	13182	11719	12004
w/Pkg. 22E (2.5-liter/automatic 3)	13194	11729	12014
w/Pkg. 26E (3.0-liter/automatic 3)	13919	12345	12630
w/Pkg. 28E (3.0-liter/automatic 4)	14002	12416	12701
LE 4-door notchback w/Pkg. 22P	13530	12076	12361
w/Pkg. 22U (2.5-liter/automatic 3)	14072	12537	12822
w/Pkg. 24U (Turbo/automatic 3)	14797	13153	13438
w/Pkg. 26U (3.0-liter/automatic 3)	14797	13153	13438
w/Pkg. 28U (3.0-liter/automatic 4)	14890	13232	13517
ES 4-door notchback w/Pkg. 23X	14441	12878	13163
w/Pkg. 23U (Turbo/5-speed)	14983	13339	13624
w/Pkg. 24U (Turbo/automatic 3)	15540	13812	14097
w/Pkg. 28U (3.0-liter/automatic 4)	15623	13883	14168
R/T 4-door notchback	18674	16603	NA
Destination charge	485	485	485

R/T low price not available at time of publication.

Standard equipment:

2.5-liter TBI 4-cylinder engine, 5-speed manual transmission, power steering, driver-side air bag, cloth reclining front bucket seats, tachometer, coolant temperature and oil pressure gauges, voltmeter, trip odometer, center console, tinted backlight, remote mirrors, visor mirrors, narrow bodyside moldings, AM/FM radio with two speakers, intermittent wipers, 185/70R14 tires. **LE** adds: 3-speed automatic transmission, rear defogger, tinted glass, Message Center, front armrest, remote trunk release, four speakers, cruise control, tilt steering column, wide bodyside moldings, floormats, added sound insulation, full wheel covers. **ES** adds: 2.5-liter turbocharged PFI engine, 5-speed manual transmission, 4-wheel disc brakes, performance suspension, leather-wrapped steering wheel, cassette player, trip computer, 205/60R15 tires on alloy wheels. **R/T** adds: 2.2-liter DOHC 16-valve turbocharged engine, rear spoiler, heated power mirrors, 205/60VR15 tires. **Base Pkgs. 21C/22D/26D:** air conditioning, rear defogger, tinted glass, floormats, four speaker radio, cruise control, tilt steering column. **Base Pkgs. 22E/26E/28E:** Pkgs. 21C/22D/26D plus power windows and locks, power mirrors, remote trunk release. **LE Pkgs. 22U/24U/26U/28U:** air conditioning, power windows and locks, power mirrors. **ES Pkgs. 23U/24U/28U:** air conditioning, power windows and locks, power mirrors.

Optional equipment:

Anti-lock 4-wheel disc brakes	899	764	791
Power Equipment Pkg., R/T	543	462	478

Prices are accurate at time of publication; subject to manufacturer's change.

	Retail Price	Dealer Invoice	Low Price
Interior Illumination Group, base	293	249	258
others	195	166	172
Illuminated entry, lighted visor mirrors, misc. lights, message center.			
Interior Convenience Group (NA base) ...	400	340	352
Overhead console, reading lamps, compass, Interior Illumination Group.			
Center armrest, base w/5-speed	81	69	71
Console w/armrest, base	155	132	136
Rear defogger, base	173	147	152
Cassette player & 4 speakers, base	155	132	136
w/seek/scan, LE	155	132	136
w/seek/scan, ES & R/T	275	234	242
Cassette player w/Infinity speakers, LE ...	430	366	378
ES & R/T	275	234	242
w/EQ, ES & RT	490	417	431
Power driver's seat (NA base)	296	252	260
50/50 split front seat, base	102	87	90
w/split folding rear seat, base	250	213	220
w/split folding rear seat, LE	61	52	54
Front bucket seats, base	148	126	130
Includes split folding rear seat.			
195/70R14 whitewall tires, base w/22D or 22E	104	88	92
base w/26- or 28E	73	62	64
205/60R15 tires, LE w/22U	177	150	156
LE w/24U, 26U or 28U	146	124	128
Requires alloy wheels.			
Alloy wheels, LE	328	279	289
Conventional spare tire, base & LE	95	81	84
Extra-cost paint	77	65	68
California emissions pkg.	102	87	90

Plymouth Sundance/ Dodge Shadow

These front-drive subcompact clones are virtually unchanged for 1992, save for some model and trim shuffling. Sundance comes as a 3- or 5-door hatchback in America and Highline versions; Shadow offers both hatchback body styles as well as a convertible. Shadow hatchbacks come in America, base, and ES trim; convertibles come only in base and ES. Shadow ES and Sundance Highline have body-colored bumpers; others have black bumpers. Sundance and Shadow America models are the lowest-priced

Plymouth Sundance America 3-door

cars with a standard driver-side air bag. On these models, a 2.2-liter 4-cylinder with 93 horsepower is the only engine offered, though it can be mated to either a 5-speed manual or 3-speed automatic transmission. Americas have limited options and are not available with such niceties as power windows, cruise control, sunroof, or tilt steering column. Sundance Highline can be ordered with the 2.2-liter four (standard) or a 100-horsepower 2.5-liter four. It comes with a 5-speed manual transmission standard, and a 3-speed automatic optional. The same combinations are available on the base Dodge Shadow. The 2.5 is standard on top-line Shadow ES, which adds a sport suspension and aero-style bodywork. The convertible is available in base and ES trim. A 152-horsepower turbocharged version of the 2.5 four is optional on ES models and on the base convertible. With any engine, a 5-speed manual transmission is standard and a 3-speed automatic is optional. Acceleration is adequate with the 2.2-liter four; it's much stronger with the turbo engine, but so is the commotion from under the hood and from the exhaust. A good compromise is the naturally aspirated 2.5, a smooth runner and reasonable performer. For a domestic car, the standard suspensions are rather firm, but deliver competent handling and a stable highway ride. Tauter still is the suspension on the sportier Shadow ES, though it's compliant enough to avoid being harsh over most surfaces. These twins offer decent room in front for tall people, but rear-seat leg room is skimpy and 6-footers are short of head room. All controls are mounted high except the stereo, which is too low to safely tune while driving. Luggage space is adequate with the rear seatback up, generous with it folded down. Rear-seat room in these twins is tight for adults, but generally, the interior is nicely packaged. Overall, not the most refined small cars, but they don't feel as light-weight as some other entry-level offerings, and all have the added safety of an air bag.

Specifications

	3-door hatchback	5-door hatchback	2-door conv.
Wheelbase, in.	97.0	97.0	97.0
Overall length, in.	171.7	171.7	171.7
Overall width, in.	67.3	67.3	67.3
Overall height, in.	52.7	52.7	52.6
Curb weight, lbs.	2615	2652	2910
Cargo vol., cu. ft.	33.3	33.3	13.2
Fuel capacity, gals.	14.0	14.0	14.0
Seating capacity	5	5	4
Front head room, in.	38.3	38.3	38.3
Front leg room, max., in.	41.5	41.5	41.5
Rear head room, in.	37.4	37.4	37.4
Rear leg room, min., in.	34.0	34.0	34.0

Powertrain layout: transverse front engine/front-wheel drive.

Engines	ohc I-4	ohc I-4	Turbo ohc I-4
Size, liters/cu. in.	2.2/135	2.5/153	2.5/153
Fuel delivery	TBI	TBI	PFI
Horsepower @ rpm	93 @ 4800	100 @ 4800	152 @ 4800
Torque (lbs./ft.) @ rpm	122 @ 3200	135 @ 2800	210 @ 2400
Availability	S[1]	S[2]	O[3]

EPA city/highway mpg

5-speed OD manual	26/32	23/31	20/26
3-speed automatic	24/28	23/27	20/25

1. Sundance/Shadow America, Highline.   2. Shadow ES, conv.   3. Shadow ES, conv.

Assembly points: Sterling Heights, Mich.; Toluca, Mexico.

Prices

Plymouth Sundance	Retail Price	Dealer Invoice	Low Price
Destination charge	$485	$485	$485

Body styles: 3- and 5-door hatchbacks. **Engines and transmissions:** 2.2- and 2.5-liter TBI 4-cylinder, 5-speed manual or 3-speed automatic transmission. Other equipment, **America:** 2.2-liter TBI 4-cylinder engine, power steering, driver-side air bag, cloth reclining front bucket seats, mini console with storage, tinted backlight, trip odometer, coolant temperature and oil pressure gauges, left remote mirror, removable shelf panel, 185/70R14 tires. **Highline** adds: AM/FM radio, cargo area carpet, added sound insulation, wheel covers.

Sundance America

	Retail Price	Dealer Invoice	Low Price
21W, 3-door, 5-speed	7984	7433	7623
22W, 3-door, automatic	8541	7907	8097
21W, 5-door, 5-speed	8384	7801	7991
22W, 5-door, automatic	8941	8274	8464
America standard equipment.			
21X, 3-door, 5-speed	9434	8666	8856
22X, 3-door, automatic	9991	9139	9329
21X, 5-door, 5-speed	9846	9043	9233
22X, 5-door, automatic	10403	9517	9707

21/22W plus air conditioning, tinted glass, rear defogger, Light Group, dual remote mirrors, AM/FM radio, visor mirrors, intermittent wipers, floormats, wheel trim rings, narrow bodyside moldings.

Sundance Highline

21A, 3-door, 2.2, 5-speed	9246	8471	8661
22A, 3-door, 2.2, automatic	9803	8945	9135
21A, 5-door, 2.2, 5-speed	9646	8831	9021
22A, 5-door, 2.2, automatic	10360	9305	9495
23A, 3-door, 2.5, 5-speed	9532	8715	8905
24A, 3-door, 2.5, automatic	10089	9188	9378
23A, 5-door, 2.5, 5-speed	9932	9075	9265
24A, 5-door, 2.5, automatic	10489	9548	9738
Highline standard equipment.			
23D, 3-door, 2.5, 5-speed	10522	9556	9746
24D, 3-door, 2.5, automatic	11079	10029	10219
23D, 5-door, 2.5, 5-speed	10937	9926	10116
24D, 5-door, 2.5, automatic	11494	10400	10590

21-24A plus air conditioning, tinted glass, rear defogger, tilt steering column, Light Group, floor console, four speakers, remote hatch release, dual-note horn, wide bodyside moldings, intermittent wipers, tachometer and 125-mph speedometer, dual remote mirrors, floormats, striping.

Air conditioning (tinted glass req.)	900	765	779
Light Group, 3-door	65	55	56
5-door	77	65	67
Overhead console, Highline	265	225	229
Includes thermometer, compass, reading lights, storage bins.			
Rear defogger	173	147	150

Prices are accurate at time of publication; subject to manufacturer's change.

	Retail Price	Dealer Invoice	Low Price
Power locks, Highline 3-door	199	169	172
Highline 5-door	240	204	208
Requires power mirrors.			
Intermittent wipers	66	56	57
Remote mirrors	69	59	60
Power mirrors, Highline w/dual mirrors . .	57	48	49
Requires power locks.			
Power driver's seat, Highline w/Pkg. D . .	296	252	256
Requires power windows, locks, and mirrors.			
Power windows, Highline 3-door	255	217	221
Highline 5-door	321	273	278
Requires power locks and mirrors.			
AM/FM radio, America	284	241	246
w/cassette player, America	489	416	423
America w/Pkg. X, Highline w/A	205	174	177
Highline w/Pkg. D	155	132	134
Infinity cassette system, Highline	430	366	372
Cruise control, Highline	224	190	194
Manual sunroof, Highline	379	322	328
Tilt steering column, Highline	148	126	128
Conventional spare tire	85	72	74
Alloy wheels, Highline	328	279	284
Floormats	46	39	40

Dodge Shadow

Destination charge	$485	$485	$485

Convertible low price not available at time of publication.

Body styles: 3- and 5-door hatchbacks, 2-door convertible. **Engines and transmissions:** 2.2- and 2.5-liter TBI 4-cylinder, 2.5-liter turbocharged PFI 4-cylinder, 5-speed manual and 3-speed automatic transmissions. **Other equipment, America:** 2.2-liter TBI 4-cylinder engine, power steering, driver-side air bag, cloth reclining front bucket seats, mini console with storage, tinted backlight, trip odometer, coolant temperature and oil pressure gauges, left remote mirror, removable shelf panel, 185/70R14 tires. **Highline** adds: AM/FM radio, cargo area carpet, added sound insulation, wheel covers. **Convertibles** add: manual folding top with vinyl boot, power windows, wide bodyside moldings, four speakers, cruise control, striping, tachometer, tilt steering column, intermittent wipers. **ES** adds to Highline: sport suspension, sill extensions, fog lamps, body-colored bumpers, rear spoiler (NA convertible), split folding rear seat, tachometer, intermittent wipers, remote mirrors, 195/60HR 15 tires on alloy wheels.

Shadow America

21W, 3-door, 5-speed	7869	7328	7518
22W, 3-door, automatic	8426	7801	7991

	Retail Price	Dealer Invoice	Low Price
21W, 5-door, 5-speed	8269	7695	7885
22W, 5-door, automatic	8826	8169	8359
America standard equipment.			
21Y, 3-door, 5-speed . . . . : .	9434	8658	8848
22Y, 3-door, automatic	9991	9131	9321
21Y, 5-door, 5-speed	9846	9036	9226
22Y, 5-door, automatic	10403	9509	9699

21/22W plus air conditioning, tinted glass, rear defogger, Light Group, dual remote mirrors, AM/FM radio, visor mirrors, intermiitent wipers, floormats, wheel trim rings, narrow bodyside moldings.

Shadow Highline

	Retail Price	Dealer Invoice	Low Price
21A, 3-door, 2.2, 5-speed	9246	8471	8661
22A, 3-door, 2.2, automatic	9803	8945	9135
21A, 5-door, 2.2, 5-speed	9646	8831	9021
22A, 5-door, 2.2, automatic	10203	9304	9494
23A, 3-door, 2.5, 5-speed	9532	8715	8905
24A, 3-door, 2.5, automatic	10089	9188	9378
23A, 5-door, 2.5, 5-speed	9932	9075	9265
24A, 5-door, 2.5, automatic	10489	9548	9738
Highline standard equipment.			
23D, 3-door, 2.5, 5-speed	10522	9956	10146
24D, 3-door, 2.5, automatic	11079	10029	10219
23D, 5-door, 2.5, 5-speed	10934	9926	10116
24D, 5-door, 2.5, automatic	11491	10400	10590

21-24A plus air conditioning, tinted glass, rear defogger, tilt steering column, Light Group, floor console, four speakers, remote hatch release, dual-note horn, wide bodyside moldings, intermittent wipers, tachometer and 125-mph speedometer, dual remote mirrors, floormats, striping.

Shadow ES

	Retail Price	Dealer Invoice	Low Price
23G, 3-door, 2.5, 5-speed	10912	9971	10161
24G, 3-door, 2.5, automatic	11469	10444	10634
23G, 5-door, 2.5, 5-speed	11234	10261	10451
24G, 5-door, 2.5, automatic	11791	10734	10924
ES standard equipment.			
23H, 3-door, 2.5, 5-speed	11833	10754	10944
24H, 3-door, 2.5, automatic	12390	11227	11417
23H, 5-door, 2.5, 5-speed	12155	11043	11233
24H, 5-door, 2.5, automatic	12712	11517	11707
25H, 3-door, turbo, 5-speed	12562	11373	11563
26H, 3-door, turbo, automatic	13119	11847	12037
25H, 5-door, turbo, 5-speed	12884	11663	11853
26H, 5-door, turbo, automatic	13441	12137	12327

23-24G plus air conditioning, tinted glass, rear defogger, tilt steering column, cruise control, Infinity cassette player, floormats.

Prices are accurate at time of publication; subject to manufacturer's change.

Shadow Convertible (Highline)

	Retail Price	Dealer Invoice	Low Price
23A, 2.5, 5-speed	13457	12261	NA
24A, 2.5, automatic	14014	12735	NA
Highline convertible standard equipment.			
23D, 2.5, 5-speed	14302	12750	NA
24D, 2.5, automatic	14589	13224	NA
25D, turbo, 5-speed	14792	13396	NA
26D, turbo, automatic	15349	13870	NA

23-24A plus air conditioning, tinted glass, dual horns, floormats, Light Group, wide bodyside moldings, four speakers, cruise control, striping, tachometer, tilt steering column, intermittent wipers.

Shadow Convertible (ES)

	Retail Price	Dealer Invoice	Low Price
23G, 2.5, 5-speed	14685	13367	NA
24G, 2.5, automatic	15242	13840	NA
ES standard equipment.			
23H, 2.5, 5-speed	15505	14064	NA
24H, 2.5, automatic	16062	14537	NA
25H, turbo, 5-speed	16234	14683	NA
26H, turbo, automatic	16971	15157	NA

23-24G plus air conditioning, tinted glass, tilt steering column, cruise control, power locks, Infinity cassette player, floormats.

Optional equipment:

Air conditioning & tinted glass	900	765	779
Light Group, 2-door	65	55	56
4-door	77	65	67
Overhead console (NA America)	265	225	229
Includes thermometer, compass, reading lights, storage bins.			
Rear defogger	173	147	150
Power locks (NA America), 3-door & conv. . .	199	169	172
5-door	240	204	208
Intermittent wipers	66	56	57
Remote mirrors	69	59	60
Power mirrors, Highline & ES	57	48	49
Requires power locks.			
Power driver's seat (NA America)	296	252	256
Requires power windows, locks, and mirrors.			
Power windows (NA America), 3-door . . .	255	217	221
5-door	321	273	278
Requires power locks and mirrors.			
AM/FM radio, America	284	241	246
w/cassette player, America	489	416	423
America w/Pkg. Y, Highline w/A	205	174	177
Highline w/D, ES w/G	155	132	134

	Retail Price	Dealer Invoice	Low Price
Infinity audio system, Highline w/Pkg. D	275	234	238
ES w/G	430	366	372
Requires power door locks.			
Cruise control (NA America)	224	190	194
Manual sunroof (NA America)	379	322	328
Tilt steering column (NA America)	148	126	128
Conventional spare tire	85	72	74
w/alloy wheel	213	181	184
Alloy wheels, Highline	328	279	284
Floormats	46	39	40
Extra-cost paint	77	65	67
California emissions pkg.	102	87	88

Pontiac Bonneville/
Buick LeSabre/
Oldsmobile Eighty Eight

Pontiac Bonneville SE

GM's front-drive full-size cars have been redesigned for
1992, and are only available in 4-door sedan body styles;
2-doors have been dropped. Wheelbase on all remains at
110.8 inches, but overall length is up by about three inches.
A driver-side air bag is standard across the board, and
traction control is a notable new available feature. All are
powered by a 170-horsepower 3.8-liter V-6 and 4-speed automatic transmission except the Bonneville SSEi, which
has a new supercharged version of the 3.8 rated at 205
horsepower. Other Bonneville models include the base SE

Prices are accurate at time of publication; subject to manufacturer's change.

and mid-level SSE; last year's LE designation has been dropped. Traction control is standard on SSEi, optional on the others. Anti-lock brakes are standard on SSE and SSEi, optional on SE with the Sport Appearance Package. To the standard driver-side air bag SSEi adds a passenger's bag, which also is an SSE option. Also standard on SSEi and optional on SSE is a heads-up instrument display. Rear-seat heating and air conditioning ducts are standard on all Bonnevilles. Buick's LeSabre comes in two models; Custom and up-level Limited. Anti-lock brakes are now standard on the Limited and optional on the base Custom. Rear-seat heater vents are optional on both. The Olds-

Specifications

	4-door notchback
Wheelbase, in.	110.8
Overall length, in.	200.6
Overall width, in.	73.6
Overall height, in.	55.5
Curb weight, lbs.	3362
Cargo vol., cu. ft.	18.1
Fuel capacity, gals.	18.0
Seating capacity	6
Front head room, in.	39.2
Front leg room, max., in.	42.0
Rear head room, in.	38.3
Rear leg room, min., in.	38.6

Powertrain layout: transverse front engine/front-wheel drive.

Engines	ohv V-6	Supercharged ohv V-6
Size, liters/cu. in.	3.8/231	3.8/231
Fuel delivery	PFI	PFI
Horsepower @ rpm	170 @ 4800	205 @ 4400
Torque (lbs./ft.) @ rpm	220 @ 3200	260 @ 2800
Availability	S	S[1]

EPA city/highway mpg

4-speed OD automatic	18/28	16/25

1. Bonneville SSEi.

Assembly point: Wentzville, Mo.

mobile Eighty Eight also comes in two versions; Royale and Royale LS. The LS comes standard with rear-seat heater ducts and anti-lock brakes, the latter of which are optional on the base model. The 170-horsepower 3.8-liter V-6 and electronically controlled 4-speed automatic combine to provide brisk performance. Under normal acceleration, the transmission is so smooth that shifts go by unnoticed, and it quickly kicks down to a lower gear when needed for passing. Base models of all offer a good ride/handling combination. The Bonneville SSE and SSEi are equipped with firmer suspensions that trade some ride comfort for greater handling prowess, as do SEs with the optional sport package and Olds Eighty Eights with the available FE3 suspension. Spacious interiors are especially accommodating to rear-seat passengers, with enough room in back to sit three across. Overall, we like the way GM has updated these cars, and they remain fine examples of the large American family sedan.

Prices

Pontiac Bonneville	Retail Price	Dealer Invoice	Low Price
SE 4-door notchback sedan	$18599	$16144	—
SSE 4-door notchback sedan	23999	20831	—
SSEi 4-door notchback sedan	28045	24343	—
Destination charge	555	555	555

Low price not available at time of publication.

Standard equipment:

SE: 3.8-liter PFI V-6, 4-speed automatic transmission, power steering, driver-side air bag, air conditioning, cloth 45/55 reclining front seats with armrest, rear armrest with cupholders, power windows, power locks, AM/FM radio, fog lamps, Pass-Key theft deterrent system, 215/65R15 tires, on alloy wheels. **SSE** adds: anti-lock brakes, variable-assist power steering, electronic leveling, 45/45 bucket seats with console, rear defogger, cassette player with EQ, Driver Information Center, 225/60R16 touring tires on alloy wheels. **SSEi** adds: supercharged 3.8-liter PFI V-6, passenger-side air bag, traction control, automatic climate control, 12-way power front seats, illuminated remote keyless entry system, Head up Display, theft-deterrent system, 225/60ZR16 tires.

Prices are accurate at time of publication; subject to manufacturer's change.

Optional equipment:

	Retail Price	Dealer Invoice	Low Price
Anti-lock brakes, SE	450	383	—
Option Pkg. 1SB, SE	383	326	—
Cruise control, rally gauges, tachometer, Lamp Group.			
Option Pkg. 1SC, SE	901	766	—
Pkg. 1SB plus power driver's seat, power mirrors, illuminated entry system, remote decklid release.			
Option Pkg. 1SD	1242	1056	—
Pkg. 1SC plus remote keyless entry system, lighted visor mirrors, Twilight Sentinel, leather-wrapped steering wheel.			
Option Pkg. 1SB, SSE	845	718	—
Passenger-side air bag, Head-up display, automatic climate control, remote keyless entry system, illuminated entry system, automatic day/night mirror, 8-speaker sound system.			
Option Pkg. R6A, SE	261	222	—
Monotone appearance pkg., 15-inch alloy wheels.			
Option Pkg. R6B, SE	424	360	—
Monotone appearance pkg., custom trim group, 225/60R16 BW touring tires on alloy wheels.			
Option Pkg. R6C, SE	200	170	—
Monotone appearance pkg., cassette player.			
Option Pkg. R6A, SSE	1835	1560	—
45/45 split front seat with leather trim, power sunroof.			
SSEi	1195	1016	—
Premium Equipment Pkg., SSE w/o Pkg. 1SB	1345	1143	—
Identical to SSE Option Pkg. 1SB.			
Convenience Group, SE w/Pkg. 1SB	213	181	—
Remote decklid release, illuminated entry system, power mirrors.			
Enhancement Group, SE w/Pkg. 1SC	206	175	—
Lighted visor mirrors, leather-wrapped steering wheel, Twilight Sentinel.			
Trailer Towing Pkg., SE	614	522	—
Engine and transmission oil coolers, sport suspension, 225/60R16 BW touring tires on alloy wheels.			
SE Sport Pkg., w/o Pkg. R6A, R6B, or R6C .	1145	973	—
w/Pkg. R6A	659	560	—
w/Pkg. R6B	551	468	—
Pkg. R6C	965	820	—
Includes monotone appearance pkg., sport suspension, anti-lock brakes, dual exhausts, 225/60R16 BW touring tires on alloy wheels.			
Traction control	175	149	—
Rear window defogger, SE & SSE	170	145	—
Heated windshield, SSE & SSEi	250	213	—
Power sunroof, SE w/o Pkg. 1SD,			
Enhancement group, & 45/45 bucket seats	1326	1127	—
SE w/Pkg. 1SD, Enhancement group, or			
45/45 bucket seats	1230	1046	—
SSE & SSEi	1216	1034	—

CONSUMER GUIDE®

	Retail Price	Dealer Invoice	Low Price
45/45 bucket seats, SE w/Pkg. 1SB or 1SC .	315	268	—
w/Pkg. 1SD	220	187	—
Includes floor and overhead consoles, lighted visor mirrors.			
45/45 articulating leather bucket seats, SSE .	1419	1206	—
Custom interior trim, SE w/1SB, 1SC, or			
1SD & w/o R6B	130	111	—
w/Option pkg. R6B	NC	NC	NC
Includes trunk security net.			
45/45 articulating leather seats, SSEi	779	662	—
Includes floor and overhead consoles with storage, power outlets.			
Power driver's seat, SE	305	259	—
Remote keyless entry system, SE & SSE .	135	115	—
Theft-deterrent system, SSE	190	162	—
Cassette player, SE	140	119	—
Cassette w/EQ, SE w/o Pkg. R6C	650	553	—
SE w/Pkg. R6C	510	434	—
AM/FM w/EQ and CD player, SE w/o Pkg. R6C	876	745	—
SE w/Pkg. R6C	736	626	—
SSE & SSEi	226	192	—
Power antenna, SE	85	72	—
Monotone appearance pkg., SE w/o Sport			
pkg. & R6A, R6B, or R6C	180	153	—
w/Sport pkg. & R6A, R6B, or R6C ...	NC	NC	NC
16-inch cross-lace alloy wheels, SE w/o			
R6A & R6B	340	289	—
SE w/R6A	34	29	—
16-inch five-blade alloy wheels, SE w/o R6A .	340	289	—
SE w/R6A	34	29	—
16-inch six-spoke alloy wheels, SE w/o R6A .	306	260	—
215/65R15 BW touring tires, SE	NC	NC	NC
215/65R15 WW touring tires, SE	76	65	—
225/60R16 BW touring tires, SE w/o Sport			
pkg. & R6B	74	63	—

Buick LeSabre

	Retail Price	Dealer Invoice	Low Price
Custom 4-door notchback	$18695	$16227	—
Limited 4-door notchback	20775	18033	—
Destination charge	555	555	555

Low price not available at time of publication.

Standard equipment:

Custom: 3.8-liter PFI V-6, 4-speed automatic transmission, power steering, air conditioning, driver-side air bag, cloth 55/45 seat with recliners and armrest, tinted glass, power windows, AM/FM radio, tilt steering column, intermittent wipers, trip odometer, Pass-Key theft deterrent system, 205/

Prices are accurate at time of publication; subject to manufacturer's change.

75R15 tires. **Limited** adds: anti-lock brakes, front storage armrest with cupholders, rear defogger, misc. lights, upgraded exterior moldings.

Optional equipment:	Retail Price	Dealer Invoice	Low Price
Anti-lock brakes, base	764	649	—
Traction control system, Ltd.	175	149	—
Premium Pkg. SC, Custom	801	681	—
Cruise control, rear defogger, white-stripe tires, front seat storage armrest, trunk net.			
Luxury Pkg. SD, Custom	1271	1080	—
Pkg. SC plus cassette player, wire wheel covers, striping, floormats.			
Prestige Pkg. SE, Custom	2254	1916	—
Pkg. SD plus anti-lock brakes, power driver's seat, power antenna, lighted visor mirror, door edge guards, remote trunk release.			
Premium Pkg. SC, Ltd.	1201	1021	—
Power driver's seat, power locks, cruise control, cassette player, power antenna, floormats, trunk net, whitewall tires.			
Luxury Pkg. SD, Ltd.	1706	1450	—
Pkg. SC plus wire wheel covers, power mirrors, remote trunk release, lighted visor mirror, front door courtesy lights, door edge guards.			
Prestige Pkg. SE, Ltd.	2611	2219	—
Pkg. SD plus UX1 audio system, power passenger seat, dual control air conditioning, remote keyless entry, cornering lamps.			
Gran Touring Pkg., w/Pkg. SC	724	615	—
w/SD/SE	484	411	—
Gran Touring suspension, 215/60R15 tires on alloy wheels, 3.06 axle ratio, leather-wrapped steering wheel, automatic level control.			
Trailer Towing Pkg, w/o Gran Touring Pkg. .	325	276	—
w/Gran Touring Pkg.	150	128	—
Engine and transmission oil coolers, automatic level control suspension.			
Gauges & tachometer, Ltd.	138	117	—
Electri-Clear windshield	250	213	—
Cassette player, Custom w/SC & Ltd. . . .	140	119	—
UX1 audio system, Custom w/SC	360	306	—
Custom w/SD/SE & Ltd. w/SC/SD	220	187	—
Includes tape search/repeat, EQ, and Concert Sound speakers.			
U1A audio system, Custom w/SC	624	530	—
Custom w/SD/SE & Ltd. w/SC/SD	484	411	—
Ltd. w/SE	264	224	—
Power antenna	85	72	—
Bodyside stripes	45	38	—
Full vinyl top	200	170	—
Power driver's seat, Custom	305	259	—
Leather/vinyl 55/45 seat, Ltd.	500	425	—
Alloy wheels, w/SC	325	276	—
w/SD/SE	85	72	—
Wire wheel covers, w/SC	240	204	—

Oldsmobile Eighty Eight Royale

	Retail Price	Dealer Invoice	Low Price
4-door notchback	$18495	$16054	—
LS 4-door notchback	21395	18571	—
Destination charge	555	555	555

Low price not available at time of publication.

Standard equipment:

3.8-liter PFI V-6, 4-speed automatic transmission, power steering, driver-side air bag, air conditioning, 55/45 cloth front seat with armrest, power windows, left remote and right manual mirrors, tinted glass, AM/FM radio, intermittent wipers, tilt steering column, Pass-Key theft-deterrent system, trip odometer, glove box and courtesy lights, 205/70R15 all-season whitewall tires. **LS** adds: anti-lock brakes, cruise control, power locks, power mirrors, front seat recliners, AM/FM cassette, power antenna, floormats, front armrest with storage.

Optional equipment:

Option Pkg. 1SB, base	1212	1030	—
Front seat recliners, front storage armrest, cruise control, power mirrors, power locks, power driver's seat, rear defogger, floormats.			
Option Pkg. 1SC	2173	1847	—
Pkg. 1SC plus anti-lock brakes, remote keyless entry system, power antenna, front and rear reading lamps, reminder package, cargo net.			
Option Pkg. 1SC, LS	1152	979	—
Automatic climate control, power driver's seat, remote keyless entry system, rear defogger, cornering lamps, reminder package.			
Option Pkg. 1SD, LS	1713	1456	—
Pkg. 1SC plus power front passenger's seat, rear seat storage armrest, lighted visor mirrors, automatic day/night mirror.			
LSS Pkg., LS	1995	1696	—
Rear defogger	170	145	—
Electriclear heated windshield, LS	250	213	—
Touring Suspension Pkg.	718	610	—
LS w/leather seats	664	564	—
Special suspension and steering, leather-wrapped steering wheel, automatic load-leveling suspension, 225/60R16 tires on alloy wheels. Requires Option Pkg. 1SB, 1SC or 1SD. Not available with wire wheel covers or 15" alloy wheels.			
Towing Pkg.	325	276	—
w/Touring Suspension Pkg.	150	128	—
HD and automatic load-leveling suspension, 3.06 axle ratio, oil cooler, high-capacity battery and cooling system. Requires Option Pkg. 1SB, 1SC or 1SD.			
Traction control system, LS	175	149	—
Engine block heater	18	15	—

Prices are accurate at time of publication; subject to manufacturer's change.

	Retail Price	Dealer Invoice	Low Price
Leather seats w/rear storage armrest, LS .	565	480	—
w/1SD	515	438	—
Striping	45	38	—
Wire wheel covers	240	204	—
Locking 15″ alloy wheels w/blackwall tires .	274	233	—
w/whitewall tires	330	281	—
Electronic instrumentation, LS	449	382	—
Requires Pkg. 1SC or 1SD.			
AM/FM cassette, base	240	204	—
AM/FM cassette w/EQ, LS	120	102	—
AM/FM cassette and CD, LS	396	337	—
AM/FM cassette and CD w/EQ, LS	516	439	—
Warranty enhancements for New York state .	25	21	—
Califonia emissions pkg.	100	85	—

Pontiac Grand Am/
Buick Skylark/
Oldsmobile Achieva

Pontiac Grand Am GT 4-door

These front-drive 2- and 4-door compacts get new styling inside and out, but except for the Achieva (which used to be called Calais), keep the same names. Wheelbases are unchanged at 103.4 inches, but length is up by about seven inches and width by about two. However, interior dimensions and trunk capacity are nearly identical to last year. All come with anti-lock brakes and automatic door locks, and unlike their predecessors, coupes and sedans have different rooflines. Grand Am is available in two versions: SE and GT. Skylark also has two models: base and GS. Achieva comes in S, SL, SC coupe, and later on, an SCX coupe. All low-line models share a new 2.3-liter "Quad OHC" 4-cylinder with 120 horsepower. A 5-speed manual transmission is standard, a 3-speed automatic optional except for the Skylark, which comes only with automatic. Skylark GS comes with a 160-horsepower 3.3-liter V-6, which is optional on the base model. On the Grand Am, GTs have last year's 2.3 Quad 4 with 180 horsepower. Optional on both SEs and GTs is a 160-horsepower 3.3-liter V-6. A 5-speed manual transmission is mandatory with the 180-horsepower Quad 4. With the optional automatic, Quad 4 horsepower drops to 160. The V-6 is available only with automatic. Oldsmobile has chosen to hold off introducing the Achieva until at least January, but when it comes, the powertrain lineup should look like this: Base S gets the 120-horsepower 2.3 with either 5-speed manual or 3-speed automatic transmission, with a 160-horsepower Quad 4 and 3-speed automatic optional. SL versions will come with the 160-horsepower Quad 4 and 3-speed automatic, and have a 160-horsepower 3.3-liter V-6 as an option. The SC coupe comes with a high-output 180-horsepower Quad 4 and 5-speed manual, but the 3-speed automatic can be ordered with either the 160-horsepower Quad 4 or the 3.3-liter V-6. Finally, the special SCX coupe will carry an even higher-output 190-horsepower Quad 4 and a 5-speed manual only. The new Quad OHC found in all base models provides adequate acceleration, and it's quiet enough at cruising speed, but the engine is coarse-sounding and too noisy above 3000 rpm. The Quad 4s are also noisy, and produce most of their power at higher engine speeds. The V-6 is more responsive to the throttle at all speeds, but isn't that much quieter. Though the instrument panels differ, all feature round gauges and a more modern, inviting look. Base suspensions offer a good combination of ride comfort and stable handling, while sport models provide sharper road manners without undue harshness. Though interior dimensions haven't changed much, the cars feel roomier in the back seat, and sedans have wider-opening rear doors that make entry and exit easier. Overall these cars are improvements over their predecessors, and while any of them would make a sensible compact choice, none really stand out as being exceptional.

Prices are accurate at time of publication; subject to manufacturer's change.

Specifications

	2-door notchback	4-door notchback
Wheelbase, in.	103.4	103.4
Overall length, in.	186.9	186.9
Overall width, in.	68.6	68.6
Overall height, in.	53.1	53.1
Curb weight, lbs.	2728	2777
Cargo vol., cu. ft.	13.2	13.2
Fuel capacity, gals.	15.2	15.2
Seating capacity	5	5
Front head room, in.	37.8	37.8
Front leg room, max., in.	43.1	43.1
Rear head room, in.	36.5	37.0
Rear leg room, min., in.	33.9	34.8

Powertrain layout: transverse front engine/front-wheel drive.

Engines

	ohc I-4	dohc I-4	dohc I-4	ohv V-6
Size, liters/cu. in.	2.3/138	2.3/138	2.3/138	3.3/204
Fuel delivery	PFI	PFI	PFI	PFI
Horsepower @ rpm	120 @ 5200	160 @ 6200	180 @ 6200	160 @ 5200
Torque (lbs./ft.) @ rpm	140 @ 3200	155 @ 5200	160 @ 5200	185 @ 2000
Availability	S[1]	S[2]	S[3]	S[4]

EPA city/highway mpg

5-speed OD manual	24/33		23/33	
3-speed automatic	24/31	22/29		19/29

1. Grand Am SE; base Skylark; Achieva S.   2. Achieva SL.   3. Grand Am GT; Achieva SC.   4. Skylark GS.

Assembly point: Lansing, Mich.

Prices

Pontiac Grand Am	Retail Price	Dealer Invoice	Low Price
SE 2-door notchback	$11899	$10685	—
SE 4-door notchback	11999	10775	—
GT 2-door notchback	13699	12302	—
GT 4-door notchback	13799	12392	—
Destination charge	475	475	475

Low price not available at time of publication.

Standard equipment:

SE: 2.3-liter OHC 4-cylinder engine, 5-speed manual transmission, anti-lock brakes, power steering, door-mounted automatic front seatbelts, cloth reclining front bucket seats, AM/FM radio, tinted glass, power locks, remote decklid release, fog lamps, trip odometer, oil level sensor, 185/75R14 tires. **GT** adds: 2.3-liter DOHC 16-valve HO Quad 4 engine (5-speed; 2.3-liter DOHC 16-valve Quad 4 with 3-speed automatic transmission), ride and handling suspension, tachometer with rally gauges, 205/55R16 tires on alloy wheels.

Optional equipment:	Retail Price	Dealer Invoice	Low Price
2.3-liter Quad 4 (non-HO), SE	410	349	—
GT w/automatic transmission (credit) . .	(140)	(119)	(119)
3.3-liter PFI V-6 engine, SE	391	332	—
GT (credit)	(90)	(77)	(77)
3-speed automatic transmission	555	472	—
Air conditioning	830	706	—
Option Pkg. 1SB, SE	565	501	—
Air conditioning, tilt steering column, intermittent wipers, cruise control.			
Option Pkg. 1SC, SE 2-door	976	854	—
SE 4-door	1041	909	—
Pkg. 1SB plus power windows, power mirrors, split folding rear seat.			
Value Option Pkg. R6A, SE 2-door	253	218	—
Cassette player, 195/65R15 tires, crosslace wheel covers.			
Value Option Pkg. R6B, SE	431	370	—
Cassette player, 195/65R15 tires on alloy wheels.			
Option Pkg. 1SB, GT	1327	1128	—
Air conditioning, tilt steering column, intermittent wipers, cruise control, variable-assist power steering.			
Option Pkg. 1SC, GT 2-door	1828	1562	—
GT 4-door	1903	1618	—
Pkg. 1SB plus split folding rear seat, power windows, power mirrors.			
Sport Interior Group	265	225	—
Driver-seat lumbar adjuster, articulated front headrests, 4-way manual seat adjuster, leather-wrapped steering wheel and shift knob, front reading lamps, rear courtesy lamps, sunvisor extensions.			
Variable-assist power steering	62	53	—
Requires tilt steering column, cruise control, intermittent wipers; not available with 185/75R14 tires.			
Rally cluster gauges, SE	111	94	—
Includes tachometer.			
Cruise control	225	191	—
Rear defogger	170	145	—
Power mirrors	86	73	—
Requires power windows.			
Power driver's seat	340	289	—
w/Sport Interior Group	305	259	—

Prices are accurate at time of publication; subject to manufacturer's change.

	Retail Price	Dealer Invoice	Low Price
Power windows, 2-door	275	234	—
4-door	340	289	—
Split folding rear seat	150	128	—
Tilt steering column	145	123	—
Intermittent wipers	65	55	—
Cassette player	140	119	—
CD player w/EQ	600	510	—
SE w/R6A or R6B	460	391	—
Extended range speakers	85	72	—
195/70R14 tires, SE	141	120	—
Includes ride and handling suspension; requires alloy wheels.			
205/55R16 tires w/sport suspension, GT	33	28	—
Crosslace wheel covers, SE	55	47	—
Alloy wheels, SE	275	234	—
Warranty enhancements for New York	25	21	—
California emissions pkg.	100	85	—

Buick Skylark

2-door notchback	$13560	$12177	—
4-door notchback	13560	12177	—
Gran Sport (GS) 2-door notchback	15555	13502	—
Gran Sport (GS) 4-door notchback	15555	13502	—
Destination charge	475	475	475

Low price not available at time of publication.

Standard equipment:

2.3-liter OHC 4-cylinder engine, 3-speed automatic transmission, anti-lock brakes, power steering, door-mounted automatic seatbelts, cloth split front bench seat (4-door), reclining bucket seats (2-door), tachometer, oil pressure and temperature gauges, voltmeter, trip odometer, AM/FM radio, tinted glass, power locks, remote fuel door and decklid release, dual outside mirrors, courtesy lamps, visor mirrors, map pockets, 185/75R15 tires. **GS** adds: 3.3-liter V-6, 4-way driver's seat with lumbar support adjuster, cloth and leather bucket seats, leather-wrapped steering wheel and shifter, Adjustable Ride Control suspension, cassette player, lighted visor mirrors, trunk net, floormats, 205/55R16 tires on alloy wheels.

Optional equipment:

3.3-liter V-6 engine, base	460	391	403
Popular Pkg. SB, base	1145	973	1002
Air conditioning, rear defogger, tilt steering column.			
Premium Pkg. SC, base	1480	1258	1295
Pkg. SB plus floormats, cruise control, intermittent wipers.			

	Retail Price	Dealer Invoice	Low Price
Luxury Pkg. SD, base 2-door	2000	1700	1750
Base 4-door	2115	1798	1851
Pkg. SC plus front seat armrest, cassette player with Concert Sound system, 4-way driver's seat adjuster, power windows.			
Prestige Pkg. SE, base 2-door	2588	2200	2265
Base 4-door	2703	2298	2365
Pkg. SD plus trunk net, lighted visor mirrors, readling lights, power antenna, power driver's seat, power mirrors.			
Popular Pkg. SB, GS	1145	973	1002
Air conditioning, rear defogger, tilt steering column.			
Premium Pkg. SC, GS	1435	1220	1256
Pkg. SB plus cruise control, intermittent wipers.			
Luxury Pkg. SD, GS 2-door	2055	1747	1798
GS 4-door	2120	1802	1855
Pkg. SC plus lighted visor mirrors, power windows, cassette player with Concert Sound system.			
Prestige Pkg. SE, GS 2-door	2623	2230	2295
GS 4-door	2688	2285	2352
Pkg. SE plus remote keyless entry, power mirrors, power antenna, power driver's seat.			
Adjustable Ride Control suspension, base .	380	323	333
Whitewall tires, base	68	58	60
195/65R15 blackwall tires, base	131	111	115
Bucket seats & floorshift, 4-door w/SB or SC	210	179	184
4-door w/SD or SE	160	136	140
Remote keyless entry system	135	115	118
CD player, w/SB or SC	624	530	546
w/SD or SE	414	352	362
Includes AM-stereo, EQ, Concert Sound speakers.			
Wheel covers, base	28	24	25
Lower accent paint, GS	195	166	171
Engine block heater	18	15	16
Warranty enhancements for New York state .	25	21	22
California emissions pkg.	100	85	88

Pontiac LeMans

Pontiac's Korean-built, front-drive subcompact entry, based on GM of Germany's Opel Kadette, receives some slight revisions for 1992. One 4-door sedan and two 3-door hatchbacks are offered (Pontiac calls its LeMans hatchbacks "Aerocoupes"), all riding a 99.2-inch wheelbase and powered by a 74-horsepower 1.6-liter four-cylinder engine. The

Prices are accurate at time of publication; subject to manufacturer's change.

1991 Pontiac LeMans 3-door

Specifications

	3-door hatchback	4-door notchback
Wheelbase, in.	99.2	99.2
Overall length, in.	163.7	172.4
Overall width, in.	65.5	65.7
Overall height, in.	53.5	53.7
Curb weight, lbs.	2191	2246
Cargo vol., cu. ft.	18.9	16.5
Fuel capacity, gals.	13.2	13.2
Seating capacity	5	5
Front head room, in.	38.8	38.8
Front leg room, max., in.	42.0	42.0
Rear head room, in.	38.0	38.0
Rear leg room, min., in.	32.8	32.8

Powertrain layout: transverse front engine/front-wheel drive.

Engines

	ohc l-4
Size, liters/cu. in.	1.6/98
Fuel delivery	TBI
Horsepower @ rpm	74 @ 5600
Torque (lbs./ft.) @ rpm	90 @ 2800
Availability	S

EPA city/highway mpg

4-speed OD manual	28/37
5-speed OD manual	31/41
3-speed automatic	26/32

Assembly point: Pupyong, South Korea.

CONSUMER GUIDE®

SE designation replaces the LE moniker used last year on the sedan and higher-line Aerocoupe, while the Value Leader Aerocoupe continues. The Value Leader comes only with a 4-speed manual transmission; SEs come standard with a 5-speed manual, and offer a 3-speed automatic as an option. Amber (instead of red) turn signals on the SE Aerocoupe and new sport-tuned exhaust for all models sums up this year's changes. Overall, LeMans lags behind most competitors in terms of technical sophistication, and doesn't offer the kind of value one might expect in a Korean-built car. The 1.6-liter engine produces only 74 horse-power—much less than most rivals—and more than its share of roughness and vibration. With manual transmission it's fairly lively, but the 3-speed automatic saps its limited strength. On the plus side, LeMans is reasonably surefooted on the road, offers more leg room and cargo space than is common in this class, and delivers high fuel economy. Nevertheless, standard and optional equipment lists are quite restricted, and the LeMans costs as much as many better-equipped, more refined competitors.

Prices

Pontiac LeMans	Retail Price	Dealer Invoice	Low Price
Aerocoupe VL 3-door hatchback	$8050	$7446	$7796
Aerocoupe SE 3-door hatchback	8750	8094	8444
SE 4-door notchback	9465	8755	9105
Destination charge	345	345	345

Standard equipment:

VL: 1.6-liter TBI 4-cylinder engine, 4-speed manual transmission, motorized front shoulder belts, reclining front bucket seats, one-piece folding rear seat, rear defogger, cargo cover, left remote mirror, bodyside moldings, trip odometer, 175/70R13 tires. **SE** adds: 5-speed manual transmission, AM/FM radio, tachometer (3-door), tinted glass, dual remote mirrors, right visor mirror (3-door), swing-out rear quarter windows (3-door).

Optional equipment:

3-speed automatic transmission, SE	475	404	413
Air conditioning, SE	705	599	613
Requires power steering.			
Power steering, SE	225	191	196
Requires air conditioning.			

Prices are accurate at time of publication; subject to manufacturer's change.

	Retail Price	Dealer Invoice	Low Price
AM/FM radio, VL	307	261	267
AM/FM cassette, VL	429	365	373
SE	122	104	106
Removable sunroof	350	298	305
Value Option Pkg. R6A, VL . . , ...	662	567	576
SE	355	306	309
Removable sunroof, AM/FM cassette, floormats.			
Floormats	33	28	29
Warranty enhancements for New York . . .	25	21	22

Saab 900

Saab 900 3-door

The top-line 900 Turbo SPG dies and detail changes are made elsewhere. Returning are 3-door hatchbacks and 4-door sedans in base, 900S, and Turbo form, and 900S and Turbo convertibles. All have front-wheel drive, anti-lock brakes, and a driver-side air bag. Base and S versions use a 2.1-liter 4-cylinder engine with 140 horsepower, Turbos have a 2.0 four with 160. Manual transmission is standard, automatic is optional. The base 900 gains standard power windows, power/heated outside mirrors, and new 16-spoke wheel covers. New 15-spoke alloy wheels are added to the 900S. Turbos get 3-spoke alloy wheels and a compact disc player/graphic equalizer. Convertible 900S models now match Turbo ragtops with the addition of a wrap-around rear spoiler, remote alarm and keyless entry, dual power front seats, and leather-covered steering wheel, shift boot, and door armrests. The 900 dates back 22 years, and they've aged pretty well. Non-turbo versions are down on power compared to others in this price class, however. Manual is the transmission of choice for wringing what power there is out of the base four, but shift action is notchy. Turbos are plenty fast, but their suspension is too stiff. The base and S are supple over bumps, firm at speed. Body lean is the rule in fast turns, but 900s grip well. There's chair-like seating for four adults. On hatchbacks and sedans, luggage space varies from ample with the rear seat up to cavernous with it folded down.

Specifications

	3-door hatchback	4-door notchback	2-door conv.
Wheelbase, in.	99.1	99.1	99.1
Overall length, in.	184.5	184.3	184.3
Overall width, in.	66.5	66.5	66.5
Overall height, in.	56.1	56.1	55.1
Curb weight, lbs.	2734	2776	2947
Cargo vol., cu. ft.	57.6	53.0	10.7
Fuel capacity, gals.	18.0	18.0	18.0
Seating capacity	5	5	4
Front head room, in.	36.8	36.8	36.8
Front leg room, max., in.	41.7	41.7	41.7
Rear head room, in.	37.4	37.4	NA
Rear leg room, min., in.	36.2	36.2	NA

Powertrain layout: longitudinal front engine/front-wheel drive.

Engines

	dohc I-4	Turbo dohc I-4
Size, liters/cu. in.	2.1/129	2.0/121
Fuel delivery	PFI	PFI
Horsepower @ rpm	140 @ 6000	160 @ 5500
Torque (lbs./ft.) @ rpm	133 @ 2900	188 @ 3000
Availability	S[1]	S[2]

EPA city/highway mpg

5-speed OD manual	20/27	21/28
3-speed automatic	19/23	19/23

1. 900, 900S.   2. Turbo.

Assembly point: Trollhattan, Sweden.

Prices are accurate at time of publication; subject to manufacturer's change.

Prices

Saab 900	Retail Price	Dealer Invoice	Low Price
3-door hatchback	$19395	—	—
4-door notchback	19995	—	—
S 3-door hatchback	23395	—	—
S 4-door notchback	23995	—	—
S 2-door convertible	30595	—	—
Turbo 3-door hatchback	28645	—	—
Turbo 2-door convertible	35345	—	—
Destination charge	440	440	440

Dealer invoice and low price not available at time of publication.

Standard equipment:

2.1-liter DOHC 16-valve PFI 4-cylinder engine, 5-speed manual transmission, anti-lock 4-wheel disc brakes, power steering, driver-side air bag, air conditioning, tachometer, coolant temperature gauge, trip odometer, analog clock, rear defogger, heated power mirrors, intermittent wipers, power windows and locks, tinted glass, driver-seat tilt/height adjustment, cloth heated reclining front bucket seats, folding rear seat, AM/FM cassette, headlamp wipers and washers, 185/65TR15 tires. **S** adds: cruise control, folding rear armrest, power sunroof, leather seating surfaces, fog lamps, alloy wheels. **Turbo** adds: 2.0-liter turbocharged engine, sport seats, CD player with EQ, 195/60VR15 tires; **convertibles** add power front seats, remote anti-theft alarm, rear spoiler, remote keyless entry system, leather-wrapped steering wheel, 185/65HR15 tires.

Optional equipment:

3-speed automatic transmission	670	—	—

Saab 9000

Like its 900 sibling, the upper-crust 9000 receives changes that are evolutionary rather than revolutionary. The biggest news is the addition of traction control on Turbo models, and a new top-of-the-line limited production 9000CD Turbo Griffin Edition. With the exception of the latter, the line is the same as last year: base 9000, 9000S, and 9000 Turbo 5-door hatchbacks; and 9000CD and 9000CD Turbo 4-door notchbacks. All ride a 105.2-inch wheelbase and come standard with a driver's air bag and

Saab 9000 Turbo 5-door

anti-lock brakes. Normally aspirated 9000s come with a 150-horsepower 2.3-liter four-cylinder, while Turbos are equipped with a 200-horsepower version of that engine. All come standard with a 5-speed manual except for CD sedans, which come standard with a 4-speed automatic. The automatic is optional on others, and a 5-speed can be special ordered on CDs (except for the Griffin Edition). Turbos with the 5-speed get a traction control system that uses brake application and throttle control to reduce wheelspin; Turbos with automatic use throttle control only. For 1992, all 9000 models get reduced scheduled maintenance and a "freeze warning" feature. In addition, the 9000 gets a power moonroof as standard equipment, and the 9000CD Turbo gets an air conditioning outlet for the rear seat. The limited production Griffin Edition (only 400 will be built) adds: Eucalyptus Green metallic paint with Taupe leather interior, special 15-inch cross-spoke alloy wheels, cellular telephone, trunk-mounted six-disc CD changer, and trip computer. Saabs are often overshadowed in the marketplace by V-6 and V-8-powered competitors, but the normally aspirated 2.3-liter four delivers adequate acceleration, while the turbo turns the 9000 into a luxury hot rod. All models offer spacious interior accommodations with very comfortable, upright seating and generous cargo capacity. Capable handling and a firm, yet compliant ride is a 9000 trademark, but turbos get a stiffer suspension that may feel too harsh to those more interested in luxury than sport.

Prices are accurate at time of publication; subject to manufacturer's change.

Specifications

	4-door notchback	5-door hatchback
Wheelbase, in.	105.2	105.2
Overall length, in.	188.2	183.7
Overall width, in.	69.4	69.4
Overall height, in.	55.9	55.9
Curb weight, lbs.	3143	3089
Cargo vol., cu. ft.	17.8	56.9
Fuel capacity, gals.	17.4	17.4
Seating capacity	5	5
Front head room, in.	38.5	38.5
Front leg room, max., in.	41.5	41.5
Rear head room, in.	37.4	37.4
Rear leg room, min., in.	38.7	38.7

Powertrain layout: transverse front engine/front-wheel drive.

Engines

	dohc I-4	Turbo dohc I-4
Size, liters/cu. in.	2.3/140	2.3/140
Fuel delivery	PFI	PFI
Horsepower @ rpm	150 @ 5500	200 @ 5000
Torque (lbs./ft.) @ rpm	157 @ 3800	244 @ 2000
Availability	S[1]	S[2]

EPA city/highway mpg

5-speed OD manual	20/26	19/26
4-speed OD automatic	17/25	17/24

1. 9000, 9000S, 9000CD.   2. 9000 Turbo S, CD Turbo, Griffin Edition.

Assembly point: Trollhattan, Sweden.

Prices

Saab 9000	Retail Price	Dealer Invoice	Low Price
5-door hatchback	$24845	—	—
S 5-door hatchback	28095	—	—
CD 4-door notchback	30195	—	—
Turbo 5-door hatchback	36045	—	—
CD Turbo 4-door notchback	36695	—	—
Griffin Edition CD Turbo 4-door notchback	42195	—	—
Destination charge	417	417	417

Dealer invoice and low price not available at time of publication.

Standard equipment:

2.3-liter DOHC 16-valve PFI 4-cylinder engine, 5-speed manual transmission, anti-lock 4-wheel disc brakes, power steering, driver-side air bag, air conditioning, AM/FM cassette, power antenna, trip computer, trip odometer, tachometer, coolant temperature gauge, front and rear reading lights, heated reclining front bucket seats, power windows and locks, heated power mirrors, velour upholstery, power moonroof, 195/65TR15 tires. **S** adds: leather upholstery, fog lights, power driver's seat, alloy wheels. **CD** adds: 5-speed manual or 4-speed automatic transmission, remote decklid release. **Turbo** adds: turbocharged engine, 5-speed manual transmission or 4-speed automatic transmission (CD only), traction control system, automatic climate control, power front seats, fog lights, upgraded audio system with EQ, 205/50ZR16 tires (hatchback), 195/65VR15 tires (CD). **Griffin Edition** adds: specific paint, leather seats, 6-disc CD changer, trip computer, cellular phone, cross-spoke alloy wheels.

Optional equipment:	Retail Price	Dealer Invoice	Low Price
4-speed automatic transmission, hatchbacks	890	—	—

Saturn

Saturn SL2 4-door

Saturn, started from scratch as General Motors' first new division in decades, is the Americanized version of a Japanese small-car builder. Its first two cars bowed last year and share no components with other GM products. Both are front-drive subcompacts in which body panels of plastic and steel are hung on a steel skeletal frame. The coupe (called the SC) has a wheelbase of 99.2 inches and

Prices are accurate at time of publication; subject to manufacturer's change.

comes in a single, sporty trim level. The more mainstream sedan rides a 102.4-inch wheelbase and ascends from the base SL through SL1 and SL2 versions. All have a 1.9-liter 4-cylinder engine, but the one in the SL and SL1 makes 85 horsepower, while the SL2 and SC coupe get a twin-cam version with 124. Manual and automatic transmission are offered with either. Anti-lock brakes are optional. Leather seat trim, new 15-inch alloy wheels, and a rear-deck spoiler are added SL2 and SC options for 1992. SL and SL1 sedans accelerate adequately with the fine-shifting 5-speed manual, but lag behind with automatic, which does its part with prompt, smooth gear changes. By contrast, the SL2

Specifications

	2-door notchback	4-door notchback
Wheelbase, in.	99.2	102.4
Overall length, in.	175.8	176.3
Overall width, in.	67.5	67.6
Overall height, in.	50.6	52.5
Curb weight, lbs.	2375	2313
Cargo vol., cu. ft.	11.3	11.9
Fuel capacity, gals.	12.8	12.8
Seating capacity	4	5
Front head room, in.	37.6	38.5
Front leg room, max., in.	42.6	42.5
Rear head room, in.	35.0	36.3
Rear leg room, min., in.	26.4	32.6

Powertrain layout: transverse front engine/front-wheel drive.

Engines	ohc I-4	dohc I-4
Size, liters/cu. in.	1.9/116	1.9/116
Fuel delivery	TBI	PFI
Horsepower @ rpm	85 @ 5000	124 @ 5600
Torque (lbs./ft.) @ rpm	107 @ 2400	122 @ 4800
Availability	S[1]	S[2]

EPA city/highway mpg

5-speed OD manual	28/38	24/33
4-speed OD automatic	26/35	23/32

1. SL, SL1.   2. SL2, Coupe.

Assembly point: Spring Hill, Tenn.

CONSUMER GUIDE®

and SC feel quick with either gear box. The suspension is slightly stiffer on the SL2 and SC, so you get a firmer ride and less body lean than on the SL and SL1 sedans. But the base models still offer a well-controlled ride with good cornering grip. Sedans offer adequate room for four adults in a cabin where most dashboard and trim pieces could have come from a Japanese subcompact. The SC coupe has adequate room in front, but the back seat is for kids only. Despite the new sound-deadening steps, Saturns still admit too much engine vibration and noise into the cabin; it's tiring on long drives. In most other ways however, these cars manage to approach the feel of comparably priced imports.

Prices

Saturn	Retail Price	Dealer Invoice	Low Price
SL 4-door notchback	$8195	$7048	—
SL1 4-door notchback	8995	7736	—
SL2 4-door notchback	10395	8939	—
SC 2-door notchback	11875	10213	—
Destination charge	275	275	275

Low price not available at time of publication.

Standard equipment:

SL: 1.9-liter TBI 4-cylinder engine, 5-speed manual transmission, motorized front shoulder belts, cloth reclining front bucket seats, 60/40 folding rear seatback, tachometer, coolant temperature gauge, trip odometer, tilt steering column, intermittent wipers, rear defogger, AM/FM radio, remote fuel door and decklid releases, door pockets, digital clock, right visor mirror, wheel covers, 175/70R14 tires. **SL1** adds: power steering, upgraded interior trim. **SL2 and SC** add: DOHC 16-valve PFI engine, driver-seat height and lumbar support adjustments, oil pressure gauge, body-colored bumpers, 195/60R15 tires on alloy wheels.

Optional equipment:

Anti-lock brakes	695	598	—
4-speed automatic transmission (NA SL) .	695	598	—
Air conditioning	795	684	—
Power sunroof (NA SL)	540	464	—
Cassette player	170	151	—
Cassette player w/equalizer	325	280	—
CD player	555	477	—
Coaxial speakers	50	43	—
Requires cassette player.			

Prices are accurate at time of publication; subject to manufacturer's change.

	Retail Price	Dealer Invoice	Low Price
Comfort & Convenience Pkg. A, SL1	250	215	—
Power door locks, right outside mirror.			
Comfort & Convenience Pkg. B, SL1	780	671	—
Power door locks, right power mirror, power windows, cruise control.			
Comfort & Convenience Pkg. B, SL2	1575	1355	—
SC	1475	1269	—
Air conditioning, power windows and locks, right outside mirror, cruise control.			
Cruise control	210	181	—
Right outside mirror, SL, SL1	30	26	—
Two-Tone paint, SL2, Coupe	155	133	—
Leather seats, SL2 & SC	610	525	—
Requies B Pkg.			
Rear spoiler, SL2 & SC	150	129	—
Teardrop alloy wheels, SL2 & SC	100	86	—

Subaru Justy

Subaru Justy GL 4WD 5-door

Subaru's entry-level minicompact remains virtually unchanged for 1992. Base 3-door hatchback is one of the least-expensive cars sold in America. Upper-level GL comes in both 3- and 5-door versions, and can be optioned with on-demand 4-wheel drive and Subaru's unique Electronic Continuously Variable Transmission (ECVT). ECVT mimics the operation of an automatic, but has an infinite spread of ratios rather than just three or four speeds. All Justys share the same 90-inch wheelbase and a 1.2-liter 3-cylinder engine, but base models get a carbureted version with 66 horsepower, while GLs have fuel injection and 73 horsepower. Overall, the Justy ranks on par with other cars in this class, though the availability of 4WD and innovative ECVT on GL models gives it a leg up on rivals. Subaru claims that the 4WD GL is the least expensive and most economical 4WD car sold in America, as even one equipped with ECVT should return better than 30 miles per gallon. ECVT provides better performance than most automatics, but its operation is not faultless; mid-range acceleration

Specifications

	3-door hatchback	5-door hatchback
Wheelbase, in.	90.0	90.0
Overall length, in.	145.5	145.5
Overall width, in.	60.4	60.4
Overall height, in.	53.7	53.7
Curb weight, lbs.	1820	2045
Cargo vol., cu. ft.	21.8	21.8
Fuel capacity, gals.	9.2	9.2
Seating capacity	4	4
Front head room, in.	38.0	38.0
Front leg room, max., in.	41.5	41.5
Rear head room, in.	37.0	37.0
Rear leg room, min., in.	30.2	30.2

Powertrain layout: transverse front engine/front-wheel drive or on-demand 4WD.

Engines

	ohc I-3	ohc I-3
Size, liters/cu. in.	1.2/73	1.2/73
Fuel delivery	2 bbl.	PFI
Horsepower @ rpm	66 @ 5200	73 @ 5600
Torque (lbs./ft.) @ rpm	70 @ 3600	71 @ 2800
Availability	S[1]	S[2]

EPA city/highway mpg

	3-door	5-door
5-speed OD manual	33/37	33/37
ECVT automatic		33/35

1. Base. 2. GL.

Assembly point: Ota City, Japan.

Prices are accurate at time of publication; subject to manufacturer's change.

tends to lag somewhat, though selecting the transmission's "sport" mode helps in this regard—at the expense of economy. Like other minicompacts, Justy is somewhat noisy, suffers a bouncy ride, and has a cramped back seat, so the availability of 4WD (at only about $800) remains Justy's biggest selling point.

Prices

Subaru Justy	Retail Price	Dealer Invoice	Low Price
3-door hatchback	$6295	—	—
GL 3-door hatchback	7699	—	—
GL 4WD 3-door hatchback	8499	—	—
GL 4WD 5-door hatchback	8599	—	—
Destination charge	395	395	395

Dealer invoice and low price not available at time of publication.

Standard equipment:

1.3-liter 2bbl. 3-cylinder engine, 5-speed manual transmission, reclining front bucket seats, one-piece folding rear seatback, remote hatch release, locking fuel door, 145SR12 tires. **GL** adds: PFI engine, uprated suspension, 50/50 folding rear seatback, rear defogger and wiper/washer, bodyside moldings, tachometer and gauges, AM/FM radio, visor mirror, cargo cover, 165/65SR13 tires.

Optional equipment:

ECVT automatic transmission, GL	535	470	490
Metallic paint	120	100	107

Subaru Legacy

A driver-side air bag and a mild facelift make news for this line of front- and 4-wheel-drive compacts. Legacy returns as a 4-door sedan in L, LS, LSi, and Sport Sedan form, and as a 5-door wagon in L and LS models. All have a 2.2-liter 4-cylinder engine that makes 130 horsepower, except in the Sport Sedan, where a turbocharger boosts it to 160. Permanently engaged 4WD is standard on Sport Sedan, optional on the others. Anti-lock brakes are stan-

Subaru Legacy L 4-door

dard on all but the base L, where it's an option. The air bag is newly standard on LS and LSi and optional on L. It is to be added to the options list of the Sport Sedan during the 1992 model run. Other new features include a "pass through" opening in the rear seat (on all but the L), a dash-mounted slide-out cupholder, and rear-seat heater ducts. The smooth 2.2 four delivers spritely acceleration with either manual or automatic transmission. On models we've driven, however, the 5-speed seemed a bit hesitant to engage during quick gear changes and was particularly reluctant to go into reverse. The Sport Sedan's turbocharged engine is even more powerful, and virtually devoid of turbo lag. Head and leg room are adequate for adults both front and rear, but the back door opening is narrow at its bottom, making it difficult to swing your feet in or out. A comfortable driving position is aided by the standard tilt steering wheel and, on LS and higher models, an adjustable-height driver's seat. All controls are well placed and easy to read. The spacious trunk is well trimmed, with a bumper-level opening and low liftover height. Overall, this is a well-equipped small car worth considering.

Specifications

	4-door notchback	5-door wagon
Wheelbase, in.	101.6	101.6
Overall length, in.	178.9	181.9
Overall width, in.	66.5	66.5

Prices are accurate at time of publication; subject to manufacturer's change.

	4-door notchback	5-door wagon
Overall height, in.	53.5	54.7
Curb weight, lbs.	2740	2860
Cargo vol., cu. ft.	14.0	71.0
Fuel capacity, gals.	15.9	15.9
Seating capacity	5	5
Front head room, in.	38.0	38.4
Front leg room, max., in.	43.1	43.1
Rear head room, in.	36.0	37.8
Rear leg room, min., in.	34.8	35.0

Powertrain layout: longitudinal front engine/front-wheel drive or permanent 4WD.

Engines	ohc flat-4	Turbo ohc flat-4
Size, liters/cu. in.	2.2/135	2.2/135
Fuel delivery	PFI	PFI
Horsepower @ rpm	130 @ 5600	160 @ 5600
Torque (lbs./ft.) @ rpm	137 @ 5600	181 @ 2800
Availability	S	S[1]

EPA city/highway mpg		
5-speed OD manual	23/30	19/25
4-speed OD automatic	22/29	18/23

1. Legacy Sport Sedan.

Assembly points: Ota City, Japan; Lafayette, Ind.

Prices

Subaru Legacy	Retail Price	Dealer Invoice	Low Price
L 4-door notchback	$11999	—	—
L 5-door wagon	12999	—	—
L 4WD 5-door wagon	14099	—	—
L Plus 4-door notchback	12999	—	—
L Plus AWD 4-door notchback	14599	—	—
L Plus 5-door wagon	14499	—	—
L Plus AWD 5-door wagon	15099	—	—
LS 4-door notchback	18299	—	—
LS 4WD 4-door notchback	19799	—	—
LS 5-door wagon	18799	—	—
LS 4WD 5-door wagon	20299	—	—

	Retail Price	Dealer Invoice	Low Price
LSi 4-door notchback	19699	—	—
LSi 4WD 4-door notchback	21199	—	—
Sport Sedan 4WD 4-door	18799	—	—
Destination charge	445	445	445

Dealer invoice and low price not available at time of publication.

Standard equipment:

L: 2.2-liter 16-valve PFI 4-cylinder engine, 5-speed manual transmission, 4-wheel disc brakes, power steering, motorized front shoulder belts, cloth reclining front bucket seats, split folding rear seat, driver-seat lumbar support adjustment, power mirrors, bodyside moldings, rear defogger, tinted glass, tachometer and gauges, remote fuel door and decklid releases, cupholder, tilt steering column, intermittent wipers, 175/70HR14 tires. **L Plus** adds: air conditioning, power windows and locks, power mirrors, AM/FM cassette with equalizer, power antenna. **LS** adds: 4-speed automatic transmission, anti-lock brakes, driver-side air bag, cruise control, driver-seat height adjustment, variable intermittent wipers, power antenna, power moonroof, rear armrest and trunk-through (4-door), lighted visor mirrors, power mirrors, leather-wrapped steering wheel and shift knob, air suspension (4WD wagon with automatic), 185/70HR14 tires on alloy wheels. **LSi** adds: leather upholstery and trim. **Sport Sedan** adds: turbocharged engine, 5-speed manual transmission, 4-wheel drive, sport seats, front air dam and rear spoiler, split folding rear seat, coin tray, full console, map lights, 195/60HR15 tires.

Optional equipment:

4-speed automatic transmission & air conditioning, L	1000	NA	NA
Anti-lock brakes & cruise control, L Plus wagon	1000	NA	NA
All other L Plus	1500	—	—
Driver-side air bag, L & L Plus	800	—	—

Subaru Loyale

These 4-door sedans and 5-door wagons are unchanged. Both are available in either front- or on-demand 4-wheel drive (not for use on dry pavement). Standard equipment includes a 90-horsepower 1.8-liter 4-cylinder engine, air conditioning, power windows and locks, power steering, rear window defogger (and wiper on the wagon), and power

Prices are accurate at time of publication; subject to manufacturer's change.

Subaru Loyale wagon

mirrors. Manual transmission is standard, automatic is optional. A lengthy list of standard features and low price make it a terrific value for the money, but Loyale is flawed by a weak, coarse engine. In front-drive models with manual transmission, it delivers passable performance. But laden with an automatic transmission and/or the extra weight of 4WD, it's somewhat overburdened. And fuel economy also suffers. Availability of 4WD, while not unique to this class, remains one of Loyale's primary virtues. It's not a permanent, self-activating system as found on Subaru's more expensive models, but it does provide extra traction in rain or snow at the push of a gearshift-mounted button. Loyale strikes a good balance in ride and handling. There is ample room for four adults—five in a pinch—though tall drivers might find leg room at a premium. Instruments and controls are clearly marked, and handy steering column stalks carry switches for the lights and wipers. Standard power windows feature "one touch" up and down operation. A Loyale may not be as refined as others in this league, but it offers a lot of value for the money.

Specifications

	4-door notchback	5-door wagon
Wheelbase, in.	97.2	97.0
Overall length, in.	174.6	176.8
Overall width, in.	65.4	65.4

	4-door notchback	5-door wagon
Overall height, in.	52.5	53.0
Curb weight, lbs.	2355	2490
Cargo vol., cu. ft.	16.0	70.3
Fuel capacity, gals.	15.9	15.9
Seating capacity	5	5
Front head room, in.	37.6	37.6
Front leg room, max., in.	41.7	41.7
Rear head room, in.	36.5	37.7
Rear leg room, min., in.	35.2	35.2

Powertrain layout: longitudinal front engine/front-wheel drive or on-demand 4WD.

Engines

	ohc flat-4
Size, liters/cu. in.	1.8/109
Fuel delivery	TBI
Horsepower @ rpm	90 @ 5200
Torque (lbs./ft.) @ rpm	101 @ 2800
Availability	S

EPA city/highway mpg

5-speed OD manual	25/32
3-speed automatic	24/26

Assembly point: Ota City, Japan.

Prices

Subaru Loyale	Retail Price	Dealer Invoice	Low Price
4-door notchback	$9799	—	—
5-door wagon	10649	—	—
4WD 4-door notchback	11149	—	—
4WD 5-door wagon	12149	—	—
Destination charge	445	445	445

Dealer invoice and low price not available at time of publication.

Standard equipment:

1.8-liter TBI 4-cylinder engine, 5-speed manual transmission, Hill Holder, power steering, air conditioning, motorized front shoulder belts, cloth reclining front bucket seats, driver-seat lumbar support adjustment, power win-

Prices are accurate at time of publication; subject to manufacturer's change.

dows and locks, AM/FM cassette, power mirrors, rear wiper/washer (wagon), remote fuel door and decklid releases, 50/50 folding rear seat (wagon), rear defogger, coin holder, console with storage, 175/70SR13 tires (4WD wagon has 165/70SR13).

Optional equipment:	Retail Price	Dealer Invoice	Low Price
3-speed automatic transmission	550	481	503

Subaru SVX

Subaru SVX

Replacing the wedge-shaped XT6 is the SVX, a sleeker coupe with more performance and luxury. Compared to the 4- and 6-cylinder, front- and 4-wheel-drive XT, the SVX is longer by four inches in wheelbase and in overall length. Its only powertrain is a 230-horsepower 3.3-liter 24-valve flat-6 engine linked to an automatic transmission. Standard is permanently engaged 4-wheel drive, anti-lock brakes, and a driver-side air bag. Automatic climate control, power windows and locks, tilt and telescoping steering wheel, and 80-watt audio system are among the standard items. SVX is an extremely competent all-weather road car. The suspension and tires furnish excellent cornering grip without a trace of harshness and the 4WD is a boon to traction and control in all conditions. The engine pulls strongly from virtually any speed. The transmission generally shifts well, but occasionally finds itself in too high a gear to provide a small speed increase without downshifting. Lots of standard amenities combine for a very comfortable driving environment. Subaru claims full 4-passenger seating, but SVX's rear seat lacks sufficient headroom for even average-sized adults, and would be short on legroom as well with tall people in front. The trunk is fairly large but the opening is quite small. Most of the side glass is fixed in place, but an unusual "window-within-a-window" slides up and down. The inner window frame leaves a line in your peripheral vision, but after a while, we didn't notice it, and overall visibility is good for a coupe.

Specifications

	2-door notchback
Wheelbase, in.	102.8
Overall length, in.	182.1
Overall width, in.	69.7
Overall height, in.	51.2
Curb weight, lbs.	3525
Cargo vol., cu. ft.	8.2
Fuel capacity, gals.	18.5
Seating capacity	4
Front head room, in.	38.0
Front leg room, max., in.	43.5
Rear head room, in.	35.0
Rear leg room, min., in.	28.1

Powertrain layout: longitudinal front engine/permanent 4WD.

Engines

	dohc flat-6
Size, liters/cu. in.	3.3/202
Fuel delivery	PFI
Horsepower @ rpm	230 @ 5400
Torque (lbs./ft.) @ rpm	224 @ 4400
Availability	S

EPA city/highway mpg

4-speed OD automatic	17/25

Assembly point: Ota City, Japan.

Prices are accurate at time of publication; subject to manufacturer's change.

Prices

Subaru SVX	Retail Price	Dealer Invoice	Low Price
3-door hatchback	$25000	—	—
Destination charge	445	445	445

Dealer invoice and low price not available at time of publication.

Standard equipment:

3.3-liter 24-valve PFI 6-cylinder engine, 4-speed automatic transmission, anti-lock 4-wheel disc brakes, limited-slip differential, power steering, driver-side air bag, motorized front shoulder belts, automatic climate control, cloth reclining front bucket seats, driver-seat height and lumbar support adjustments, tilt steering column, power windows and locks, remote keyless entry system, AM/FM cassette with power diversity antenna, tinted glass, variable-intermittent wipers, rear washer/wiper, power mirrors, tachometer and gauges, remote fuel door and decklid releases, rear defogger, folding rear seatback, lighted visor mirrors, map lights, illuminated entry sytem, 225/50VR16 tires on alloy wheels.

Optional equipment:

Touring Pkg.	3000	NA	NA

Leather seats, leather-wrapped steering wheel and shifter, power driver's seat, premium stereo with CD player, power moonroof, heated outside mirrors, speed-sensitive power steering.

Rear spoiler, w/Touring Pkg.	350	NA	NA

Suzuki Sidekick and Samurai

Suzuki trims model offerings in both its Samurai and Sidekick sport-utility lines, and 4-door Sidekicks get a horse-power boost. Sidekick shares its 2-door convertible body with the similar Geo Tracker. The 5-door hardtop is exclusive to Sidekick. All 5-door models have 4WD and come in JX or JLX trim. For 1992, 5-doors get a revised 1.6-liter 4-cylinder engine for an increase of 15 horsepower, to 95; 2-doors retain the 80-horsepower version. Also exclusive to the 5-door is a new automatic transmission option with four speeds; a 3-speed automatic remains optional on 4WD 2-doors. A 5-speed manual is standard. New this year for 4WD Sidekicks are standard automatic locking front hubs.

Suzuki Sidekick convertible

And all Sidekicks gain anti-lock rear brakes that work in 2WD only, plus a redesigned instrument panel. The smaller Samurai loses its 2WD JS model, leaving only the price-leading 2WD JA and 4WD JL offerings. Both retain the basic open Samurai body first seen back in 1985 (the hardtop has since disappeared), a 1.3-liter overhead-cam 4-cylinder engine with 66 horsepower, 5-speed manual transmission (an automatic isn't offered) and, on the JL, part-time 4WD. This year's big change is eliminating the JL's previously standard back seat. The JS was already a 2-seater. With their underpowered engine and rock-hard suspension, Samurais are slow, bouncy, and feel rather unstable. The larger and more popular Sidekick has adequate power for around-town duty and off-road excursions, but you've really got to push it to stay abreast of freeway traffic. Even with the 4-door's added power, there's little reserve muscle for merging or passing. The tall stance and narrow body dictate low cornering speeds; even then body lean is substantial. The cabin is functional, but the door crowds the driver's left shoulder. And wind, road, and engine noise are quite intrusive. The 4-door model is intended as an inexpensive 4WD family vehicle, but interior space is a bit tight for that purpose, and the small size and lightweight construction of both models give us pause from a safety standpoint. We've never recommended mini 4 × 4s as everyday transportation because they suffer too many shortcomings compared to cars of the same price.

Prices are accurate at time of publication; subject to manufacturer's change.

Specifications

	Sidekick 2-door soft top	Sidekick 4-door wagon	Samurai 2-door soft top
Wheelbase, in.	86.6	97.6	79.9
Overall length, in.	142.5	158.7	135.0
Overall width, in.	64.2	64.6	60.2
Overall height, in.	65.6	66.5	64.6
Curb weight, lbs.	NA	NA	2094
Cargo vol., cu. ft.	32.9	46.4	31.1
Fuel capacity, gals.	11.1	14.5	10.6
Seating capacity	4	4	2
Front head room, in.	39.5	40.6	38.6
Front leg room, max., in.	42.1	42.1	40.0
Rear head room, in.	39.0	40.0	NA
Rear leg room, min., in.	31.7	32.7	NA

Powertrain layout: longitudinal front engine/rear-wheel drive or on-demand 4WD.

Engines

	ohc I-4	ohc I-4	ohc I-4
Size, liters/cu. in.	1.6/97	1.6/97	1.3/79
Fuel delivery	TBI	PFI	TBI
Horsepower @ rpm	80 @ 5400	95 @ 5600	66 @ 6000
Torque (lbs./ft.) @ rpm	94 @ 3000	98 @ 4000	76 @ 3500
Availability	S[1]	S[2]	S[3]

EPA city/highway mpg

5-speed OD manual	25/27	24/26	28/29
3-speed automatic	23/24		
4-speed OD automatic		22/26	

1. 2-door Sidekick.   2. 4-door Sidekick.   3. Samurai.

Assembly points: Ingersoll, Ontario, Canada; Hamamatsu, Japan.

Prices

Suzuki Sidekick	Retail Price	Dealer Invoice	Low Price
JS 2WD 2-door soft top, 5-speed	$10699	—	—
JX 4WD 2-door soft top, 5-speed	11999	—	—
JX 4WD 2-door soft top, automatic	12599	—	—
JX 4WD 5-door hard top, 5-speed	12499	—	—

	Retail Price	Dealer Invoice	Low Price
JX 4WD 5-door hard top, automatic	13349	—	—
JLX 4WD 5-door hard top, 5-speed	13699	—	—
JLX 4WD 5-door hard top, automatic ...	14549	—	—
Destination charge, 2-door	280	280	280
4-door	295	295	295

Dealer invoice and low price not available at time of publication.

Standard equipment:

JS: 1.6-liter TBI 4-cylinder engine, 5-speed manual transmission, anti-lock rear brakes, vinyl reclining front bucket seats, dual outside mirrors, 195/75R15 tires. **JX** adds: 16-valve engine (4-doors), 5-speed manual or 3-speed automatic transmission (4-speed automatic on 4-doors), power steering, AM/FM cassette, tachometer, day/night mirror, cloth upholstery, power mirrors, cigarette lighter, rear defogger (4-door), bodyside moldings (4-door). **JLX** adds: rear seat, power windows and locks, rear wiper/washer, tilt steering column, remote fuel door release.

Optional equipment:

Air conditioning	722	NA	—
Tilt steering column	NA	NA	NA
Chrome wheels	150	NA	—
Kenwood speakers	377	NA	—
Floormats	55	NA	—
Metallic paint	NA	NA	NA

OTHER OPTIONS are available as dealer-installed accessories.

Suzuki Samurai

JA 2WD	$6299	—	—
JL 4WD	8199	—	—
Destination charge	270	270	270

Dealer invoice and low price not available at time of publication.

Standard equipment:

JA: 1.3-liter TBI 4-cylinder engine, vinyl front bucket seats, 205/70R15 tires. **JL** adds: 2-speed transfer case, day/night mirror, tinted glass, carpet, wheel center caps.

OPTIONS are available as dealer-installed accessories.

Prices are accurate at time of publication; subject to manufacturer's change.

Suzuki Swift

Suzuki Swift 3-door

Suzuki's subcompact 3-door hatchbacks and 4-door sedans receive some minor styling revisions and new features for 1992. Three-door hatchbacks are built on a 89.2-inch wheelbase and offered in base GA and high-performance GT form. Four-door sedans are offered in base GA and upscale GS versions riding a 93.1-inch wheelbase. Power for all but the GT is provided by a single-cam 1.3-liter 4-cylinder engine generating 70 horsepower; GTs get a twin-cam version of that engine with 100 horsepower. A 5-speed manual transmission is standard across the line, with a 3-speed automatic optional on all but the GT. All models get redesigned front and rear facias and a new dashboard design. GTs get new 7-spoke full-wheel hubcaps, and GS 4-doors get power steering and redesigned full-wheel hubcaps. Suzuki also builds the similar Geo Metro, though that model carries a smaller 55-horsepower 1.0-liter 3-cylinder engine. As might be expected, Swift's trump card is fuel economy. We averaged nearly 36 mpg in around-town driving with a 1990 4-door, and over 31 mpg with a "pocket rocket" GT, both of which are nearly identical to the current models. However, their small size and light weight make them susceptible to potholes and strong crosswinds, and they would likely suffer in a confrontation with a larger vehicle (which means virtually any other car on the road). All Swifts lack sufficient sound insulation to muffle road and engine noise; the little 4-cylinder in particular puts

CONSUMER GUIDE®

up quite a commotion as it growls and snarls its way through traffic. Though these Suzukis make for decent little runabouts, larger, more substantial cars like the Honda Civic and Mazda 323/Protege cost only a bit more and are nearly as stingy with fuel.

Specifications

	3-door hatchback	4-door notchback
Wheelbase, in.	89.2	93.1
Overall length, in.	147.4	161.2
Overall width, in.	62.0	62.0
Overall height, in.	53.1	54.3
Curb weight, lbs.	1721	1853
Cargo vol., cu. ft.	15.4	11.5
Fuel capacity, gals.	10.6	10.6
Seating capacity	4	4
Front head room, in.	37.8	39.1
Front leg room, max., in.	42.5	42.5
Rear head room, in.	36.5	37.4
Rear leg room, min., in.	29.8	32.0

Powertrain layout: transverse front engine/front-wheel drive.

Engines

	ohc I-4	dohc I-4
Size, liters/cu. in.	1.3/79	1.3/79
Fuel delivery	TBI	PFI
Horsepower @ rpm	70 @ 6000	100 @ 6500
Torque (lbs./ft.) @ rpm	74 @ 3300	83 @ 5000
Availability	S[1]	S[2]

EPA city/highway mpg

5-speed OD manual	46/50	28/35
3-speed automatic	36/39	

1. GA, 4-doors.   2. GT.

Assembly points: Ingersoll, Ontario, Canada; Hamamatsu, Japan.

Prices

Suzuki Swift	Retail Price	Dealer Invoice	Low Price
GA 3-door hatchback, 5-speed	$6899	—	—
GA 3-door hatchback, automatic	7499	—	—

Prices are accurate at time of publication; subject to manufacturer's change.

	Retail Price	Dealer Invoice	Low Price
GT 3-door hatchback, 5-speed	9599	—	—
GA 4-door notchback, 5-speed	7699	—	—
GA 4-door notchback, automatic	8299	—	—
GS 4-door notchback, 5-speed	9099	—	—
GS 4-door notchback, automatic	9699	—	—
Destination charge	270	270	270

Dealer invoice and low price not available at time of publication.

Standard equipment:

GA: 1.3-liter TBI 4-cylinder engine, 5-speed manual or 3-speed automatic transmission, power steering (4-doors), cloth and vinyl reclining front bucket seats, split folding rear seat, tinted glass, 155/70R13 tires. **GS** adds: AM/FM cassette, tachometer, rear defogger, day/night mirror, door pockets, remote fuel door and decklid/hatch releases, power mirrors. **GT** adds: DOHC 16-valve PFI engine, 4-wheel disc brakes, sport suspension, sport seats, rear wiper/washer, front air dam and sill extensions, 175/60R14 tires.

Optional equipment:

Air conditioning	699	NA	—
Kenwood speakers	429	NA	—
Floormats	55	NA	—
Metallic paint	NA	NA	NA

OTHER OPTIONS are available as dealer-installed accessories.

Toyota Camry

Camry is redesigned and gains a standard driver-side air bag. Wheelbase is longer by less than an inch, but the body is longer by six and wider by two, and curb weights are up 250 pounds. Deluxe, LE, and new XLE 4-door sedans are offered. Due in spring is a 5-door wagon and a sporty SE sedan. Manual transmission is standard on the Deluxe; all others use automatic. Anti-lock brakes are optional. Camry again shares its front-drive chassis with the entry-level Lexus but has different styling and fewer standard features than the more-expensive ES 300. Standard is a 135-horsepower 2.2-liter 4-cylinder that offers adequate acceleration, but feels sluggish in the 30-55 mph range with the automatic transmission. Optional is the 185-horsepower 3.0-liter V-6 used in the ES 300. It has ample low-

Toyota Camry XLE V-6

speed acceleration, plenty of passing power, and is remarkably quiet. The automatic changes gears with a slight vibration at low speeds but is otherwise smooth and quick to downshift. The new Camry rides firmly over bumps, but doesn't jar. It's composed on the highway, stable and secure in corners. Noise is well muffled. Adults have plenty of leg room front and back, though the rear seatback is stiff and too reclined. Some front head room is lost on LE and XLE models with the power moonroof, though it's still adequate. Wider rear doors improve entry/exit. The lid of the roomy trunk opens at bumper level and the split rear seatback folds down. All controls are within easy reach. Camry remains a bit smaller than the arch-rival Honda Accord, but it's long on features, driving appeal, and quality feel.

Specifications

	4-door notchback
Wheelbase, in.	103.1
Overall length, in.	187.8
Overall width, in.	69.7
Overall height, in.	55.1
Curb weight, lbs.	2943
Cargo vol., cu. ft.	14.9
Fuel capacity, gals.	18.5
Seating capacity	5
Front head room, in.	38.4
Front leg room, max., in.	43.5
Rear head room, in.	37.1
Rear leg room, min., in.	35.0

Powertrain layout: transverse front engine/front-wheel drive.

Prices are accurate at time of publication; subject to manufacturer's change.

Engines

	dohc I-4	dohc V-6
Size, liters/cu. in.	2.2/132	3.0/180
Fuel delivery	PFI	PFI
Horsepower @ rpm	135 @ 5400	185 @ 5200
Torque (lbs./ft.) @ rpm	145 @ 4400	195 @ 4400
Availability	S	O
EPA city/highway mpg		
5-speed OD manual	22/29	19/26
4-speed OD automatic	21/27	18/25

Assembly points: Georgetown, Ky.; Tsutsumi, Japan.

Prices

Toyota Camry	Retail Price	Dealer Invoice	Low Price
DLX 4-door notchback, 5-speed	$14368	—	—
DLX 4-door notchback, automatic	15168	—	—
LE 4-door notchback, automatic	16998	—	—
XLE 4-door notchback, automatic	18848	—	—
DLX V6 4-door notchback, automatic	16808	—	—
LE V6 4-door notchback, automatic	18638	—	—
XLE V6 4-door notchback, automatic	20508	—	—

Dealer invoice and low price not available at time of publication.

Dealer invoice and destination charge may vary by region.

Standard equipment:

DLX: 2.2-liter DOHC 16-valve PFI 4-cylinder engine, 5-speed manual or 4-speed automatic transmission, driver-side air bag, power steering, tachometer, coolant temperature gauge, trip odometer, cloth reclining front bucket seats, split folding rear seat with armrest, remote fuel door and decklid releases, rear defogger, dual outside mirrors, front door pockets, tilt steering column, intermittent wipers, AM/FM radio, tinted glass, 195/70HR14 tires. **LE adds:** power mirrors, 5-way adjustable driver's seat, cruise control, power windows and locks, air conditioning, cassette player. **XLE** adds: power moonroof, 7-way power driver-seat lumbar support adjuster, illuminated entry, map lights, lighted visor mirrors, variable-intermittent wipers, alloy wheels.

Optional equipment:

Anti-lock brakes, 4-cyl.	1245	—	—
V6	1130	—	—

	Retail Price	Dealer Invoice	Low Price
Air conditioning	870	—	—
Leather trim, XLE	950	—	—
Alloy wheels, LE.	400	—	—
LE V6	420	—	—
Moonroof, LE	900	—	—
Includes map lights.			
Cruise control, DLX	230	—	—
AM/FM cassette, DLX	150	—	—
Includes power antenna.			
Premium AM/FM cassette, LE & XLE	290	—	—
Includes power antenna.			
CD player, XLE	990	—	—
California emissions pkg.	100	—	—

Toyota Celica

Toyota Celica GT-S 3-door

All models get a restyled nose and new taillamps and the GT is now available with anti-lock brakes. Also, wheel diameter increases on the ST from 13 inches to 14, and on the GT from 14 inches to 15. GT models also gain standard front fog lamps and a rear spoiler, and—except on the convertible—ABS as an option. ABS remains optional on all others except the ST. All STs are 2-door coupes with a 103-horsepower 1.6-liter 4-cylinder engine. The GT adds a 3-door hatchback and 2-door convertible with a 135-horsepower 2.2 four. The GT-S has the 2.2 and is a hatchback. Celica All-Trac Turbo is a hatchback with a 200-horsepower

Prices are accurate at time of publication; subject to manufacturer's change.

turbocharged 2.0 four and permanently engaged 4-wheel drive; all other Celicas have front-wheel drive. Manual transmission is standard; automatic is optional except on All-Trac Turbo. A driver-side air bag is standard. The ST feels underpowered with automatic and is no more than adequate with the 5-speed. GTs are quite lively with manual and responsive even with automatic. All have capable handling and roadholding; GT and GT-S are quite sporty. The All-Trac has tenacious grip and abundant power. The convertible suffers fewer body quivers than most ragtops. Celica occupants feel bumps, but in ride comfort and overall feel, these are as refined as any car in the class, though some testers say tire roar and exhaust noise are intrusive on long trips. The dash is a model of efficiency, but the cabin has a closed-in feeling and subpar visibility. Tall drivers must recline the seatback for adequate head room, while the rear seat is for small kids. The rather large cargo area suffers from a high liftover.

Specifications

	2-door notchback	3-door hatchback	2-door conv.
Wheelbase, in.	99.4	99.4	99.4
Overall length, in.	176.0	173.6	176.0
Overall width, in.	67.1	67.1	67.1
Overall height, in.	50.6	50.6	50.6
Curb weight, lbs.	2447	2646[1]	2844
Cargo vol., cu. ft.	12.6	24.7	12.6
Fuel capacity, gals.	15.9	15.9[2]	15.9
Seating capacity	4	4	4
Front head room, in.	37.7	37.7	37.7
Front leg room, max., in.	42.9	42.9	42.9
Rear head room, in.	33.0	33.0	33.0
Rear leg room, min., in.	26.8	26.8	26.8

1. 3219 lbs., All-Trac.   2. 18.0, All-Trac.

Powertrain layout: transverse front engine/front-wheel drive or permanent 4WD (All-Trac).

Engines	dohc l-4	dohc l-4	Turbo dohc l-4
Size, liters/cu. in.	1.6/97	2.2/132	2.0/122
Fuel delivery	PFI	PFI	PFI
Horsepower @ rpm	103 @ 6000	135 @ 5400	200 @ 6000

	dohc I-4	dohc I-4	Turbo dohc I-4
Torque (lbs./ft.) @ rpm	102 @ 3200	140 @ 4400	200 @ 3200
Availability	S[1]	S[2]	S[3]

EPA city/highway mpg

5-speed OD manual	25/32	22/29	19/24
4-speed OD automatic	24/31	21/28	

1. ST. 2. GT, GT-S. 3. All-Trac.

Assembly point: Tahara, Japan.

Prices

Toyota Celica	Retail Price	Dealer Invoice	Low Price
ST 2-door notchback, 5-speed	$13378	—	—
ST 2-door notchback, automatic	14088	—	—
GT 2-door notchback, 5-speed	15708	—	—
GT 2-door notchback, automatic	16418	—	—
GT 2-door convertible, 5-speed	20468	—	—
GT 2-door convertible, automatic	21178	—	—
GT 3-door hatchback, 5-speed	15838	—	—
GT 3-door hatchback, automatic	16548	—	—
GT-S 3-door hatchback, 5-speed	17328	—	—
GT-S 3-door hatchback, automatic	18128	—	—
All-Trac Turbo 3-door hatchback, 5-speed .	22048	—	—

Dealer invoice and low price not available at time of publication.
Dealer invoice and destination charge may vary by region.

Standard equipment:

ST: 1.6-liter DOHC 16-valve PFI 4-cylinder engine, 5-speed manual or 4-speed automatic transmission, power steering, driver-side air bag, cloth reclining front bucket seats, center console with armrest, dual cup holders, rear defogger, remote fuel door and decklid/hatch releases, coolant temperature gauge, tachometer, trip odometer, intermittent wipers, tinted glass, dual outside mirrors, AM/FM radio, 185/70R14 tires with full-size spare. **GT** adds: 2.2-liter engine, power antenna, power mirrors, tilt steering column, bodyside moldings, 50/50 split folding rear seat, cargo cover (3-door), full wheel covers, 185/65R15 tires; **convertible** has power top, power rear quarter windows. **GT-S** adds: 4-wheel disc brakes, front air dam with fog lights, rear spoiler, voltmeter, cassette player, sport seats, tilt/telescopic steering column with memory, variable-intermittent wipers, 215/50VR15 tires on alloy wheels. **All-Trac Turbo** adds: 2.0-liter turbocharged, intercooled engine, permanent 4-wheel drive, power windows and locks, tilt steering column, rear wiper/washer, cruise control.

Prices are accurate at time of publication; subject to manufacturer's change.

Optional equipment:	Retail Price	Dealer Invoice	Low Price
Anti-lock brakes, GT 2-door	1360	NA	—
GT & GT-S 3-door	1360	NA	—
All-Trac	1130	NA	—
Includes cruise control (std. All-Trac).			
Manual air conditioning, ST & GT	870	NA	—
Automatic climate control, GT-S & All-Trac .	1050	NA	—
Alloy wheels, GT	420	NA	—
GT Convertible	400	NA	—
Power Pkg., GT & GT-S	450	NA	—
Power windows and locks.			
Leather trim, GT 2-door	1420	NA	—
GT-S	1175	NA	—
All-Trac	1120	NA	—
Includes power driver's seat, power windows and locks; not available on convertible.			
Sunroof	700	NA	—
Cruise control, ST/GT 2-doors, GT-S 3-door	230	NA	—
GT 3-door	365	NA	—
Includes variable-intermittent wipers, rear wiper/washer (3-doors).			
Cassette player, ST	150	NA	—
GT	180	NA	—
Includes four speakers with ST, six speakers with GT.			
Premium audio system w/cassette, GT exc.			
conv.	470	NA	—
Conv.	430	NA	—
GT-S & All-Trac	290	NA	—
Premium audio system w/CD, GT exc. conv.	1375	NA	—
Conv.	1305	NA	—
GT-S & All-Trac	1195	NA	—
CQ Convenience Pkg., ST	140	NA	—
Tilt steering column, driver-seat height adjustment.			
Value Pkg., GT 2-door	995	NA	—
GT 3-door	1130	NA	—
GT-S	2125	NA	—
GT & GT-S: power windows and locks, cruise control, air conditioning, cassette player, variable-intermittent wipers, floormats. GT-S: sunroof, anti-lock brakes, automatic climate control.			

Toyota Corolla

The LE sedan is no longer offered with manual transmission, and the 2-door coupe body style is replaced in Toyota's lineup by the Paseo (see separate report). Corolla returns as a 4-door in base, Deluxe, and LE trim, and as a 5-door

1991 Toyota Corolla DX wagon

wagon in Deluxe dress. All have front-wheel drive except the All-Trac wagon, which has permanently engaged 4-wheel drive. All have a 102-horsepower 1.6-liter 4-cylinder engine. Manual transmission is standard, automatic is optional (it's standard on the LE sedan). The sedan shares its design with the Geo Prizm and some are built alongside the Prizm at a Toyota-General Motors plant in California. Corolla's suspension soaks up rough roads with impressive resiliency. Acceleration is pretty uninspired, and it's hurt more by an automatic transmission that's too anxious to shift into the higher gears, and downshifts harshly after a delay. The engine growls loudly in acceleration, exhaust noise is noticeable even when cruising, and tire rumble isn't at all well muffled. The soft suspension that does so much for ride allows ample body lean in corners and gets little help from the skinny tires. The cabin is roomier than many rivals', but the bucket seats don't have much rearward travel, so tall drivers might be cramped. And rear leg room is short unless the front seats are well forward. The gauges are unobstructed and the high-mounted controls are easy to reach while driving. Along with its Prizm clone, Corolla is functional, economical, well-built and should be reliable. The wagon enhances its utility appeal, especially in All-Trac form.

Prices are accurate at time of publication; subject to manufacturer's change.

Specifications

	4-door notchback	5-door wagon
Wheelbase, in.	95.7	95.7
Overall length, in.	170.3	171.5
Overall width, in.	65.2	65.2
Overall height, in.	52.4	54.5
Curb weight, lbs.	2253	2299[1]
Cargo vol., cu. ft.	12.7	64.5
Fuel capacity, gals.	13.2	13.2
Seating capacity	5	5
Front head room, in.	38.4	39.6
Front leg room, max., in.	40.9	40.9
Rear head room, in.	36.4	39.3
Rear leg room, min., in.	31.6	31.6

1. 2639 lbs., All-Trac.

Powertrain layout: transverse front engine/front-wheel drive or permanent 4WD (All-Trac).

Engines

	dohc I-4
Size, liters/cu. in.	1.6/97
Fuel delivery	PFI
Horsepower @ rpm	102 @ 5800
Torque (lbs./ft.) @ rpm	101 @ 4800
Availability	S

EPA city/highway mpg

5-speed OD manual	28/33
3-speed automatic	26/29
4-speed OD automatic	26/33

Assembly points: Fremont, Calif.; Cambridge, Ontario, Canada; Takaoka, Japan.

Prices

Toyota Corolla	Retail Price	Dealer Invoice	Low Price
4-door notchback, 5-speed	$9418	—	—
4-door notchback, automatic	9918	—	—
Deluxe 4-door notchback, 5-speed	10408	—	—
Deluxe 4-door notchback, automatic	10908	—	—
LE 4-door notchback, automatic	12598	—	—

	Retail Price	Dealer Invoice	Low Price
Deluxe 5-door wagon, 5-speed	11078	—	—
Deluxe 5-door wagon, automatic	11578	—	—
Deluxe All-Trac wagon, 5-speed	12688	—	—
Deluxe All-Trac wagon, automatic	13498	—	—

Dealer invoice and low price not available at time of publication.

Dealer invoice and destination charge may vary by region.

Standard equipment:

1.6-liter DOHC 16-valve PFI 4-cylinder engine, 5-speed manual or 3-speed automatic transmission, door-mounted automatic front shoulder belts, cloth reclining front bucket seats, console with storage, coolant temperature gauge, trip odometer, door pockets, 155SR13 tires. **Deluxe** adds: rear defogger, remote fuel door and decklid releases, intermittent wipers, split folding rear seat (wagon). **All-Trac wagon** has permanent 4-wheel drive, 5-speed manual or 4-speed automatic transmission, mud guards, rear wiper, 165SR13 tires. **LE** adds: 4-speed automatic transmission, power steering, dual remote mirrors, AM/FM radio, 6-way driver's seat with lumbar support adjustment, split folding rear seatback, tachometer, tilt steering column, full wheel covers, 175/70SR13 tires.

Optional equipment:

	Retail Price	Dealer Invoice	Low Price
Air conditioning	820	NA	NA
Power steering (std. LE)	250	NA	NA
Alloy wheels, LE	410	NA	NA
Includes 175/70R13 tires, mud guards.			
Exterior Appearance Pkg., Deluxe 4-door & All-Trac	85	NA	NA
Tilt steering column, Deluxe & All-Trac . .	120	NA	NA
Sunroof, Deluxe, LE, & All-Trac	550	NA	NA
Includes map lights, visor mirrors.			
Fabric seats, wagons	70	NA	NA
Rear wiper, 2WD wagon	135	NA	NA
Audio Accommodation Pkg., All-Trac	115	NA	NA
AM/FM radio w/2 speakers, wagons	210	NA	NA
AM/FM radio w/4 speakers (std. LE; NA wagon)	340	NA	NA
AM/FM cassette w/2 speakers, 2WD wagon .	390	NA	NA
All-Trac	490	NA	NA
w/4 speakers, base & Deluxe 4-doors . .	490	NA	NA
w/4 speakers, LE	150	NA	NA
Power Pkg., LE	560	NA	NA
Power windows and locks.			
Tachometer, Deluxe w/5-speed, All-Trac . .	60	NA	NA
Cruise control, Deluxe & LE	230	NA	NA
Includes variable-intermittent wipers.			

Prices are accurate at time of publication; subject to manufacturer's change.

	Retail Price	Dealer Invoice	Low Price
Split folding rear seat, Deluxe 4-door . . .	110	NA	NA
Value Pkg., Deluxe 4-door	514	NA	NA
2WD wagon	524	NA	NA
All-Trac	580	NA	NA
LE	719	NA	NA

Deluxe: power steering, AM/FM cassette with 4 speakers (4-door; 2 speakers on wagon), digital clock, split folding rear seat, floormats, fabric seats (wagon). LE adds: air conditioning, power windows and locks, cruise control, variable-intermittent wipers, floormats.

	Retail Price	Dealer Invoice	Low Price
Two-tone paint, All-Trac	235	NA	NA
All Weather Guard Pkg., base 4-door . . .	160	NA	NA
2WD wagon	190	NA	NA
Deluxe & LE 4-doors	55	NA	NA

HD battery, rear defogger, HD heater and boost ventilator, rear wiper (2WD wagon).

	Retail Price	Dealer Invoice	Low Price
California emissions pkg.	75	NA	NA

Toyota Cressida

Toyota Cressida

Toyota's rear-drive premium sedan is unchanged for 1992. Cressida comes only as a 4-door notchback sedan in one trim level. Its 190-horsepower 3.0-liter 6-cylinder engine is derived from the inline-6 used in the Supra sports car. A 4-speed automatic with electronic shift controls is the only transmission. Anti-lock brakes are optional; a driver-side air bag is not offered. Cressida is one of the more conservatively styled cars in its class, and one of the very few with rear-wheel drive. The upright body design doesn't translate into a wealth of usable passenger room; both the Acura Legend and Nissan Maxima are larger inside, for example. And its trunk space is paltry for this market. Acceleration is competitive with most in the class, however, and the engine is very quiet. Cressida's transmission does its part with prompt, smooth shifts up and down the speed range. Braking is good, and exceptional with the optional ABS. The rear-drive configuration gives up some wet-weather traction, though overall, handling and grip are predictable, and more than adequate for Cressida's mission. So is the firm but supple ride. Simple, feather-touch controls, comfortable seats, and good outward visibility are interior highlights.

Specifications

	4-door notchback
Wheelbase, in.	105.6
Overall length, in.	189.6
Overall width, in.	67.3
Overall height, in.	54.5
Curb weight, lbs.	3439
Cargo vol., cu. ft.	12.5
Fuel capacity, gals.	18.5
Seating capacity	5
Front head room, in.	38.4
Front leg room, max., in.	42.8
Rear head room, in.	37.1
Rear leg room, min., in.	35.0

Powertrain layout: longitudinal front engine/rear-wheel drive.

Engines	dohc I-6
Size, liters/cu. in.	3.0/180
Fuel delivery	PFI
Horsepower @ rpm	190 @ 5600
Torque (lbs./ft.) @ rpm	185 @ 4400
Availability	S

EPA city/highway mpg	
4-speed OD automatic	19/24

Assembly point: Motomachi, Japan.

Prices are accurate at time of publication; subject to manufacturer's change.

Prices

Toyota Cressida	Retail Price	Dealer Invoice	Low Price
4-door notchback	$23488	—	—

Dealer invoice and low price not available at time of publication.

Dealer invoice and destination charge may vary by region.

Standard equipment:

3.0-liter DOHC 24-valve PFI 6-cylinder engine, 4-speed automatic transmission, power steering, 4-wheel disc brakes, motorized front shoulder belts, automatic climate control, reclining front bucket seats, cruise control, variable-intermittent wipers, trip odometer, coolant temperature gauge, tachometer, AM/FM cassette with EQ, diversity power antenna, power windows and locks, heated power mirrors, tilt/telescopic steering column, theft-deterrent system, 205/60R15 tires.

Optional equipment:

Anti-lock brakes	1130	NA	NA
Power glass moonroof	900	NA	NA
Includes map lights.			
Power Seat Pkg.	880	NA	NA
NA with leather seats.			
Leather seats	1830	NA	NA
CD player	700	NA	NA
California emissions pkg.	100	NA	NA

Toyota MR2

Toyota's mid-engine, rear-drive 2-seat MR2 returns unchanged as a base model with a 130-horsepower 2.2-liter 4-cylinder engine and a turbocharged version with a 200-horsepower 2.0-liter four. Manual transmission is standard; automatic is optional for non-turbos. A driver-side air bag is standard; anti-lock brakes are optional. The chief advantage of a mid-engine design is a near-even weight distribution for enhanced balance and handling. Indeed, MR2 corners flatly and is very responsive in changes of direction. Pour on the power too early in a turn, however, and MR2's tail snaps sideways with little warning, especially on wet pavement and particularly in the turbo model. Access to the engine is limited, cargo space is slim, and with the

Toyota MR2

engine directly behind the passenger compartment, you hear plenty of mechanical noise. Acceleration with the base 2.2 four is quite satisfying. The turbo is a seriously fast car, but we'd have trouble spending the extra money for it. Power is best above 3000 rpm with either engine, so we prefer manual transmission for spirited driving. Stopping power is good with the standard 4-wheel disc brakes, though we wouldn't be without the ABS. A short wheelbase, stiff springs, and limited suspension travel make the ride choppy. There's plenty of shoulder and leg room, though those over 6-feet tall brush the headliner with the space-robbing T-tops or removable sunroof. Visibility is poor over the shoulders. Instruments and controls are simple and convenient. Overall, a fast, fun, solid sports car.

Specifications

	2-door notchback
Wheelbase, in.	94.5
Overall length, in.	164.2
Overall width, in.	66.9
Overall height, in.	48.8
Curb weight, lbs.	2559[1]
Cargo vol., cu. ft.	6.6
Fuel capacity, gals.	14.3
Seating capacity	2
Front head room, in.	37.5
Front leg room, max., in.	43.3

Prices are accurate at time of publication; subject to manufacturer's change.

	2-door notchback
Rear head room, in.	—
Rear leg room, min., in.	—

1. 2758 lbs., Turbo.

Powertrain layout: transverse mid engine/rear-wheel drive.

Engines	dohc I-4	Turbo dohc I-4
Size, liters/cu. in.	2.2/132	2.0/122
Fuel delivery	PFI	PFI
Horsepower @ rpm	130 @ 5400	200 @ 6000
Torque (lbs./ft.) @ rpm	140 @ 4400	200 @ 3200
Availability	S	S
EPA city/highway mpg		
5-speed OD manual	22/28	20/27
4-speed OD automatic	22/29	

Assembly point: Sagamihara, Japan.

Prices

Toyota MR2	Retail Price	Dealer Invoice	Low Price
2-door notchback, 5-speed	$16048	—	—
2-door notchback, automatic	16848	—	—
2-door notchback w/T-bar roof, 5-speed . .	16998	—	—
Turbo 2-door notchback, 5-speed	19378	—	—
Turbo w/T-bar roof, 5-speed	20278	—	—

Dealer invoice and low price not available at time of publication.

Dealer invoice and destination charge may vary by region.

Standard equipment:

2.2-liter DOHC 16-valve PFI 4-cylinder engine, 5-speed manual or 4-speed automatic transmission, 4-wheel disc brakes, driver-side air bag, cloth reclining bucket seats, tilt steering column, AM/FM radio, tachometer, coolant temperature gauge, trip odometer, 195/60HR14 front and 205/60HR14 rear tires on alloy wheels. **Turbo** adds: 2.0-liter turbocharged engine, AM/FM cassette, power mirrors, rear spoiler, V-rated tires.

Optional equipment:

Anti-lock brakes	1130	NA	—
Electro-hydraulic power steering	600	NA	—

	Retail Price	Dealer Invoice	Low Price
Air conditioning	NA	NA	NA
Pop-up/removable sunroof	380	NA	—
Power Pkg., base	575	NA	—
Turbo	465	NA	—
Power windows and locks, power mirrors (std. Turbo).			
Cruise control & intermittent wipers	265	NA	—
Rear spoiler, base	225	NA	—
Theft deterrent system	165	NA	—
Alloy wheels, base	400	NA	—
Leather Trim Pkg., base	1750	NA	—
Turbo	1275	NA	—
Seven-way leather seats, leather interior trim, power windows and locks, power mirrors, center storage box.			
AM/FM cassette, base	260	NA	—
Premium AM/FM cassette, base	635	NA	—
Base w/T-bar roof	570	NA	—
Turbo	310	NA	—
Includes seven speakers, biamplified woofer, power antenna.			
Premium AM/FM cassette w/CD player, base	1335	NA	—
Base w/T-bar roof	1270	NA	—
Turbo	1010	NA	—
California emissions pkg.	100	NA	—

Toyota Paseo

The front-drive Paseo replaces the 2-door Corollas in Toyota's lineup. It's smaller and less expensive than the Celica and competes against such coupes as the Geo Storm and Hyundai Scoupe. Paseo is derived from the subcompact Tercel and shares its wheelbase and 1.5-liter 4-cylinder engine, though horsepower here is 100, 12 more than in Tercel. Manual transmission is standard, automatic is optional. Paseo has a firmer suspension than Tercel and standard 14-inch wheels instead of 13s. Power steering, tachometer, and folding rear seat are standard. Acceleration is more than adequate with manual transmission. Automatics aren't as peppy, but fuel economy is excellent with either gearbox. The ride is pleasantly supple and controlled. Paseo feels agile and competent in most maneuvers, though tight turns bring on lots of body lean and plowing from the front tires. The engine vibrates under

Prices are accurate at time of publication; subject to manufacturer's change.

Toyota Paseo

throttle, there's an annoying exhaust resonance around 4000 rpm, and tires roar and the body drums on coarse pavement. The back seat holds only toddlers. The front buckets are comfortable, but tall people may be short of front leg room, and there's no excess head space, especially with the optional sunroof. A simple dashboard is marred by a steering wheel that's mounted too high and doesn't tilt. Thick roof pillars hinder over-the-shoulder visibility. The trunk is good sized for this class, but the opening narrows at the bumper, which complicates packing. Smaller and noisier than the 2-door Corollas it replaces, Paseo's strengths are excellent highway mileage, a comfortable ride, and pretty good value for the money.

Specifications

	2-door notchback
Wheelbase, in.	93.7
Overall length, in.	163.2
Overall width, in.	65.2
Overall height, in.	50.2
Curb weight, lbs.	2075
Cargo vol., cu. ft.	7.7
Fuel capacity, gals.	11.9
Seating capacity	4
Front head room, in.	37.7
Front leg room, max., in.	41.1

	2-door notchback
Rear head room, in.	32.0
Rear leg room, min., in.	30.0

Powertrain layout: transverse front engine/front-wheel drive.

Engines

	dohc I-4
Size, liters/cu. in.	1.5/90
Fuel delivery	PFI
Horsepower @ rpm	100 @ 6400
Torque (lbs./ft.) @ rpm	91 @ 3200
Availability	S

EPA city/highway mpg

5-speed OD manual	28/34
4-speed OD automatic	26/32

Assembly point: Takaoka, Japan.

Prices

Toyota Paseo	Retail Price	Dealer Invoice	Low Price
2-door notchback, 5-speed	$10338	—	—
2-door notchback, automatic	11138	—	—

Dealer invoice and low price not available at time of publication.

Dealer invoice and destination charge may vary by region.

Standard equipment:

1.5-liter DOHC 16-valve PFI 4-cylinder engine, 5-speed manual or 4-speed automatic transmission, power steering, automatic front shoulder belts, cloth sport seats, tinted glass, tachometer, trip odometer, digital clock, intermittent wipers, AM/FM radio, rear defogger, cup holders, remote trunk and fuel door openers, folding rear seat, full wheel covers, 175/65R14 tires.

Optional equipment:

Air conditioning	800	NA	—
Cruise control	230	NA	—
Glass sunroof	380	NA	—
AM/FM cassette w/4 speakers	280	NA	—
All Weather Guard Pkg	55	46	—
HD battery, rear defogger w/timer, heater.			
Alloy wheels	455	NA	—
Includes 185/60R14 all-season tires.			

Prices are accurate at time of publication; subject to manufacturer's change.

	Retail Price	Dealer Invoice	Low Price
Rear spoiler	285	NA	—
185/60R14 tires	55	NA	—
California emissions	75	NA	—

Toyota Previa

Toyota Previa Deluxe

Previa gains a standard driver-side air bag, under-dash knee bolsters, and a center stoplamp to become the first minivan to meet all passenger-car safety standards. Introduced last year, Previa returns in Deluxe and top-line LE versions. Both are available with rear-wheel drive or permanently engaged 4-wheel drive, called All-Trac. The only engine is a 138-horsepower 2.4-liter 4-cylinder mounted below the front seats. Manual transmission is standard on Deluxe models; automatic is optional on Deluxe and standard on LE. Anti-lock brakes now are optional on Deluxe as well as LE models; power windows, locks and mirrors are standard on LE; and the optional middle captain's chairs now swivel 180 degrees. Previa easily keeps pace with traffic around town, but there's too little power for quick passing above about 40 mph. The engine is somewhat coarse. The heavier All-Tracs are a bit less responsive, but have better wet-weather traction than rear-drive versions. Previa is stable on the road and easily absorbs most bumps. Getting in or out is easy. The roomy cabin holds seven without cramping and has adequate cargo space with all seats in place. You must stoop over the engine bulge to move from the front seats to the rear. The split rear bench hinges outward, a clever alternative to removable seats. Climate-system switches are poorly marked, and it's easy to accidentally hit the "Overdrive Off" button on the tip of the automatic-transmission lever. Previa is even more attractive with the new safety features. But powertrain harshness remains a weak point, and the LE models are pricey, so look for a Deluxe.

Specifications

	4-door van
Wheelbase, in.	112.8
Overall length, in.	187.0
Overall width, in.	70.8
Overall height, in.	68.7
Curb weight, lbs.	3455[1]
Cargo vol., cu. ft.	157.8
Fuel capacity, gals.	19.8
Seating capacity	7
Front head room, in.	39.4
Front leg room, max., in.	40.1
Rear head room, in.	38.5
Rear leg room, min., in.	36.6

1. 3670 lbs., All-Trac.

Powertrain layout: longitudinal mid engine/rear-wheel drive or permanently engaged 4WD.

Engines

	dohc I-4
Size, liters/cu. in.	2.4/149
Fuel delivery	PFI
Horsepower @ rpm	138 @ 5000
Torque (lbs./ft.) @ rpm	154 @ 4000
Availability	S

EPA city/highway mpg

5-speed OD manual	18/22
4-speed OD automatic	17/22

Assembly point: Kariya, Japan.

Prices are accurate at time of publication; subject to manufacturer's change.

Prices

Toyota Previa	Retail Price	Dealer Invoice	Low Price
Deluxe 2WD, 5-speed	$16518	$14123	$15321
Deluxe 2WD, automatic	17318	14807	16063
LE 2WD, automatic	21448	18231	19840
Deluxe All-Trac, 5-speed	19128	16259	17694
Deluxe All-Trac, automatic	20018	17015	18517
LE All-Trac, automatic	24058	20449	22254

Dealer invoice and destination charge may vary by region.

Standard equipment:

Deluxe: 2.4-liter DOHC 16-valve PFI 4-cylinder engine, 5-speed manual or 4-speed automatic transmission, driver-side air bag, power steering, tilt steering column, cloth reclining front bucket seats, 3-passenger middle seat, tinted glass, digital clock, dual outside mirrors, bodyside moldings, full carpet, full wheel covers, P205/75R14 tires. **LE** adds: dual air conditioning, 4-wheel disc brakes, power windows and locks, power mirrors, fold-down third seat, cruise control, rear defogger, power locks, AM/FM radio, intermittent wipers, P215/65R15 tires with full-size spare.

Optional equipment:

Anti-lock brakes, Deluxe	1405	1124	1265
LE	1130	904	1017
Dual air conditioning, Deluxe	1500	1200	1350
Convenience Pkg., Deluxe	710	568	639
Rear defogger, fold-down third seat.			
Power Pkg., Deluxe	655	524	590
Power windows and locks, power mirrors.			
Rear wiper & cruise control, Deluxe w/5-speed	455	367	411
Deluxe w/automatic	395	319	357
Privacy glass, LE	365	292	329
Cruise control, Deluxe w/5-speed	300	240	270
Includes tachometer.			
Deluxe w/automatic	240	192	216
AM/FM cassette, Deluxe	530	397	464
LE	190	142	166
Premium AM/FM cassette, LE	500	375	438
Premium AM/FM cassette w/CD, LE	1230	922	1076
Dual sunroofs, LE	1470	1176	1323
Captain's chairs w/armrests, LE	750	600	675
Fold-down third seat, Deluxe	600	480	540
Theft deterrent system, Deluxe	165	132	149
LE	410	328	369
Alloy wheels, LE	420	336	378

Toyota Supra

Toyota Supra Turbo

Revised shift points for the optional automatic transmission is the only change of note to this rear-drive 2+2. Supra carries on as a base coupe with a 200-horsepower 3.0-liter inline 6-cylinder engine or as a coupe or targa-top SportRoof model with a turbocharged 3.0 rated at 232 horsepower. A 5-speed manual transmission is standard; a 4-speed automatic is optional, and Toyota says its new shift points improve performance and smoothness. A driver-side air bag is standard. Anti-lock brakes are standard on Turbo, optional on base. Introduced as a 1986 model, the current Supra is ancient compared to its primary rival, the Nissan 300ZX, which was redesigned for 1990. Toyota reportedly will introduce a redesigned new-generation Supra for 1993, but the current model still has its appeal. With a base curb weight of nearly 3500 pounds, Supra's more of a grand-touring machine than a pure sports car. It's not really nimble around town, but wide tires and a low stance give it impressive cornering power, and the firm suspension confidently tackles demanding roads. Rear drive and wide tires doom it to poor traction in snow, however, and even in rain, it takes a sensitive throttle foot to keep the rear end from slipping sideways in turns. Engine and wind noise are low on the highway, but road noise is high, partly because of the aggressive tire tread. Entry and exit are compromised by Supra's low build and doors that need a lot of space to open. Once aboard, you'll find supportive front seats, a comfortable driving position, simple gauges, and conve-

Prices are accurate at time of publication; subject to manufacturer's change.

nient controls. The child-sized rear seat is there for those who can't justify buying a strict 2-seater, but even with the rear seats folded, the cargo area is shallow.

Specifications

	3-door hatchback
Wheelbase, in.	102.2
Overall length, in.	181.9
Overall width, in.	68.7
Overall height, in.	51.2
Curb weight, lbs.	3463
Cargo vol., cu. ft.	12.8
Fuel capacity, gals.	18.5
Seating capacity	4
Front head room, in.	37.5
Front leg room, max., in.	43.6
Rear head room, in.	33.9
Rear leg room, min., in.	24.7

Powertrain layout: longitudinal front engine/rear-wheel drive.

Engines

	dohc I-6	Turbo dohc I-6
Size, liters/cu. in.	3.0/180	3.0/180
Fuel delivery	PFI	PFI
Horsepower @ rpm	200 @ 6000	232 @ 5600
Torque (lbs./ft.) @ rpm	188 @ 3600	254 @ 3200
Availability	S	S

EPA city/highway mpg

5-speed OD manual	18/23	17/23
4-speed OD automatic	18/23	18/23

Assembly point: Tahara, Japan.

Prices

Toyota Supra	Retail Price	Dealer Invoice	Low Price
3-door hatchback, 5-speed	$25280	—	—
3-door hatchback, automatic	26080	—	—
Turbo 3-door hatchback, 5-speed	28750	—	—
Turbo 3-door hatchback, automatic	29550	—	—

	Retail Price	Dealer Invoice	Low Price
Turbo w/SportRoof, 5-speed	29770	—	—
Turbo w/SportRoof, automatic	30570	—	—

Dealer invoice and low price not available at time of publication.

Dealer invoice and destination charge may vary by region.

Standard equipment:

3.0-liter DOHC 24-valve PFI 6-cylinder engine, 5- speed manual or 4-speed automatic transmission, power steering, 4-wheel disc brakes, driver-side air bag, automatic climate control, power windows and locks, heated power mirrors, cupholder, tilt/telescopic steering column, fog lights, theft deterrent system, bodyside moldings, tachometer, coolant temperature and oil pressure gauges, voltmeter, trip odometer, variable intermittent wipers, cruise control, console with storage and padded armrest, cloth sport seats, driver's seat power lumbar and lateral support adjustments, folding rear seatbacks, lighted visor mirrors, remote fuel door and hatch releases, illuminated entry system, tinted glass, rear defogger, cargo cover, AM/FM cassette with EQ, diversity power antenna, 225/50ZR16 Goodyear Eagle GS-D tires on alloy wheels. **Turbo** adds: turbocharged, intercooled engine, anti-lock brakes, speed-sensitive power steering, oil cooler, turbo boost gauge, limited-slip differential.

Optional equipment:

Anti-lock brakes (std. Turbo)	1130	NA	—
Sports Pkg., base	795	NA	—
Turbo	360	NA	—
Limited-slip differential, speed-sensitive power steering, electronically modulated suspension.			
White Appearance Pkg.	40	NA	—
Leather Trim Pkg.	1100	NA	—
CD player	680	NA	—
CD player w/sub-woofer	825	NA	—
Sunroof	700	NA	—
California emissions pkg.	100	NA	—

Toyota Tercel

Toyota's least-expensive model was redesigned for 1991 and returns unchanged. The 2-door comes in entry-level Standard trim and mid-line Deluxe guise; the 4-door in Deluxe and top-line LE dress. The only engine is an 82-horsepower 1.5-liter 4-cylinder that drives the front wheels. Manual transmission is mandatory on the Standard model; automatic

Prices are accurate at time of publication; subject to manufacturer's change.

Toyota Tercel DX 2-door

is optional on the others. Acceleration around town is adequate, even with the automatic. Tercel is a little quicker with the easy-shifting manual, though there's never an abundance of passing power. The engine's growl under throttle quiets to a tolerable level at cruising, but most roads bring out lots of tire noise and suspension thumping. Combined with a somewhat harsh ride, Tercel's a poor choice for long-distance travel. Petite dimensions and a tight turning circle are allies in close quarters. The narrow all-season tires have good traction in the wet, though they squeal easily in tight turns on dry pavement. There's ample room in front. Rear-seaters over 5-foot-10 will be cramped. No complaints about the driving position, but some testers say the front seats are too hard. You must take your eyes from the road to tune the low-set radio. Tercel's door-mounted front shoulder belts extend and retract with the doors and make entry/exit awkward when carrying parcels. The trunk has a convenient bumper-height opening and a flat floor. The split folding rear seat standard on LE and optional on the 2-door Deluxe folds down, but doesn't lie flat. Tercel is a well-made, economical subcompact that should be reliable. Deluxe and Standard models offer the best value.

Specifications

	2-door notchback	4-door notchback
Wheelbase, in.	93.7	93.7
Overall length, in.	161.8	161.8

	2-door notchback	4-door notchback
Overall width, in.	64.8	64.8
Overall height, in.	53.2	53.2
Curb weight, lbs.	1950	2005
Cargo vol., cu. ft.	10.7	10.7
Fuel capacity, gals.	11.9	11.9
Seating capacity	5	5
Front head room, in.	38.7	38.2
Front leg room, max., in.	41.2	41.2
Rear head room, in.	36.7	36.1
Rear leg room, min., in.	31.9	31.9

Powertrain layout: transverse front engine/front-wheel drive.

Engines

	ohc I-4
Size, liters/cu. in.	1.5/89
Fuel delivery	PFI
Horsepower @ rpm	82 @ 5200
Torque (lbs./ft.) @ rpm	89 @ 4400
Availability	S

EPA city/highway mpg

4-speed OD manual	32/37
5-speed OD manual	29/36
3-speed automatic	26/29

Assembly point: Takaoka, Japan.

Prices

Toyota Tercel	Retail Price	Dealer Invoice	Low Price
Standard 2-door notchback, 4-speed	$6998	—	—
DX 2-door notchback, 5-speed	8428	—	—
DX 2-door notchback, automatic	8928	—	—
DX 4-door notchback, 5-speed	8528	—	—
DX 4-door notchback, automatic	9028	—	—
LE 4-door notchback, 5-speed	9908	—	—
LE 4-door notchback, automatic	10408	—	—

Dealer invoice and low price not available at time of publication.

Dealer invoice and destination charge may vary by region.

Prices are accurate at time of publication; subject to manufacturer's change.

Standard equipment:

Standard: 1.5-liter PFI 4-cylinder engine, 4-speed manual transmission, door-mounted automatic front shoulder belts, vinyl reclining front bucket seats, coolant temperature gauge, trip odometer, left outside mirror, center console, 145/80R13 tires. **DX** adds: 5-speed manual or 3-speed automatic transmission, fabric upholstery, dual outside mirrors, rear quarter pockets (2-door), 155SR13 tires. **LE** adds: 60/40 folding rear seatback, upgraded upholstery, tinted glass, cupholders, rear defogger, remote mirrors, intermittent wipers, digital clock, remote fuel door and decklid releases, AM/FM radio, bodyside moldings.

Optional equipment:	Retail Price	Dealer Invoice	Low Price
Air conditioning	800	NA	NA
Rear defogger (std. LE)	35	NA	NA
Power steering (NA Standard)	250	NA	NA
Convenience Pkg., DX 2-door	235	NA	NA
Intermittent wipers, digital clock, remote mirrors, 60/40 folding rear seatback, remote fuel door and decklid releases.			
Exterior Appearance Pkg., DX	185	NA	NA
Body-colored bumpers, bodyside molding, tinted glass.			
AM/FM radio w/2 speakers (std. LE)	210	NA	NA
w/4 speakers, DX	340	NA	NA
LE	130	NA	NA
AM/FM cassette w/4 speakers, Deluxe . . .	490	NA	NA
LE	280	NA	NA
Tachometer, LE w/5-speed	60	NA	NA
All Weather Guard Pkg., Standard & DX . .	90	NA	NA
LE	55	NA	NA
HD battery, rear defogger, heater.			
California emissions pkg.	70	NA	NA

Toyota 4Runner

The grille, front bumper, and aero-style headlamps are new, and power steering and a rear wiper/washer are made standard. Plus, this compact sport-utility now stores its spare tire under the rear of the body instead of on an outside carrier. Five-door models offer a 2.4-liter 4-cylinder engine rated at 116 horsepower, or a 3.0-liter V-6 rated at 150. It's available with rear drive or 4-wheel drive, and with manual or automatic transmission. A 3-door model comes only with 4WD, V-6, and manual transmission. The V-6 4×4s have rear anti-lock brakes and 4WDemand,

Toyota 4Runner SR5 5-door

which allows changing in or out of 4WD at speeds up to 50 mph. With the 4-cylinder engine, the vehicle must be stopped to engage 4WD, though 4WDemand and rear ABS are optional. All models have seats for five. Leather trim is a new option on V-6 5-doors. The 4-cylinder is just too weak to move this rather heavy wagon with any authority. Even the V-6 requires lots of throttle to deliver acceptable acceleration. 4Runner rides as comfortably as some cars and takes corners more like a big station wagon than a truck-based sport-utility. However, entry/exit is hampered by one of the tallest step-up heights in the sport-utility field—about two feet. Head room is at a premium for those over six feet, and some occupants say the seats are mounted too low for optimal comfort. Cargo space is good with the rear seat up, generous with it down. The 4Runner enjoys good assembly quality and Toyota's reputation for reliability, but it's pricier, slower, and less roomy than some rivals.

Specifications

	3-door wagon	5-door wagon
Wheelbase, in.	103.3	103.3
Overall length, in.	176.0	176.0
Overall width, in.	66.5	66.5
Overall height, in.	66.1	66.1
Curb weight, lbs.	4050	3740
Cargo vol., cu. ft.	78.3	78.3
Fuel capacity, gals.	17.2	17.2

Prices are accurate at time of publication; subject to manufacturer's change.

	3-door wagon	5-door wagon
Seating capacity	5	5
Front head room, in.	38.7	38.7
Front leg room, max., in.	41.5	41.5
Rear head room, in.	38.3	38.3
Rear leg room, min., in.	31.6	31.6

Powertrain layout: longitudinal front engine/rear-wheel drive or on-demand 4WD.

Engines

	ohc I-4	ohc V-6
Size, liters/cu. in.	2.4/144	3.0/180
Fuel delivery	PFI	PFI
Horsepower @ rpm	116 @ 4800	150 @ 4800
Torque (lbs./ft.) @ rpm	140 @ 2800	180 @ 3400
Availability	S	O[1]

EPA city/highway mpg

5-speed OD manual	19/22	15/18
4-speed OD automatic	18/20	14/16

1. Std. 3-door.

Assembly point: Toyota City, Japan.

Prices

Toyota 4Runner	Retail Price	Dealer Invoice	Low Price
4WD 3-door wagon, V6, 5-speed	$20428	—	—
2WD 5-door wagon, V6, automatic	19198	—	—
4WD 5-door wagon, 5-speed	18018	—	—
4WD 5-door wagon, automatic	19118	—	—
5-door wagon w/4WDemand, 5-speed	18218	—	—
4WD 5-door wagon, V6, 5-speed	19928	—	—
4WD 5-door wagon, V6, automatic	20978	—	—

Dealer invoice and low price not available at time of publication.

Dealer invoice and destination charge may vary by region.

Standard equipment:

2.4-liter PFI 4-cylinder engine, 5-speed manual or 4-speed automatic transmission, rear-wheel drive or on-demand 4WD, power steering, reclining front bucket seats, split folding rear seat, tachometer, coolant temperature and oil pressure gauges voltmeter, trip odometer, remote fuel door release, power tailgate window, rear wiper/washer, 225/75R15 tires. **V6** adds: 3.0-liter PFI V-6, 4WDemand (allows engagment of 4WD at speeds up to 50 mph), anti-lock rear brakes, power steering, intermittent wipers, AM/FM radio, rear defogger, tilt steering column.

Optional equipment:

	Retail Price	Dealer Invoice	Low Price
Anti-lock rear brakes, 4-door w/4-cyl. . . .	250	212	231
Air conditioning, 5-doors	840	—	—
AM/FM radio, w/4-cyl.	340	—	—
AM/FM cassette, 4-cyl.	550	—	—
V6	210	157	184
Premium AM/FM cassette, V6	595	—	—
CD player, V6	1295	—	—
Power antenna, V6	65	—	—
Sunroof	770	—	—
Tilt steering column, 4-cyl.	155	—	—
Alloy wheels & 31" tires, 4WD V6	880	—	—
Alloy wheels w/225/75R15 tires	490	—	—
Chrome Pkg.	230	184	207
Chrome Pkg. 2, V6	230	184	207
Cruise Control Pkg.	310	—	—
Includes Lighting Pkg.			
Cruise Control Pkg. 2, V6 5-doors	255	—	—
Includes leather-wrapped steering wheel.			
Power Pkg., 5-doors	705	—	—
3-door	585	—	—
Power windows and locks, power mirrors.			
Rear heater	150	120	135
Two-Tone Paint Pkg.	430	344	387
Sports Pkg. SX, 5-door	440	352	396
Cloth sport seats, rear privacy glass, Sports Pkg. w/bronze glass.			
V6 5-door	440	352	396
All Weather Guard Pkg., 4WD 4-cyl.	165	134	150
V6	55	46	51
Includes rear defogger and HD battery.			
Leather seat Pkg., V6 4-door	1390	—	—
Includes privacy glass.			
Value Pkg. 1, V6 4-door	1249	—	—
4-cyl. 4-door	1799	—	—
Air conditioning, Chrome Pkg., power windows and locks, power mirrors, cruise control, cassette player (4-cyl.), floormats.			
Value Pkg. 2, V6 4-door	1249	—	—
Value Pkg. 1 plus modified rear chrome bumper; requires alloy wheels.			
Value Pkg. 3, V6 4-door	1194	—	—
Value Pkg. 1 with leather-wrapped steering wheel; requires alloy wheels and leather seats.			

Prices are accurate at time of publication; subject to manufacturer's change.

Volkswagen Cabriolet

Volkswagen Cabriolet Carat

Last year's Etienne Aigner designer edition gets the ax, three-point seat belts replace lap belts in the back seat, the base model gets full wheel covers, and the radio now turns off with the ignition switch. Otherwise, Volkswagen's convertible, now in its 13th season, carries on unchanged. Based on the mid-Seventies Rabbit design that was superceded by the Golf in 1985, it rides a 94.5-inch wheelbase and is powered by a 94-horsepower 1.8-liter four-cylinder engine. A 5-speed manual transmission is standard, a 3-speed automatic optional. Base and up-level Carat versions are available, the latter offering leather interior, cruise control, alloy wheels, and an optional power top. A driver-side air bag is standard, but anti-lock brakes are not available. The age-old design will likely be replaced next year with a version based on the new Golf scheduled to debut in the fall. Despite its age, the Cabriolet makes a pretty good showing of itself. Handling is satisfyingly sporting-like, acceleration is brisk (though much more so with the 5-speed manual than the 3-speed automatic), and aided by its integral roll bar, the body is more rigid than many newer ragtops. Dashboard controls are easy to reach and the seating position is comfortable. However, the top takes up a lot of rear seat room and reduces the trunk to nearly useless proportions. The back seat can be folded down to increase the cargo space, but the roll bar blocks passage to the rear area. The expanse of material at the rear corners limits visibility when the top is up, and it is so tall when it's folded down that shorter drivers can only see the roofs of the cars that are following. Yet despite its drawbacks, the Cabriolet is a fun little car that stacks up well against newer rivals.

Specifications

	2-door conv.
Wheelbase, in.	94.5
Overall length, in.	153.1
Overall width, in.	64.6
Overall height, in.	55.6
Curb weight, lbs.	2307
Cargo vol., cu. ft.	6.5
Fuel capacity, gals.	13.8
Seating capacity	4
Front head room, in.	37.4
Front leg room, max., in.	39.4
Rear head room, in.	33.0
Rear leg room, min., in.	31.8

Powertrain layout: transverse front engine/front-wheel drive .

Engines

	ohc I-4
Size, liters/cu. in.	1.8/109
Fuel delivery	PFI
Horsepower @ rpm	94 @ 5400
Torque (lbs./ft.) @ rpm	100 @ 3000
Availability	S

EPA city/highway mpg

5-speed OD manual	25/32
3-speed automatic	23/28

Assembly point: Onsabrück, Germany.

Prices

Volkswagen Cabriolet	Retail Price	Dealer Invoice	Low Price
2-door convertible	$17320	$15368	$16344
Carat 2-door convertible	18950	16811	17881
Destination charge	370	370	370

Prices are accurate at time of publication; subject to manufacturer's change.

CONSUMER GUIDE®

Standard equipment:

1.8-liter PFI 4-cylinder engine, 5-speed manual transmission, power steering, driver-side air bag, cloth reclining front bucket seats, driver's seat height adjustment, tachometer, coolant temperature gauge, oil temperature and pressure gauges, voltmeter, trip odometer, AM/FM cassette, power windows, door pockets, remote mirrors, intermittent wipers, rear defogger, tinted glass, 185/70HR14 tires. **Carat** adds: leather sport seats, leather-wrapped steering wheel and shift knob, cruise control, alloy wheels.

Optional equipment:	Retail Price	Dealer Invoice	Low Price
3-speed automatic transmission	545	506	526
Air conditioning	860	739	800
Power roof, Carat & Aigner	795	684	740
Metallic paint, base & Carat	170	146	158
California emissions	100	102	100

Volkswagen Corrado

Volkswagen Corrado

Following a short 1992 model run, the front-drive Corrado G60 sport coupe will be replaced by a version boasting a new V-6 powertrain. Until then, the Corrado continues virtually unchanged. Riding a 97.3-inch wheelbase, it comes only as a 3-door hatchback in one trim level with few options. Standard are a supercharged 158-horsepower 1.8-liter 4-cylinder engine, 5-speed manual transmission, and 4-wheel disc brakes. A 4-speed automatic and anti-lock brakes are optional. Corrados come with 205/50VR15 tires on alloy wheels, and an unusual rear spoiler that extends automatically above 45 mph to reduce aerodynamic lift, and retracts when speeds drop below 12 mph. The new version, to be introduced around March of 1992, will carry a narrow-angle V-6 displacing 2.8 liters and rated at 178 horsepower. Standard equipment will include an electronic differential lock, anti-lock brakes, alarm system, velour interior, and restyled hood and grille. The Corrado's super-charged engine doesn't really show its muscle until 3000 rpm or so, which means that the car feels weak coming off the line and when a surge of power is needed around town. However, response on the highway is outstanding. As is expected in a sport coupe, handling is crisp with good cornering grip. Front seats are firm and supportive, front head-room is adequate, but the rear seat has insufficient room for adults. Visibility to the rear is obstructed, particularly when the tail-mounted spoiler pops up at speed. In its current guise, the Corrado is well equipped, but seems pricey compared to others in this league.

Specifications

	3-door hatchback
Wheelbase, in.	97.3
Overall length, in.	159.4
Overall width, in.	65.9
Overall height, in.	51.9
Curb weight, lbs.	2675
Cargo vol., cu. ft.	30.0
Fuel capacity, gals.	14.5
Seating capacity	4
Front head room, in.	37.0
Front leg room, max., in.	41.7
Rear head room, in.	35.0
Rear leg room, min., in.	31.2

Powertrain layout: transverse front engine/front-wheel drive.

Engines

	Supercharged ohc I-4
Size, liters/cu. in.	1.8/109
Fuel delivery	PFI
Horsepower @ rpm	158 @ 5600
Torque (lbs./ft.) @ rpm	166 @ 4000
Availability	S

Prices are accurate at time of publication; subject to manufacturer's change.

	Supercharged ohc I-4
EPA city/highway mpg	
5-speed OD manual	20/28
4-speed OD automatic	19/27

Assembly point: Onsabrück, Germany.

Prices

	Retail Price	Dealer Invoice	Low Price
Volkswagen Corrado			
3-door hatchback	$19860	$17517	$18689
Destination charge	370	370	370

Standard equipment:

1.8-liter supercharged PFI 4-cylinder engine, 5-speed manual transmission, 4-wheel disc brakes, motorized front shoulder belts, velour height-adjustable bucket seats, split folding rear seat, air conditioning, cruise control, power windows and locks, power mirrors, AM/FM cassette, tachometer, coolant temperature and oil pressure gauges, voltmeter, trip odometer, tilt steering column, rear defogger, tinted glass, leather-wrapped steering wheel and shift knob, cargo cover, visor mirrors (lighted right), speed-activated retractable rear spoiler, fog lamps, intermittent wipers, rear wiper/washer, 205/50VR15 tires on alloy wheels.

Optional equipment:

4-speed automatic transmission	795	761	835
Anti-lock brakes	835	852	835
Power sunroof	725	624	675
Alarm system	195	168	182
Leather interior	740	637	689
Metallic paint	170	146	158
California emissions	100	102	100

Volkswagen Fox

Last year Volkswagen dropped the Fox 3-door station wagon and GL Sport model from its entry-level front-wheel-drive subcompact line, leaving just the base 2-door sedan and GL 4-door sedan. Both carry over with few changes for 1992. Riding a 92.8-inch wheelbase, the Fox is powered by an 81-horsepower 1.8-liter four-cylinder engine. Base 2-doors come with a 4-speed manual; GL 4-doors with a 5-

Volkswagen Fox 2-door

speed manual. No automatic transmission is offered. Biggest News for 1992: Volkswagen finally rewired the radio so that it turns off with the ignition. The base Fox offers a bit more flair than most entry-level cars in this class, and the GL adds some worthwhile amenities in addition to two more doors. The GL's 5-speed has closer gear ratios that help in around-town driving, while the base model's 4-speed has a tall top gear that makes shifting down to third mandatory for highway passing. Both models handle with agility, but the manual steering is quite heavy at low speeds, and power steering isn't offered. That and the omission of an automatic transmission option has undoubtedly hurt Fox sales. Inside, leg room is ample in front, adequate in the rear. Head room, however, is tight, and taller drivers may find their heads brushing against the ceiling. Relatively thin, upright roof pillars aid visibility, which is good to all directions. Interior storage space includes a deep glovebox, door map pockets, and a large dashboard shelf. The trunk is rather small, and the spare tire, mounted against one wall, takes up some usable width. Fox has had a hard time competing in a market dominated by Japanese manufacturers, but it is a fun-to-drive subcompact that you may be able to get at a bargain price.

Specifications

	2-door notchback	4-door notchback
Wheelbase, in.	92.8	92.8
Overall length, in.	163.4	163.4

Prices are accurate at time of publication; subject to manufacturer's change.

	2-door notchback	4-door notchback
Overall width, in.	63.0	63.0
Overall height, in.	53.7	53.7
Curb weight, lbs.	2172	2238
Cargo vol., cu. ft.	9.9	9.9
Fuel capacity, gals.	12.4	12.4
Seating capacity	4	4
Front head room, in.	36.6	36.6
Front leg room, max., in.	41.1	41.1
Rear head room, in.	31.9	31.9
Rear leg room, min., in.	30.2	30.2

Powertrain layout: transverse front engine/front-wheel drive.

Engines

	ohc I-4
Size, liters/cu. in.	1.8/109
Fuel delivery	PFI
Horsepower @ rpm	81 @ 5500
Torque (lbs./ft.) @ rpm	93 @ 3250
Availability	S

EPA city/highway mpg

4-speed OD manual	25/32
5-speed OD manual	25/33

Assembly point: Sao Paulo, Brazil.

Prices

Volkswagen Fox	Retail Price	Dealer Invoice	Low Price
2-door notchback	$7370	$6820	$7095
GL 4-door notchback	8560	7787	8174
Destination charge	320	320	320

Standard equipment:

1.8-liter PFI 4-cylinder engine, 4-speed manual transmission, cloth reclining front bucket seats, left remote mirror, rear defogger, intermittent wipers, console with coin box and storage bin, analog clock, 155/80SR13 tires. **GL** adds: 5-speed manual transmission, upgraded carpet, velour upholstery, digital clock, door pockets, map light, tachometer, right visor mirror, tinted glass, wide bodyside molding, 175/70SR13 tires.

Optional equipment:

	Retail Price	Dealer Invoice	Low Price
Air conditioning	715	615	665
Heavy-duty cooling	90	78	84
Metallic paint	165	142	154
AM/FM cassette	430	370	400
Sound system preparation	115	99	107

Volkswagen Golf/Jetta

Volkswagen Jetta Carat

The Jetta's 2-door body style is dropped for 1992, but otherwise, the front-drive Golf and Jetta carry on with few changes. Jetta, now offered only as a 4-door notchback sedan, comes in GL, Carat, and GLI 16V versions. Plus, there's a new diesel version, which VW calls the ECOdiesel. Golf comes in GL trim as a 3-door or a 5-door hatchback, and as the 3-door GTI and GTI 16V models. GL versions have a 100-horsepower 1.8-liter 4-cylinder engine. Jetta Carat and Golf GTI get a 105-horsepower version. GLI 16V and GTI 16V share a 134-horsepower 2.0-liter four. Manual transmission is standard on all and automatic is optional except on the 16V and ECOdiesel. VW says the 59-horsepower ECOdiesel 1.6-liter turbocharged diesel engine emits fewer pollutants than Jetta's previous diesel engine. On all 1992 models, radios have been rewired so that they turn off with the ignition switch; previously, they could be left on after the ignition was turned off. Redesigned Golf/Jettas are due out in the fall of 1992 as 1993 models. Even the

Prices are accurate at time of publication; subject to manufacturer's change.

base Golf and Jetta GLs possess competent, well-balanced road manners, while the GLI and GTI 16Vs offer vivid performance. These car work best with manual transmission. All are roomy inside considering their subcompact dimensions, with adequate space in back for two adults. Jetta has a huge trunk, Golf a large cargo bay. Golf and Jetta carry a design that dates back nearly 10 years, and they look boxy compared to Japanese competitors. But these are roomy, economical cars that deliver European performance at a reasonable price.

Specifications

	Jetta 4-door notchback	Golf 3-door hatchback	Golf 5-door hatchback
Wheelbase, in.	97.3	97.3	97.3
Overall length, in.	172.6	159.1	159.1
Overall width, in.	66.1	65.5	65.5
Overall height, in.	55.7	55.7	55.7
Curb weight, lbs.	2330	2320	2375
Cargo vol., cu. ft.	16.6	86.9	86.9
Fuel capacity, gals.	14.5	14.5	14.5
Seating capacity	5	5	5
Front head room, in.	38.1	38.1	38.1
Front leg room, max., in.	39.5	39.5	39.5
Rear head room, in.	37.1	37.5	37.5
Rear leg room, min., in.	35.1	34.4	34.4

Powertrain layout: transverse front engine/front-wheel drive.

Engines	ohc I-4	ohc I-4	dohc I-4	Turbo-diesel ohc I-4
Size, liters/cu. in.	1.8/109	1.8/109	2.0/121	1.6/97
Fuel delivery	PFI	PFI	PFI	PFI
Horsepower @ rpm	100 @ 5400	105 @ 5400	134 @ 5800	59 @ 4800
Torque (lbs./ft.) @ rpm	107 @ 3400	110 @ 3400	133 @ 4400	81 @ 2000
Availability	S[1]	S[2]	S[3]	S[4]
EPA city/highway mpg				
5-speed OD manual	25/32	25/32	21/28	37/40
3-speed automatic	23/28	23/28		

1. GL models.   2. GTI 8V, Carat.   3. GTI 16V, GLI 16V.   4. Jetta ECOdiesel.

Assembly points: Puebla, Mexico; Wolfsburg, Germany.

Prices

Volkswagen Golf/Jetta	Retail Price	Dealer Invoice	Low Price
Golf GL 3-door hatchback	$9640	$8668	$9154
Golf GL 5-door hatchback	9950	8945	9448
Golf GTI 3-door hatchback	11100	9983	10542
Golf GTI 16V 3-door hatchback	13910	12281	13096
Jetta GL 4-door notchback	11370	10045	10708
Jetta GL ECOdiesel 4-door notchback	11670	10484	11077
Jetta Carat 4-door notchback	12390	10943	11667
Jetta GLI 16V 4-door notchback	15480	13663	14572
Destination charge	370	370	370

Standard equipment:

GL: 1.8-liter PFI 4-cylinder engine, 5-speed manual transmission, power steering (Jetta), door-mounted front shoulder belts, cloth reclining front bucket seats, driver-seat height adjustment (Jetta), console with storage (Jetta), rear defogger, intermittent wipers, tinted glass, front door pockets, tilt steering column, remote mirrors, bodyside moldings, radio prep (speakers, wiring, and antenna), tachometer, coolant temperature gauge, trip odometer, right visor mirror, 175/70SR13 tires (Golf), 185/60HR14 tires (Jetta). **ECOdiesel** has 1.6-liter turbo diesel engine. **Carat** adds: power windows and locks, power mirrors, visor mirrors with lighted right, full wheel covers. **GTI** adds to GL: power steering, sport suspension, sport seats, console with storage, tilt steering column, fog lights, 185/60HR14 tires. **GTI 16V** and **GLI 16V** add: 2.0-liter DOHC 16-valve engine, 4-wheel disc brakes (GTI), sport suspension, Recaro front seats, AM/FM cassette (GLI), leather-wrapped steering wheel, trip computer, 195/50VR15 tires on alloy wheels (GTI), 185/55VR15 tires on BBS alloy wheels (GLI).

Optional equipment:

3-speed automatic transmission	545	506	526
Anti-lock brakes, GLI 16V	835	852	835
Air conditioning	840	723	782
Power steering, Golf GL	285	245	265
Cruise control	235	202	219
AM/FM cassette	340	279	310
w/6 active speakers, Jetta	495	426	461
Manual sliding sunroof	425	366	396
Alloy wheels, Carat	380	327	354
Metallic clearcoat paint	170	146	158
California emissions pkg.	100	102	100

Prices are accurate at time of publication; subject to manufacturer's change.

Volkswagen Passat

Volkswagen Passat GL 4-door

VW's flagship front-drive compact line grows from two to
five entries for 1992, and gains a new 2.8-liter V-6 engine
in addition to the 2.0-liter four used previously. Like last
year, 4-door sedans and 5-door wagons will be offered, all
again riding a 103.3-inch wheelbase. Previously, both body
styles were offered only in GL trim; this year, a "decon-
tented" CL 4-door is added, along with V-6-powered versions of the GL sedan and wagon. The base powertrain
remains a 134-horsepower 2.0-liter four coupled to a 5-
speed manual transmission. A 4-speed automatic is optional. The 4-cylinder engine is standard in the CL sedan
and GL sedan and wagon. Top-of-the-line sedans and
wagons will offer a new 2.8-liter V-6 with 172 horsepower,
along with electronic differential lock, anti-lock brakes (optional on the 4-cylinder GLs), 15-inch BBS alloy wheels,
fog lamps, trip computer, alarm system, and programmable
intermittent wipers. We have not yet had a chance to drive
a Passat with the new V-6. However, the 4-cylinder models
with 5-speed manual accelerate quite briskly, and offer a
firm suspension that delivers good handling with stable
control, but also a ride that might seem overly firm to
some. Unfortunately, the 4-speed automatic is one of the
most ill-mannered transmissions we've ever encountered.
It shifts harshly, both up through the gears and down, and
holds third gear far too long before shifting into fourth.
Depress the throttle to gain a bit more speed on the high-

way, and little happens until the pedal is almost floored, at which time the transmission kicks all the way down to second and the car shoots forward. Passat will comfortably hold four (five in a pinch), with ample leg and head room front and rear. The rear seatback also has an angle adjustment, and can be folded down to expand the already-cavernous trunk. Dashboard controls are easy to reach.

Specifications

	4-door notchback	5-door wagon
Wheelbase, in.	103.3	103.3
Overall length, in.	180.0	179.9
Overall width, in.	67.1	67.1
Overall height, in.	56.2	56.2
Curb weight, lbs.	2985	3029
Cargo vol., cu. ft.	14.2	68.9
Fuel capacity, gals.	18.5	18.5
Seating capacity	5	5
Front head room, in.	38.2	38.7
Front leg room, max., in.	42.5	42.5
Rear head room, in.	37.4	39.0
Rear leg room, min., in.	38.2	38.2

Powertrain layout: transverse front engine/front-wheel drive.

Engines

	dohc I-4
Size, liters/cu. in.	2.0/121
Fuel delivery	PFI
Horsepower @ rpm	134 @ 5800
Torque (lbs./ft.) @ rpm	133 @ 4400
Availability	S

EPA city/highway mpg

5-speed OD manual	21/30
4-speed OD automatic	20/29

Assembly point: Emden, Germany.

Prices

Volkswagen Passat	Retail Price	Dealer Invoice	Low Price
GL 4-door notchback	$17550	$15484	$16517
GL 5-door wagon	17970	15853	16912

Prices are accurate at time of publication; subject to manufacturer's change.

CONSUMER GUIDE®

	Retail Price	Dealer Invoice	Low Price
Destination charge	340	340	340

Standard equipment:

2.0-liter DOHC 16-valve 4-cylinder engine, 5-speed manual transmission, 4-wheel disc brakes, power steering, motorized front shoulder belts, cloth reclining front bucket seats with height, lumbar, and thigh support adjustments, air conditioning, 60/40 folding rear seatback, power windows and locks, cruise control, power mirrors, AM/FM radio, rear armrest, console with storage, tachometer, coolant temperature gauge, trip odometer, digital clock, rear defogger, tinted glass, front door and seatback pockets, remote mirrors, tilt steering column, bodyside moldings, radio prep (speakers, wiring, antenna), cargo cover and rear wiper/washer (wagon), 195/60VR14 tires.

Optional equipment:

4-speed automatic transmission	795	761	778
Anti-lock brakes	835	852	835
Power sunroof	725	624	675
Leather upholstery	740	637	689
Forged alloy wheels	600	516	558
Metallic paint	170	146	158
California emissions pkg.	100	102	100
Cold Climate Package	270	232	251

Includes heated front seats and washer nozzles.

Volco 240

Anti-lock brakes are now standard on all Volvos, and the up-level 240 GL sedan has been reinstated to Volvo's entry-level premium sedan/wagon 240 series after a two-year absence. Otherwise, the line continues with few changes. The venerable rear-wheel-drive 240 is offered in 4-door sedan (base and new GL versions) and 5-door wagon (base only) body styles, all on a 104.3-inch wheelbase. Power comes from a 114-horsepower 2.3-liter four-cylinder engine coupled to either a 5-speed manual or 4-speed automatic transmission. A driver-side air bag and anti-lock brakes are standard on all 240s. The new GL will add a sunroof, heated outside mirrors, and other amenities not found on the base model. It will be differentiated visually by having a chrome grille in place of the base model's matte black grille. The 240 series has been around a long time, and

Volvo 240

though its styling might be somewhat out of date, it has an excellent reputation for durability and safety—and a loyal following. In most performance categories, the 240 is adequate but hardly as stimulating as most competitors. One exception: Acceleration with the automatic transmission is tepid, so heavy throttle application is required to keep abreast of traffic. Handling is competent, with a ride that is firm and stable. Relatively thin roof pillars allow good visibility. Interiors offer four adults plenty of room, and wagons have cavernous cargo area. While the 240 is hardly a standout in its class, if you buy a car with the intention of keeping it for a long time, it may be one of your better choices.

Specifications

	4-door notchback	5-door wagon
Wheelbase, in.	104.3	104.3
Overall length, in.	189.9	190.7
Overall width, in.	67.3	67.7
Overall height, in.	56.3	57.5
Curb weight, lbs.	2919	3051
Cargo vol., cu. ft.	14.0	76.0
Fuel capacity, gals.	15.8	15.8
Seating capacity	5	5
Front head room, in.	37.9	37.9
Front leg room, max., in.	40.1	40.1
Rear head room, in.	36.1	36.8
Rear leg room, min., in.	36.4	36.4

Powertrain layout: longitudinal front engine/rear-wheel drive.

Prices are accurate at time of publication; subject to manufacturer's change.

Engines

	ohc I-4
Size, liters/cu. in.	2.3/141
Fuel delivery	PFI
Horsepower @ rpm	114 @ 5400
Torque (lbs./ft.) @ rpm	136 @ 2750
Availability	S

EPA city/highway mpg

5-speed OD manual	21/28
4-speed OD automatic	20/25

Assembly point: Torslanda, Sweden.

Prices

Volvo 240	Retail Price	Dealer Invoice	Low Price
4-door notchback, 5-speed	$20820	—	—
4-door notchback, automatic	21495	—	—
5-door wagon, 5-speed	21320	—	—
5-door wagon, automatic	21995	—	—
GL 4-door notchback, 5-speed	21495	—	—
GL 4-door notchback, automatic	22170	—	—
Destination charge	395	395	395

Dealer invoice and low price not available at time of publication.

Standard equipment:

2.3-liter PFI 4-cylinder engine, 5-speed manual or 4-speed automatic transmission, 4-wheel anti-lock disc brakes, power steering, driver-side air bag, cloth reclining heated front seats, air conditioning, power windows and locks, remote outside mirrors, AM/FM cassette, tachometer, coolant temperature gauge, trip odometer, intermittent wipers, 185/70R14T tires. **GL** adds: sunroof, heated front seats, heated power mirrors, power antenna.

Optional equipment:

Limited-slip differential	315	—	—
Cruise control	NA	—	—
Vinyl upholstery, wagon	NA	—	—
Leather upholstery	595	—	—
Metallic paint	265	—	—
California emissions pkg.	125	—	—

Volvo 740

Volvo 740

Anti-lock brakes are now standard on all Volvos, and all 740s also come with an automatic locking differential this year. The 740 Turbo sedan and the Bertone-styled Coupe, at one time known as the 780, have both been dropped, but otherwise there are few changes to Volvo's mid-level offerings. The company's rear-wheel-drive premium sedans and wagons ride a 109.1-inch wheelbase. Model choices include base sedan and wagon, and Turbo wagon. The base models carry the same 114-horsepower 2.3-liter four cylinder engine as found in Volvo's 240-series cars, while the Turbo wagon comes with a 162-horsepower version of that engine. A 4-speed automatic is the only transmission offered. All 740s have a driver-side air bag and anti-lock brakes as standard equipment. Base 740s now have power mirrors, which were already standard on the Turbo wagon. Turbo wagons also get automatic climate control, power sunroof, and wider tires on alloy wheels. With only 114 horsepower, the base 740 doesn't strike us as any kind of bargain. The Turbo wagon, with its added features and 162 horsepower, seems like a much better deal, even though it's quite a bit more expensive than its normally aspirated counterpart. Unlike many turbos, boost comes in quickly and smoothly even at lower speeds, providing brisk acceleration whether around town or on the highway. By comparison, the base model delivers leisurely acceleration and passing response. All, however, handle capably with a firm, controlled ride. Both the sedans and wagons have roomy, functional interiors, while wagons add a huge cargo area. The automatic locking differential, standard on all models this year, should make these rear-wheel-drive Volvos more capable in the rain and snow. They look and feel more modern than the aging 240 series cars, and share Volvo's enviable reputation for safety and durability.

Specifications

	4-door notchback	5-door wagon
Wheelbase, in.	109.1	109.1
Overall length, in.	189.3	189.3
Overall width, in.	69.3	69.3
Overall height, in.	55.5	56.5
Curb weight, lbs.	2954	3082
Cargo vol., cu. ft.	16.8	74.9
Fuel capacity, gals.	15.8	15.8
Seating capacity	5	5
Front head room, in.	38.6	38.6
Front leg room, max., in.	41.0	41.0
Rear head room, in.	37.1	37.6
Rear leg room, min., in.	34.7	34.7

Powertrain layout: longitudinal front engine/rear-wheel drive.

Engines	ohc I-4	Turbo ohc I-4
Size, liters/cu. in.	2.3/141	2.3/141
Fuel delivery	PFI	PFI
Horsepower @ rpm	114 @ 5400	162 @ 4800
Torque (lbs./ft.) @ rpm	136 @ 2750	195 @ 3450
Availability	S[1]	S[2]

EPA city/highway mpg

4-speed OD automatic	20/28	19/22

1. 740, 740 GL.   2. 740 Turbo.

Assembly points: Ghent, Belgium; Halifax, Nova Scotia, Canada.

Prices

Volvo 740	Retail Price	Dealer Invoice	Low Price
740 4-door notchback	$24285	—	—
740 5-door wagon	24965	—	—

	Retail Price	Dealer Invoice	Low Price
740 GL 5-door wagon	25765	—	—
740 Turbo wagon	27795	—	—
Destination charge	380	380	380

Dealer invoice and low price not available at time of publication.

Standard equipment:

2.3-liter PFI 4-cylinder engine, 4-speed automatic transmission, 4-wheel anti-lock disc brakes, Automatic Locking Differential, power steering, driver-side air bag, cloth reclining heated front seats, air conditioning, power windows and locks, remote outside mirrors, AM/FM cassette, tachometer, coolant temperature gauge, trip odometer, intermittent wipers, 185/65R15 tires. **740 Turbo** adds: turbocharged engine, automatic climate control, power sunroof, 195/60R15 tires on alloy wheels.

Optional equipment:

Leather upholstery	895	NA	—
Cruise control	NA	NA	—
Sunroof, wagons	NA	NA	—
Metallic paint	265	NA	—

Volve 940/960

Volvo's 900-series 4-door sedans and 5-door wagons gain a new 960 variant to replace the former 940 SE flagship. Though they share the same platform and many body panels with Volvo's 700-series cars, the 900s are differentiated by a sloping rear window and higher rear deck. The 940 GL sedan has a 114-horsepower 2.3-liter 4-cylinder engine. Discontinued for 1992 is the 940 GLE, along with its 153-horsepower 2.3 four. The 940 Turbo sedan and wagon keep their 162-horsepower 2.3 four. The new 960 sedans and wagons use a new 2.9-liter inline-6 rated at 201 horsepower. Automatic is the only transmission offered on any of these cars. Anti-lock brakes, a driver-side air bag, and automatic locking differential are standard across the line. Acceleration with the 940 GL is sedate; there's too little muscle for its size—and price. The 940 Turbo models have more than enough power. The 960 is quicker still, and being smoother than either of the fours, is more in keeping with this price level. With any engine, the transmission changes gears crisply without being harsh or abrupt. The firm sus-

Prices are accurate at time of publication; subject to manufacturer's change.

Volvo 940 GLE

pension provides a stable, well-controlled ride, and the 940 has a tight 32.2-foot turning circle that makes it more maneuverable than most similarly-sized sedans. Like the 740-series cars, interior space is generous and wagons have tremendous cargo capacity. The 940 and new 960 carry Volvo's reputation for durability and safety, but also consider such standouts as the Acura Legend and Cadillac Seville in this class.

Specifications

	4-door notchback	5-door wagon
Wheelbase, in.	109.1	109.1
Overall length, in.	191.7	189.3
Overall width, in.	69.3	69.3
Overall height, in.	55.5	56.5
Curb weight, lbs.	3009	3177
Cargo vol., cu. ft.	16.8	74.9
Fuel capacity, gals.	15.8	15.8
Seating capacity	5	5
Front head room, in.	38.6	38.6
Front leg room, max., in.	41.0	41.0
Rear head room, in.	37.1	37.6
Rear leg room, min., in.	34.7	34.7

Powertrain layout: longitudinal front engine/rear-wheel drive.

Engines	ohc I-4	Turbo ohc I-4	dohc V-6
Size, liters/cu. in.	2.3/141	2.3/141	2.9/178
Fuel delivery	PFI	PFI	PFI

	ohc I-4	Turbo ohc I-4	ohc V-6
Horsepower @ rpm	114 @ 5400	162 @ 4800	201 @ 6000
Torque (lbs./ft.) @ rpm	136 @ 2750	195 @ 3450	197 @ 4300
Availability	S[1]	S[2]	S[3]
EPA city/highway mpg			
4-speed OD automatic	20/28	19/22	18/26

1. 940 GL.　2. 940 Turbo.　3. 960.

Assembly points: Kalmar, Sweden; Uddevalla, Sweden; Ghent, Belgium; Halifax, Nova Scotia, Canada.

Prices

Volvo 940/960	Retail Price	Dealer Invoice	Low Price
940 GL 4-door notchback	$24995	—	—
940 Turbo 4-door notchback	30795	—	—
940 Turbo wagon	31475	—	—
960 4-door notchback	33975	—	—
960 wagon	34655	—	—
Destination charge	380	380	380

Dealer invoice and low price not available at time of publication.

Standard equipment:

940 GL: 2.3-liter PFI 4-cylinder engine, 4-speed automatic transmission, 4-wheel anti-lock disc brakes, Automatic Locking Differential, power steering, driver-side air bag, cloth reclining heated front seats, integrated rear child seat, automatic climate control, power windows and locks, remote outside mirrors, AM/FM cassette, tachometer, coolant temperature gauge, trip odometer, sunroof, intermittent wipers, 185/65HR15 tires. **940 Turbo** adds: turbocharged engine, power mirrors, 205/55VR16 tires on alloy wheels. **960** adds: 2.9-liter DOHC 24-valve PFI V-6, leather upholstery, 8-way power driver-seat with memory, cruise control, 195/65VR15 tires on 20-spoke alloy wheels.

Optional equipment:

Leather upholstery, 940	895	—	—
Power driver-seat, 940	NA	—	—
Requires leather upholstery.			
Cruise control, 940 GL	NA	—	—
Metallic paint, 940	265	—	—
California emissions	125	—	—

Prices are accurate at time of publication; subject to manufacturer's change.

RATINGS CHART

SCALE 5 = Exceptional; 4 = Above average; 3 = Average; 2 = Below average; 1 = Poor

MAKE AND MODEL	Performance							Accommodations						Workmanship		Value	TOTAL
	Acceleration	Economy	Driveability	Ride	Steering/handling	Braking	Noise	Driver seating	Instruments/controls	Visibility	Room/comfort	Entry/exit	Cargo room	Exterior	Interior		
Acura Integra (GS 3-dr)	4	3	4	3	4	5	3	4	4	4	3	3	3	4	4	4	59
Acura Legend (Sedan)	5	2	4	4	4	5	4	3	4	4	4	4	4	4	4	4	63
Acura NSX	5	2	4	3	5	5	2	4	4	3	3	2	1	5	4	3	55
Acura Vigor	4	3	4	4	4	5	3	3	4	4	3	4	4	5	3	3	61
Audi 80 and 100 (100)	4	3	3	3	4	5	4	4	4	4	4	4	4	4	5	3	61
BMW 3-Series (325i)	4	3	4	4	4	5	3	3	4	5	4	4	3	5	4	3	62
BMW 5-Series (525i)	3	3	3	4	4	5	3	3	4	4	3	4	4	5	4	3	60
BMW 7-Series and 850i (735i)	5	2	4	4	4	5	4	4	4	4	4	4	4	4	5	3	64
Buick Park Ave/ Oldsmobile Ninety Eight	4	2	5	4	3	5	4	4	4	4	4	4	4	5	4	3	63
Buick Regal (3.8, ABS)	4	2	4	3	4	5	3	4	2	4	3	4	4	4	4	3	58

Model															
Buick Roadmaster/Chevrolet Caprice/Oldsmobile Custom Cruiser (sedan)	4	1	4	4	3	5	4	3	4	3	5	4	4	4	3	59
Cadillac Allante	4	2	4	3	4	5	3	4	3	3	3	2	4	4	2	53
Cadillac Brougham (5.7)	4	1	4	3	2	4	4	3	2	3	5	4	4	3	3	54
Cadillac De Ville/Fleetwood (4-dr)	5	2	5	3	3	5	4	4	3	3	5	4	4	5	4	64
Cadillac Eldorado and Seville (Seville)	5	2	5	3	4	5	4	4	3	4	4	3	5	4	3	61
Chevrolet Astro/GMC Safari (AWD)	3	1	4	2	3	5	3	3	3	5	2	5	4	4	3	53
Chevrolet Beretta/Corsica (Beretta GT)	4	2	3	3	4	5	3	3	4	3	3	3	4	4	4	56
Chevrolet Camaro/Pontiac Firebird (Z28)	5	1	3	3	4	4	2	3	2	2	2	2	3	3	3	44
Chevrolet Cavalier/Pontiac Sunbird (Cavalier 2-dr)	3	4	4	3	3	5	3	3	4	3	3	3	4	4	4	56
Chevrolet Corvette (LT1)	5	1	3	2	5	5	2	3	2	3	2	2	4	4	3	48
Chevrolet Lumina/Oldsmobile Cutlass Supreme/Pontiac Grand Prix (Euro 4-dr)	3	2	3	3	4	5	3	3	4	4	4	4	4	3	3	55

RATINGS CHART

SCALE 5 = Exceptional; 4 = Above average; 3 = Average; 2 = Below average; 1 = Poor

MAKE AND MODEL	Performance							Accommodations						Workmanship		Value	TOTAL
	Acceleration	Economy	Driveability	Ride	Steering/handling	Braking	Noise	Driver seating	Instruments/controls	Visibility	Room/comfort	Entry/exit	Cargo room	Exterior	Interior		
Chevrolet Lumina APV/ Oldsmobile Silhouette/ Pontiac Trans Sport (3.8-liter V-6)	4	2	4	4	4	5	3	3	3	2	5	3	5	4	3	3	57
Chevrolet S10 Blazer/ GMC Jimmy/Oldsmobile Bravada	4	2	3	2	3	5	3	3	3	4	4	4	4	3	3	4	54
Chrysler Imperial/ New Yorker Fifth Avenue	4	2	3	3	3	5	4	3	3	3	4	4	4	4	4	3	56
Chrysler LeBaron (conv)	4	2	3	3	4	3	3	4	3	3	3	3	2	3	3	3	49
Dodge Caravan/Plymouth Voyager/Chrysler Town & Country (Grand Caravan)	4	2	3	3	4	5	3	3	4	4	5	3	5	4	4	4	60

Model																			Total
Dodge/Plymouth Colt and Eagle Summit (3-dr)	3	4	4	3	3	3	3	2	3	4	4	2	3	3	4	4	4	3	53
Dodge Daytona (ES/V-6)	4	3	4	3	4	3	3	2	3	3	2	2	2	3	4	4	4	3	50
Dodge Dynasty/Chrysler New Yorker Salon (3.3, ABS)	4	2	3	3	3	5	4	4	3	3	4	4	3	3	4	4	4	3	56
Eagle Premier/Dodge Monaco (Premier ES)	4	2	4	4	4	4	3	3	4	2	4	4	4	2	4	3	3	3	57
Ford Aerostar (4WD)	4	2	4	2	4	4	3	3	4	3	2	5	2	3	4	4	4	3	55
Ford Escort/Mercury Tracer (Escort 5-dr)	3	4	3	4	3	3	3	3	3	4	5	3	4	3	4	3	3	4	56
Ford Explorer/Mazda Navajo (Explorer 5-d)	4	1	4	3	4	4	3	3	3	4	4	4	4	4	4	4	4	4	59
Ford Festiva	3	5	2	3	3	4	3	2	4	4	2	2	4	3	4	3	3	3	52
Ford Mustang (GT 3-dr)	5	1	4	2	4	3	4	2	3	3	3	3	3	3	4	3	3	4	49
Ford Probe (LX, ABS)	4	3	3	3	4	5	4	2	3	3	2	3	3	3	4	4	4	3	53
Ford Taurus/Mercury Sable (3.8, ABS)	4	2	4	3	4	5	3	3	3	4	4	4	4	3	4	4	4	4	59
Geo Metro (3-dr)	3	5	4	2	3	4	4	1	4	3	2	3	5	3	4	3	3	3	50
Geo Prizm (LSi)	3	4	3	4	3	3	3	3	3	4	3	3	5	4	4	4	4	4	56
Geo Storm (GSi)	4	3	4	3	4	4	4	2	3	3	2	3	2	3	4	4	4	3	51
Geo Tracker (conv)	3	3	3	2	3	4	3	1	3	4	3	2	3	4	3	3	3	3	45
Honda Accord (EX 4-dr)	4	3	3	4	4	5	4	4	4	4	4	4	5	4	4	4	4	4	64

RATINGS CHART

SCALE 5 = Exceptional; 4 = Above average; 3 = Average; 2 = Below average; 1 = Poor

MAKE AND MODEL	Performance							Accommodations						Workmanship		Value	TOTAL
	Acceleration	Economy	Driveability	Ride	Steering/handling	Braking	Noise	Driver seating	Instruments/controls	Visibility	Room/comfort	Entry/exit	Cargo room	Exterior	Interior		
Honda Civic (EX 4-dr)	3	4	4	3	4	5	3	4	4	3	4	3	3	4	4	3	58
Honda Prelude (Si)	4	4	4	3	4	5	3	4	3	3	2	2	2	4	4	3	54
Hyundai Elantra	3	3	4	2	3	3	2	3	4	5	3	3	4	3	4	4	53
Hyundai Excel/Scoupe (Scoupe LS)	2	4	3	3	4	3	3	4	4	4	2	2	4	4	4	4	54
Hyundai Sonata (4-cyl)	3	3	4	3	4	3	3	4	3	3	4	4	4	4	4	4	57
Infiniti G20 (automatic)	4	3	3	3	4	5	3	4	4	4	4	4	3	4	4	3	59
Infiniti M30 (conv)	4	2	4	3	4	5	3	4	4	2	3	3	2	5	4	3	55
Infiniti Q45	5	2	4	4	4	5	3	4	4	4	4	4	3	4	4	3	61
Isuzu Rodeo (LS 4WD)	3	2	4	3	3	4	3	4	3	3	4	3	4	4	3	4	55

Jaguar Sedan and XJS (Sovereign)	4	2	4	5	4	5	5	3	3	4	3	3	4	3	3	5	4	3	61
Jeep Cherokee (5-dr, ABS)	4	1	4	4	3	5	5	3	3	4	3	4	3	4	4	4	4	4	57
Jeep Wrangler (4.0)	4	1	4	2	3	3	3	2	2	3	3	3	2	3	3	3	3	3	44
Lexus ES 300	4	3	4	4	4	5	4	4	4	3	4	4	3	4	3	5	5	3	63
Lexus LS 400	5	2	5	5	4	5	5	4	4	4	4	4	3	4	3	5	5	4	68
Lexus SC 300/400 (400)	5	2	4	4	4	5	3	4	3	4	2	3	2	4	3	5	5	4	60
Lincoln Continental	4	2	4	4	4	5	3	4	3	4	4	4	4	4	4	4	4	3	60
Lincoln Mark VII	5	1	4	3	3	5	4	3	3	3	3	3	3	5	4	5	5	4	58
Lincoln Town Car	4	2	4	4	3	5	5	3	3	3	3	5	4	5	4	5	4	3	62
Mazda Miata	4	4	4	3	4	4	2	4	4	4	3	3	1	4	4	4	4	5	57
Mazda MPV (V-6)	4	2	4	3	3	4	3	4	3	4	3	4	4	4	4	4	4	4	57
Mazda MX-3	4	3	4	3	4	3	3	4	3	4	2	3	3	4	3	4	4	4	55
Mazda 323/Protege (Protege LX)	4	4	4	3	4	4	2	4	4	4	3	3	3	4	3	4	3	4	57
Mazda 626/MX-6 (626)	3	3	3	3	3	4	3	3	4	4	4	4	4	4	4	4	3	3	56
Mazda 929	4	2	4	4	4	5	4	3	4	4	4	4	3	4	4	4	4	3	60
Mercedes-Benz S-Class (500SEL)	5	1	4	5	4	5	5	4	3	3	5	4	4	5	4	5	5	2	65
Mercedes-Benz 190E (2.3)	4	2	3	4	4	5	3	4	4	4	3	3	3	5	4	5	5	3	59

RATINGS CHART

SCALE 5 = Exceptional; 4 = Above average; 3 = Average; 2 = Below average; 1 = Poor

MAKE AND MODEL	Performance							Accommodations						Workmanship		Value	TOTAL
	Acceleration	Economy	Driveability	Ride	Steering/handling	Braking	Noise	Driver seating	Instruments/controls	Visibility	Room/comfort	Entry/exit	Cargo room	Exterior	Interior		
Mercedes-Benz 300/400/500 (300E)	4	2	4	4	4	5	4	4	4	4	4	4	4	5	5	3	64
Mercedes-Benz 300/500SL	5	1	4	3	4	5	3	4	5	4	4	4	3	5	5	3	62
Mercury Capri (XR2)	4	3	4	3	4	4	2	4	4	3	3	3	2	4	3	4	54
Mercury Cougar/Ford Thunderbird (Cougar XR7)	4	1	3	3	4	5	4	4	4	3	4	3	3	4	4	3	56
Mercury Grand Marquis/Ford Crown Victoria	4	2	4	4	3	5	5	4	4	3	5	5	4	4	4	4	64
Mercury Topaz/Ford Tempo (Topaz LTS)	4	3	4	3	3	3	3	4	3	4	3	3	3	4	4	4	55
Mitsubishi Diamante (LS)	4	2	4	3	4	5	3	4	2	4	4	4	4	4	4	3	58

Model														Total
Mitsubishi Eclipse/Eagle Talon/Plymouth Laser (Eclipse GS DOHC)	4	3	4	2	4	4	2	4	4	2	2	2	4	51
Mitsubishi Expo/Eagle Summit Wgn/Plymouth Colt Vista (Expo SP)	3	3	4	3	4	3	4	3	4	5	5	3	4	59
Mitsubishi Galant (LS)	3	4	4	3	3	3	3	4	4	4	4	3	4	59
Mitsubishi Mirage (4-dr)	3	3	3	3	3	3	3	3	4	3	3	3	3	53
Mitsubishi Precis	2	5	3	3	3	2	2	3	4	5	3	3	4	53
Mitsubishi 3000GT/Dodge Stealth (VR-4)	5	2	3	2	5	3	3	4	3	2	2	2	3	50
Nissan Maxima (SE)	5	2	4	4	4	5	4	4	4	4	4	4	4	64
Nissan NX 1600/2000 (2000)	4	4	4	3	4	5	2	4	4	2	2	3	4	56
Nissan Pathfinder	3	2	4	4	3	4	3	3	3	3	3	4	3	55
Nissan Sentra (GXE, ABS)	3	4	3	3	4	5	3	3	4	5	3	3	4	58
Nissan Stanza (GXE, ABS)	4	3	4	3	4	4	3	4	4	3	3	3	4	59
Nissan 240SX (SE)	4	3	4	2	4	4	2	3	4	2	2	3	3	50
Nissan 300ZX (Turbo)	5	2	3	2	5	5	2	4	4	2	3	3	3	54
Oldsmobile Cutlass Ciera/Buick Century (V-6)	4	2	4	3	3	3	3	3	4	4	4	4	4	56
Oldsmobile Toronado/Buick Riviera (Trofeo)	4	2	5	3	4	5	4	4	4	3	3	5	3	59

RATINGS CHART

SCALE 5 = Exceptional; 4 = Above average; 3 = Average; 2 = Below average; 1 = Poor

MAKE AND MODEL	Performance							Accommodations						Workmanship		Value	TOTAL
	Acceleration	Economy	Driveability	Ride	Steering/handling	Braking	Noise	Driver seating	Instruments/controls	Visibility	Room/comfort	Entry/exit	Cargo room	Exterior	Interior		
Plymouth Acclaim/Dodge Spirit (Acclaim 4-cyl)	3	3	3	3	3	4	2	4	3	4	4	4	4	4	4	4	56
Plymouth Sundance/Dodge Shadow (America)	3	3	3	3	4	3	2	4	3	3	3	3	4	4	3	5	53
Pontiac Bonneville/Buick LeSabre/Oldsmobile Eighty Eight	4	2	5	4	3	5	4	3	4	4	4	4	4	4	5	4	63
Pontiac Grand Am/Buick Skylark/Oldsmobile Achieva (Quad 4)	4	3	4	3	4	5	2	4	4	3	3	3	3	4	4	4	57
Pontiac LeMans (LE)	2	4	3	3	4	3	2	3	4	4	3	3	3	4	3	3	51
Saab 900 (Turbo 3-dr)	5	3	4	3	4	5	3	4	3	3	4	3	4	4	3	3	58
Saab 9000 (CD Turbo)	5	2	4	3	5	5	3	4	3	4	4	4	4	4	4	3	61

Saturn (SL2 4-dr)	4	4	3	3	4	4	2	4	3	3	4	4	57
Subaru Justy (ECVT)	3	5	3	2	3	3	2	4	5	2	3	3	50
Subaru Legacy (4WD 4-dr)	4	3	3	4	4	3	3	4	4	3	4	4	58
Subaru Loyale (4WD wgn)	2	3	3	3	4	3	3	3	5	4	4	4	56
Subaru SVX	5	3	4	3	5	5	3	3	3	4	4	3	56
Suzuki Sidekick and Samurai (Sidekick 4-dr)	2	3	3	3	3	3	2	4	3	3	4	3	49
Suzuki Swift (GT)	4	4	2	4	4	4	4	5	2	3	3	3	51
Toyota Camry (V-6, ABS)	4	3	4	4	5	4	3	4	4	5	4	4	64
Toyota Celica (GT)	3	4	3	4	5	3	4	2	2	5	4	3	51
Toyota Corolla (LE 4-dr)	3	4	4	3	4	3	4	5	3	4	4	4	56
Toyota Cressida (ABS)	4	2	4	4	5	4	3	5	4	4	4	4	63
Toyota MR2	4	4	3	4	4	4	4	3	2	1	4	4	54
Toyota Paseo	4	5	4	4	4	4	4	4	2	3	4	4	56
Toyota Previa (LE, ABS)	3	2	4	3	5	3	3	4	5	5	4	4	60
Toyota Supra (Turbo)	5	2	2	4	5	5	4	3	2	3	4	4	54
Toyota Tercel (2-dr)	3	4	3	3	4	4	3	5	3	3	4	3	55
Toyota 4Runner (V-6/5-dr)	3	1	4	4	4	4	3	4	4	2	4	3	56
Volkswagen Cabriolet	4	4	4	3	4	3	4	2	3	4	4	3	52
Volkswagen Corrado (ABS)	4	3	2	4	5	3	4	2	3	3	4	3	51

RATINGS CHART

SCALE 5 = Exceptional; 4 = Above average; 3 = Average; 2 = Below average; 1 = Poor

MAKE AND MODEL	Performance						Accommodations						Workmanship			TOTAL
	Acceleration	Economy	Driveability	Ride	Steering/handling	Braking	Noise	Driver seating	Instruments/controls	Visibility	Room/comfort	Entry/exit	Cargo room	Exterior	Interior	Value	
Volkswagen Fox (2-dr)	3	4	4	3	3	4	3	3	3	5	3	3	2	4	3	4	54
Volkswagen Golf/Jetta (Jetta GL)	3	3	3	3	4	4	3	4	4	3	3	3	4	4	4	4	56
Volkswagen Passat (4-dr, ABS)	4	3	3	3	4	5	3	3	4	3	4	4	4	4	4	3	58
Volvo 240 (wgn)	3	3	4	3	3	4	2	4	3	5	4	4	4	5	4	3	58
Volvo 740 (4-dr)	3	2	4	3	4	5	3	3	4	4	4	4	4	5	4	3	59
Volvo 940/960 (960)	4	2	4	4	4	5	3	3	4	4	4	4	4	5	3	3	60

JAN 2 4 1992